The British army of
William III, 1689–1702

JOHN CHILDS

The British army of William III, 1689–1702

MANCHESTER
UNIVERSITY PRESS

© John Childs 1987

Published by Manchester University Press
Oxford Road, Manchester M13 9PL, UK
and 27 South Main Street, Wolfeboro, NH 03894-2069, USA

British Library cataloguing in publication data
Childs, John
  The British army of William III, 1689–1702.
  1. Great Britain,   *Army* – History   2. Great
  Britain – History, Military – Stuarts,
  1603–1714
  I. Title
  355'.00941   UA649

Library of Congress cataloging in publication data
Childs, John Charles Roger.
  The British Army of William III, 1689–1702.
  1. Great Britain.   Army – History – 17th century.
  2. Great Britain. Army – History – 18th century.
  3. Great Britain – History, Military – Stuarts,
  1603–1714.   I. Title.
  UA649.C54   1987   355'.00941   87–11054

ISBN 0–7190–1987–7 hardback

Photoset in Linotron Sabon by
Northern Phototypesetting Co, Bolton
Printed and bound in Great Britain by
Anchor Brendon Limited, Tiptree, Essex

CONTENTS

PREFACE

Ten years have elapsed since the publication of the first volume of my trilogy devoted to the social and political history of the British army during the reigns of Charles II, James II, and William III. As the project now leaves my hands there is a tinge of sadness at the departure of the many characters whom one has come to know so well. Not that it has dominated my life. Far from it, for no history can ever be as important as the present day and the future. The hundreds of hours spent leaning over an ancient typewriter or, more frequently, staring out of the window towards Beamsley Beacon and lower Wharfedale have witnessed exhilaration, boredom, intellectual smugness, and depression. However, the sensation which lives in the memory is a penumbra of simultaneous moods ranging from the certainty that the enterprise is vitally important, to the feeling that it is entirely without point or purpose. Which has been ultimately triumphant is a difficult question to answer. There lingers an aftertaste of acute dissatisfaction with the numerous lacunae and errors which have been caused by my own incompetence and the variable quality of the surviving evidence, as well as an emptiness in wondering what it all adds up to. I am also conscious of being far too modern in my concern for the plight of the common soldier.

Archival research has now become a hideously expensive business, especially for those with families to support and who live outside the south-east of England and the Thames valley. The little that I have accomplished has only been made possible through the generous financial assistance of the British Academy, the Twenty-Seven Foundation, and the Staff Research Fund of the University of Leeds. Being a lone and independent spirit I have incurred few debts although

I must record my thanks to Mr. David Chandler for general encouragement and for the loan of a typescript of an article long before its publication; to Sir Humphry Tollemache for guiding me around his family archives; and to Major F. W. Woodward for information about the fortifications of Plymouth. Dr David Hayton most kindly allowed me to consult the typescript of his edition of the parliamentary diaries of Salwey Winnington and William Cowper prior to its publication by the Royal Historical Society. Dr Paul Hopkins located the 'missing' volume of the Blathwayt Papers and directed my attention towards the archives of Westminster Cathedral. One of the few pleasures derived from the preparation of this book has been to work in the Dutch archives where I have been fortunate to experience the friendliness and helpfulness of the staffs of the Algemeen Rijksarchief in The Hague, the Gemeentearchief of Amsterdam, and the Gemeente Archief 's-Gravenhage. My wife and sons will be delighted that this protracted task has reached a conclusion although they will now have to endure the shadow of a weightier presence, the Duke of Marlborough.

John Childs
Ilkley, 17 November 1986.

ABBREVIATIONS

The following abbreviations have been employed in the footnotes at the end of each chapter.

Add. MSS.	Additional Manuscript
App.	Appendix
ARA	Algemeen Rijksarchief, The Hague
BCRO	Berkshire County Record Office, Reading
BL	British Library
Bod. Lib.	Bodleian Library, Oxford
BTRO	Berwick-upon-Tweed Record Office
CCRO	Chester City Record Office
CJ	*Journals of the House of Commons*
CSPC	*Calendar of State Papers Colonial, America and West Indies*
CSPD	*Calendar of State Papers Domestic*
CTP	*Calendar of Treasury Papers*
CTrB	*Calendar of Treasury Books*
DCRO	Dorset County Record Office, Dorchester
EHR	*English Historical Review*
GAA	Gemeentearchief, Amsterdam
GCRO	Gloucestershire County Record Office, Gloucester
Harl. MSS.	Harleian Manuscripts, British Library
HCRO	Kingston-upon-Hull City Record Office
HJ	*Historical Journal*
HMC	*Reports of the Royal Commission on Historical Manuscripts*
HP	*The House of Commons, 1660–1690*, ed. B. D. Henning (London, 1983), 3 vols.

JBS	*Journal of British Studies*
JMH	*Journal of Modern History*
JSAHR	*Journal of the Society for Army Historical Research*
LCA	Leeds City Archives
LG	*London Gazette*
LJ	*Journals of the House of Lords*
LUL	Leeds University Library
Luttrell	Narcissus Luttrell, *A Brief Historical Relation of State Affairs from September 1678 to April 1714* (Oxford, 1857), 6 vols.
MSS.	Manuscript
NLI	National Library of Ireland, Dublin
NLW	National Library of Wales, Aberystwyth
NRO	Northamptonshire County Record Office, Northampton
n.s.	new series
o.s.	old series
PCRO	Portsmouth City Record Office
PHSL	*Proceedings of the Huguenot Society of London*
PRO	Public Record Office, London
RPCS	*Registers of the Privy Council of Scotland*
SP	State Papers, Public Record Office, London
SR	*Statutes of the Realm*
SRO	Scottish Record Office, Edinburgh
Steele	*A Bibliography of Royal Proclamations of the Tudor and Stuart Sovereigns, 1485–1714*, ed. Robert Steele (Oxford, 1910), 2 vols.
TRHS	*Transactions of the Royal Historical Society*
WCA	Westminster Cathedral Archives, London
WO	War Office Papers, Public Record Office, London

NOTE ON DATES

All dates in the text and footnotes are given in the English Old Style which was ten days behind the Continental New Style until 1700, and eleven days thereafter. In cases where a letter or paper cited was written in Europe, then both old and new style dates have been given, i.e. 5/15 February 1697, and 5/16 February 1701. As in modern usage, the new year has been taken to begin on 1 January and not on 25 March.

For 'Cesca, Michael, and Robert

INTRODUCTION

This, the final volume of the trilogy of studies covering the social and political history of the British army between 1660 and 1702, describes the organisation, administration, command structure, and personnel of the army within the British Isles during the reign of William III. It is also concerned with civil-military relations, military law, and the part played by the standing forces in the confused politics of the 1690s. With the exception of the Brest expedition in 1694, no attempt has been made to discuss in any depth or detail the military operations upon which sections of the army were engaged in the Low Countries, Ireland, Scotland, and in the West Indies and the North American colonies. This omission has been quite deliberate. In the first place, the operational history of the Nine Years' War is somewhat tedious, especially that of the campaigns in the Spanish Netherlands. Secondly, their reiteration is unnecessary for the purposes of this work. The inclusion of a chapter about the attack on Brest can be justified by the facts that it was a purely British operation as well as a shining example of the political pressures which were brought to bear upon the regular troops. At some time in the future, attention will be given to writing a detailed military history of the British army's role in the campaigns of King William's War but, in the meantime, a number of authorities provide sufficient accounts. Colonel Walton does his best, with the aid of vivid descriptions, to bring the campaigns in the Low Countries to life;[1] Dr Simms has penned an excellent and concise record of the Jacobite Wars in Ireland; Dr Hopkins has recently compiled a close study of the Jacobite Wars in Scotland;[2] and W. T. Morgan and D. E. Leach have investigated the war in the West Indies and in North America.[3] In preparing the penultimate chapter on the administration

of the British corps in the allied army in Flanders, which is partially
intended to serve as a bridge into the projected military history of the
Nine Years' War, I have relied quite heavily upon L. M. Waddell's
doctoral dissertation.[4] It is regrettable that this fine piece of research
has never been published in substantial form.

In the face of an officer corps which probably involved something in
the region of ten thousand men between 1689 and 1702, of whom five
thousand were holding active commissions at any one time, the proso-
pographical approach which was used extensively in the first two parts
of the trilogy, most particularly in the second, has been abandoned.
Without the aid of a computer and a team of research assistants, mass
biography on such a scale has proved to be impractical. Wherever
possible, familiar characters have been welcomed back onto the stage
and their subsequent careers and attitudes have provided a series of
unifying threads, but William's large officer corps cannot be grasped
and understood in quite the same way as the smaller and more
tractable institutions of the restoration monarchs. It was simply too
big and amorphous. On the other hand, more information has come to
light about the nature of the common soldier enabling his profile to be
more confidently sketched. Again, as in the previous volumes, no
principal, bedrock source of manuscript material has been discovered.
The War Office collection in the Public Record Office is surprisingly
incomplete and unhelpful, mainly because the secretary-at-war,
William Blathwayt, took most of his official papers into his own
private archive when he retired in 1704. However, these documents,
which are now housed in the British Library, consist of correspondence rather than the continuous runs of administrative orders, circu-
lars, and statistics which are so essential in trying to establish how an
institution functioned.[5] Consequently, the researcher's net has been
cast far and wide with rewarding catches from a number of local
record offices. In view of the general dearth of secondary literature
relating to the reign of William III, and this especially applies to the
history of the army, a separate bibliography has not been provided.
Instead, extensive footnotes have been employed which initially introduce both printed and manuscript sources by their full titles and
thereafter refer to reduced versions. Works and archives which are
repeatedly cited have their shortened forms established in the list of
abbreviations.

In the summer of 1685, James II greatly augmented his small
standing army to cope with the invasion by the Dukes of Monmouth
and Argyll but, instead of demobilising these levies after the successful

Battle of Sedgemoor, he retained them and began to demonstrate signs of governing with and through a standing army in the manner of an absolute monarch. By 1687, the army looked to be a potential instrument for the creation of a catholic autocracy in England. Not only did the anglican gentry and aristocracy view this possible development with disfavour, but even the career, professional army officers grew uneasy and began to fear for their own futures and commissions. They were markedly influenced by the precedent of the almost total purge of protestant officers from the Irish army by the Duke of Tyrconnel. These developments coincided with the international ambitions of William of Orange. The Dutchman was able to play upon this restlessness in some of James II's officer corps and orchestrate a small but highly effective conspiracy which undertook to organise mass desertions when the Dutch invasion occurred. Although the promises were far in excess of the achievement, the army conspiracy wrecked the army's command structure and, more importantly, destroyed the few remaining ounces of James II's self-confidence. In completing the downfall of James II and in ushering William and Mary towards the throne, the Restoration army reduced itself to a scarcely recognisable rabble. Its shameful retreat from Salisbury Plain along the Thames valley to the western outskirts of London brought about the final disintegration of the old Stuart army.

Notes

1 Clifford Walton, *The History of the British Standing Army, 1660–1700* (London, 1894).
2 J. G. Simms, *Jacobite Ireland, 1685–1691* (London, 1969); Paul Hopkins, *Glencoe and the end of the Highland War* (Edinburgh, 1986); James M. Hill, *Celtic Warfare, 1595–1763* (Edinburgh, 1986), pp. 64–79.
3 W. T. Morgan, 'The British West Indies during King William's War, 1689–1697', *JMH*, ii. (1930), pp. 378–409; D. E. Leach, *Arms for Empire; a military history of the British colonies in North America, 1607–1763* (New York, 1973), pp. 80–115.
4 Louis M. Waddell, 'The administration of the English Army in Flanders and Brabant from 1689 to 1697', (Doctoral Dissertation, University of North Carolina, 1971).
5 William Blathwayt's military papers are to be found in BL, Add. MSS. 9, 719–35 and 38,694–707. One volume, formerly no. 9,450 in the manuscripts of Sir Thomas Phillipps – 'Lord Cutts's Letters' – escaped the clutches of the British Library and is now in the possession of Mr Richard Moore, of Whatlington, Sussex.

I

Reformation and renaissance

Chaos. Utter chaos. Deserted by some of its senior officers, leaderless, and without structure, support or orders, the British army had ceased to exist. In September 1688, the entire Scottish army of 2,964 men had marched into England to combat the threat of a Dutch invasion, whilst a further reinforcement of 2,820 soldiers had sailed across St George's Channel from Ireland. Now, English, Scots, and Irish, both protestant and catholic, milled around in total confusion. James II was no longer the effective monarch yet the Prince of Orange's constitutional status was decidedly uncertain. On 10 December 1688, James II had written a badly worded letter to the Earl of Feversham, the commander-in-chief of the royal army, which the lethargic general had interpreted as a directive to disband the force under his control. This only amounted to some 4,000 men in and around Uxbridge, the rest having melted away, deserted to William, or remained paralysed in their garrisons and quarters. Spread throughout the length and breadth of southern and central England, the army had degenerated into an untidy rabble, unsure of whether it had been disbanded or was still a legal entity. Unofficered groups of Irish catholic soldiers tried to reach Liverpool, Chester and Whitehaven in an effort to return to their own country, but this only succeeded in giving some credence to the 'Irish Alarms' which swept from London and the south-east through the Midlands into Lancashire and Chesire during the middle and latter part of December. Lord George Livingstone, the acting commander of the Scottish troops in England, could see the writing on the wall and marched his men back over the Cheviots into relative sanity and order.

James's old army had been disgraced and humiliated. It had also been defeated. Although it had not fought a battle with the invader, it had lost the campaign of propaganda and morale, the principal weapons of William of Orange. A conspiracy of desertion, limited in scope but well orchestrated, had ripped the guts out of the higher command structure of the royal army at the vital moment and shattered the confidence of the king in the one seemingly reliable pillar of his regime. From Salisbury, James had dragged his dejected regiments back along the Thames valley to their final and wretched 'disbandment' at Uxbridge, a march which had resulted in the disintegration of the army. William had won a military and political victory without having to engage the main forces of his opponent; few bloody and 'decisive' battles have achieved such significant results. However much the English generals and senior officers tried to cloud the issue, the naked truth was that their army had been smashed in the field. Had the King failed his army, or had the army let down its master?

Undoubtedly, the army under James had suffered from divided loyalties. Everywhere had been causes for internal friction: protestant and catholic; English and Irish; courtier and professional officers. Yet, despite James's threats to remodel the officer corps in the summer of 1688, despite his preference for the professional and catholic officer, when faced with the Dutch invasion in November 1688 the huge majority of the army remained loyal to their legitimate sovereign. There was a conspiracy amongst some of the more senior officers and there can be little doubt that this was instrumental in shredding what little was left of James's self-confidence at Salisbury, but if the King could have shrugged off the desertions his army would, in all probability, have stood by him and fought the Dutch invader. It was the senior and professional career officers who conspired with and deserted to William in November and December 1688, those who saw their commissions and futures threatened by a possible catholicisation of the English establishment. Most of the subaltern officers and the rank and file were not involved. The experience of Captain Edwin Sandys of the Royal Horse Guards gives a typical illustration of the pressures felt by army officers in 1688. In the middle of the summer, James invited Sandys

into his closet [and] began to talk about this and that and at last told him what he would do for him and how great a commander he should be if he would but be a catholic. To whom the captain replied, in a big hoarse voice as he always spoke, 'I understand your majesty well enough. I fear God and I honour the King, as I ought, but I am not a man that is given to change.' Which unexpected answer so stopped the King's mouth that he had not a word to say.

Within a few days after, the captain went to the Earl of Oxford [colonel of the Royal Horse Guards], and would needs have given his commission up and gone into Holland &c., but the Earl would not accept of it, but whispered him in the ear, saying, 'These things will not last long', meaning these actions of the King. And just about a quarter of a year after, the Revolution happened.

Yet for all this, when it [the Revolution] was happening, yet this good captain got into Windsor Castle and kept it for the King until he run out of land.[1]

Despite this great reservoir of loyalty and national hatred of the Dutch, the conspiracy amongst some senior army officers made certain that James was rendered incapable of employing his one resource. Even before Salisbury, James's buoyancy had suffered a number of hammer blows. All the calculations about family fealty and the timing of the invasion had fallen to pieces when William had stepped onto the sands of Torbay on 5 November. The army conspiracy was then sufficient to drive James into a state of nervous collapse.

He saw King James ride backward and forward continually with a languishing look, his hat hanging over his eyes and a handkerchief continually in one hand to dry the blood of his nose for he continually bled. If he and the soldiers did but chance to hear a trumpet or even a post-horn they were always upon a surprise, and all fit to run away, and at last they did so. All the nights there was nothing but tumult and every question that was asked, 'Where are the enemy?' 'How far off are they?' 'Which way are they going?', and such like.

In stark contrast to this sad portrait of a declining king, when William came ashore he was naturally worried and wearing 'his own hair, which was long and black, and looked as to his face very pale and wan'. However, as the campaign developed to his complete satisfaction, 'he got a wig and looks as brisk and as good a colour as anyone'.[2]

It is tempting to see the reduction of James II's forty thousand men into a gaggle of stragglers as the end of the old Stuart army and interpret the Phoenix of the 1690s as virtually a new creation. Like all worthwhile temptations, it is partially irresistible. James II had used his expanded armed forces to enforce his religious and political policies in England, so much so that he was prepared to employ army officers as justices of the peace, deputy-lieutenants, and local election agents. More menacingly, he had applied military pressure to recalcitrant boroughs, institutions, and individuals in a manner which smelled horribly of garlic and cheap wine. Louis XIV did that sort of thing, not English kings. James II's employment of the army as a coercive political police force had brought to mind the days of

Cromwell and the Interregnum when England had first been subjected to regimes which relied upon armed force as both a political power base and as a means of political and religious enforcement. To a large extent, the invasion of William of Orange brought this sinister development to an end. On the other hand, there was a great continuity between the old army of James II and the army of William III in terms of personnel, organisation, and tradition.

William of Orange's expedition of 1688 had been invited to England to help remedy the manifest abuses in the political and religious systems, at least that was the English version. However great the blow to the army's prestige and self-confidence, however humiliating was the reality of a successful foreign invasion, William's intervention had given the English political nation the opportunity to terminate, once and for all, the absolutist tendencies of the Restoration monarchs. The defeat of the army was the price that had to be paid. Yet William's own objectives had been entirely different. His main purpose in crossing the North Sea had been to secure England for the protestant alliance in Europe and to prevent her from sliding into the French camp. Once that had been accomplished, there remained the business of protecting his wife's claim to the throne and making sure that the resources of the British Isles – military, naval, commercial and financial – were deployed in the correct political direction. One of the things which William did not want to discover was that the flight of his predecessor had left the majority of public affairs in a shambles. In the first place William had expected sizeable sections of the English army to desert to him *en masse* and was annoyed when only officers rode into his camp, but he was even more furious at Feversham's disbandment of the residue of James's army. Time was of the essence. D'Humière's French troops were already nibbling at the Spanish Netherlands and few could fail to see that the French would make their major effort in that theatre in 1689. William needed to be free of the irritations of England in order to turn his full attention to deal with the French menace. Instead of finding a country ready to engage in a major foreign war, William was faced with political confusion, divided loyalties and a military muddle. The army required reorganisation from top to bottom.

The only real method of solving the army's problems in 1688 and 1689 would have been to disband the entire formation and start again from scratch. This had been the solution adopted by Charles II in 1660 when he had been faced with a similar situation, but William did not enjoy the luxuries of time and peace. With a war in Ireland, a rebellion in Scotland, and a conflagration in Flanders, William was obliged to throw the English and Scottish armies straight into action making such corrections to the officer corps and improvements in training and administration as were possible in the field. William III's English army was not new. It embodied most of the faults of its predecessors and was essentially a hugely expanded version of the armies of Charles II and James II. William was never able to execute a thorough and radical reform of his British armed forces; he compromised and improvised under the anvil of war. In the end, he created a system which just about worked but it was a hand to mouth affair.[3]

Lord Cavendish's horse had been raised during the emergency of November 1688 and was formally commissioned by the Prince of Orange on 31 December. As the colonel was a staunch whig he was adjudged politically acceptable and was reinstated in his command, whilst his lieutenant-colonel, John Coke, possessed impeccable credentials. For his outspoken criticism of James II's address to the House of Commons on 18 November 1685, Coke had been stripped of his captaincy in Princess Anne of Denmark's regiment of foot.[4] Coke was one of the first protestant martyrs. In the confusion following the flight of James, the political reliability of the field officers mattered more than the state of the regiment. The latter was deplorable. John Depretit, the agent, informed the colonel that most of the troopers were 'very careless about their horses and duty, uncivil in their quarters, and saucy to their officers'. Trooper Doncaster had grievously assaulted a gentleman as he sat peacefully by his own fireside. Troopers Salter, Bradford, Buxton, and the Sutton brothers messed together but refused to pay one farthing for their hay and oats even though their pay was up-to-date. To crown it all, Trumpeter John Cook could not play his instrument.[5]

Such faintly comic cameos of indiscipline and disorganisation could have been repeated for the majority of the new regiments scattered across the midlands and the south of England. However, there was a further complication in the process of bringing order to the army. Many of the soldiers who had assisted the principal supporters of William of Orange during the invasion had been irregulars. Dover Castle had been seized by a disorderly collection of three hundred sailors, townsmen, and yokels under the dubious leadership of two master mariners, a brewer, a soldier, and two bakers. The Prince of Orange had to offer this gang financial recompense for their outlays before they agreed to hand over the Castle to some Kent militia under Colonel Wickfield.[6] The Earl of Danby's private army in Yorkshire comprised another threat to the restoration of law and order. In a move calculated to resolve this problem and to burst Danby's political bubble, William instructed the self-appointed satrap of the north to thank all the gentlemen and volunteers who had turned out at York and to ask them to go home and ready themselves to support the Orange interest in the coming parliamentary elections. Danby was also ordered to disband his irregular foot in York 'keeping only just so many as is absolutely required to keep the town of York in peace and good order'. At Nottingham, the Earl of Devonshire's irregular officers were given the Prince of Orange's commission whilst their men were granted the option of engagement in the regular army or a free discharge.[7]

Before the army in the provinces could be reorganised, the central administration had to be put on an even keel. The last marching order in the name of James II had been issued from the War Office by the secretary-at-war, William Blathwayt, on 4 December 1688. Like many other government officials, Blathwayt was unsure of his position in the wake of James's flight and William initially trusted no one who was not Dutch or demonstrably not English. From 14 to 31 December, William's personal secretary, Constantijn Huygens, ran the War Office from St James's Palace and not until late in January 1689 did Blathwayt begin to resume control of military administration. By 2 February he was functioning reasonably smoothly although there were potential rivals for his position. His deputy and judge-advocate general, George Clarke, was being encouraged by David Crawford, the deputy commissary-general of the musters, to challenge for the post before Blathwayt was firmly back in the saddle. In the event, Clarke did not act on Crawford's advice and he was to remain as Blathwayt's reliable subordinate for the rest of the reign. Blathwayt's resumption of office came just in time. A major riot had occurred in the vital fortress of Berwick-on-Tweed on 14 December, caused by an unpaid soldiery seizing free quarter from the townspeople. Further trouble was only averted by the mayor and Major Edward Nott reaching an agreement whereby the town paid the soldiers' subsistence money until cash arrived from London.[8] With the reins of administration resting in the experienced and competent hands of a civil servant who enjoyed the distinction of having been suspected of complicity in the pro-Williamite conspiracy of 1688, the Prince of Orange was able to set about the massive task of bringing the English army into a state of operational effectiveness. There were three main difficulties: how to restore religious harmony in the ranks; how to secure the loyalty of the officers and men to the new regime; and how to build up numbers and morale.

The solution to the first problem was fairly straightforward, at least in theory. Native catholics and Irish catholics were cashiered. The Lords, meeting in the Guildhall, had issued an order on 14 December 1688 instructing all Irish officers and soldiers to return to their original formations where their subsistence would continue to be paid until other arrangements could be made. In the meantime they were to be disarmed and their weapons were deposited in the Ordnance stores in the Tower of London. Any Irishman who refused to comply was to be treated as a vagabond.[9] As quickly as possible, the Irish regiments were gathered into southern England. The Irish Guards marched into Lewes where they joined Colonel Anthony Hamilton's infantry, whilst Roger MacElligott's foot was billetted in and around Chichester. On the last day of the eventful year of 1688, Colonel John Beaumont, the governor of Portsmouth, was ordered to take two detachments of Sir John Talbot's horse and one party from Sir John Fenwick's cavalry regiment and march to East Grinstead, Lewes, and Chichester. These troopers were entrusted with the task of disarming the three catholic Irish regiments under John Butler, Anthony Hamilton, and Roger MacElligott and of escorting them to Portsmouth. The Irish Guards, a predominantly protestant regiment, were also ordered to come into Portsmouth. Once all the four corps had arrived, any catholics in the Irish Guards were attached to the other three regiments and the few protestants in the catholic formations were drafted into the Guards. From Portsmouth, the three catholic regiments were then bundled onto transport ships and taken to the Isle of Wight where they came under the suzerainty of the governor, Sir Robert Holmes.

To assist Holmes in guarding the Irish, four companies from the Portsmouth garrison were sent over the water to reinforce the existing garrison of six companies. Altogether, some 1,500 catholic Irish were herded onto this vast prisoner-of-war camp. Formal disbandment followed on 8 and 9 January 1689.[10] The Irishmen reacted vigorously to their incarceration – the 250 dragoons of Colonel John Butler's regiment had ridden into Portsmouth disarmed but defiantly carrying sticks – and many did their best to escape to France and Ireland.[11] With just ten companies to watch the entire coastline of the Isle of Wight and only a few small cruisers stationed offshore, it was not difficult for the more determined to slip away. Their escape was made easier by a number of French privateers and small men-of-war which kept close to the southern shore of the island.[12] By April 1689, 300 had got away, including Colonel Roger MacElligott who had taken passage for France before proceeding to join James II in Ireland. The long-term solution of how to dispose of the remaining Irish was traditional; sell them into foreign service. The Prince of Orange negotiated an agreement with Leopold I, the Holy Roman Emperor, for a regiment of 1,800 catholic Irish to fight for the Imperial armies in Hungary. Not only did this remove the unwanted addition to the population of the Isle of Wight, but it enabled William to do a good turn for his ally and provide him with some extra troops which would be needed if Leopold was to make an effective military showing in Hungary as well as combatting French incursions into the Rhineland. Initially, Leopold had asked for 2,000 men but William could offer no more than 1,800. By 4 April, there were only 1,200 left on the Isle of Wight and Blathwayt wrote to Holmes and Dennis MacGillicuddy, the commander of the prospective regiment, to expedite the embarkation of the soldiers.[13] They had been packed aboard their transports by 24 April and subsequently arrived in Hamburg where they deserted in droves.[14] Some were promptly recaptured but others made their way to Rotterdam from where many were recruited into the French army in Flanders, an embarrassment which William had been anxious to avoid. The agreement with Leopold had specifically requested that the Irish be sent to fight in far-off Hungary and not in Flanders or on the Rhine.[15] So low had the numbers in the Irish regiment become by 1691 that William dispatched 500 replacements from amongst the Jacobite army in Ireland following the Treaty of Limerick. In the Isle of Wight, the Irish left mountains of debts for quarters and subsistence as well as deserters 'skulking in the bushes and coppices'.[16]

Not all the Irish catholic soldiers in England could be dealt with by sending them from a prison camp on the Isle of Wight into exile on the plains of the Danube. In small groups or individually the disbanded Irish wandered towards north-west England searching for succour, sympathy and a passage home. Three hundred meandered into Coventry on 27 December 1688 with neither money nor arms. The local authorities treated them very gingerly, providing 200 lbs of beef, before gently persuading them to march back to their regiments.[17] Colonel John Butler and several other officers were arrested in Whitehaven and taken to the security of Carlisle Castle.[18] 'There is continually passing of disbanded soldiers towards the seaports, probably for Ireland', wrote Robert Harley, 'and it is thought they often rifle the posts'.[19] On the following day, the mayors of Carlisle, Whitehaven, Liverpool, Chester, Holyhead, Beaumaris, Milford

Haven, Bristol, Minehead, St Ives, and Padstow were instructed by the
Earl of Shrewsbury to discover and apprehend all Irish catholics trying
to escape back to Ireland. These measures were designed not to punish
the Irish but to clear up a messy situation. Indeed, the Irish were more
frightened than frightening, adrift in an alien country, the servants of a
discredited religion and king. Shrewsbury showed considerable sympathy for these unfortunates, pointing out to magistrates that many of
those who might be arrested would have no means of support, in
which case each man was to be given sixpence a day and all ex-officers
were to receive half-pay.[20] It took a considerable time to weed all the
catholics, both English and Irish, from the ranks of the new army. Six
companies of the Duke of Bolton's regiment marched from Barnstaple
to Plymouth in November 1689 in order to serve on the fleet as
marines. *En route,* some of the soldiers were found to be catholics and
were duly disarmed and arrested. As late as March 1690, a Captain
Body who was on active service in Flanders was exposed as a follower
of Rome. Rather embarrassed, Shrewsbury allowed Marlborough to
decide the man's fate.[21] In the same month, north and central
Lancashire echoed to rumours of disbanded Irish soldiers living in
papists' houses and some companies of foot were sent to investigate
the problem, if problem there really was. A little later, Irish soldiers
were still to be found locked up in Preston gaol. Even in 1697, an
impoverished informer was able to gain limited headway with stories
about catholics creeping into the army, particularly into the regiment
of Colonel Richard Coote. The accusations were found to be
groundless but their mere existence demonstrated that a professional
informer still found the issue potentially profitable.[22]

The termination of the Jacobite wars in Ireland brought the Williamite government face to face with the problem of disposing of yet
more disbanded catholic soldiers. Twelve thousand were dispatched
to fight in the French armies, forming the basis of the Irish Brigade, but
many remained in Ireland after the settlement and took the option to
serve in the forces of William III. This arrangement did not last for
long. Eighteen regiments of these catholic leftovers were disbanded
early in 1692 and 2,000 of the better officers and men were temporarily retained and then sent into the service of the Holy Roman
Emperor. So anxious was William to be clear of the Irish that he footed
the bill for transport and provisions himself and virtually presented
the troops to Leopold as a free gift.[23] The officers received £300 to
cover their travelling expenses and nine officers and two non-commissioned officers were allowed to delay in Ireland to regain their

health before sailing to join their regiment.[24] William also gave his unreserved support to a scheme to allow Irish Jacobite officers to recruit mercenary companies in Ireland and then take them to fight for the catholic allied powers or for Venice in the Morea.[25] That William allowed these arrangements to proceed illustrates his desperation to be rid of the Irish problem, for they put the clock back by thirty years to the days when individual captains had been allowed to contract personally with hiring powers rather than being obliged to work through government agencies.[26] William ran the distinct risk of reopening Ireland as a reservoir for international recruiters, particularly the French, yet he was responding to a real need. Blathwayt reported to Nottingham that hordes of impoverished Irish officers were crossing over to Flanders and imploring the king to give them some employment. William wanted this traffic stopped at source as they were nothing but a nuisance and could not be given commissions in any case being of the wrong religion. Nottingham replied that he would do his best to prevent them leaving for Flanders but their starvation and poverty made them desperate for work.[27]

Compared to the other woes which beset the army, the disposal of the Irish catholics in 1689 and 1691 was relatively simple; they were readily identifiable and it was not difficult to complete the necessary purges. It was far less easy to decide which protestant officers and men were still basically loyal to James II, which favoured William III, and which had a foot in both camps. Equally taxing was the reorganisation of the old royal army along more modern and professional lines. The first project for William and Blathwayt was to ensure the loyalty of the majority of the army towards the new regime. This was complicated. In the first place, the bulk of the rank and file had not altered their allegiance in 1688 but had remained faithful to James II. Grudgingly, in most cases, they had accepted their fate and recognised the *fait accompli* but it could never be claimed that they had welcomed the arrival and enthronement of William of Orange and they certainly showed few signs of enthusiasm for the new order. The officer corps was badly divided. Only about one-third of James II's officers were, ultimately, to serve consistently with the armies of William III; another third retired from military life unable to compromise their oaths of allegiance and yet unwilling to act treasonably; whilst the remainder took up arms for their old master in Scotland and Ireland. William was forced to enter a life and death struggle with Louis XIV, equipped with the most unpromising human material in the shape of a sullen soldiery and a split officer corps. Even worse, William placed little trust even in those officers who had altered their allegiance and openly avowed the Orangist cause. Old Marshal Schomberg took a very dim view of officers who changed their coats in mid-campaign and William himself knew enough of English politics to realise that what had been accomplished against James II might well be achieved against him in the future. With a history of civil wars, republics, a restoration, an exclusion crisis, a catholic monarch, and a political revolution, England was the contemporary byword for instability and the army had scarcely acted as an innocent spectator in many of these events. William felt keenly that no English politician or solider was to be fully trusted but he did not possess enough Dutchmen or Germans to officer all the new regiments of the English army. He was obliged to work with unedifying native talent.

Paradoxically, the one saving grace of the supposedly amateur and inefficient English army during the winter of the Revolution was professionalism. Just as the professionalism of Southwell, Pepys, Robert Yard, Blathwayt, Godolphin, and Stephen Fox gave continuity and strength to the civil service, so the professionalism of many of James II's old officers provided cohesion during these dark months. One of the most important features of the army under James II had been the return of scores of British officers on foreign service to their home establishments. English, Irish, and Scottish officers who had fought for France, the Dutch Republic, Spain, and the Holy Roman Empire were welcomed back and these gentlemen brought with them both technical expertise and the attitudes of the international military brotherhood. In Europe, the officers of the new standing armies were international, mercenary, and itinerant. They were well accustomed to changing employers at the end of a campaigning season or a war and were little concerned with the niceties of religious or political scruple. Sir John Lanier, Charles Trelawney, Percy Kirke, John Churchill, John Coy, Thomas Langston, and many others were able to transfer their allegiance from James to William without jarring their consciences. For them it was merely a change of paymaster. It was worth their while to remain in the British army as a major international war had just commenced in which England promised to be fully involved giving the professional officers every opportunity for advancement and profit. This corps of officers, tightly-knit, personally acquainted and interconnected helped to hold the forces together. Without their contribution, unconscious and vaguely dishonourable though it was, William might well have been without any English army at all in the spring of 1689.[28]

If the reorganisation of the army was to be successful, then the initial step was to remove the troops as far from the political currents of London as possible. Duties in the capital were taken over by the Dutch and German troops which had crossed the North Sea with the Prince of Orange. Orders were sent to all regiments banishing them into the outer darkness of the provinces. As a number of corps were without field officers or recognisable headquarters, these instructions were published twice in the *London Gazette* between 17 and 24 December 1688.[29] The Life Guards had to swallow their pride and quarter in Maidstone, Chelmsford and St Albans, whilst the First Foot Guards and the Coldstreamers were obliged to endure exile in Portsmouth, Tilbury, Rochester, Dover, and Maidstone. Every regiment of James II's army which had been in England for the campaign of 1688 was given a town to act as its base, even those formations which had been scarcely recruited by the time of the Dutch landing. To these regimental headquarters, officers and men were ordered to report, providing a focus for deserters and stragglers and a depot for recruitment and administration. Security in London and the ceremonial duties in Whitehall and the royal palaces, which had once been the cherished preserve of the horse and foot guards, were assumed by Dutch soldiers.

The next stage was to bring in 'lost' weapons. From the moment of the beginning of the withdrawal from Salisbury, deserters had stolen away from the royal army until Feversham's disbandment at Uxbridge had completed the untidy process of disintegration. The men, in most cases, had escaped complete with their arms, uniforms, and equipment, most of which were then promptly sold to civilians, criminals, and publicans in return for much needed ready cash. A proclamation of 21 December 1688 rather piously hoped that all persons who had purchased arms from deserters or disbanded soldiers would bring them to the Ordnance stores at Uxbridge, Hounslow, or the Tower. Clearly the new owners were reluctant to part with their property as the proclamation was repeated on 28 February 1689 and on 1 April the Ordnance Office offered five shillings for a returned flintlock musket, carbine or pair of pistols, and half a crown for a matchlock.[30] Some weapons had been seized by civilian authorities during the emergency of November and December 1688. The mayors of Chester and Carlisle were instructed by Blathwayt to return all confiscated arms and accoutrements which had been taken from catholic soldiers.[31] In all probability, only a fraction of the missing guns were regained by the Ordnance, a factor which contributed to the shortages of basic weapons experienced by the British corps in Flanders during the summer of 1689.

With depots established for the regiments and steps taken to gather in lost weapons, the process of reconstruction continued with the purging of the officer corps. Wherever possible, political trustees of William were sent to 'regulate' the regiments which had lost their commanding officers. Lord Delamere, a man of no military experience, took command of Lieutenant-General Robert Werden's horse after he had refused to take employment under the new regime. Delamere was then expected to remove the Jacobite and suspect officers and set about improving discipline, recruitment, quarters, and efficiency.[32] Colonel Richard Hamilton, an Irish catholic, was confined to the Tower of London on 31 December 1688 and his regiment was entrusted to Lieutenant-Colonel John Coy, a seasoned veteran professional who had fought in France and Tangier. Once Coy had received his commission, several officers and 'a large number of men' were cashiered, presumably because of their religion or uncertain allegiance.[33] On the same day as Hamilton's confinement, the 'catholic' Earl of Peterborough was relieved of the colonelcy of his cavalry regiment and Edward Villiers, another hardened campaigner who had learned his trade in France during the 1670s, stepped into his shoes.[34] Colonel Solomon Richards, who had been appointed by James II on 27 September 1688, was recommissioned by William on 31 December. Richards was an Irish non-conformist who had been the lieutenant-colonel of Oliver Cromwell's own regiment during the 1650s and had become governor of Wexford in 1659, in addition to owning a 3,000 acre estate in Solsborough. Within one month of accepting William's commission, Richard had replaced his major, John Jones, and four subalterns. Richards himself did not last long but he fell from grace for committing military misdemeanours rather than from political disloyalty; he returned with his regiment from before Londonderry in May 1689 saying that the town was indefensible and a lost cause. William disagreed and sacked him for pusillanimity.[35] The old Earl of Oxford was restored to the command of the prestigious Royal Horse Guards and the Earl of Shrewsbury and Lord Lumley were given back commissions which James II had confiscated. Lord Wiltshire, another political trustee, was given the colonelcy of a new regiment.[36] Even in those formations which gave the appearance of being loyal and trustworthy, William took no chances. After receiving fulsome praise for keeping his battalion of the Scots Guards in order during their march to Ipswich, Major James Maitland was asked by

Blathwayt to 'send an account in writing of what may concern the regiment and of what officers are removing and fit to be preferred'.[37] Maitland was another officer distinguished by his known loyalty and was rapidly promoted reaching a full colonelcy in 1694. By June 1689, a committee of the House of Lords which had been appointed to regulate the army, had dismissed over 200 officers for making false musters and had found three priests in one regiment.[38] Old Sir Charles Littleton, now reaching the end of his career as colonel of Prince George of Denmark's maritime regiment of foot, wrote an anguished letter to Christopher, Lord Hatton, which gives a depiction of the severity of the purge.

I am yet in suspense how my regiment will be disposed, for we are treated so hardly, both in words and deeds, about it. Though we are not broke, I can't think they care to keep us. They will not allow us, what they do to others, to make our recruits, and tell us withal the King is so dissatisfied with the officers about the deserting of the soldiers that, as a mark of his displeasure, this hardship is put upon us. I have plainly told Lord Churchill, who is now Lord Marlborough, we think we deserve better usage as being the regiment whose officers have stuck best together in the service of any in the army, there being none but the lieutenant-colonel and one captain who have quitted it. But I do so despise the opinion I hear is had of me, that I did privately contrive the meeting and deserting at Brandford [Brentford] etc. as the playing such a double game, when I had this king's commission, that I am weary of serving any longer and am very willing to resign to those they can be better assured of.

On 16 April, Littleton's regiment was broken and the men were drafted into the Royal Fusiliers, Marlborough's corps.[39]

Henry Cornwall laid down his commission on the day that the Prince of Orange entered London. It was a purely personal decision and his two sons, Robert and Wolfran, served the new colonel, William Stewart, throughout the reign.[40] Over the period of the Revolution, the Queen's Foot under Charles Trelawney replaced the lieutenant-colonel, the major and eleven other officers out of an officer complement of forty.[41] Of the thirty-three officers serving with the Royal Dragoons on 1 January 1689, only twelve were still with the regiment one year later.[42] Eight of the twenty-four captains in the First Foot Guards retired between 5 November 1688 and April 1689.[43] Close on the heels of the disgrace of Colonel Solomon Richards, Blathwayt ordered Charles Trelawney to inspect the regiment and dismiss any officer who might be suspect and then fill up the vacancies with the nominees of the new Irish protestant colonel, Sir George St George.[44] Sir John Reresby noted on 17 March 1689 that within the space of four days, seventy officers had resigned their commissions.[45] Where he could and when the candidate was worth the effort, William tried to persuade senior officers to join his cause. No stone was left unturned to tempt Colonel Theophilus Oglethorpe, a veteran who had trained under Turenne in France, to cross the floor but he would have none of it and retired to his house at Godalming from where he dabbled in Jacobite intrigue.[46] Lord Forbes's Irish regiment of foot, the future Royal Irish Regiment, lost 500 officers and men in the wake of William's order to disband all catholics; just 130 officers and men remained. Forbes himself resigned during the winter of 1688–9 on the grounds that he could not break his oath of allegiance to James II. His major, Sir John Edgeworth, replaced him but a series of financial scandals soon brought about his downfall. The Earl of Meath stepped into the breach on 1 May 1689, and within a few weeks had introduced forty-one new officers, virtually the entire commissioned strength of the regiment.[47]

The turmoil in the Royal Irish Regiment brings to light another aspect of the purge: it was often a two, or even three stage affair. Politically amenable peers and gentlemen were thrown into the gaps created by the resignations of the senior officers who were unable to break their bonds to James II, regardless of their martial abilities. Once the immediate crisis was over, William was able to search around for more competent soldiers. Henry Cornwall's foot passed through the hands of Oliver Nicholas and John Cunningham before reaching William Stewart on 1 May 1689. Henry Wharton was politically of the right mould but no soldier and his tenure of a foot regiment lasted for just eleven months. Lord Delamere's horse was promptly transferred to the command of a highly experienced professional, Theodore Russell.[48]

Despite the purges of the officer corps, the army continued discontented and potentially disloyal. Both the Marquis of Halifax and John Evelyn realised that the remnants of James II's army constituted a pool of possible Jacobite support should there be an invasion from France, Scotland, or Ireland. The English army was 'not in order' and 'not firm' in the Orange interest and neither was it so weakened in numbers that it had ceased to pose a physical threat to the Prince.[49] Desertions among the rank and file were commonplace. The troopers from Lord Brandon's and Lord Miremont's regiments of horse were disbanded and incorporated into other regiments but the majority deserted with their horses before they reached their new formations.[50]

In the evening I visited Lord Burlington, where was Sir John Reresby. He said, his brother, a captain in the Duke of Grafton's regiment of guards [Edmund Reresby, younger brother of Sir John, captain in the First Foot Guards] was come from Oxford with six companies of that regiment [four hundred men] in order to go to Gravesend. That they quartered that night at Branford [Brentford]. That the captain was come to town to give the Duke of Grafton an account that he had not above forty men in his company. That the rest had not above fifteen or twenty men apiece. That they run daily away and declared publicly that they would go neither into Holland, nor Ireland, nor fight against King James.

On receiving this news, William listened to stories that the desertions from the First Foot Guards had occurred with Reresby's connivance and encouragement and Edmund was cashiered and put under temporary house arrest.[51] These mass desertions did not stem solely from loyalty to the old king, but often from more immediate concerns. International war meant service, wounds, and death overseas. The soldiers were also restless and demoralised from the inglorious role that they had been called upon to play during the Revolution. The guards, in particular, felt bitter and insulted at the Dutch troops taking over their traditional functions of protecting the monarch in Whitehall and Westminster.[52] Guards officers found themselves removed from the centre of patronage and fashion and the rankers, who were virtually permanent residents of London, were wrenched away from lucrative part-time employments.

William then proceeded to rub salt into these wounds. When the States-General panicked and asked for the return of the Dutch troops in order to defend the Spanish Netherlands, William seized the opportunity to rid himself of some of the troublesome old regiments from James II's army. On 19 February, he enforced an oath of fidelity on all officers and soldiers which bound them to the Prince and to obey the orders of any generals or senior officers set over them.[53] After reviewing all eighteen Dutch regiments in England on Hyde Park on 19 February, William ordered 3,000 Dutch guards to remain in England and 6,000 Dutch line troops to prepare to embark for Holland. To make up the difference of 3,000 men, William ordered two battalions of the Coldstream Guards, the Royal Scots, Prince George of Denmark's foot, Charles Churchill's battalion, the Royal Fusiliers, and Robert Hodges's battalion to ready themselves to depart for the Dutch Republic and, everyone presumed, for the war in the Spanish Netherlands. Just to make matters worse, William ordered honoraria to be paid to all the Dutch forces in England in recognition of their services, ranging from £200 for a colonel down to £2 10s. for a private soldier. William was able to dress up this insensitive act by explaining that the gifts were in the spirit of the address of thanks to the armed forces voted by the House of Commons on 1 February, even though the Commons had intended their gratitude to extend mainly to the British troops. The king sounded a trifle more convincing when he stated that the British battalions were but the first instalment of the 10,000 British soldiers who were to go to the United Provinces under the 'articles separés' of the Anglo-Dutch Mutual Defence Treaty of 3 March 1678.[54]

Humiliated, insulted, demoralised, with their officers changing nearly every week, and about to be shipped off to an unwanted foreign war, it was remarkable that no major mutiny had occurred. Grievances continued to pile up. Because the battalions earmarked for Holland were replacing the Dutch troops remaining in England, there was widespread concern that the British soldiers would be entered on the Dutch establishment where rates of pay were lower. To allay this fear, William issued a proclamation on 4 April 1689 assuring all British regiments serving in the Low Countries that they would remain on the English establishment and receive English wages.[55]

On 13 March 1689, Colonel Sir Charles Littleton received orders in his quarters at Brentford to march his regiment of foot to Greenwich ready for embarkation for Holland. When these instructions were read before the assembled regiment that morning, the grenadier company refused to comply. Littleton and his officers were staggered by this overt mutiny but after a mixture of promises and threats they succeeded in persuading the remainder of the battalion to march, leaving the grenadiers and Lieutenant Baggot's company behind in Brentford. The 'rump column' crossed the Thames at the first ferry where another group deserted and returned to Brentford. Littleton's men spent the night of 13 March at Croydon from where the colonel sent an officer to the local justice of the peace and high constable to arrest the mutineers at Brentford; this had a salutary effect and during the evening some of the Brentford deserters rejoined the battalion. However, by the end of the eventful 13 March, Littleton had lost 150 out of his paper strength of 600. Unfortunately, during the late evening the Royal Scottish Regiment of Horse arrived to take up quarters in Croydon. This regiment was in an even worse condition than Littleton's as a number of troops had already mutinied and were marching back towards the Scottish border. Mutineers from both regiments intermingled and another 100 men had disappeared by dawn. By 15 March Littleton had calmed his men down but he informed Blathwayt that embarkation was out of the question. The men's grievances, the colonel explained, were threefold. They feared that they would have to serve under Dutch officers; that they would receive Dutch rates of pay; and they felt that they were being banished from England whilst the Dutch troops remained to 'eat up the fat of the land'. Blathwayt and William responded by cancelling the embarkation order and disbanding both Littleton's foot and the Royal Scottish Horse before the end of March, drafting the few loyal men who remained with the colours into other regiments.[56]

Tension also mounted amongst the other regiments as they marched towards Gravesend, Ipswich, and Harwich to take ship for the Netherlands. A number of men in the Coldstream Guards refused to go abroad and deserted but it was in the ranks of the Royal Scots that the heaviest storm broke. Until 1678, the Royal Scots had fought in France as a mercenary regiment and there were many officers and men still with the formation in 1689 who had a very clear image of the dangers and tribulations of continental warfare. The regiment arrived in Ipswich, their projected port of embarkation, on Saturday 13 March and on Sunday they settled down in the parish church of St Mary le Tower to hear a sermon by the lecturer to the Ipswich corporation, Thomas Alexander. The fact that Alexander had been appointed in 1687 gives some indication of his religious and political convictions. Alexander's address to a soldiery which was heavily infested with Jacobites and catholics was inflammatory.[57] Immediately after the service, the 1,400 men of the Royal Scots gathered on the Cornhill where two captains and some of the grenadiers disarmed the officers and seized the regimental pay-chest. After firing a few guns in the air and limbering-up four light cannon, they set off for Scotland and home. Just half a mile outside Ipswich, the mutineers held a mass meeting at which they resolved to march north and fight for King James. A further delay allowed for the election of officers and then the hopeless and pathetic march began. Buoyed up with a false optimism, the rebels announced that the Royal Fusiliers at Harwich would join the mutiny but no one stirred, although news of the trouble in the Royal Scottish Horse and Littleton's foot at Brentford and Croydon clearly reached the Scotsmen and gave them additional hope.[58] The revolt of the Royal Scots, Littleton's and the Royal Scottish Horse may well have been the prelude to an orchestrated rising amongst James II's old regiments but, in the event, not enough common soldiers demonstrated the courage of their convictions.

William Harbord, paymaster of the forces in Ireland, acquainted the House of Commons with the situation on 15 March and the nervous members immediately addressed William to suppress the outbreak and issue a proclamation declaring the mutineers to be rebels and traitors. Jack Howe, the whig member for Cirencester, was insistent that only Dutch troops should be used to apprehend the mutineers for 'I know not which else to trust'. His advice was duly followed and two Dutch horse regiments and one of dragoons set off up the Great North Road to intercept the Royal Scots on their road from East Anglia into Lincolnshire.[59] Only just over half the regiment had deserted in the first place and at least 600 Royal Scots had meekly boarded their transports at Ipswich and sailed out of the Orwell for Holland.[60] As the mutineers journeyed northwards, stragglers and deserters gradually reduced their numbers until by the time they reached Swaton Common in Lincolnshire, only about 550 were left. Out of the grey dawn of 19 March, the Dutch dragoons swept into the rear of the mutineers' cantonment as the two Dutch cavalry regiments simultaneously pinned their front. Outnumbered by some four to one and unable to deploy their four small cannon, the mutineers surrendered without a fight. A party of forty or fifty mutineers was travelling in advance of the main body to arrange billets but they were surprised by the dragoons as they were collecting straw and victuals into Falkingham church. One sergeant tried to resist but a hail of fire cut him down and his companions dropped their weapons.[61] The whole affair had lasted for just six days.

The Royal Scots were an old regiment with a proud tradition. Their colonel during James II's reign had been the catholic Earl of Dumbarton, making the formation into something of a flagship for James's aims of military catholicism and professionalism. Sensibly, showing his customary good judgement in public affairs, William realised that lenient treatment would prove more beneficial than severity. Two days after the surrender, the paymaster-general of the English army, the Earl of Ranelagh, sent an agent into Lincolnshire with sufficient funds to pay the subsistence of the 520 remaining mutineers on their march to London. Although Godart van Ginckel, the commander of the victorious Dutch cavalry, was given permission to tie the Royal Scots together, this proved unnecessary and the journey south was peaceful enough. The majority of the soldiers suffered a short incarceration in the Bridewell in Clerkenwell but within a week they had been shipped from Tower Wharf for Holland. That was their punishment. Twelve captains and seven lieutenants went to Newgate but, in the end, only one captain was executed on Tower Hill and the rest were pardoned and cashiered.[62] By contemporary standards, these scarcely counted as punishments. Despite all the confusion of the process of the Revolution in the army, the mutiny of the Royal Scots was the only mass desertion and it was basically caused by the awful prospect of having to fight in Flanders. The mutineers, whatever they may have said on the Cornhill in Ipswich, were not initially inspired by notions of loyalty to the old king. Their complaints were more obvious and military in nature. The demoralising defeat in November and December 1688 was a far more important factor in creating discontent amongst the private soldiery than any higher principles of loyalty and allegiance. Such matters were of deep and abiding concern to the officers but their men were affected by more immediate and practical issues. After years of soft living under Charles II and James II, the British soldiers did not want to put their lives at risk in Flanders for a Dutchman who had just given them a sound thrashing.

Not only could William take some comfort in the quick suppression of the mutiny and the fact that the other regiments destined for Flanders had not followed the example of the Royal Scots, but it was clear that not everyone in the army was against him. The Duke of Northumberland, captain of the second troop of the Life Guard, presented William with an address from his officers and troopers assuring him of their faithfulness and willingness to serve. A similar petition from the officers and men of the whig Earl of Monmouth's regiment reached William on 16 March, probably in response to the news of the mutiny of the Royal Scots.[63] Blathwayt was able to write to Major James Maitland of the Scots Guards to tell him how 'extremely well satisfied' was the king with the 'orderly marching and dutiful behaviour' of the battalion under his command.[64] On the Sandhill in the centre of Newcastle upon Tyne stood an equestrian statue of James II which bore the inscription, 'the statue of the first catholic king erected by the first catholic mayor'. This was too much for the Royal Dragoons to stomach and their colonel, Anthony Heyford, an army conspirator in 1688, ordered it to be pulled down. Captain Robert Killigrew's troop duly obliged after which the customary riot ensued and the mob pelted the bronze with stones. Soldiers joined happily in the celebrations of the coronation of William and Mary in Cambridge, the officers dining with members of the corporation and university and the soldiers parading through the town.[65] Lieutenant-Colonel James Purcell of Henry Cornwall's foot, resigned his commission at the Revolution and took service with the Jacobite forces in Ireland. By the end of February 1689, Purcell had changed his mind and gave up his Jacobite commission, pestering William for employment. He was unsuccessful simply because he was a catholic.[66]

However, examples of overt army loyalty to William and Mary were the exception rather than the rule.

Our affairs at home fright us more than those abroad. The old army is rather grown worse than mended. I have a letter from my corporation [Cirencester] that the soldiers quartered there will not let the people make bonfires at proclaiming the king, and they are not checked by their officers.

So thundered Jack Howe in the House of Commons on 25 February. That same night he received a further letter from Circencester, 'which acquaints me . . . that the soldiers are so insolent there that, contrary to the interest of the king and queen, they proclaim King James . . . they drank King William's and Queen Mary's damnation'.[67] Sir John Fenwick, Lord Griffin, Theophilus Oglethorpe, Sir Thomas Haggerston, and Colonel Heneage Finch, all ex-officers, were arrested during the spring and early summer of 1689 on suspicion of Jacobite activities. Captain Robert Minors, the governor of Upnor Castle, and some of his garrison officers were taken into custody for 'drinking extravagant healths and speaking reflectingly of his majesty'. Two officers were sent to the Marshalsea for toasting King James during a training camp on Blackheath in August 1690. Two months earlier, Lieutenant-Colonel John Vaughan of Lord Colchester's regiment was gaoled and cashiered on the grounds that he favoured the return of James II.[68] Once the 10,000 British troops had reached Waldeck's allied army in the Spanish Netherlands, they deserted in prodigious numbers and one historian has ventured to suggest that Maréchal d'Humières risked the attack on the town of Walcourt on 15/25 August 1689 safe in the reasonable assumption that the British soldiers were so low in morale and so suspect in their loyalty to William that they would not fight.[69] Certainly, the French invasion plans for 1692 were based upon the idea that the English army and navy would desert William III.[70] Jacobites in France mentioned particularly the Queen's horse, the First Foot Guards, the Earl of Bath's foot, and William Selwyn's foot as potentially unstable. The reputation which the British army awarded itself in 1688 lasted for many years.

Quite how much of the purge of the officer corps during 1689 was under William's direct control is open to question. William was not well acquainted with the majority of the English officers although he knew intimately those gentlemen who had served with the Anglo-

Dutch Brigade. Furthermore, William was fully occupied with a great range of public affairs in 1689 and it would have been almost impossible for him to have conducted personally the restructuring of the army. The aged Duke of Schomberg was placed in overall command of the British and foreign forces in England but his ignorance of the minutiae of English martial life was more profound than William's and his position was merely notional. The German confided to the Earl of Ailesbury that Lord Churchill 'proposes all about the army' and that Bentinck 'is the secretary to write all'. Of the latter point there is little doubt. Bentinck was a close associate of Count Solms, the commander of the Dutch Blue Guards and one of William's right-hand men in military matters. Also, hardly any of the correspondence concerning the alterations in the officer corps during the first half of 1689 passed through the hands of either Huygens or Blathwayt. Both the War Office papers and Huygens's diary are bare of such material. The verity of the former point is more difficult to assess. Ailesbury partially clouds the issue by suggesting that Churchill made a handsome profit out of the selling of commissions and from accepting douceurs and bribes.[71] This was a standard accusation to throw against Churchill whose avarice and ambition did not endear him to his colleagues and contemporaries and whose entire career was riddled with speculation and rumour about financial misdeeds. Himself a committed Jacobite, Ailesbury cannot be relied upon to make impartial judgements about a man whose personal loyalties were dubious and who had been instrumental in ousting James II. Yet, despite all these caveats, Ailesbury's assessment does make some sense. Probably Churchill acted as an adviser to William, putting forward names for appointment and promotion. If this was the case, then both Churchill and the king were pushing in the same direction; William desired a professional and loyal officer corps whilst Churchill wanted to build up his own circle of clientage by drawing upon his contacts amongst the professionals. William's wishes and Churchill's ambition worked for the good of the army, although their motives were utterly dissimilar. However, Churchill's executive influence must have been somewhat limited. From late May 1689, he was stationed in Flanders at the head of the British corps in Waldeck's army and the real power in purging the officer corps then passed to the special committee of the House of Lords and the Commissioners for Reforming the Abuses in the Army.

One way to secure the loyalty and obedience of the old army was to guarantee regularity of pay. A proclamation of 18 January 1689

announced that trustworthy officers had been assigned to all regiments and that, provided all muster rolls had been returned to the
commissary-general of the musters within ten days, all arrears of pay
upto 1 January 1689 would be met 'forthwith'.[72] On 1 February, the
House of Commons chimed in with its own effort to persuade the
army that its correct allegiance lay with the new regime. The House
resolved *nemine contradicente,*

That the thanks of this House be given to the officers, soldiers and marines in
the army and the fleet for having testified their steady adherence to the
protestant religion and been instrumental in delivering this kingdom from
popery and slavery; and also to all such who have appeared in arms for that
purpose.

These fine words were read to each regiment and Marshal Schomberg
returned the army's expressions of gratitude to the House of
Commons three days later.[73]

Still the quest for accurate information on the state of the army
continued. Blathwayt sent a circular to all colonels asking for details of
how many weapons their regiments possessed and how many of these
were defective.[74] Another round-robin of 21 February instructed each
regimental commander to render a written account of his effective
strength and his unit's readiness to march.[75] As battalions of foot
waited at Preston for orders to embark for Ireland, Captain Anthony
Stoughton 'received an express to give a faithful account upon word
and honour what effective men there are in these companies'.[76] By the
end of January 1689, six cavalry regiments and three infantry formations had been disbanded and the reliable officers and men had
been distributed amongst other corps, but none of these measures
produced noticeably satisfactory results from William's point of
view.[77] As Sir John Reresby watched seventeen regiments march north
towards the Scottish border on 1 April 1689, he observed that many of
the battalions were 'unarmed, unclothed, and without sufficient pay to
clear their arrears'. Sir John, an old soldier himself, could not resist the
waspish remark that although there was a shortage of money for the
army, navy, and general government of the country, there seemed to
be plenty to splash around on the coronation of William and Mary.
The letters from Lieutenant-Colonel Simon Pack of the Princess of
Denmark's foot must have increased the unease felt at the condition of
the army. Pack described his command as 'good' but 'unclothed'. He
had tendered the new oaths to all his men,

not one refusing, after which I spoke to them concerning the nature of their

oath and the necessity of a most religious observance of it as good protestants
. . . and was followed with the greatest shouts imaginable and as much joy as
ever I saw in any men. So that I have a human assurance these men are for the
king's service if they are not spoiled through neglect and ill usage. Now Sir,
give me leave to tell you our miserable condition and the danger their good
humour will not continue long: our subsistence is witheld from us through
want of due returns, not only before we marched but even at our departure
. . . they are now marching without one farthing of subsistence.[78]

In other words, the loyalty of the rank and file to William and Mary
could now, just about, be guaranteed but administrative chaos
coupled with fraud and indiscipline by the officers might still blow
down the fragile edifice. The solution to the problem of how to
discover the real facts about the state of the army lay, in typical seventeenth century fashion, in the establishment of a special commission.

Under the dignity of the Great Seal, a commission 'for reforming
the abuses in the army' was appointed on 10 May 1689. Politically, it
was unmistakably whig. Nominally in the chair was the Duke of
Schomberg, but the effective work was undertaken by the Earl of
Devonshire, the lord steward of the household; the Earl of Monmouth, a treasury commissioner and colonel of a newly-raised regiment; Lord Lumley, a colonel of horse and a gentlemen of the king's
bedchamber; Thomas Wharton, the comptroller of the household and
member of parliament for Buckinghamshire; William Harbord, paymaster of the forces in Ireland and member of parliament for Launce-
ston; Major-General Sir John Lanier, who was then besieging Edinburgh Castle; Major-General Percy Kirke; and Brigadier-General
Charles Trelawney. In addition, the commissioners enjoyed the
technical expertise of Charles Toll, deputy-paymaster in England;
George Clarke, judge-advocate-general in England and personal
secretary to Prince George of Denmark; and David Crawford, the
deputy commissary-general of the musters. The background for the
commissioners' work was laid down in a proclamation of 13 May
which simply stated that some officers had committed false musters
and had detained part of their soldiers' pay. The commissioners had
been instructed to investigate. They were charged with inspecting
every regiment in its quarters to ascertain the numbers of men, their
ages, physical fitness, and length of service; the state of their clothes
and horses; their discipline and behaviour in their billets; and whether
they were actually paying for their board and lodging. If need arose,
the commissioners were given the power to disband whole regiments
or move formations to alternative quarters. The pay of all officers and

soldiers found guilty of taking free quarter was to be stopped until the debts incurred had been met. The commissioners were also asked to consult with local gentry and householders from regions through which troops had recently marched to see whether any of the men or their officers had demonstrated disloyalty to the government. In addition, they had to enquire into the regularity of the musters and to assess the extent of the arrears of pay. Finally, the gentlemen were exhorted to report regularly to Whitehall and not to hesitate to disband any officer, soldier, troop, company, or regiment which looked to be either technically or politically deficient. It was to be the first general inspection of the army in England.

Travelling in coaches and six, the commissioners set off into the summer sunshine of 1689 keeping to an itinerary publicly announced in the *London Gazette*. Knees must have trembled as colonels and captains read of the approach of the august gentlemen but the advance notice gave some commanders just enough time to put a temporary gloss on the condition of their commands. From London, the commission drove to Huntingdon, Hull, York, Durham, Newcastle, Morpeth, and Berwick. Pausing to draw breath they then plunged through Hexham to Carlisle, and onto Penrith, Kendal, Lancaster, Preston, Warrington, Chester, Shrewsbury, Stafford and Northampton.[79] As the commissioners dashed around, Blathwayt wrote to Ginckel, commanding the forces in northern England with his headquarters at Berwick-upon-Tweed, ordering him to move his units to the places directed by the inspectors. The secretary at war also informed the commissioners of changes in regimental quarters so that they could adjust their route.[80] What did this grand tour of inspection achieve? Very little. This huge fact-finding mission merely revealed some of the detail of what was already suspected. George Clarke admitted that the commission turned out very few officers simply because most of the Jacobite and non-juring officers had already left the service. Many of those whose loyalties were known to be ambiguous could not be cashiered as it had already become extremely difficult to find suitable replacements, especially amongst field and senior officers. The majority of company commanders from the old army were past masters at filling up their ranks with 'faggots' at the last possible moment before a muster and they could smell the presence of a deputy-commissary at a considerable distance. The advance notice given of the impending arrival of the commissioners gave these technicians of the false muster ample time and opportunity to make certain that the inspectors went back to London with no clear idea of how many men there really were in the army. Some overall impression of the true state of the forces was gained but the all-important detail was lacking. The Earl of Monmouth cynically observed to John Locke that one of the new regiments 'wanted nothing to be complete but clothes, boots, arms, horses, men and officers'.[81] Although there was a kernel of truth in this, Monmouth was referring to the cavalry unit of Lord Delamere, a man for whom he had nothing but contempt. Despite the attendance of the commissioners, the Earl of Roscommon's foot left Salisbury with its quarters unpaid, its pay in arrears, and with its clothing incomplete. About the shifting of men from one regiment to another, the commissioners could do nothing but declare a moratorium. All soldiers who had deserted from their old regiments before 13 December 1688 and had since joined new formations were to remain with their new units, whereas those who had moved after that date were to return to their initial regiments.[82]

Perhaps there was little for the commission to achieve. The majority of officers had already sorted out their personal political and religious stances well before May 1689 under the immediate pressure of the Revolution, the new oaths, and the wars in Scotland and Ireland. The commission's real concern had been with the prevalence of false musters; the fact that the king seemed to be paying large sums of money for non-existent soldiers. To an extent, even this problem was incapable of solution. If the loyalty of the army was to be sufficiently guaranteed to enable William to further his European ambitions, then blood money had to be paid to the officers. As Charles II had discovered, once false musters had crept into the system and had been honoured with the semi-official stamp of approval, they were the very devil to excise. Moreover, William had no intention of radically reforming the operation and administration of the British army. He wanted a force which could operate effectively in the field even if it was blemished by financial malpractice and inefficient procedures. The commission of 1689 was a political gesture towards the whigs and the anti-standing army lobby. The political purge of the officer corps had occurred by May 1689 and William was not deeply interested in further disturbing the British army by a deep investigation into its shadey regimental dealings. Not surprisingly, the commission of 1689 was intended to discover very little and duly obliged the monarch. With his profound knowledge of the French, Dutch, German, and Scandinavian armies, William probably recognised the limitations of central control over a late seventeenth century army and was far more aware than English politicians that there still existed a balance of interests between a king and his army officers.[83]

William had escaped relatively lightly. The confusion of the winter of the Revolution gave little cause for optimism and yet 10,000 British troops were in Flanders by the end of May 1689, a major mutiny had been crushed, and by August, Schomberg had landed in Ireland with a corps of twelve British regiments. They were not good troops and their officers were sometimes more distinguished by their political rather than their military training, but a British army was in being and in the field. For two years it needed to be bolstered by Dutch reinforcements and Danish mercenaries, but it slowly improved.

Notes

1   John Childs, *The Army, James II, and the Glorious Revolution* (Manchester, 1980), pp. 168–206; *The Diary of Abraham de la Pryme*, ed. Charles Jackson (Surtees Society, 1870), pp. 43–4.

2   *Pryme's Diary*, pp. 21–2, 7 Jan. 1692. Pryme was quoting Thomas Bennet of St John's College, Cambridge, who was actually in Salisbury in Nov.–Dec. 1688.

3   Childs, *The Army, James II, and the Glorious Revolution*, p. 187; S. B. Baxter, *William III* (London, 1966), pp. 250–1, 284–5.

4   *English Army Lists and Commission Registers, 1660–1714*, ed. Charles Dalton (London, 1892–1904), ii. 247; Childs, *The Army, James II, and the Glorious Revolution*, pp. 13, 47; *HP*, ii. 100–101.

5   *HMC, Cowper MSS.*, ii. 346–7, 30 Dec. 1688, Oxford.

6   *CSPD 1689–90*, p. 28.

7   *Correspondentie van Willem III en van Hans Willem Bentinck*, ed. N. Japikse (The Hague, 1932–7), iii. 83–4, 12 Dec. 1688, Prince of Orange to Earl of Danby; Colley Cibber, *An Apology for the life of Mr Colley Cibber*, ed. R. W. Rowe (London, 1899), i. 70–1.

8   Louis M. Waddell, 'The administration of the English army in Flanders and Brabant from 1689 to 1697' (Doctoral Dissertation, University of North Carolina, 1971), pp. 56–63; PRO, WO 5/5, ff. 1–60; BTRO, GM 14, ff. 165–7; BL, Egerton MSS. 2,618, f. 156.

9   Steele, i. 473.

10   WO 5/5, ff. 2–14; J. L. Garland, 'The regiment of MacElligott, 1688–1689', *Irish Sword*, i. (1949), p. 124; Luttrell, i. 493; John Davis, *The History of the Second Queen's Royal Regiment* (London, 1887–95), ii. 85.

11   *HMC, Le Fleming MSS.*, p. 232.

12   *CSPD 1689–90*, p. 6, 21 Feb. 1689, Sir Robert Holmes to Earl of Shrewsbury.

13   WO 4/1, f. 65; *CSPD 1689–90*, p. 44.

14   WO 5/5, ff. 151–2.

15   *HMC, Finch MSS.*, ii. 223.

16   *HMC, 4th Report, App.*, p. 324; Luttrell, i. 525, 543, 554; *HMC, Le*

Fleming MSS., pp. 241–2; Richard Ollard, *Man of War; Sir Robert Holmes and the Restoration Navy* (London, 1969), p. 206.

17 HMC, *Le Fleming MSS.*, p. 231.
18 WO5/5, f. 69; *CSPD 1689–90*, p. 4.
19 HMC, *Portland MSS.*, iii. 433, 15 Mar. 1689.
20 *CSPD 1689–90*, p. 26.
21 HMC, *Downshire MSS.*, 320; *CSPD 1689–90*, p. 504.
22 HMC, *Kenyon MSS.*, pp. 238, 240, 24 Mar. & 6 May 1690; *Letters illustrative of the reign of William III from 1696 to 1708, addressed to the Duke of Shrewsbury by James Vernon, secretary of state*, ed. G. P. R. James (London, 1841), i. 300, 302, 331.
23 HMC, *Finch MSS.*, iv. 23–50; J. G. Simms, *Jacobite Ireland, 1685–1691* (London, 1969), p. 260; for the history of the Irish Brigades in France, see, J. C. O'Callaghan, *History of the Irish Brigades in the service of France* (Shannon, 1969).
24 *CTP 1557–1696*, p. 317, 31 Aug. 1693.
25 HMC, *Finch MSS.*, iv. 54, 1 Apr. 1692.
26 John Childs, 'The British Brigade in France, 1672–1678', *History*, lxix. (1984), p. 386.
27 HMC, *Finch MSS.*, iv. 444, 455.
28 For the rise of professionalism in the British army, see, John Childs, *The Army of Charles II* (London, 1976), pp. 25–37; Childs, *The Army, James II, and the Glorious Revolution*, pp. 27–8, 119–37; Fritz Redlich, *The German Military Enterpriser and his work force* (Wiesbaden, 1964–5), 2 vols.
29 *LG*, nos. 2411, 2412.
30 Steele, i. 474, 478.
31 WO 5/5, ff. 76, 90, 23 Feb. & 5 Mar. 1689.
32 *The Portledge Papers*, ed. R. J. Kerr & Ida Coffin Duncan (London, 1928), p. 57, 1 Jan. 1689; *HP*, iii. 689–90.
33 R. L. Pomeroy, *The Regimental History from 1685 to 1922 of the 5th Princess Charlotte of Wales' Dragoon Guards* (London, 1924), i. 6.
34 R. Whyte & A. H. Atteridge, *A History of the Queen's Bays, the 2nd Dragoon Guards, 1685–1929* (London, 1930), p. 33; NLW, Herbert MSS. HM2 14/7a, p. 84.
35 F. J. Hebbert, 'The Richards brothers', *Irish Sword*, xii. (1975), p. 200; HMC, *Portland MSS.*, iii. 427, 31 Jan. 1689; Henry Horwitz, *Parliament, Policy, and Politics in the Reign of William III* (Manchester, 1977), p. 31; *Calendar of the Orrery Papers*, ed. Edward MacLysaght (Dublin, 1941), p. 372.
36 *Portledge Papers*, p. 56.
37 WO 4/1, f. 64, 19 Mar. 1689.
38 HMC, *Le Fleming MSS.*, pp. 244–5.
39 *Correspondence of the Family of Hatton*, ed. E. M. Thompson (Camden Society, 1878), ii. 129–30; WO 5/5, f. 108.
40 F. L. Petre, *The History of the Norfolk Regiment, 1685–1914* (Norwich, 1924), i. 7.

41 L. I. Cowper, *The King's Own, the story of a Royal Regiment, 1680–1914* (Oxford, 1939), i. 53.
42 C. T. Atkinson, *History of the Royal Dragoons, 1661–1934* (Glasgow, 1934), pp. 56–7.
43 F. W. Hamilton, *The Origin and History of the First or Grenadier Guards* (London, 1874), i. 332–3.
44 WO 4/1, f. 68; WO 5/5, f. 250.
45 *The Memoirs of Sir John Reresby,* ed. Andrew Browning (Glasgow, 1936), p. 566.
46 A. A. Ettinger, *James Edward Oglethorpe, Imperial Idealist* (Oxford, 1936), pp. 32–3; *HP,* iii. 170–1; *CSPD 1673–5,* p. 567.
47 G. Le M. Gretton, *The Campaigns and History of the Royal Irish Regiment from 1684 to 1902* (Edinburgh & London, 1911), pp. 3–4.
48 Dalton, *Army Lists,* iii. 1–9.
49 Reresby, *Memoirs,* p. 571; *The Diary of John Evelyn,* ed. E. S. de Beer (Oxford, 1955), iv. 620, 629, 631.
50 WO 5/5, f. 34, 9 Jan. 1689, Constantijn Huygens to Colonel Edward Villiers.
51 *The State Letters of Henry, Earl of Clarendon, Lord Lieutenant of Ireland during the reign of King James the second, and his lordship's Diary for the years 1687, 1688, 1689, and 1690,* ed. Richard Powney (Oxford & Dublin, 1765), ii. 329, 10 Mar. 1689; Reresby, *Memoirs,* pp. 563–4.
52 Hamilton, *Grenadier Guards,* i. 325–30; Bod. Lib. Ballard MSS. 39, f. 57, 14 Mar. 1689, 'YG' to Arthur Charlett.
53 WO 5/5, f. 73, 19 Feb. 1689.
54 H. R. Knight, *Historical Records of the Buffs, East Kent Regiment, 3rd Foot* (London, 1905), i. 279, 283; Luttrell, i. 503–4; *HMC, Kenyon MSS.,* p. 218; Clarendon, *Diary,* ii. 322; Hamilton, *Grenadier Guards,* i. 329–30; DCRO, D60/X12.
55 Knight, *The Buffs,* i. 283; Steele, i. 478–9.
56 Charles D. Ellestad, 'The mutinies of 1689', *JSAHR,* liii. (1975), pp. 9–12.
57 *Letters of Humphrey Prideaux to John Ellis,* ed. E. M. Thompson (Camden Society, 1875), p. 153, 27 June 1692; J. R. Western, *Monarchy and Revolution; the English State in the 1680s* (London, 1972), p. 143; BL, Add. MSS. 38,695, ff. 146–8.
58 Paul Rapin de Thoyras, completed by Thomas Lediard, *The History of England* (London, 1732–7), iii. 353.
59 *CJ,* x. 49–50; Anchitell Grey, *Debates of the House of Commons, from the year 1667 to 1694* (London, 1763), ix. 164–6; Reresby, *Memoirs,* p. 565; Luttrell, i. 511; *CSPD 1689–90,* p. 27; F. B. Maurice, *The History of the Scots Guards* (London, 1934), i. 74.
60 P. L. Müller, *Wilhelm III von Oranien und Georg Friedrich von Waldeck* (The Hague, 1873–80), ii. 147, 15 Mar. 1689, William III to Waldeck.
61 *HMC, Cowper MSS.,* ii. 352, 20 Mar. 1689, Edward King to mayor of

Lincoln; Luttrell, i. 514.

62 *CSPD 1689–90*, pp. 43, 45, 186; Luttrell, i. 515, 566; *HMC, Le Fleming MSS.*, p. 244; WO 5/5, f. 114; WO 4/1, f. 64.

63 Luttrell, i. 505, 512.

64 WO 4/1, f. 125, 19 Mar. 1689.

65 *HMC, Cowper MSS.*, ii. 356; *CSPD 1689–90*, p. 115; *The Diary of Samuel Newton, Alderman of Cambridge, 1662–1717*, ed. J. E. Foster (Cambridge Antiquarian Society, 1890), pp. 99–101.

66 SP 63/340, f. 167.

67 Grey, *Debates*, ix. 110, 112.

68 Luttrell, i. 586; ii. 58, 88; *CSPD 1689–90*, pp. 71, 118, 145; *CSPD 1690–1*, p. 4.

69 Müller, ii. 163–4; Knight, *The Buffs*, i. 293.

70 Geoffrey Symcox, *The Crisis of French Sea Power, 1688–1697* (The Hague, 1974), p. 122; James Macpherson, *Original Papers containing the secret history of Great Britain, from the Restoration to the accession of the House of Hanover* (London, 1775), i. 460, 484.

71 *The Memoirs of Thomas, Earl of Ailesbury*, ed. W. E. Buckley (Roxburghe Club, 1890), ii. 244–5; *HMC, Dartmouth MSS.*, i. 249; *Journal van Constantijn Huygens, den zoon, van 21 October 1688 tot 2 Sept. 1696* (Utrecht, 1876), i. 1–98.

72 Steele, i. 476; WO 5/5, f. 43; Luttrell, i. 497.

73 *CJ*, x. 16, 18; WO 5/5, f. 61.

74 WO 4/1, f. 62, 26 Jan. 1689.

75 *HMC, Coke MSS.*, p. 351; WO 5/5, f. 74, 21 Feb. 1689.

76 *Diary of Thomas Bellingham, an officer under William III*, ed. Anthony Hewitson (Preston, 1908), p. 54, 26 Feb. 1689.

77 WO 5/5, ff. 9–23; L. Edye, *Historical Records of the Royal Marines* (London, 1893), i. 298–303.

78 Reresby, *Memoirs*, p. 570; BL, Add. MSS. 38,695, ff. 152–5, 1 & 6 Apr. 1689.

79 BL, Harl. MSS. 7018, ff. 251–4; *CSPD 1689–90*, pp. 97–8; *HMC, Leyborne–Popham MSS.*, pp. 268–70; *LG*, nos. 2455, 2458; Steele, i. 481; *CTrB 1689–92*, pp. 126, 128; Lediard, iii. 377.

80 BL, Harl. MSS. 7018, f. 251; WO 5/5, ff. 162–3; WO 4/1, ff. 70, 72.

81 HCRO, L. 1524; *The Correspondence of John Locke*, ed. E. S. de Beer (Oxford, 1976 cont.), iii. 637–8, 9 Jun. 1689, Newcastle upon Tyne; Horwitz, *Parliament, Policy and Politics*, p. 91.

82 *Locke Correspondence*, iii. 643, 1 Jul. 1689, Salisbury, Dr Adrian Thomas to John Locke.

83 Childs, *Army of Charles II*, pp. 104–9; John Childs, *Armies and Warfare in Europe, 1648 to 1789* (Manchester, 1982), pp. 78–9.

II

The officers

Lieutenant John Guyon of the Royal Fusiliers had kicked off his shoes and stockings at the end of a hard day and was relaxing on a camp bed in the tent of his lieutenant-colonel, John Shrimpton. It was ten o'clock in the evening. In barged Lieutenant John Day of the same regiment. 'Whose tent is this?' he demanded. 'It is my tent,' replied the recumbent Guyon. 'No, it is not.' 'Yes, by God, it is,' answered Guyon in a rising temper, to which Day responded, 'No, by God, it is not'. Guyon had by now got off the bed and faced his accuser. 'Yes, by God, it is, as long as I lie in it.' 'How can that be?' enquired Day. 'Yes it is,' said Guyon, 'for it is the colonel's tent and as long as I lie in it, it is mine'. 'By God,' shouted Day, 'you might have given me a more civil answer'. 'How do you mean?' 'Not to answer me so crossly,' snapped Day, 'but to answer me more like a gentleman'. At this, Guyon's temper cracked. 'He is a dog that says I do not answer him like a gentleman.' 'You are a dog and a villain for saying so, and so come out,' spat Day.

Guyon seized his sword from the table and followed Day out into the night. In the ensuing brawl – it cannot be dignified with the title duel – Guyon beat Day to the ground and broke his sword. Despite the efforts of Lieutenant Gervase Holland to separate them, Guyon picked up the hilt of the broken weapon and repeatedly hit Day over the head. One week later, Lieutenant John Day died from his injuries, the victim of a senseless quarrel which he himself had started. Guyon was court-martialled and sentenced to death, but he was later reprieved and cashiered from the army.[1]

If this sordid incident had occurred in 1689 when William III's army was riddled with amateurism and divided allegiances, it might be more comprehensible, but it did not. It took place in the Cockelberg camp, south of Brussels, in the last year of the War of the Grand Alliance when peace negotiations were nearing completion and it represented the behaviour of a supposedly honed and professional officer corps. This juvenile behaviour, typical though it was of the age, was no better than that of the officers who had served under Charles II and James II. Perhaps it was partially caused by the pressure of active service – the Royal Fusiliers had fought at Namur in 1695 – or the boredom of camp life. Perhaps it was symptomatic of a deeper malaise.

Lionel Copley of Wadworth in Yorkshire, came from a family which enjoyed the political patronage of the Osbornes. Under the guidance of the Earl of Danby, Lionel Copley had secured a captaincy in the Irish Foot Guards in 1674 and had then transferred into the prestigious First Foot Guards in England two years later. On 31 December 1681, he was granted the lucrative and important post of lieutenant-governor of Hull and, in this capacity, he played a vital role in bringing about the capture of Hull for the Orange interest during the Revolution in 1688. Copley's patron, Danby, become governor of Hull on 1 April 1689 and set about creating 'a place of retreat, and whereby to make his terms, should there be any change of times'. Danby's agent in this task was Lionel Copley and he set about running Hull like a police state. Between 1689 and 1691, he committed a series of arbitrary and illegal acts. John Baker's horse and saddle were stolen by soldiers, his cattle were impounded in Hull blockhouse, and the military encroached upon his lands. Casting covetous eyes upon the house and 'brewing vessels' of Thomas Sawbosworth, Copley had him arrested by a file of musketeers and locked in the provost-marshal's house for eleven days. When this failed to persuade Sawbosworth to part with his goods, Copley made out that he was a deserter from the army and threw him into the town gaol to await trial at the next assizes. During the General Election of 1690, Copley drew out the town guard in front of the Guildhall in contravention of all custom and government instruction. Lieutenant-governor Copley was also anxious to benefit from the trade of the city and so he levied an unofficial and personal tax of one farthing per ton on shipping which entered and left the port 'to the great oppression of several masters'. As if this litany of crime was insufficient, Copley also interfered with the posts. On a number of occasions he seized the mail 'and caused the same to be brought to his own house or to a tavern, where he opened and embezzled, destroyed or otherwise disposed of several letters'. When a complaint was lodged with John Wildman, the postmaster-general, Copley's response was to arrest the deputy-postmaster of

Hull, George Mawson, and tie him,

neck and heels, with that extreme violence, that the blood gushed out of his
nose and mouth and kept him in that intolerable posture for two hours and a
half, till the petitioner was utterly deprived of sense and put in extreme hazard
of his life, and remains to this day miserably crippled, disabled in his limbs,
and impaired in his sight.

Petitions were sent to the House of Commons and Copley was
summoned to appear before the honourable members but Danby's
protection proved adequate and no official action was taken against
him. In 1691, Copley was quietly removed from Hull and sent off to
govern Maryland where he died two years later.[2]

Major James Menzies, commanding Lord Lindsey's regiment of
foot in Glasgow, also seriously abused his privileged position. He
arrested a number of citizens in October 1694 claiming that they were
deserters. Complaints were lodged with the magistrates who duly
ordered Menzies to bring the men before them but Menzies refused
their request on two separate occasions. As a compromise, a conference was arranged in the town clerk's office between Major Menzies
and three of his captains, the provost, two baillies, and the town clerk,
Robert Park. The meeting opened with the provost politely asking that
the prisoners be brought before them and in this he was quietly
supported by Park. Menzies then completely lost control of himself
and hit Park with his cane. A brawl ensued which ended with Captain
Jervis holding Park down as Menzies drew his sword and ran him
through. Robert Park died instantly. The major then hurried to the
guardhouse and drew up the duty company in three files to block the
road whilst he leapt onto his horse and fled. The hue and cry spread
out in pursuit of the major and later that day, John Gillespie, John
Anderson, and Robert Stevenson found Menzies skulking in a garden
at Rainfield. They challenged him to surrender but, again, Menzies
drew his sword upon which the three men took no chances and shot
him dead. Gillespie, Anderson, and Stevenson were tried for murder in
December 1694 but they were acquitted.[3]

Arbitary, arrogant, overbearing, childish, quarrelsome, and
regarding themselves as above the law, the army officers of William III
did not inspire great affection or confidence. William was a soldier–
king in the European tradition with a great interest in the fighting
abilities of armed forces but his achievements in the British army were
strictly limited. By 1697 it was much larger and the officers did have
considerable experience of active service but it remained, by modern

standards, a Jekyll and Hyde; brave and effective, yet amateur and weak. It was truly an institution in transition, and it was small wonder that the anti-standing army lobby in English political life gained, rather than lost ground during the reign of Dutch William. Few officers devoted more time to their martial duties than was absolutely necessary. To judge from the observations of Thomas Bellingham, an aide-de-camp to William in Ireland, as the troops billetted around Preston in 1689 to await shipment across St George's Channel, the officers lived the life of Reilly. They played cards, drank, arranged bowls matches, went for walks, organised horse races and cock-fights, shot at the butts, dined, danced and generally idled their time away. If the officers were lounging about like this, one hesitates to imagine what the men were getting up to. Now and again the officers gathered their men from their quarters and taverns and went through a few basic exercises. When the army went into winter quarters in Flanders, those officers who could not escape back to England created their own imitations of London society in the unlikely surroundings of Ghent, Bruges, Malines, Nieuport, and Ostend. They set up casinos, hired travelling players, and held balls and banquets. Yet, all of this was supposed to be beneficial to a young man or, at least it had no worse effects upon evolving personalities than an Oxford education.

Your brother Michael hath been here ever since a little before Christmas last, who is very much improved; stammering little, swearing nor taking any tobacco at all, and being very free from drinking, which are very great accomplishments in a camp, as well as in a college.[4]

On the other hand, a single campaigning season in the West Indies could wipe out a colonel, his wife, his daughter, and most of his officers and soldiers.[5]

Charles II had 442 commissioned officers in his English army in 1684, with a further 175 commissions in Scotland and 406 in Ireland. By the time of the emergency of November 1688, James II had increased his officer corps to 1,869 in England, whilst the Scottish and Irish establishments remained virtually unchanged. After the expansion of the forces in the winter of 1693–1694, William III could boast of 5,000 commissioned officers on all three establishments. It is very difficult and dangerous to generalise about such a large body of men; they were a very disparate bunch indeed. Aristocrats, gentry, younger sons of titled and landed families, mingled with tradesmen and even a few from lower social orders. Captain Henry Mordaunt complained to the House of Commons on 21 November 1692 that 'trumpeters and corporals have been made officers'.[6] Throughout the reign there was a shortage of good and capable officers. Nearly all the professionals who served overseas had been absorbed into the army of James II by 1687 and the augmentation of the forces to face the Dutch in November 1688 was only officered by scraping the bottom of the barrel. After the flight of James II, this pool of officers was decimated leaving William the unenviable task of hugely increasing his army with an inadequate supply of commanders. There is an impression that this shortage of officer material continued all through the War of the Grand Alliance. To an extent, the anti-standing army tradition developed a reticence amongst the landed gentry about sending their sons into the forces whilst the certainty of a major disbandment at the end of hostilities made the taking of a commission something of a financial gamble. Sir James Lesley's regiment of foot was without both a lieutenant-colonel and a major in September 1689 and Rupert Billingsley was asked to 'fill-in' until a new major 'could be found'. A 'paucity' of officers with the army in Flanders were reported in October 1695 in the wake of the siege of Namur and officers who had been dismissed for quite serious offences reappeared in commissioned ranks after indecently short intervals. Lieutenant-Colonel Francis Edgeworth of the Royal Irish was broken over a clothing fraud on 1 May 1689 but was recommissioned as major of the same regiment on 1 October. Likewise, Captain Euvert de Meausse Saurency of the First Foot Guards was cashiered for 'insulting' Lord Coningsby but he was given a captain's place in Lord Donegal's foot in June 1701.[7]

William Tomson, a London haberdasher, became a captain of foot; Colonel John Courthope was a lawyer and a member of the Middle Temple; Lietenant James Thomas of the second Marine regiment married the widow of Edmund Ludlow and so acquired an estate worth more than £3,000 a year. Thomas was thirty and Mrs Ludlow admitted to sixty-two.[8] It was still a time when a gentleman volunteered for military service treating it as a part of the 'grand tour' and of his general education. Maurice Thompson, 'a fool of £4,000', was badly wounded whilst serving as a volunteer at the siege of Namur in 1695. Danby's son, the Marquis of Carmarthen and a naval officer, went to Flanders in July 1696 'to make the campaign'.[9] Around the officer corps lay a penumbra of regimental chaplains, quartermasters and surgeons. All these places were commissioned but they did not enjoy full officer-status; they more closely resembled the position of modern warrant officers. Regimental chaplaincies were generally taken by young clergymen, the military equivalent of a curacy.

William Sawle, the chaplain of James Stanley's foot, petitioned for his arrears of pay on 11 June 1698 so that he could meet the charges of taking up a living which had been recently conferred upon him. Doubtless, regimental chaplaincies were also of some interest to older clergy who could gain no preferment and lacked patronage. Their duties were not onerous. Indeed, there is every suggestion that some chaplains combined their military duties with civilian employment and were frequently absent from their soldierly flocks. The most famous chaplain of the reign, Edward D'Auvergne, was the rector of St Brelade on the island of Jersey as well as chaplain to the Royal Scots. Garrisons in England had their spiritual needs attended to by the local parish priest. When with his regiment, the chaplain was not overworked. He was obliged to read the common prayer once a day, although how this was to be accomplished when the formation was quartered in small groups over a wide area was not mentioned, preach once a week, and administer the sacrament four times a year. Chaplains in Ireland treated their martial duties so lightly that on 29 July 1697 the Lords Justices forbade beneficed clergymen from becoming regimental chaplains.[10] It was clearly a relatively attractive position. Work was light, the salary amounted to £120 per annum, and there was a good chance of catching the eye of the king or another effective patron. D'Auvergne was made one of the chaplains to the king in 1699. For highflyers, the army was a useful path to serious preferment. In March 1692, John Wickhart was created chaplain-general to the British forces in Flanders at a daily wage of ten shillings and within three years he had risen to become Dean of Westminster. His successor, Richard Willis, ended his life as Bishop of Winchester.[11]

If there was dissension within the officer corps of William III, it arose principally from professional rather than from social or political origins. To begin with, questions of loyalty did arouse considerable passions. On 3 April 1689, there was a duel between an officer of James II's army and a newly commissioned officer 'about the two kings', but these matters were settled relatively quickly.[12] Thereafter, friction centred upon a subject not unknown in English society; gentlemen versus professionals. In the time of Charles II there had only been room on the home establishments for the career professionals during the periods when the army had been expanded for war, and most of their lives were spent fighting abroad as mercenaries. When James II brought the majority of these men back into England during peacetime to command his enlarged armed forces, the question of a professional army which was consequently remote from the sympathies of parliament and landed society raised its head and was one of the principal causes of political concern during James's short reign. The Glorious Revolution did not solve this problem, in fact it accentuated it. A large number of the old professionals who had dominated the military scene between 1660 and 1688 faded from view. Hugh Mackay and Sir John Lanier were killed at Steenkirk in 1692, Percy Kirke died from fever in the same year, Thomas Langston retired in 1690, Sir John Fenwick and Theophilus Oglethorpe turned Jacobite, and Charles Trelawney resigned his regiment in 1692 and was put out to grass as governor of Dublin. However, not all the familiar faces disappeared. Many of the old guard from the Anglo-Dutch service, the brigade in France, and Tangier, were still rising through the ranks in 1689 or were ripe for senior commands. Edmund Mayne, Hatton Compton, John and Charles Churchill, John Coy, Edward and Godfrey Lloyd, Samuel Venner, Thomas Talmash, John Cutts, and Edward Villiers were the up and coming professionals, the men who dominated the field and general commissions during the War of the Grand Alliance. However, the majority of the subalterns' places went to young and new men. Some naturally came from old military families, many were from the gentry and aristocracy anxious to serve king and country, but large numbers came from either the middling and lesser gentry or from commercial roots. This latter category looked upon the army as a career, a way to earn their living, and constituted the new professionals. Charles Wills began his distinguished path to military fame as a captain in Thomas Erle's foot in 1691; John Webb started a soldier's life in the First Foot Guards in 1689; and George Wade entered the Earl of Bath's foot as a humble ensign in 1690.

Initially, the landed classes were not unduly concerned. A war had to be fought and officers had to command the army, but the war went on and on and the army and its officers became more important and more numerous, both politically and socially. Peace in 1697 did not bring an end to the problem for although the army was disbanded the professional officers did not sail overseas to search for a living but took half-pay and waited in idleness for the advent of the next war. Professional army officers had become a factor in English society, both in time of war and peace. The new permanence of a professional military order had created a new political and social interest by 1702, just as the rise of the City of London had formed another political focus to challenge the ancient hegemony of land and breeding.[13] The oil of gentlemen officers and the water of professionals did not mix well, even though the latter were militarily far more important. After all, it was the professionals who were retained under the half-pay system not the gentlemen. It was professionals who formed the continuous, experienced officer corps which began in the Nine Years' War, fought through the War of the Spanish Succession, and then stretched out into the eighteenth century.

If it is his Majesty's pleasure not to restore my lieutenant-colonel (John Ward, who had been court-martialled), my choice is Major (William) Purefoy of Brewer's. . . . I like Purefoy because he serves not just for his bread, but for love of king and country and for honour. As for my major (Charles Wills), I shall be silent. I could only wish gentlemen might serve with gentlemen, old soldiers, as they style themselves, with old soldiers, for when they are mixed they seldom agree, so, by consequence, the service suffers.[14]

This leads into a maze of complexity. What did Colonel Thomas Saunderson mean in his use of the terms 'gentleman' and 'old soldier', what was his definition of the gentleman and the professional officer? His choice for a new lieutenant-colonel to replace John Ward, a gentleman with colonel plantations, lay between Charles Wills, the son of an impoverished farmer and therefore reliant on his army pay, and William Purefoy of a well-established Cornish landed family. Ward was clearly a gentleman and Wills was obviously a professional or 'old soldier', but what of Purefoy who went onto the half-pay list in 1697? Was he a 'gentleman–professional' in the same mould as John Churchill? The key can only be found by altering the application of the label 'professional'. Up to this point, a professional officer has been identified as a soldier who looked to his sword to earn his daily bread and, consequently, was mainly to be discovered fighting overseas but returning to the British Isles on the occasions when the army was augmented for war. As we have seen, the huge majority of these men returned to England, Ireland, and Scotland permanently during the reign of James II and added considerable martial expertise to the armies of William III. After 1689, this use of the term 'professional' has to be abandoned because from this date professional officers served principally on the British establishments and cannot be identified by their foreign service; gentlemen and professionals were now part of the same establishment and, accordingly, the nature and perception of the professional officer underwent a subtle but distinct transformation.

The officer profession had not suddenly sprung into existence in 1689. Aristocrats and gentlemen had long displayed considerable martial pretensions which surfaced during the Wars of the Roses, Elizabethan and Jacobean jousting, and in the Civil Wars. Both before and after the Civil Wars there had been hundreds of English gentry and nobility on foreign service in Germany, Russia, Sweden, France, and the United Provinces. The expansion of the officers corps after the Revolution was the final and official flowering of a long-term trend and it released a considerable reservoir of aptitude and talent ready for employment in 1689. The English landed classes may have been opposed to the maintenance of a standing army but they were not offended by the military profession nor were they necessarily against military institutions. Most of them were, after all, connected with the militia. However, the English political élite was horrified by the notion of a standing army and there lay the new distinction between the gentleman and the professional officer. A gentleman would fight for his sovereign, religion, and country, would take a commission in the army in time of war or insurrection, would serve in his county trained band, would even sit in parliament and vote for wartime taxation and supervise its assessment and collection, but he was utterly sickened by the idea of retaining a standing army in years of peace. All he could see were the ghosts of Cromwell and James II, and the living menace of Louis XIV. Professionals were those officers who were prepared to serve in a peacetime regular army and who were unconvinced by the propaganda of the anti-standing army movement. The professional could thus be a noble, a gentleman, or a commoner, rich or poor, but he was positively distinguished by his attitude towards the retention of a peacetime establishment. The professional had become a 'career officer'.[15] Such a change did not occur overnight and William III's reign witnessed the phasing out of the old, foreign-service professionals, and their steady replacement by the new, younger, career officers of the future.

The British officers of King William were not necessarily good soldiers. A certain political stance or a lifetime of service on foreign stations guaranteed neither competence nor ability and professionalism had little to do with martial capabilities. Men did not, and do not, join armies because they were demonstrably excellent at soldiering; they took commissions because they wished to follow their particular career for whatever personal reason. In some cases, the new officers did turn out to be future generals – Charles Wills was a fine example – but most were glad to achieve the pinnacle of an ultimate promotion to field rank. Similarly, under the pressures of war, rank amateurs can discover that they are superb soldiers, a category in which Oliver Cromwell was the outstanding example. William himself thought very little of the expertise of any member of the British officer corps, whether gentleman or professional. Even those like Kirke and Talmash who had spent all their lives in the service of one state or another, failed when given independent commands. The king was firmly of the opinion that 'the humour and character of a peer of England do not agree very well with the discipline to which a colonel must be subject', and he described the Captain of the Second Troop of the Life Guards, the Duke of Northumberland, as 'a great blockhead'. When William used the word professional, he meant Dutch, German, Huguenot, or a British officer who had served in the Anglo-Dutch Brigade.[16] William was accustomed to the Dutch system where officers took little leave and were promoted on merit.

In British military affairs, William was not a reformer. His purpose in invading England in 1688 had been to acquire and then to use the resources of the British Isles in his struggle against Louis XIV. He required an English army which simply worked and to achieve this he was prepared to adapt and to improvise but he was not prepared to waste valuable time and money in undertaking a radical reform. Without a family and without obvious dynastic ambition, William often thought in terms of immediate expediency rather than planning for the distant future. New regulations were passed as and when they became necessary. One of the results of this hand to mouth approach was that abuses which had been painfully apparent under Charles II and James II continued to fester but provided that they did not impair the operational efficiency of the army in the field, William either turned a blind eye towards them or swept them under the carpet by issuing new edicts which he failed to enforce. The principal ills which affected the officer corps were the granting of commissions to children, general indiscipline, the making of false musters, and taking unofficial leave of absence.

Child commissions were usually given to the offspring of senior or distinguished officers as a form of reward. Percy Kirke's son, of the same christian name, was made an ensign in his father's regiment at the tender age of twelve months on 3 May 1684. His senior by just six months was George, Lord Ettrick, the son and heir of James II's favourite, the Earl of Dumbarton, when he was created a company commander in the Royal Scots on 23 October 1688. Little Lord Ettrick lost his commission in December 1688, not because William forbade the practice of granting child commissions, but because of his father's flight to France.[17] Kirke's son became a captain on his sixth birthday in 1689 and eventually assumed regimental duties when he had reached the dizzy heights of senior regimental captain. At twenty-four he was a lieutenant-colonel and a full colonel three years later. Richard Hill, the murderer of the actor William Mountford, was commissioned into Viscount Lisburne's foot when he was just twelve years of age whilst James, the son and heir of Brigadier James Ferguson, colonel of the Cameronians, was gazetted ensign on his fourth birthday. In recognition of his outstanding services to William of Orange, Hugh Mackay's twelve year old son was given a company on 1 September 1692 after his father's death at Steenkirk. He grew into a man of no great ability and died a major in the Dutch army at the age of twenty-eight. The Earl of Monmouth wheedled his infant son into an ensign's place on 1 January 1694, naturally in his lordship's own regiment. One very young boy, Carey, the son of Captain Peter Godby of Thomas Fairfax's foot, was commissioned ensign in 1696 but he was forced out of his place during the disbandment of the following year and re-entered the army at a more sensible age in 1709.[18] Some more senior officers did have reservations about making children into army officers. When the king offered a commission to Brigadier William Selwyn's eleven year old son, it was politely refused.[19] Child officers, though, were very much the exception. Most young men taking subaltern's commissions did so in their late teens and early twenties. At the other end of the scale there was no retirement age and although William disliked elderly officers, the purchase system gave him no real opportunity for enforcing discharges. Sir Francis Compton, lieutenant-colonel of the prestigious Royal Horse Guards, was still serving, aged seventy, in 1699 but he was clearly a man of exceptional physical stamina having just married a girl of seventeen.[20] His colonel, the Earl of Oxford, was but a mere seventy-three.

The late seventeenth century was an age of considerable social violence. Many men, and women, carried arms as a matter of everyday course and there was a tendency for the complex rules of a brittle social etiquette to break with a frightening crack. Amongst gentlemen this led to duelling. Army officers, officially armed and engaged in a profession of controlled violence, were some of the worst offenders. Duels were monotonously frequent and although repeatedly banned by royal command there was no discernible diminution during the reign. It would be both tedious and pointless to list all the recorded duels involving army officers during William's reign but some of the more notable, or where a reason for the quarrel can be detected, are more worthy of mention. Officers of Lord Berkeley's regiment of dragoons were dining at the lodgings of Captain Edward Mortimer when, at four o'clock, in burst Captain Thomas Lloyd who had left the regiment under a cloud but a fortnight before. The party broke up and as various members were walking across the market place in Louvain, Lloyd accused Major Giles Spicer of having run him down to Lieutenant-Colonel Francis Hawley. Spicer denied this and an argument ensued, swords were drawn and Spicer wounded Lloyd in the thigh. Lloyd died soon afterwards. Spicer was duly court-martialled but was acquitted as the court felt that he had only acted in self-defence. Hawley also put in a good word for Spicer, an old comrade-in-arms from the days of Charles II and the expedition to Flanders in 1678.[21] Captain Edward Parry of John Churchill's regiment and a Captain Cary travelled fifty miles in order to inflict mortal wounds on one another.[22] Whilst the allied army was rushing by forced marches to deflect the French from crossing the Scheldt at Pont-de-Pierre near Oudenarde, Sandy Dundas still found time to kill Cornet Conway of Polwarth's regiment in a duel.[23] Colonel Sir Richard Atkins was convinced that his wife had been sleeping with a beau who went by the unlikely name of Medlicot. Atkins met this glorious specimen of humanity in a coffee shop, walked with him to the Temple and then offered him a challenge. True to his type, Medlicot declined the invitation whereupon Atkins knocked him down with his cane. One month later, Lady Atkins was again causing her husband anxiety. This time the supposed correspondent was Lord James Howard, a brother of the Duke of Norfolk, a man of sterner stuff who was happy to oblige the pugilistic Sir Richard, but 'after some few passes, his lordship having the advantage, they friendly drank a glass of wine together, my lord denying the accusation laid to his charge'.[24] Captain William Hill of the Coldstream Guards was stupid enough to offend Lord Mohun; John, Lord Cutts, and Major Henry Holmes squabbled about rumours of political skulduggery on the Isle of Wight; and one lieutenant killed another in Chester.[25]

Perhaps one of the more celebrated duels of the 1690s was that which ended in the death of Conway Seymour, the eldest son of Sir Edward Seymour. At the age of twenty-four, Conway Seymour was 'a new set-up, vain young fop, who made a great éclat about the town by his spendid equipage, not setting any bounds to his pompous living'. On Sunday 4 June 1699, he met with Captain George Kirke of the Royal Horse Guards in St James's Park. They were both drunk and, 'calling one another beaus at a distance, they challenged, and went out of the park to fight', where Seymour was wounded in the neck. After a week, he seemed to be on the road to recovery when he decided 'to go on a debauch, eating of fruit and drinking four or five glasses of burgundy wine after'. This unhappy concoction caused him to vomit, reopening his wound, infection set in, and he died. Kirke was found guilty of manslaughter, burnt in the hand and temporarily suspended from his commission. However, it made little difference to his career and he rose to become the major of the Royal Horse Guards in 1704.[26] On the morning of Saturday 21 December 1700, Major-General William Stewart and Captain Thomas Bellew duelled in London. As they had both been badly wounded in their right hands during the war, they agreed to fight with pistols. They held their fire until they were within two yards of each other and then Stewart fired – and missed. Bellew breathed a sigh of relief and sportingly threw away his gun saying that he had no wish to kill the general.[27]

Silly and childish though they were, duels only hurt the officers involved and they had little effect on the overall operational efficiency of the army, whereas false musters most certainly did. The mustering system was crucial to the functioning of a seventeenth century army as it was the sole means by which the crown ensured that it actually possessed the soldiers for which it was paying and that it was not being defrauded by its agents, the officers. It also gave the crown an up to date record of how many soldiers it had in pay at any one time. In theory, the system was simplicity itself and had changed little since the days of Elizabeth I. On a given day, a deputy commissary of the musters paraded the troop or company and inspected the men present to make sure that the numbers and the names matched the signed list which had been presented to him by the unit's officers. If all was in order, then he counter-signed the muster roll and posted it off to the paymaster-general in London who duly issued pay according to the strength shown on the roll. What could go wrong? The answer, unfortunately, was just about everything. Musters were conducted once every two months but between those days captains habitually maintained their commands at well below establishment, pocketing the wages of the absent men, and then filled them up especially for muster-day by hiring 'faggotts' off the street or by putting their servants into uniform. Soldiers could be persuaded to respond to two names during roll-call, and men who had long been in their graves found themselves miraculously resurrected.[28] False musters proved impossible to eradicate. Partly this was because limited false musters were officially permitted. The agent of each regiment was paid by one fictitious man in each troop or company, most colonels enjoyed the luxury of the wages from one 'dead-pay' from all their sub-units, and the right of officers to possess servants was open to huge abuse. During the chaos of 1688 and early 1689, false musters boomed. In Flanders, throughout the war, the muster system collapsed entirely. No detailed musters were held and, at best, the men were counted by two muster-masters to make sure that the total on parade bore a vague resemblance to the total on the muster roll. Who was actually on parade was never investigated. Perhaps any seventeenth century mustering system, even the superior French method, could not have kept adequate records of men whilst on active service with the constant changes caused by death, sickness, desertion, and recruitment. In Flanders, the Williamite government had to accept the unpalatable truth that it could be, and was, grossly swindled by its colonels and company commanders.[29]

In England, Ireland, and Scotland, the government did its best to control the damage caused by false musters. On 29 November 1689, a proclamation introduced regulations for the Scottish musters. Any officers found guilty of making bogus returns were to be cashiered and obliged to repay the embezzled funds and all the 'faggotts' employed by such officers were to be whipped and burnt in the cheek. Servants could not be mustered and any non-commissioned officer who exposed a false muster was to receive a reward of five hundred marks and any common soldier, two hundred. Above all else, the muster rolls had to give personal details of each man listed: his place of birth, where he had been levied, and his trade before enlistment. The muster rolls were to be made out in triplicate – one copy going to the clerk of the Treasury for the issue of pay, one to be retained by the muster-master general, and one to be kept in the regimental archive.[30] A similar set of regulations was included in the first renewal of the English Mutiny Act on 20 December 1689, with one important addition. As the company officers and the deputy commissaries obviously connived at false musters, perhaps the presence of a third party might guarantee fair play. Accordingly, the local justice of the peace or mayor of a corporate borough had to be notified of any muster within his area and he was then obliged to be present and referee the whole affair.[31] This merely revealed a further snag; many justices were also army officers. Accordingly, the Mutiny Act of 20 December 1690 insisted that the umpiring justice could not be an officer and in the boroughs of Westminster and Southwark matters had become so bad that two law officers had to attend each muster.[32] Additional regulations were brought in on 30 May 1690 insisting that all soldiers absent from musters because of sickness or furlough had to be represented by properly attested certificates. None of this seems to have had much appreciable effect upon the occurrence of false musters. Scottish muster rolls in 1698 contained nothing but bare names; no places of birth, occupations, or personal details. English rolls in 1691 were equally unsatisfactory.[33] The increasingly draconian regulations included penalties against officers, soldiers, commissaries, and civilians who in any way aided or abetted false musters and were enshrined in the various renewals of the Mutiny Act, but the only real answer lay in Edward Sackville's suggestion of higher rates of pay for company officers.[34]

Despite all the preventative medicine, the disease continued throughout the reign in England, Ireland and Scotland. In all probability just the very worst cases came before the court-martial. Only when a subordinate – officer, non-commissioned officer, or soldier – informed on his captain could official action be taken. As most company officers benefited from the rake-off on false musters and the commissary was unable to hear or see straight with a few guineas in his pocket, the chances of detecting chicanery were slight indeed. Even the regulation insisting that local magistrates oversee the conduct of musters came to nought as they mostly failed to materialise and refused to dirty their civilian hands with army business. The Mutiny Act of 1695–6 imposed a fine of five pounds upon any justice who neglected to attend a muster.[35] When accusations were made, the informants were usually motivated by pique, the prospects of rewards, or both. Charges laid by soldiers or non-commissioned officers generally failed because they were unable to prove their cases through insufficient evidence; in other words, they did not have access to the precious, parchment muster rolls.[36] When an action was brought by a fellow officer then the chances of a successful prosecution increased enormously simply because he could secure the relevant muster rolls, he could read, he understood the workings of the court martial, and the presiding officers were more likely to accept the word of a gentleman than that of a low-born corporal.[37] Interestingly, the epidemic of false musters also infected the Dutch and Huguenot regiments serving on the English and Irish establishments.[38]

Apart from false musters, the financial indiscipline of senior officers had other, more ingenious outlets. When Lord Forbes resigned the command of the Royal Irish because of his allegiance to James II, the colonelcy fell to his major, Sir John Edgeworth, who was duly commissioned on 1 March 1689. Edgeworth rubbed his hands with glee for 'he was in much haste to grow rich', and set about defrauding the clothing account of his new regiment. He bought old clothes from soldiers who had been disbanded at Uxbridge and Salisbury and sent them to his regiment's quarters at Chester whilst stopping his men's pay as if the clothing had been in pristine condition. Unfortunately, the king got to hear of this and sent two inspectors to investigate. They found that the new clothes of the Royal Irish had already seen considerable service and Edgeworth was cashiered along with his three sons, Lieutenant-Colonel Francis, and Captains Ambrose and Robert.[39] Few cases of financial irregularity were as spectacular as this. Most of the accusations made against colonels by subordinates hinted that money for the payment of quarters and subsistence was being held back by the colonel for his own, temporary profit. Colonel François du Cambon, the commander of one of the Huguenot regiments, was temporarily suspended for this offence in 1693, as were Colonels Samuel Venner and Henry Rowe in 1695.[40] Colonel Rechteren of a Dutch foot regiment, was accused of financial mismanagement by some of his officers in February 1695; his court-martial only found enough evidence to warrant Rechteren's suspension but William restored him to his command. However, Greibe, his German adjutant, then brought a civil action for debt of £580 and Rechteren was arrested and carried to Newgate.[41]

Matters came to a head in 1695. During the year, an increasing number of senior officers found themselves begrimed with accusations of defrauding their men, caused, partly, by the weakening economy and the growing currency crisis. The people of Royston in Cambridgeshire, delivered a petition to the House of Commons on 23 January 1695. They complained that Captain Henry Cartwright's company of Ferdinando Hastings's regiment of foot had demanded sums of money over and above those legally set for their provisions and their quarters. Every week, the company had insisted that the town pay 17s 6d to the lieutenant, 14s to the ensign, 6s to the two sergeants, 4s 6d to each of the three corporals, and 3s to each of the sixty private soldiers. If they refused to pay up, then the soldiers threatened to distrain upon their goods and chattels. In addition, Royston was still smarting at having received no money for quartering two companies of the notorious Sir John Edgeworth's Royal Irish in 1689. Colonel Hastings, Major Anthony de Moncal, and assorted captains and ensigns, along with the regimental agent, Tracy Pauncefoot, were summoned to the bar of the House of Commons and examined. The truth rapidly came out that Agent Pauncefoot had the pay of Cartwright's company in his hands but had neglected to issue it. This had left Cartwright's men without funds and so they had tried to raise their own pay from amongst the miserable inhabitants of Royston. Clearly, this required further investigation as a regimental agent was the personal employee of the colonel and was responsible solely to the colonel. The House appointed a committee which took and considered evidence until 5 April 1695. In the interim, a circular order was issued by Blathwayt to all colonels instructing them to make absolutely certain that every penny was passed on to company captains and that the officers within each regiment accounted fully with one another. When the committee presented its report to the Commons, it made sad and depressing reading. Many regimental agents detained the subsistence money in their own hands and used it to finance their personal, short-term investments. To cover their tracks, they bitterly informed their officers and soldiers that no pay had yet been issued but generously offered to make them a loan until such time as the paymaster-general should send the balance of pay. Effectively, agents were lending soldiers their own, legitimate pay at interest. To disguise these operations, agents entered 'great deductions under the head of contingencies' in their accounts. More specifically, Hastings had compelled his officers to buy their uniforms from him at extortionate prices 'by confining and threatening those who would not comply therewith'. Hastings also took bribes in return for recommending men for commissions and failed to make proper accounts with his company commanders. Pauncefoot helped himself to 2s in the £1 of all regimental moneys and had cheated the entire regiment out of a royal bounty of five hundred guineas. Hastings was cashiered and Pauncefoot was gaoled.[42]

Strangely, despite these revelations and the fact that the cancer of corruption reached right up to Treasury Secretary Henry Guy, very little was done to regulate the activities of agents and colonels in accounting with their regiments. Even the objectionable Pauncefoot, and his brother Edward, made a comeback in regimental agency before the end of the reign. Lieutenant-Colonel Mountjoy Mortimer of the Earl of Essex's dragoons was cashiered for identical offences in 1696 and Major-General Isaac de la Melonière and Sir Bevil Grenville were both court-martialled but acquitted in 1697.[43] Financial frauds by senior officers bothered junior officers, deeply concerned private soldiers, horrified civilians and parliament, but they did not seem to worry the king. Again, where the fighting performance of the army was not unduly affected William seemed relatively content to leave well alone.

Keeping officers at their posts was a difficult task. Technically, any officer wishing to take leave had to secure a pass from the secretary at war and the approval of his colonel but this was only complied with if the proposed absence coincided with a muster. In this case, a certificate from the secretary at war had to be produced to the commissary in order for the absent officer to be included on the muster roll and so receive his pay for the preceding two months. If leave of absence did not include a muster day then the formality of acquiring a pass was dispensed with and officers on duty in England, Ireland, and Scotland seem to have come and gone very much as they pleased.[44] Officers serving in Flanders often returned to the British Isles during the winter months to recruit their regiments and during this time they helped themselves to periods of unofficial leave. They were usually summoned back to their overseas commands in late March or early April.[45] In England though, unofficial leave was a serious problem and led to units being severely under-officered and ill-disciplined. To William, such slovenliness was typical of the amateur soldiers of England and was directly contrary to the practice in the United Provinces. As early as 20 February 1689, Blathwayt sent a circular to all colonels complaining that there were far too many officers absent without leave and reminding them that leave was only permissible if the officer was in receipt of a certificate given under the sign manual and commissaries were forbidden to muster an officer without such a document being produced.[46] Nothing much happened. On 17 October 1691, Colonel Sir George St George wrote in astonishment to Blathwayt that, 'there are more of my officers now in town than I have known and yet none of them without some reasonable pretence of business'. From Portsmouth in 1692, the Earl of Monmouth observed that Colonel Tobias Purcell's foot was short of five captains as it embarked for Guernsey and Ferdinando Hasting's battalion possessed just three captains when it marched into Portsmouth garrison from its quarters in Winchester, Salisbury, and Rumsey.[47] Despite repeated attempts to enforce the regulations, when the expeditionary force left Ireland for Holland in June 1701 not enough officers could be found.[48]

In trying to assess the martial competence of William III's officers it is easier to discover examples of ineptitude and irresolution than illustrations of ability and bravery. Partially this can be explained by the fact that the incidence of failure is far more noteworthy than everyday normality but historians can only travel where the evidence

leads. To begin with, William refused to believe that any British officer
had even the remotest idea of what he was doing. The simple business
of setting up a camp near Whitehaven for the horse and a camp near
Liverpool for the foot before their embarkation for Ireland in June
1689 was not allowed to proceed until the Dutch quartermaster-
general, Scravemoer, had inspected the sites and supervised all the
arrangements.[49] Colonel John Hales bore out all William's prejudices
when he lamented to Blathwayt on 12 July 1692 that, 'I am not fond of
fighting'. He was sacked shortly afterwards.[50] Squabbles about precedence amongst the colonels dominated the ill-fated attempt to raid St
Malo in 1692. The king's solution was simple. Whoever had the older
commission, provided that it had been signed by William either as
Prince of Orange or as king, was to have seniority, but this did not
prevent an almighty row between the three captains of the Life Guards
after the Earl of Scarborough sold his commission in 1699.[51]
Supposedly, the Earl of Macclesfield boasted that he only admitted
into his regiment of horse officers with military experience but he
could not have been too particular as one of his captains was the
infamous duellist, Lord Mohun. There were periodic reports of insu-
bordination and 'disrespectful words' being addressed to a senior by a
more junior officer, and even one instance of cowardice in the face of
the enemy.[52] William, Lord O'Brien bemoaned the fact that he could
not 'with honour' avoid having to go to Flanders although he would
much rather have remained in England. Lord Galway's horse was
encumbered with half-pay officers, officers with one arm or one leg,
officers with seven children, officers in ill-health, officers who spent
half their time as paymasters for pensions, and all this in an active
service unit commanded by one of William's Dutch trustees. Bishop
Burnet thought that the surrender of the garrisons at Dixmuyde and
Deynse in 1695 was symptomatic of a deep malaise within the British
army, a condition produced by its performance in 1688 and by
William's disinterest and distrust. Although the feeble defence of the
two Flanders towns can be attributed to other causes, there is some
truth in Burnet's remark, especially when the poor performance in the
field is linked with the corruption scandal of the same year. The army
did not fully recover its morale and confidence until Marlborough
took command in 1701, banishing foreign generals and commanders-
in-chief for good.[53] Overgeneralisations, though, are always a dangerous indulgence – young Michael Fleming revelled in army life.

I have lately received a letter from your brother Michael, who is in great heart,
and likes the King's camp in Flanders very well, being there well paid and

having there all kinds of provisions in great plenty.[54]

But then, Fleming was very young, very junior, and very impressionable.

Every effort was made to ensure that the new regiments of 1693 and 1694 were commanded by colonels from either gentry and aristocratic stock or who were personally known to William through service in the Anglo-Dutch Brigade. The former were supported by experienced lieutenant-colonels and majors. Officers who were competent but personally difficult were moved from regiment to regiment until they found a niche which fitted both their abilities and their characters. In Flanders, at least, a respectable standard of military efficiency was expected.[55] Some officers were good, some were bad, and some were average. What is clear is that the army did not suffer from a malaise of corruption amongst its officers but from William's indifference. Corruption there certainly was but it was not widespread and tended to be concentrated largely in some of the regiments which spent most of their time in England and were not employed in Flanders. The British army suffered from a lack of leadership, no encouragement, and from the absence of radical reform and imaginative administration. Blathwayt was a pen-pusher and a paper-shifter; he was not a creative administrator in the mould of Samuel Pepys. William was a soldier–king and he had done much to reform the Dutch army during the 1680s but he did not try to repeat this process with the British army in the ensuing decade. Regulations were issued when the principal faults of the British officer corps became glaringly obvious but there was no consistent effort to follow up these exhortations, no system for springing surprise checks and inspections, and few new ideas. The army existed, it grew larger, and it served William's international purposes; that was as much as the king expected and as much as he received in return. Captain Henry Mordaunt's complaint to his fellow members of the House of Commons that 'I wish the king would reward and punish more than he does' neatly encapsulated the reciprocal indifference.[56] There was neither training nor instruction for junior officers whilst the draconian measures with which William had mastered the Dutch officer corps in the 1670s and 1680s were never translated into the British establishment. Many of the new officers of 1689 and 1690 came from the ranks of the Life Guard, a reservoir of trainee officers, but there was no equivalent of the procedure in the Netherlands whereby two companies of cadets were permanently attached to the Blue Guards and to the other regiments of

William's Dutch *garde du corps*. If it had not been for the abundant supply of qualified Huguenot refugees in England in 1689 and 1690, the rapid augmentation of the army for the war in Flanders, Scotland, and Ireland might well have proved nearly impossible to implement. Training was acquired in the field by the seat of the breeches; what counted was experience. The simple ability to raise recruits entitled a man to a subaltern's commission, twenty volunteers proving sufficient to secure an ensign's place in 1693. Sir Edward Dering spent £5,000 of his own money in recruiting, clothing, paying, and equipping a foot regiment for service in Ireland in 1689 for which outlay he was rewarded with a colonel's commission. His son was still searching for compensation from the government in 1720. For British officers, there was no equivalent of the Brussels Military Academy. On 22 April 1689 a new clause was proposed for insertion into the Bill for regulating hackney carriages.

Whereas there is no sufficient provision made within this kingdom for instructing young men in military exercises, for want whereof great numbers are sent abroad, to the apparent hazard of their being perverted in their religion; which might be prevented and great sums spent among foreigners might remain in England, if an academy for teaching military exercises (existed) in or near London or Westminster: Be it enacted for the aforesaid purposes, and to the end that English gentlemen may learn the said exercises at reasonable rates:
That a moiety of the revenue that shall arise yearly by virtue of this act shall be employed by their Majesties in purchasing land in or near London and Westminster, and erecting thereupon an academy wherein military exercises are to be taught, and after the yearly sum of £400, part of the revenue arising by virtue of this act, shall be applied towards the maintenance and salaries of the masters and repairs of the buildings; the academy to be always under the care of five commissioners to be appointed by their Majesties.

This enlightened endeavour to provide basic education for Britain's future officers was lost when the entire bill was 'laid aside' later in the year. Fortunately, there were some young men who just loved fighting, like the Earl of Marchmont who put off his wedding when he heard the news of the investment of Ath in 1697 and dashed across the North Sea to join in the fun. This was regarded as especially noteworthy as the marriage was the end product of a love-match.[57] In a system where experience amounted to the basic qualification for promotion, the purchasing of commissions and the consequent reliance upon seniority to decide preferment had some merit. It tended to retard the progress of those with natural ability but no money, yet it allowed the ordinary, plodding, competent company officer, the backbone of all armies who possessed modest financial means, to proceed by measured steps up the rungs of the ladder of regimental rank as he slowly developed experience, maturity, and confidence. Whilst it was far from the ideal method of managing an officer corps, the results which it achieved in the field were uniformly adequate and history has witnessed a number of inferior procedures for creating and advancing army officers.

To have led troops across to William during the campaign of 1688 or to have been an active conspirator in William's interest was insufficient qualification to gain rapid promotion and military honours after 1689. Certainly, no conspirator suffered through his activities but none did spectacularly well, with the spasmodic exception of John Churchill. Charles Trelawney remained a brigadier throughout the reign, Percy Kirke stayed a major-general and blotted his copybook before Londonderry in 1689, whilst John Lanier and Thomas Langston continued their slow rise to prominence. Thomas Talmash was given the colonelcy of the Coldstream Guards but then he had not been a conspirator, rather a loyal member of the prestigious Anglo-Dutch Brigade. William's policy in 1689 was to give the colonelcies of both newly-raised regiments and those of James II whose commanders had resigned or been dismissed to aristocrats and upper gentry who had demonstrated a loyalty to the new regime and who possessed sufficient territorial interest to raise new recruits rapidly. Not many of these political colonels retained their regiments for long. Lord Herbert commanded his regiment for just one month, Lord Lovelace for seven, and the unsuitable Earl of Roscommon died in mid-September 1689. When Sir John Guise resigned his battalion in mid-September 1689, William breathed a sigh of relief and gave his place to Lieutenant-Colonel John Foulkes, an Anglo-Dutch veteran. Guise had proved singularly incompetent.[58] Their replacements tended to be serving officers who had experience with the army in England, or who had fought in the Anglo-Dutch Brigade. The latter were particularly favoured. John Cutts, Thomas Talmash, William Selwyn, Samuel Venner, Charles O'Hara, Theodore Russell, Francis Fergus O'Farrell, Henry Erskine, Sir Thomas Livingstone, Robert Goodwin, Edward Dutton Colt, Godfrey and Edward Lloyd, George Lauder, Sir Henry Bellasise and the Earl of Oxford; the list of new colonels read like the roll call of the Anglo-Dutch Brigade. Unfortunately for William, the Anglo-Dutch Brigade had only consisted of six regiments and could not possibly have contained enough senior officers to form the entire basis of the expanded army in England. Some of the 'political' colonels of 1689 continued in their commands, gaining a little military experience with the passage of time. The Duke of Bolton came to command two battalions, the Earl of Monmouth and Peterborough clung onto his cavalry regiment until 1694, and the Earl of Scarborough sold out in 1699. New and untried officers had also to be promoted. Robert Byerley 'had never seen a pistol fired' when he came to command a dragoon regiment in 1689 and he left the regimental accounts in total confusion on his resignation three years later. William III's colonels were a mixture of gentry and aristocrats and career professionals, with the latter showing an increasing domination.

Between 1689 and 1697, the war years, the acquisition of a colonelcy was far from easy. For the eleven new battalions of foot and the four new regiments of cavalry raised during the winter of 1693–4, there were a number of suitors. The Earl of Warwick and Holland, Lord Mountjoy, Lord Sherborne, Sir William Waller, Lord Blaney, Oliver Cromwell, the Earl of Arran and John Manley were all rumoured to have 'put in' for the vacancies. Only Lord Mountjoy and the Earl of Arran were successful. John Manley was probably interested for all the wrong reasons as he was experiencing serious financial difficulties and looked upon the proprietorship of a regiment as a means of making easy money.[59] If colonelcies were hard to come by on account of the money which could be made from them and the political clout and patronage which they engendered, the opposite was true for the lower commissions. So desperate was the situation in 1689 that likely young gentlemen were approached and asked whether they would consider taking a commission. Other suitable candidates took commissions just to try out army life. Edmund Wyndham trained for the law but became an officer in the Duke of Bolton's foot for four years before returning to the legal profession. Dour Scots convenanters like Lieutenant-Colonel William Maxwell or John Blackader joined the army largely from religious motivation. 'Yea, now is the time when those that are for Christ and those that are for Anti-Christ are opposing themselves one to another'. Subalterns' commissions in the Guards and other prestigious regiments were competitive all through the war, but until the great disbandment began in 1697 it was neither difficult nor expensive for a father to place his son in a line formation. By the end of 1697, the coming of demobilisation and half-pay had put all commissions at premium value and when a humble lieutenant in the First Foot Guards died in 1700 there were a great many 'solicitors' for his place, including candidates supported by James Vernon and the Earl of Dorset.[60]

Whether belonging to a colonel or an ensign, all commissions had to be purchased. Theoretically, the purchase system operated as a graduated series of investments. On entering the army, the new officer paid a sum of money for his commission directly to the officer whose retirement had created the vacancy. When the new officer eventually received promotion, he did not sell his initial commission but paid the monetary difference between the value of his old commission and his new one directly to the officer who was leaving the service. Other officers who received promotion because of that same retirement also paid the difference in value between their old and new places, all of this money going to make up the full value of the commission of the retiring officer. To take an example. If a captaincy was worth £1,800, a lieutenancy £700, and an ensigncy £450, then the retiring captain's eighteen hundred pounds was composed of the lieutenant paying him £1,100 for his promotion, the ensign £250 for his elevation, and £450 from the ensign for his new commission. Only when an officer actually left the services did he sell his commission; until that time he merely added to his investment with each higher rank achieved.[61]

Purchase was as much a political as a military necessity. It ensured that the British army remained a collection of regiments rather than becoming a monolithic whole.[62] Also, the purchase of commissions acted as some real proof against political interference in the officer corps. James II had endeavoured to disregard the property rights of purchase when he had dismissed officers for political reasons, and this fear for the sanctity of property lay at the root of the army desertions in 1688. Although William tried to abolish purchase and institute promotion on merit, as in the Dutch army, his failure effectively secured the political loyalty of the British officer corps. Purchase made certain that only those who could afford it and enjoyed the approved social and political background became members of the army élite. Purchase further ensured that changes in the composition of the officer corps were slow. Thus equipped with officers of the correct political and social hue, the army did not pose too much of a threat to the liberties of the nation. Much of the concern about James II's army had arisen through the king's use of professional officers rather than gentlemen in the higher echelons of command. Purchase guaranteed that the army did not become an immediate prey to political faction as the nature and composition of the officer complement within each regiment could not be affected with each shift in the Whig and Tory wind. This was only true in the case of regimental ranks. The appointment of general officers was often directly political, but these were not purchasable ranks but commissions in the gift of the king or government. During William's reign, the cost of commissions was relatively low. The anti-standing army sentiments displayed in 1688–9 and again in 1697–9, may have dissuaded some of the landed orders from buying commissions for their sons. This, if only for William's tenure of the throne, made the officer corps somewhat cosmopolitan and kept commission prices under control.[63] William loathed the very idea of purchase and did his best to stamp it out but, as with so much else in the army, he failed utterly. From 19 February 1689, all officers had to swear that neither they nor anyone on their behalf had given 'anything' in order to obtain their commissions. Although this oath was further refined in 1693 and 1694 before being incorporated into the 1695 Mutiny Act, it had no affect on the situation, and the trade in commissions continued at all regimental levels.[64] By 1691, a further complication had set in – colonels were accepting bribes before they even got round to selling the commissions to the lucky candidates. The patronage of the governor of Inniskilling was said to be worth £150 and Colonel John Foulkes thought it worth his while to let it be known that he did not accept douceurs for recommending young men for places in his regiment. According to the Earl of Monmouth and Peterborough, there were two coffee houses in the Charing Cross region of London which specialised in broking army commissions and colonels used these agencies to rake in as much money as they possibly could both through sweeteners and straight purchase.[65] William stood very little chance of putting a stop to purchase. There was far too much continuity between the old army and the new, too much money had already been invested, and William relied for military guidance in 1689 upon those officers who were heavily involved in profiting from the system. Technically, the only money which should have passed hands during the issuing of a commission was the fee due to the secretary at war in England and the chief secretary in Ireland.[66]

Information about the actual cost of commissions is hard to discover as most arrangements were made verbally and were not committed to paper. Obviously, there was an enormous variance between Guards formations and line regiments, between horse and foot, and between permanent units and those raised solely for the duration of the war. The latter obviously charged the lowest commission prices and it is possible, although unprovable, that the officers of these wartime regiments paid little or nothing for their positions when they were first raised except, perhaps, for a little present to the colonel.

Thereafter, and bearing in mind that the regiments raised during the winter of 1693–4 were only in existence for three years, little or no purchase seems to have occurred. However, if a unit could show a history which stretched back into the reigns of James II and Charles II or came from the Anglo-Dutch Brigade, then there was an excellent chance of it surviving a disbandment and so commission prices were correspondingly high. An ensign's place probably cost between £200 and £400 and a captain's commission might have fetched anything from £500 to £1,000. Colonelcies ranged from the £2,000, which Colonel John Coy raised when he sold his dragoon regiment to the Earl of Arran, to the £12,000 paid by the Earl of Albemarle for the captaincy of the First Troop of the Life Guards in 1699.[67] Miscalculations could occur. If a regiment found itself disbanded after the peace of 1697 against all expectations, then the financial loss of all the officers was heavy. This was one of the reasons why commission prices in the Horse and Foot Guards were so high; the investment was vitually without risk whilst in all other regiments there was an element of poker in buying a commission during a war.

Once in the army, by fair means or foul, the next obstacle was to achieve promotion. Family interest was vital. Lieutenant-General William Stewart's regiment of foot read like his family tree; one of his sons was the lieutenant-colonel, another was the major, and nine other relatives held commissions out of a total officer complement of forty-one. Brigadier William Selwyn made it a point of sanctimonious and pious honour that he had not filled his regiment with his own children. 'During the war, I considered his Majesty's service so much, that of three sons not one has a commission in my regiment, though I had several precedents to have a full company'.[68] It was possible to rise from the ranks, and Sir Charles O'Hara of the First Foot Guards recommended a sergeant for an ensign's place adding the important proviso that the sergeant was really a gentleman as one of his cousins was a commissioned officer.[69] However, it was patronage which elevated junior officers into captaincies and field commissions, and the best form of patronage was family connection. The Earl of Nottingham asked Blathwayt to promote the interests of his cousin, Christopher Yelverton, pointing out that a vacant company had recently appeared in the First Foot Guards on the death of Charles Rogers. Yelverton was unsuccessful, as Lord Sidney, a personal friend and favourite of the king, put forward one of his relatives, Gilbert Primrose, and he won. William recommended the unlucky Yelverton to come over to Flanders and show his mettle in the field, advice which he took as he distinguished himself at Steenkirk 'and I hope will obtain his desires upon the present vacancies in the Guards'. Nothing like a good battle to ease the promotion stakes.[70] Soldiers who fought hard impressed William. Christopher Codrington gained his captaincy in the Guards after performing sterling service at the siege of Namur in 1695.[71] Sir Daniel Fleming summed it all up very neatly.

My son Michael is, I thank God, very hearty at Dendermonde in Flanders and hopes to be advanced, considering the many vacancies there, and here in England. He was at great charge in listing, passing, and marching above twenty able soldiers from Kendal to London; and he got no pay for himself until he arrived in Flanders. He hath been an ensign a year, he hath behaved himself well in the Battle of Landen and elsewhere in Flanders, and he hopes to be preferred. If you shall be pleased to speak for him to Colonel [James] Stanley, a member of your house, and to Mr Blathwayt, probably it may prove much to my son's advantage.

This was not quite enough to tip the scales in Michael Fleming's favour as he wrote to his father on 18 March 1694, asking for some money for 'if one can but appear handsome in the camp it goes a great way in his preferment'. This did the trick and by 24 July 1694, Michael Fleming was listed Colonel Stanley's captain-lieutenant. Although personal soliciting on behalf of candidates for subalterns' places was the standard form, William tended to reserve to his own judgement the appointment of field and general officers regardless of the most vigorous canvassing. Despite the recommendation by the Lords Justices of Ireland of Lieutenant-Colonel Henry Pearce of Sir Henry Bellasise's foot for the command of one of the new regiments in 1694, William ignored their suggestion.[72]

Promotion by seniority of commission within the regiment was already well established and altered little between William's reign and the end of the eighteenth century. When a vacancy occurred, the eldest ensign moved up to become the youngest lieutenant, whilst the eldest lieutenant, who was usually the captain-lieutenant in command of the colonel's own company, advanced to the position of most junior captain. If the unit had any cadets attached to it, then the eldest and most deserving, or the best connected, took the junior ensign's place. In a formation without a gaggle of cadets, gentlemen volunteers, and other hangers-on, the youngest ensign's vacancy went to an outsider.[73] The right to nominate to subaltern vacancies rested with the colonel. A colonel wrote to Blathwayt giving his choice and Blathwayt then contacted the King to check that all was in order. When William was absent in Flanders or the United Provinces, subaltern promotions and new commissions in England had to be vetted by the Board of General Officers and then given final approval by the Lords Justices.[74] The promotion and appointment of field officers was much more a question of dictation by the king through the medium of Blathwayt. Colonels were still asked to suggest the names of suitable officers for field commissions within their own regiments but this did not imply the virtual guarantee of nomination. The final decision rested very much with William and even when he was abroad the commissions of all field and general officers had to be personally approved and decided upon by himself. There was, of course, a huge amount of lobbying and arm-twisting but William tried to ensure that his British regiments were commanded and administered by his own appointees. Colonel Hugh Wyndham wrote to Blathywayt that 'the King had ordered me to take a captain of Langston's in the room of Mark Le Bas'.[75] When Sir Henry Bellasise's lietuenant-colonel, Robert Tempest, died in 1699, the colonel was only able to 'recommend' a successor from the half-pay list. Naturally, he suggested the name of Thomas Handiside, an old Anglo-Dutch officer, whom he knew would be acceptable to the king.[76] William's absolute control over field appointments came as a nasty shock to Colonel Godfrey Lloyd in 1692 after he had assumed that he would take over the regiment previously directed by the unsoldierly John Hales. Despite being one of the favoured from the magic circle of the Anglo-Dutch Brigade, Lloyd was told that he was to command one of the Duke of Bolton's battalions and was duly packed off to the West Indies.[77] After the two major disbandments between 1697 and 1699, the competition for all commissions at all levels increased to fever pitch. The merest rumour that a serving officer was ill was enough to bring a cascade of letters of patronage tumbling onto Blathwayt's desk. This could lead the secretary at war into committing some unfortunate faux pas. In October 1698, he promised the commission of captain to Dampierre Breval in Belcastel's Huguenot regiment on the assumption that the incumbent would die. He rather unsportingly recovered.[78]

Apart from the political colonels of 1689, William looked for experience and proven competence when promoting and creating field officers. The king rarely elevated gentlemen to senior positions in the army who were without sufficient military prowess and ability; the army was not dominated by military ignorami as had not infrequently been the case during the reign of Charles II and, to a lessor extent, during that of his successor. Major James Wood and Major Robert Bruce, who both wrote to William Carstares trying to enlist his support for their promotion to the lieutenant-colonelcy of Lord Strathnaver's regiment, were experienced officers. Wood had been a captain in Scotland, England, Ireland, and Flanders for five years, and major in Flanders for four. Bruce said simply that he had been a major for 'long enough'.[79] After John, Lord Cutts had been awarded the Coldstream Guards following the death of Thomas Talmash in 1694, his old foot regiment was given to Lieutenant-Colonel William Seymour of the Coldstreamers, a son of Sir Edward Seymour, with ten years service under his belt. The death of Colonel Edward Lloyd in the same year saw the elevation of Lieutenant-Colonel Thomas Fairfax of Lord Castleton's regiment, a direct descendant of the parliamentary general who had been in the army for a decade. This was the typical pattern. The majority of the colonels of the eleven new battalions of foot and four regiments of cavalry which were raised in the winter of 1693–4, were already experienced field officers and the few who did not hold martial distinction were propped up by excellent lieutenant-colonels and majors. The most inexperienced of these new colonels was the Earl of Denbigh, but even he had risen through the ranks to become lieutenant-governor of Carlisle in 1685.[80] Although the fifteen new formations gave over five hundred opportunities to 'deserving' gentlemen to become subalterns, Goodwin Wharton's appointment as lieutenant-colonel of the Earl of Macclesfield's horse was the only example of a military ignoramus being granted a field commission for political reasons. The half-mad Wharton owed his preferment to the patronage of Lord Macclesfield and also to divine intervention as 'the Lord said I should finish all and be a colonel and a general in three quarters of a year.' More realistically, Wharton was being rewarded for his prominent performances in the House of Commons. Macclesfield himself was a political appointee who gave off the scent of the year – moderate whig – but he was also a well-tried officer from a decidedly military family. William did not compromise the quality of his regimental field officers by allowing political considerations to exercise undue weight in dictating their selection.[81]

Thomas Talmash was a whig but William employed him because he was a member of the Anglo-Dutch Brigade and a highly competent commander. Charles Trelawney's name was mentioned by the Tories as a possible successor to Talmash but William was not interested in a man who had resigned over the issue of foreign officers in 1692.[82] Marlborough's disgrace in 1692 was partly political in origin in that William suspected him of having Jacobite connections and of turning Princess Anne against her sister, but the most important misdemeanour from William's point of view was Marlborough's role in alienating the British officer corps from the Dutch and German generals.[83] Brigadier Thomas Erle was essentially a whig and trimmed to every political wind that blew, but he was also an able and accomplished general officer. Most of the general officers and colonels were whig – Rivers, Scarborough, Ormonde, Romney, Talmash, Cutts, Denbigh, Peterborough, Macclesfield, Fairfax, Selwyn, and Stewart – but political complexion was not obtrusive within the army. The army had been reformed by whigs officers in 1689 and with the restrictions of the purchase system and the failure of Carmarthen and the Tories in 1693, it remained basically a whig preserve for the remainder of the reign.

Not that this really mattered in strategic terms. The army and its officers had very little part in deciding strategic issues and so little opportunity arose for the army to concern itself with whig and tory squabbles over the direction of the British war effort. In Flanders, the British army was no more than a single corps in the midst of an international force where strategy was the concern of the political leaders of the confederacy. The only area in which English politicians and soldiers were relatively free to decide their own strategic priorities was in colonial operations and descents on the French coast, a process which resulted in the disaster at Brest in 1694. Naturally, the likes of Macclesfield and Peterborough were happy to recommend their whig friends for senior commissions in their own units, but they still had to be men of proven military ability. William promoted virtually no-one merely on the grounds of his politics. Political considerations functioned only on the very fringes of the Williamite army and the king was strong enough to police his own officer selection. If William had been forced to operate through an English commander-in-chief or some other form of agency, then his objective of retaining an apolitical aspect to the officer corps may well have failed. Marlborough, in Anne's reign, usually placed military efficiency before political considerations and it was only after his fall that the descent into the maelstrom of political purging began. There were no Jack Hills in William's time. This relative elevation of the army above the day-to-day hurly-burly of party strife was reflected in the low numbers of officers who were members of the House of Commons. Throughout the period between 1689 and 1702, only seventy-one serving officers sat in the House and in any one parliament there were never more than thirty-nine serving officers and never less than thirty-one. In contrast, eighty-nine army and navy officers had sat in James II's parliament and

Charles II usually had over forty serving officers in all his parliamentary sessions. Naturally, nothing in the late seventeenth century political scene was straightforward. Lord Cutts reported in 1697 that there were several 'cunning, intriguing, and deceitful men' in the army, including some of the general officers, 'allied to very busy men in both Houses of Parliament'. Neither was Cutts himself averse to using his position as Governor of the Isle of Wight to influence parliamentary elections in the royal interest.[84]

Similarly with Jacobitism. There were rumours that army officers had Jacobite sympathies and, if King James ever re-entered England, then they would bring over their commands, but no hard evidence was ever produced and no Jacobite officer ever surfaced to cause real alarm. The purges of 1689 and the new military oaths were pretty thorough, resulting in the flight of the genuinely Jacobite officers to fight for their old sovereign in Scotland and Ireland. Richard Ingoldsby came under suspicion of Jacobitism in 1698 but nothing could be proved against him.[85] An anonymous letter to the Earl of Portland on 1 May 1692 suggested that a considerable number of officers were 'already engaged' on James II's side and had been vouched for by Marlborough. The list included Sir John Lanier, Thomas Langston, Charles Trelawney, John Coy, John Hales, Zachariah Tiffin, Richard Brewer, Charles Churchill, and Lewis and Rupert Billingsley. This was a list of the old professional clique from France in the 1670s, an extension of the Rose Tavern plotters and the Association of Protestant Officers. If they were involved in Jacobite plotting it had little to do with affection for James II. Their concern was with the favour shown by William III to Dutch and German general officers and the corresponding lack of opportunities for promotion and rewards for aspiring British candidates. Their complaints, even if there was substances in the charges, were identical with those which had animated them to conspire against James II in 1688; they were career officers and they saw their progress being blocked, this time by the Dutch rather than the catholics and the Irish.[86] More information came into London on 5 May 1692 from Admiral Russell off Portsmouth. Thomas Langston's regiment was quartered at Canterbury and several troopers had recently drunk the health of James II upon their knees and Russell rather suspected that the infection may have gone deeper into the army as a whole. Russell certainly thought that Jacobite agents provocateurs had been busy amongst the soldiery in England and stirring them up 'with an opinion that their comrades were hardly used when not paid'. Major William Mathews of the

Coldstream Guards was suspected 'to be for the descent', and his brother, Colonel Edward Mathews of the Royal Dragoons, regarded him as quite capable of treachery. Faced with this information, Queen Mary had no option but to act. She showed the evidence to the Duke of Leinster, the Earl of Portland, Lord Sidney, and the Board of General Officers, all of whom advised her to arrest the supposed conspirators. John Hales, John Langston, William Culliford, Thomas Pownall, William Brereton, Edmund Mayne, Anthony Rodney, and Charles Williams were clapped into Newgate but they were all released after a short period of detention and allowed to continue with their army careers. No substantive evidence could be found against any one of them. That is not to suggest that they were all innocent and whiter than white, but no one had said too much and no one had committed the cardinal sin of putting pen to paper.

That is not to say that there were no Jacobites in the army following the purges and resignations of 1689. Chaplain Alexander Shields of the Cameronians reported on 28 April 1691 from Bruges, that many of the old officers from James II's time were still serving in both the Royal Scots and the infantry regiment of Francis Fergus O'Farrell. A number of these gentlemen had already deserted to the French and 'we wish they were all gone, the less treachery were to be feared when action is required'. A certain 'Mr. Hornby', a Jacobite agent, reported to Henry Browne at St Germains on 13 May 1691, that Major Charles Fox of Robert Hodges's foot had agreed 'to come over to the King on the first occasion'. Nothing came of the promise, if promise there ever had been, and this turned into yet another figment of Jacobite wishful thinking. Charles Fox had been one of the few company officers of Charles Trelawney's foot who had remained loyal to James in 1688, but he had swum with the tide after his sovereign's flight and joined Robert Hodges's regiment as a captain in December of that year. Promotion to major had followed in March 1689 and a further elevation to lieutenant-colonel occurred on 1 January 1692. Clearly, Fox was a possible candidate for Jacobite pressure and propaganda but his vague undertaking was never put into effect. Similarly, Lieutenant-Colonel Lewis Billingsley of the Life Guard told the Jacobite intriguer Captain David Floyd in 1691 that he promised 'to return to his duty whenever a fair occasion is offered'. By 1693, even these meaningless 'assurances' from isolated army officers had evaporated and the coterie at St Germains were clutching at the straws of amazingly vacant and factless intelligence summaries.

[an English corps of thirteen battalions in Flanders, hardly amounting to seven thousand men], desert daily, officers as well as soldiers, and I am afraid they have but too much mind to return to their old master. Thirteen officers went away together not long since, which has put us in a great fright for the rest, and the enemy is as diligent to entice them away as we are to preserve them steady in their duty.

Jacobites were still hovering around the allied army in Flanders in 1694 but the pressure of individual officers with dubious personal allegiances never amounted to a basic instability in the entire army. The 'fair occasions' for desertion always reached into the eternal sunset and when desertions by non-commissioned officers and private soldiers did occur, unshakeable allegiance to the old king was the last motive to be suspected. William III's British army officers might have corresponded with James II's exiled court from time to time – Colonels Lord Sidney, the Duke of Ormonde, and the Earl of Marlborough were most certainly guilty of this crime – but they did not go over to the other side. Even their correspondence with St Germains was non-committal and usually consisted of stating the obvious and of passing on information which was already common knowledge. Marlborough was hardly breaking new ground when he informed David Floyd in the spring of 1691 that he

advises sending men as well as stores to Ireland for the Prince of Orange intends to push hard to reduce it early. But any ill success, he thinks, will break the Confederacy and mind those in England of their duty to their natural sovereign.

Had James II demonstrated any real drive to regain his lost throne or convinced his potential military and political supporters in Great Britain that he could mount a realistic and practical attempt, then many of the dilettante Jacobites in the British army might well have reconsidered their positions but they were never placed in this awkward and embarrassing predicament. James II stood no chance of regaining his inheritance after the Boyne and the hard-headed and politically sensitive army officers gave him no commitment in return. There were suggestions that the surrenders of the allied garrisons in Dixmuyde and Deynse in late July and early August 1695 were caused by Jacobite intrigue, but no evidence could be produced and the shameful episodes resulted from nothing more uncommon or sinister than loss of nerve and poor judgement. Serving officers had no part in the Assassination Plot of 1696 and in the aftermath of its discovery the army swore the Oath of Association quickly and without fuss.[87]

The pay of a colonel of foot was £410 per annum but to this could be added another £140 in allowances for servants and probably as much again from the proceeds of fictitious musters and other quasi-legal perquisites. A colonel of dragoons earned about the same but the commander of a cavalry formation received well over six hundred pounds in basic pay alone. A captain of foot earned £170 a year, and an ensign's salary amounted to a meagre £66; a captain of horse was paid £346 a year and a cornet £209. The three troops of the Life Guard were in an altogether different category with a gentleman private being paid four shillings a day, as much as a lieutenant in a line infantry regiment. Also, the officers of the two regiments of English Foot Guards, the First and the Coldstream, were granted additional pay in 1690 and 1691 raising a colonel to a basic salary of £681, a captain to £285, and an ensign to £106.[88] Many colonels were pluralists holding general rank or posts in the Ordnance Office or in the navy in addition to their regimental places.[89] All cavalry and dragoon officers enjoyed forage allowances and every officer was entitled to a daily allowance for servants, ranging from a single batman for an ensign of foot to four for a colonel of horse. In the field, all officers enjoyed a graduated scale of free daily bread rations with which to feed their servants but, more often, these were sold to the hungry soldiery on the open market realising yet more cash for the officers' pockets. Overall a captaincy in the Foot Guards might have been worth as much as £600 or £700 a year, a captain in a line cavalry regiment would have taken home a sum in the region of £400, whilst a captain of foot in a marching battalion enjoyed a remuneration of around £200. They needed every penny.[90]

In the first place, outside the hallowed ranks of the horse and foot guards and below the rank of colonel, or possibly lieutenant-colonel, the majority of the officers of the line regiments were from gentry rather than aristocratic origins. Most were younger sons without inheritances, obliged to make their own ways in the world, and the majority of line officers left the army either on the bread line or actually in debt.[91] As early as the spring of 1689, Blathwayt reported that many of the junior officers were so poor that they could not afford to take up their posts in Flanders when ordered. Their pay was in arrears and the tallies which they had been given in lieu of wages were only redeemable at a discount of forty per cent.[92] When the pay of the soldiery was in arrears, its customary condition, then officers were expected to dip into their own pockets to provide their men with basic subsistence until funds arrived from the paymaster. In 1692, the company officers of the First Foot Guards were hard put to find three weeks' support for their charges. The lowest ranks – cornets, ensigns, and lieutenants – had a struggle to make ends meet on their meagre remuneration. A regimental adjutant was paid but four shillings a day, and Sir Charles O'Hara reckoned that the job could only be performed by a company officer in addition to his normal duties so that the adjutant could receive double pay and so have enough to live on. The implication here was that unless an officer was attached to a company then he was outside the regular round of perquisites, false musters, servant allowances, forage allowances, horse allowances, and all the swindles that boosted the pay of company officers from ensign to general. On the other hand, an adjutant's place was much sought after when the great disbandment was in the offing in 1697 for if a regiment was going to remain in existence than it had to have an adjutant whereas any number of its companies might be reformed.[93]

The wealth of individuals colonels varied enormously. Colonel Robert Hodges, whose first recorded commission was as a captain-lieutenant of dragoons in 1678 and who served with the Royal Scots in Tangier, prophetically wrote his will before the battle of Steenkirk in 1692. He was owed £997 from his battalion's officers, mostly for clothing debts, and another £234 in personal pay from the paymaster-general. Hodges had no personal fortune and his finances were tied up entirely with those of his command. On the other hand, Colonel Richard Cunningham, another professional like Hodges but this time with a background in the Anglo-Dutch Brigade, left the modest fortune of £2,500 when he died in 1696. Neither Hodges nor Cunningham qualified as gentlemen, but Colonel Richard Leveson most certainly did and he left an estate worth £25,000 at his death in 1699. The Earl of Argyll, captain and colonel of the Scottish Life Guards, dipped into his pocket to the tune of £400 to support his troopers otherwise they would have been 'entirely in disorder'.[94] Similarly, not all junior officers were poverty-stricken. Cornet John Westrop of the Queen's Dragoons inherited an estate in Ireland valued at £400 a year, although it must be admitted that this happy occurrence was enough to make him resign his commission.[95]

Officers' pay was almost permanently in arrear. Ensign William Crammond of Sir David Colyear's foot with the British corps in Flanders in 1689, received his wages every four weeks but he got less than two shillings a day rather than the three shillings to which he was entitled. If the soldiers were not paid on time, and in Flanders the men were usually given their subsistence and not their full wages, then the officers had no money with which to reimburse the regimental clothing account, the contingency fund, or the 'necessaries' fund. The result was steadily mounting debt. Ensign Richard Gore of the Coldstream Guards was owed £171 1s 7d by the government for the period between 14 October 1694 and 25 March 1699, nearly two years' full pay. When the great disbandment began in 1697, William was faced with massive arrears of pay due to his officers and no ready cash with which to meet them and this, more than any other factor, brought the half-pay scheme into existence.[96] All regimental officers were paid a weekly subsistence, ranging from 10s 6d for an ensign of foot, to 14s 0d for a lieutenant, to £5 1s 6d for a colonel. The balance of full pay was issued as and when it became available but, as the war went on, full pay became a rarity and officers had to provide both for themselves and for their men from their basic subsistence. Perhaps fittingly, the pay of general officers was not only permanently in arrear but was frequently not issued at all and during the disbandment after the Peace of Rijkswijk the balances due to the generals were given the lowest priority by the paymasters. Gregory King reckoned that the four thousand military families in England in 1688 received an average annual income of £60, about the same as the better-off parish clergy but still very much towards the bottom of the league table of professions.[97]

The end of the War of the Grand Alliance was the death-knell to the careers of many officers, or so it seemed. The three Scottish regiments which formed the remnants of the old Anglo-Dutch Brigade, returned to the United Provinces. Some redundant officers wandered across Europe to take service with the Holy Roman Empire, or into the Baltic lands to seek employment with the Swedish and Polish forces. A few artillerymen, mostly Scottish, went into the Russian service and accompanied Peter the Great back to Muscovy after his tour of western Europe, but the vast majority of officers faced unemployment.[98] All they had to look forward to was poverty and the termination of a possibly promising career. 'The poor subalterns', mused Sir Charles O'Hara as he officiated at the breaking of Thomas Erle's foot on 3 March 1698, 'are in a miserable condition but I know not how to help them and their poverty puts me in mind of my own.' Colonel Thomas Brudenell was about to disband his own foot battalion, a doleful task, but before he did so he tried to do something for his junior officers, by representing

the miserable condition of my subaltern officers, who had laid out what little money they had to accoutre themselves well upon their going for Ireland, and now must be forced to beg their way to London. If something be not sent to them upon account of their arrears, or advance of half-pay, I must beg you to assist them in this, for I am sure it would move your compassion to see the miserable condition they are in.[99]

Lieutenant Charles Burton, late of the Marines, found himself in prison for a debt of £100, a sum of money which he could easily have paid if his arrears had been met. Matters were taken just a little further by Captain John Bellingham in 1699 who tried his hand, very unsuccessfully, at forging £40 notes out of £5 bills but 'he had practiced very little being found out in time'. He had also undertaken a little highway robbery to supplement his income.[100]

Half-pay dated back to 1641 when it was an act of royal grace and favour. Half-pay was given to some officers after the major disbandments during the reign of Charles II in 1667, 1674 and 1679, with the recipients being attached to standing regiments as reformadoes and given responsibility for training and drill. When the army was augmented, the half-pay officers were the first to receive the new commissions. The remuneration was exactly half of their establishment pay and it was met quarterly by the paymaster-general.[101] William continued to use the half-pay system from the very beginning of his reign. On 17 July 1689, all the officers who had been evicted from their commissions in Ireland by Tyrconnel during the reign of James II and who had still not found employment, were admitted to half-pay; a total of 169 officers benefited but most did not stay long on the half-pay list being quickly found employment in the enlarged army. William III's half-pay was different to that of Charles II in just one minor respect. Between 1689 and 1697, half-pay amounted to a little more than fifty per cent of establishment rates as the full allowance for servants was permitted.[102] Temporary half-pay was given to the officers of Luke Lillingston's disbanded battalion in 1695, but they were rapidly swallowed up into other formations.[103]

Whatever pious words one may be tempted to write about the use of the half-pay system in 1697, the overwhelming compulsion was the financial position of the government. Certainly, during the War of the Grand Alliance the British army had built up a strong corps of trained and experienced officers whom William III was anxious to retain because he well knew that the Peace of Rijkswijk was nothing more than a truce and that war with France would break out again sooner rather than later. William did not want the British armed forces to fall back into their old habits. The emphasis of the disbandment of 1697–9 was upon men not upon officers; even though infantry

companies were reduced to forty or forty-five men, the full comple-
ments of officers were maintained whilst the Scottish establishment
was adjusted to accommodate as many officers as possible. To an
extent, the actual machinery of disbandment tended to achieve the
objective of keeping the trained and competent officers without the
unconscious assistance of half-pay. The youngest regiments were
always the first to be axed and in those regiments which were continued but contracted in size, it was the youngest troops and companies
which made way. This policy concentrated age, seniority, and experience into the peacetime regiments by dispensing first with relative
youth and inexperience.[104] Obviously, the sheer scale of the disbandments which followed the Nine Years' War made something of a
nonsense of this argument, but there remained some merit in it. The
standing regiments which survived the political butchery were officered with a wealth of experience and talent which provided an
excellent foundation for the augmentation of the army during the War
of the Spanish Succession.

The common soldiers and the non-commissioned officers were
relatively cheap to disband; the officers were the very opposite. Subsistence money had been issued fairly regularly during the war, even in
the dark days of 1696, but officers' full pay and clearings had dropped
into dismal arrears. Paying off the officers in 1697 and meeting the
debts for quarters would have been an unimaginably expensive operation and well beyond the resources of the strained public purse.
Half-pay, or retaining officers until sufficient funds could be
discovered to meet their arrears in full, was the only workable solution.[105] The Lords Justices decided upon half-pay for just this reason
on 6 November 1697, when they were faced with a bill for £22,000 to
pay off the officers and quarters of a single regiment of cavalry. The
Commons concurred on 18 January 1698, agreeing to provide half-
pay for all disbanded officers until they had either been paid their
arrears or had been 'otherwise provided for'. One year later, these
provisions were tightened to include only those 'natural-born subjects
of the king' who had been disbanded after 10 September 1697, the
date of the Peace of Rijkswijk, and who had served in English regiments. The Commons also addressed the king to fill all future vacancies in the few remaining standing regiments from the half-pay list, a
request with which it proved impossible to comply.[106] Technically,
this xenophobic attitude engendered by the New Country Party would
have excluded from half-pay both Scottish and English officers who
had served in Scottish regiments. The Commons partially dealt with

this anomaly on 14 March 1700 when it allowed half-pay for English officers who had fought in Scottish regiments, but the native Scots remained without funds even though a lenient view was usually taken of their plight.[107]

Between February 1698, the date of the introduction of half-pay, and 14 March 1700, forty-nine vacancies occurred in the army of which a mere eighteen were filled by officers on the half-pay list. Clearly, the spirit of the Commons' address of 27 April 1699 asking the king to fill all future vacant commissions from the half-pay list was being evaded, but William had never made any reply to that address as parliament had been prorogued on 4 May 1699. William had committed himself to nothing. There were large numbers of officers on the half-pay list whom William had no wish to retain: the lazy, the incompetent, the disobedient, the superannuated, and those who had spent the entire war in recruiting depots in Ireland and had not seen a shot fired in anger. Also, to have closed every vacancy with a half-pay officer would have permitted no new blood to have entered the army, an unhealthy state of affairs for any institution. Also, the system of regimental seniority militated against the half-pay officers. When a retirement, death, or internal promotion created a vacancy, then all the existing company officers moved up one rung on the ladder of rank, leaving any potential gap at the very bottom in the form of an ensign's or a cornet's commission. Such a place was of little attraction to a half-pay captain, or even a lieutenant. Fortunately, the re-expansion of the army for war in 1701 absorbed the half-pay officers.[108]

At each successive stage of the disbandment in 1697, 1698, and 1699, more and more officers were added to the half-pay account until it was costing in the region of £70,000 per annum.[109] Six hundred and thirty-five officers were drawing half-pay by the end of 1698 in England, with a further five hundred in Ireland and another forty-three receiving their allowance from the naval establishment through the marine regiments. The rates of half-pay were not ungenerous for the higher ranks but woefully inadequate for the subalterns. A colonel of horse drew £1 0s 6d a day, and a colonel of foot had twelve shillings; a cavalry captain received 10s 6d, and an infantry captain five shillings; a cornet of horse took home seven shillings a day, but an ensign in a marching regiment struggled along on a daily wage of just 1s 10d. Variable though the rates were, they seem to have been paid fairly regularly, at least by seventeenth century standards. By the end of December 1700, the half-pay list was only three months in arrears.[110] Both the king and the Commons took a fairly broad and

and generous view of half-pay and did their best to include officers under its umbrella. Lieutenant Fenwick resigned his commission in 1698 because of the after effects of wounds and tried to make a living in civvy street. He failed but with the support of Brigadier William Selwyn, he successfully applied to be included on the half-pay list.[111] Half-pay was a mere financial expedient but it did have the accidental effect of keeping the British officer corps roughly intact during the five years of peace between 1697 and 1702. William clearly understood the financial necessity but was happy to enjoy the military fruits. That the king should have wanted to retain the majority of his British officer corps was seen as little short of remarkable by many serving officers as they had grown convinced during the course of the war that he only had time for foreign officers and regarded the British as distinctly second class. From the point of view of the House of Commons, the acceptance of half-pay was inconsistent. Robert Harley and Paul Foley, heading their New Country Party, decimated the army between 1697 and 1700, reducing it to a mere shell in accordance with the howls of the anti-standing army movement, and yet the huge corpus of half-pay officers represented a vastly enlarged peacetime army, potentially an infinitely greater political danger than the skeletal establishment which they permitted to continue. Half-pay also meant that the political interest group of the army had come to stay, regardless of the actual size of the peacetime formation.

Englishmen did not care for foreigners. Whilst quartered in Hoddesdon in 1690, two Dutch colonels were lucky to escape with their lives. One Charles Fox assaulted them both and John Clark 'wilfully' drove his coach and horse straight at the Dutchmen whereby one was 'dangerously hurt and bruised'.[112] English army officers did not react quite as violently as this to the presence of foreigners, but the sentiments were much the same. William had a litany of motives for preferring German and Dutch to British senior officers during the earlier part of his reign. British officers were constantly looking over their shoulders towards St Germain and none of them, with the exception of Marlborough, prosecuted the Irish wars with much enthusiasm as they were fighting their annointed king and their recent comrades-in-arms. William did not fear such pusillanimity from European generals, nor with the Dutch formations and the mercenary units composed of Danes, Huguenots, Brandenburgers, and Württembergers. They were only too anxious to finish the war as quickly as possible and escape back to the civilisation of the continent, and their commanders – Galway, Ginckel, Solms, and Württemberg – could be relied upon to fight with some vigour and directness. As far as the British were concerned, William only trusted their professional abilities if they had served under him in the Anglo-Dutch Brigade. He was prepared to employ Hugh MacKay on independent command in Scotland in 1689, and forgive him the defeat at Killiecrankie, because he knew him well and had a high regard for his proven potential. Thomas Talmash fell into the same category. As other British senior officers gained more experience – Ormonde, Cutts, Marlborough, Erle – then they would rise through the ranks, provided that they kept their political credentials reasonably polished and did not dally with St Germain too overtly. Given the time and patience to build up trust and convince William that they could develop into effective field commanders, the British generals would receive their rewards before the end of the war. Marlborough, with his towering ambition had neither time nor patience. His demand to William that only English generals should command English troops really meant that only Marlborough should command the English troops. William was not prepared to risk his brittle European confederacy by submitting to the ego of one man. In his eyes, Marlborough had still to prove himself as a prospective commander-in-chief even though he had done well at Walcourt, Cork, and Kinsale, but then so had Talmash at Athlone and Aughrim. Furthermore, Marlborough was relatively low-born and William could not be certain how the aristocratic and royal generals in his allied armies in Flanders – Vaudemont, Württemberg, and the Elector of Bavaria – would take to sharing command with a parvenu. Talmash did have the advantage of high-birth but so too did the Duke of Ormonde who was also William's cousin, an important factor with William who had a good seventeenth century belief in the benefits of family. Waldeck, Nassau, Overkirk, and Zuylestein were all cousins of the king. If and when William did feel the need to appoint a full English general then it was more likely to be Talmash than Marlborough. When Marlborough began to press his claims too hard then he had to be sacrificed. Fortunately for William, the known Jacobite intrigues of Marlborough and his wife provided sufficient excuse to remove him from his commissions without creating additional animosity amongst the British officers towards foreigners.[113]

However, English generals and colonels did feel persecuted. Both Hugh Mackay and Thomas Talmash felt that William did not give them sufficient credit for their performances during the Irish wars, and Marlborough complained, with some justification, that his planning and execution of the Cork expedition in 1690 were worthy of some real mark of appreciation. William, though, had not become king of England in order to favour the English. During the early years of his reign, he was aloof in all his dealings with Englishmen, both politicians and soldiers. He worked, as he had always done, through a small circle of personal military and political advisers and he was not the man to change the habits of a successful lifetime in order to humour the likes of Marlborough and a few amateur English officers. Rather than risking a direct attack on William over this issue, the British general officers chose Henrik Trajectinus, Graaf van Solms, a lieutenant-general in the Dutch army and the colonel of William's Blue Guards. Solms had recommended William to break five English regiments in Ireland in January 1691 because of their poor condition. Solms was 'a proud, haughty man and not at all grateful to your men nor treats your officers with any civility'. Solms had apparently ignored William's orders to support the British vanguard at Steenkirk in 1692, and had quietly watched as the soldiers were butchered a mere half mile away. William sat even further back and bit his nails in rage as he cursed that he could not have his orders obeyed. Solms was an aristocrat, a professional soldier, a Dutchman, and a great-uncle of the king. Solms was the ideal target but he was only the personification of the much wider complaint that William was using England and the English solely for his own ends. The country was being exploited by William III just as it had been exploited by James II; William III was also 'failing to oblige' the English gentry, politicians and soldiers. Even Talmash, one of the very few English generals for whom William felt any regard, blotted his copybook by threatening to resign both his colonelcy of the Coldstream Guards and his commission as major-general out of pique for William's penchant for Dutch officers, and it took a two hour interview and a promotion to lieutenant-general to secure Talmash's continuance. It did, however, wreck the relationship.[114]

The House of Commons proved to be the forum for the public airing of the hatred of foreign officers. Sir Thomas Clarges and Colonel John Granville opened the campaign for the country interest on 30 December 1691, arguing that the employment of so many foreign officers was a great discouragement to the English and a blight on their ambitions. Richard Hampden responded with a more whiggish point-of-view. 'I think it is for your interest to have foreigners rather than natives, for whereby your own men will not be bred soldiers and so prevent the fear of a standing army, which I am against.'[115] There matters rested until the principal parliamentary debate began on 21 November 1692, in the wake of the Steenkirk campaign. The country whigs discovered themselves to be in an awkward situation. They were naturally opposed to permanent forces but they had to approve of a standing army commanded by English officers if they were to use this particular stick with which to chastise the Marquis of Carmarthen, the Tories, and the king. Enviably adroit footwork allowed Sir Peter Colleton to side-step this issue by admitting that there were plenty of English generals and they were preferable to foreigners, 'who cannot have that affection for England. When King James set up to overthrow parliaments and property, the English officers gave up their commands. . . . I move that "None but natives should command Englishmen".' Sir Edward Seymour countered this emotive effusion by pointing out the sad truth that there were few Englishmen fit to be generals 'and will you think to discharge and send away foreigners till you have generals of your own?' From his practical experience, Captain Henry Mordaunt was able to tell the House that he had 'served under foreigners who did very well', whilst Sir John Lowther added that the reigns of the four Stuart monarchs had resulted in four lost generations of general officers, making foreign commanders therefore indispensable. Besides, it was the prerogative of the crown to appoint general officers, not the business of the parliament. The Earl of Ranelagh, the paymaster-general of the army, then rose to his feet to present the debate with some much needed evidence. For the coming campaign in 1693, two out of five lieutenant-generals with the British army were to be English, Thomas Talmash and the Earl of Oxford, and the other three – Schomberg, Overkirk, and Leinster – were to be naturalised. Three of the five major-generals were natives: Ormonde, Scarborough, and Sir Henry Bellasise; whilst another three English major-generals, Sir John Lanier, Percy Kirke, and Sir Robert Douglas, had died during 1692. Six of the ten brigadiers also qualified as English. As yet, said Ranelagh, no full generals had been appointed in the British army for 1693. When faced with this set of facts which indicated that there was not really a problem except for the unbridled ambitions of a few men, Clarges rather weakly suggested that the king could not know about suitable English candidates for high command as he was surrounded by a circle of foreign advisers. Thomas Erle admitted that his four years' service as a colonel did not even qualify him for that rank let alone a general's commission, and then Henry Cornwall, sensing that the wide attack on foreign officers lacked substance, rounded on Count Solms for his conduct at Steenkirk. From this point, the debate lost focus and degenerated into a slanging match about the relative merits and demerits of Solms and

Talmash.[116]

It was an old problem. Feversham, in James's reign, had been an unpopular commander-in-chief because he was a Frenchman who spoke English with a music-hall accent; Schomberg's command of the British Brigade in Portugal in the 1660s and his command of the corps for the descent on the coast of Zealand in 1673 had been deeply resented. Very little resulted from the parliamentary debate. The Lords addressed the king to leave 20,000 British troops in England in 1693 under an English general and requested that no foreign general be permitted to command English soldiers. William said that 'he would consider of it'. This effectively ended the matter as William would never have consented to interference in his right to appoint officers in his own armies, and the House of Commons had to wait until after the Peace of Rijkswijk in 1697 before they could return to the assault.[117] On 16 December 1698, the Commons voted to exclude all foreign officers from the home establishment. The precise motives remain unclear. Xenophobia did not help but, probably, it had more to do with resuming the failed campaign of 1692–3 and offering a public snub to William. It may well have been an attempt to make the English army truly national and so less likely to pose a constitutional threat within England, but the central point was that by 1698 there were ample English officers available to fill all the general ranks in the forces. The length of the war had solved the difficulty.[118] The fact that there were one hundred and eleven foreigners riding as gentlemen privates in the sacred Life Guards, the seminary of future officers, nearly a third of the total, seems to have passed unnoticed. It did not matter. Talmash was dead and Marlborough had been reinstated, and they had been the real agitators.[119]

William's British officer corps during the War of the Grand Alliance was a hybrid. Composed of aristocrats, gentry, professional officers and courtiers, it claimed numerous links with the armies and traditions of Charles II and James II yet possessed its own novel features. The most significant of these was its size. Although the maximum number of officers serving at any one time was around 5,000 in 1694, far more men than this passed through the military machine during the course of the hostilities. A conservative estimate suggests that somewhere between 8,000 and 10,000 men served as officers thus bringing a sizeable proportion of British landed families into close contact with the standing army. The military profession permeated into British society arousing both violent resentment and antagonism but also a growing sense of acceptability.

Notes

1 WO 89/1, ff. 291–302, 14/24 July 1697, Cockelberg Camp, evidence of Gervase Holland; WO 92/1, fragment.

2 HCRO, L. 1524, Petition of John Baker to the House of Commons; *CJ*, x. 191, 265–8; Andrew Browning, *Thomas Osborne, Earl of Danby and Duke of Leeds* (Glasgow, 1944–51), i. 477–8; Charles Dalton, *Irish Army Lists, 1661–1685* (London, 1907), p. 99; SP 29/415, ff. 156–7; Dalton, *Army Lists,* i. 188, 289; ii. 37; H. C. Foxcroft, *The Life and Letters of Sir George Savile, Bart., First Marquis of Halifax* (London, 1898), ii. 211, n. 5; *The History and Proceedings of the House of Commons from the Restoration to the Present Time*, ed. Richard Chandler (London, 1741–4), ii. 352–3.

3 Peter Burke, *Celebrated Naval and Military Trials* (London, 1876), pp. 63–72.

4 *Diary of Thomas Bellingham*, pp. 40 et passim; V. T. Harlow, *Christopher Codrington, 1668–1710* (Oxford, 1928), p. 74; *The Flemings in Oxford*, ed. J. R. Magrath (Oxford Historical Society, 1904–24), iii. 201–2; *HMC, Le Fleming MSS.,* p. 335, 8 Feb. 1694, Sir Daniel Fleming to Rev. George Fleming. Michael Fleming was a lieutenant in Colonel Hon. James Stanley's foot.

5 Luttrell, iv. 543, referring to Colonel Francis Collingwood and his regiment of foot.

6 Grey, *Debates*, x. 252–3.

7 WO 4/1, f. 75; *HMC, Frankland–Russell–Astley MSS.,* pp. 86–7; Dalton, *Army Lists,* iii. 58–9, 390; Robert Parker, *Memoirs of the most remarkable military transactions from the year 1683 to 1718* (London, 1747), p. 14; Luttrell, v. 77.

8 Waddell, p. 329; Harlow, *Codrington*, pp. 74–5; *Portledge Papers*, p. 188.

9 *The Lexington Papers*, ed. H. M. Sutton (London, 1851), p. 116; BCRO, Trumbull Add. MSS. 103.

10 *CTP 1697–1702*, p. 169; Steele, ii. 164.

11 Luttrell, ix. 522; Sir John Smyth, *In this Sign Conquer: the Story of the Army Chaplains* (London, 1968), pp. 23–4.

12 Luttrell, i. 518.

13 G. S. Holmes, *Augustan England: Professions, State and Society, 1680–1730* (London, 1982), pp. 262–5.

14 2/12 Aug. 1697, Colonel Thomas Saunderson to Blathwayt, quoted in, Waddell, pp. 301–2.

15 On the military profession in 16th and 17th century England; see: A. J. Loomie, 'Gondomar's selection of English officers in 1622', *EHR*, lxxxviii. (1973), pp. 574–81; J. W. Stoye, *English Travellers Abroad, 1604–1667* (London, 1952), pp. 29–30, 239–67; Ian Roy, 'England turned Germany? The aftermath of the Civil War in its European context', *TRHS*, 5th series, xxviii. (1978), p. 130; P. R. Newman, *Royalist Officers in England and Wales, 1642–1660* (New York,

1981); P. R. Newman, 'The Royalist Officer Corps, 1642–1660: army command as reflection of social structure', *HJ*, xxvi. (1983), pp. 945–58; Childs, *Army of Charles II*, pp. 21–46; Childs, *The Army, James II and the Glorious Revolution*, pp. 18–55, 119–37.

16 Foxcroft, *Halifax*, ii. 205–8, 'Spencer House Journals, 28 Mar. 1689'.
17 Dalton, *Army Lists*, iv. 292–4, 297.
18 H. M. WALKER, *A History of the Northumberland Fusiliers, 1674–1902* (London, 1919), pp. 41–2.
19 BL, Add. MSS. 9,735, f. 63, 10 Oct. 1698, Selwyn to Blathwayt.
20 Luttrell, iv. 518, 577.
21 BL, Add. MSS. 9,723, ff. 41, 43, 20/30 Mar. 1692; Luttrell, ii. 417.
22 Luttrell, ii. 604.
23 *HMC, Marchmont MSS.*, p. 125, 19/29 Aug. 1694, Master of Polwarth to Lord Polwarth.
24 Luttrell, iii. 494, 506.
25 *HMC, Portland MSS.*, iii. 592; *CSPD 1697*, pp. 382, 512; CCRO, QCO/1/16/42, 27 Mar. 1698.
26 Evelyn, *Diary*, v. 331; *Vernon Correspondence*, ii. 302, 311, 422; Dalton, *Army Lists*, iii. 21.
27 Luttrell, iv. 721.
28 HCRO, L. 1524.
29 Waddell, pp. 45–9.
30 Steele, ii. 436–7.
31 *SR*, vi. 146–8, 1 William & Mary, session 2, c. 4.
32 *SR*, vi. 230, 2 William & Mary, session 2, c. 6.
33 *LG*, no. 2564; SRO, E. 100/8/13–52; Churchill College, Cambridge, Erle–Drax MSS., 4/17, f. 1.
34 Clifford Walton, *History of the British Standing Army, 1660–1700* (London, 1894), p. 804; *Acts of the Parliaments of Scotland* (Edinburgh, 1844–75), ix. 255–9; *Parliamentary Diary of Narcissus Luttrell*, ed. Henry Horwitz (Oxford, 1972), p. 40.
35 *SR*, vi. 586–9, 7 William & Mary, c. 8.
36 Luttrell, ii. 313; iii. 193; iv. 85; *CSPD 1696*, pp. 48–9; *CSPD 1698*, p. 355.
37 Luttrell, iii. 133; *CSPD 1695*, p. 241; WO 71/13, ff. 5–7.
38 *CSPD 1694–5*, p. 234; Luttrell, iii. 373, 393, 396.
39 Parker, *Memoirs*, p. 14; Dalton, *Army Lists*, iii. 58–9, 412; NLI, MSS. 4,166, Diary of Brigadier Robert Stearne, f. 6.
40 Luttrell, iii. 32; C. T. Atkinson, *The South Wales Borderers, 24th Foot, 1689–1937* (Cambridge, 1937), p. 26; *CSPD 1695*, p. 316.
41 WO 71/13, f. 14; Luttrell, iii. 457, 477; *CSPD 1695*, p. 320.
42 *CJ*, xi. 202, 213, 224; Gilbert Burnet, *History of His Own Time* (Oxford, 1833), iv. 259–60; Horwitz, *Parliament, Policy and Politics*, pp. 146–7; Sir Henry Everett, *The History of the Somerset Light Infantry [Prince Albert's], 1685–1914* (London, 1934), pp. 33–6; Lediard, iii. 447–8; BL, Add. MSS. 38,700, f. 28, 10 Feb. 1695.
43 Luttrell, iv. 66–7, 254; *CSPD 1696*, p. 338; *CSPD 1697*, p. 54.

44 BL, Add. MSS. 9,727, ff. 56, 66, 115, 135, 193; BL, Add. MSS. 9,728, f. 70; *CSPD 1696*, p. 3.
45 Luttrell, iii. 56; *CSPD 1694–5*, p. 63.
46 WO 5/5, f. 77.
47 BL, Add. MSS. 9,727, f. 30; *HMC, Finch MSS.*, iv. 98, 100.
48 WO 5/8, f. 32; BL, Add. MSS. 9,727, ff. 195–6; *CSPD 1700–1702*, p. 371.
49 WO 4/1, f. 72, 22 June 1689.
50 BL, Add. MSS. 9,727, ff. 46–7.
51 Knight, *The Buffs*, i. 313; *HMC, Finch MSS.*, iv. 331; Luttrell, iv. 507.
52 Luttrell, iii. 280; WO 89/1, ff. 128–34.
53 *The Inchiquin Manuscripts*, ed. J. Ainsworth (Dublin, Irish Manu-scripts Commission, 1961), p. 32; *CSPD 1694–5*, p. 366; Burnet, *History*, iv. 275.
54 *Flemings in Oxford*, iii. 124, 23 June 1693, Sir Daniel to Roger Fleming.
55 *State Papers and Letters addressed to William Carstares*, ed. Joseph M'Cormick (Edinburgh, 1774), p. 160; BL, Add. MSS. 9,755, ff. 47–8; BL, Add. MSS. 9,730, f. 87.
56 Grey, *Debates*, x. 252–3, 21 Nov. 1692.
57 *CSPD 1697*, p. 124; *HMC, Le Fleming MSS.*, p. 331; Basil Williams, *Stanhope, a study in eighteenth century war and diplomacy* (Oxford, 1932), pp. 9–15; ARA, Raad van State, 1896/2, f. 10; *CSPD 1700–1702*, pp. 540–1; *CJ*, x. 97, 112, 129; *Carstares*, p. 201; BL, Add. MSS. 63,629, f. 1; LCA, Temple Newsam MSS., TN/P02/2A/II/26, Petition of William Dering; BL, Add. MSS. 38,699, f. 24. On various attempts to found private military academies in England dur-ing this period see W. H. Manchée, 'The Fouberts and their Royal Academy', *PHSL*, xvi. (1938–41), pp. 77–97.
58 Western, *Monarchy and Revolution*, p. 338; H. A. Wyndham, *A Family History: the Wyndhams of Somerset, Sussex, and Wiltshire* (Oxford, 1950), pp. 14–15; *HMC, Portland MSS.*, iii. 431; Waddell, pp. 304–6.
59 Luttrell, iii, 240, 242; *HP*, iii. 13–14.
60 *Flemings in Oxford*, ii. p. xi.; *Carstares*, pp. 271–2; *CSPD 1700–1702*, p. 128, 8 Oct. 1700; Wyndham, *Family History*, p. 14; *One of King William's Men: being leaves from the diary of Colonel William Maxwell of Cardoness, 1685–1697*, ed. H. M. B. Reid (Edinburgh, 1898), pp. 168–70.
61 This paragraph has been substantially based upon A. P. C. Bruce, *The Purchase System in the British Army, 1660–1871* (London, 1980), pp. 5, 17–20.
62 J. H. Bassett, 'The purchase system in the British Army, 1660–1871', (Doctoral Dissertation, University of Boston, 1969), p. 215.
63 J. H. Plumb, *The Growth of Political Stability in England, 1675–1725* (Harmondsworth, 1969), p. 126.
64 WO 5/5, f. 73; Walton, p. 854; BL, Add. MSS. 21,494, f. 23; *SR*, vi.

587–9, 6 & 7 William & Mary, c. 8.

65 Walton, pp. 452–3; *HMC, Finch MSS.,* iv. 98.

66 *HMC, Bath MSS.,* iii. 144–5, 24 July 1697, Joshua Dawson to Mathew Prior.

67 Walton, p. 455; Luttrell, iv. 492, 494; Pomeroy, *5th Dragoon Guards,* i. 21–2.

68 Dalton, *Army Lists,* v. 68; BL, Add. MSS. 9,755, f. 59, 23 Sept. 1698, Selwyn to Blathwayt.

69 BL, Add. MSS. 9,723, f. 93, 19–29 Apr. 1692, Breda, Sir Charles O'Hara to Blathwayt.

70 *HMC, Finch MSS.,* iv. 20, 30, 41, 345.

71 Harlow,*Codrington,* p. 79; *The Life and Times of Anthony Wood, antiquary of Oxford, 1632–1695, described by himself,* ed. Andrew Clark (Oxford Historical Society, 1891–1900), iii. 487.

72 *Flemings in Oxford,* iii. 146–7, 19 Jan. 1694, Sir Daniel Fleming to Sir John Lowther; *HMC, Le Fleming MSS.,* p. 334; DCRO, D60/X20.

73 *Seafield Correspondence from 1685 to 1708,* ed. James Grant (Edinburgh, Scottish History Society, 1912), p. 231, 19 May 1698, Brigadier R. Maitland to Earl of Findlater; John Shy, *Toward Lexington* (Princeton, 1965), pp. 343–71.

74 *CSPD 1695,* p. 38; BL, Add. MSS. 9,724, f. 102; BL, Add. MSS. 9,728, f. 115; *CSPD 1697,* p. 139.

75 BL, Add. MSS. 9,724, f. 52.

76 BL, Add. MSS. 9,731, f. 95; ARA, Raad van State, 1928, f. 347; *Papers Illustrating the History of the Scots Brigade in the Service of the United Netherlands, 1572–1782,* ed. James Ferguson (Edinburgh, Scottish History Society, 1899), i. 515.

77 BL, Add. MSS. 9,727, ff. 52–3.

78 BL, Add. MSS. 9,728, f. 82; BL, Add. MSS. 9,755, f. 67.

79 *Carstares,* pp. 328–9, 8 & 10 Aug. 1697.

80 Horwitz, *Parliament, Policy, and Politics,* pp. 127–8; Dalton, *Army Lists,* i. 15, 37, 90, 102, 181; ii. 37, 42.

81 J. Kent Clark, *Goodwin Wharton* (Oxford, 1984), p. 288; BL, Add. MSS. 20,007, f. 87.

82 *CSPD 1694–5,* p. 222, 13 July 1694, Earl of Shrewsbury to the king.

83 Edward Gregg, *Queen Anne* (London, 1980), pp. 84–8; Baxter, *William III,* pp. 299–300.

84 Robert Walcott, *English Politics in the Early Eighteenth Century* (Oxford, 1956), pp. 24–5, 28–9, 165–7; *HP,* i. 10; Horwitz, *Parliament, Policy, and Politics,* pp. 358–66; *HMC, Frankland–Russell–Astley MSS.,* pp. 83, 85, 91–2.

85 Waddell, pp. 306–7.

86 *HMC, Finch MSS.,* iv. 114–15. One hundred and ten officers were listed.

87 *County of Buckingham, Calendar to the Sessions Records,* ed. William Le Hardy (Aylesbury, 1933–6), ii. 160, 197; *HMC, Finch MSS.,* iv. 122–5, 137; DRCO, D60/X43, 9 Mar. 1694, Sir John Trenchard to Sir

Henry Bellasise; Luttrell, ii. 444–5, 448–9; iv. 27; S. H. F. Johnston, 'A Scots chaplain in Flanders, 1691–1697', *JSAHR*, xxvii. (1949), p. 5; WCA, Browne MSS., ff. 75, 101, 220, 250, 257a–f; WCA, Old Brotherhood MSS., iii. f. 232; Paul Hopkins, 'Sham plots and real plots in the 1690s', in, *Ideology and Conspiracy: Aspects of Jacobitism, 1689–1759,* ed. Eveline Cruickshanks (Edinburgh, 1982), p. 93; Jane Garrett, *The Triumphs of Providence: the Assassination Plot, 1696* (Cambridge, 1980); BL, Add. MSS. 63,629, ff. 30–1, Account of the siege of Dixmuyde by a Dutch officer.

88   BL, Harl. MSS. 7,437, ff. 16, 18; see Appendix A.
89   *Parliamentary Diary of Luttrell,* p. 297, 6 Dec. 1692.
90   Williams, *Stanhope,* p. 7; Holmes, *Augustan England,* pp. 266–7; Harlow, *Codrington,* p. 79.
91   Waddell, pp. 318–19.
92   Ailesbury, *Memoirs,* i. 241.
93   BL, Add. MSS. 9,723, ff. 26, 29, 39, 55, 62; *Seafield Correspondence,* pp. 200–201.
94   Waddell, pp. 308–10; *Carstares,* pp. 349–50.
95   Luttrell, iv. 526; Dalton, *Army Lists,* iv. 59.
96   BL, Add. MSS. 29,878, Ensign William Crammond's Diary; NRO, ASL 238, Ashley of Ashby St Ledger Collection, 10/20 Dec. 1699.
97   Gregory King, *Natural and Political Observations and Conclusions upon the State and Condition of England* (London, 1973), pp. 48–9; Erle–Drax MSS., 2/47, ff. 2, 4; DCRO, Ilchester MSS., D. 124, Box 278.
98   Luttrell, iv. 280, 285, 427; Dalton, *Army Lists,* iv. pp. xix–xx.
99   BL, Add. MSS. 9,755, ff. 16, 22.
100 Edye, *Royal Marines,* i. 589; *Vernon Correspondence,* ii. 334, 5 Aug. 1699, James Vernon to Shrewsbury.
101 Alan J. Guy, *Oeconomy and Discipline: Officership and Administration in the British Army, 1714–63* (Manchester, 1985), pp. 99–100; WO 33/10, f. 145, 'Memorandum on half-pay, pensions, etc.'.
102 BL, Harl. MSS. 7,439, ff. 11–14; *HMC, Le Fleming MSS.,* p. 243; Walton, p. 839.
103 *HMC, Downshire MSS.,* i. 470–1.
104 *CSPD 1698,* p. 30; *CSPD 1700–1702,* p. 153.
105 *Vernon Correspondence,* i. 464; Cowper, *King's Own,* i. 88.
106 Godfrey Davies, 'The reduction of the army after the Peace of Ryswick', *JSAHR,* xxvii. (1950), pp. 20–1; Luttrell, iv. 623; *Acts of the Parliaments of Scotland,* x. 241, app. 72; *CSPD 1697,* p. 462.
107 *Vernon Correspondence,* ii. 54, 58–9; *CJ,* xiii. 103–5, 282–4.
108 *Inchiquin Manuscripts,* p. 61; *CSPD 1700–1702,* pp. 128, 346.
109 Bod. Lib. Rawlinson MSS. A. 245, f. 24a.
110 *CJ,* xii. 564–82, 634; Steele, ii. 176.
111 BL, Add. MSS. 9,755, f. 34.
112 *Hertford County Records: Notes and Extracts from the Sessions Rolls, 1581–1698,* ed. W. J. Hardy (Hertford, 1905), i. 387.

113 D. C. A. Agnew, *Henri de Ruvigny, Earl of Galway* (Edinburgh, 1864), pp. 42–3; Baxter, *William III*, pp. 298–9; Waddell, pp. 195–200; Burnet, *History*, iv. 152–3; *Correspondentie van Willem III en van Hans Willem Bentinck*, ed. N. Japikse (The Hague, 1927–8), i. 63; *Parliamentary Diary of Luttrell*, pp. 255–6.

114 John Carswell, *The Old Cause* (London, 1954), pp. 191–2; E. D. H. Tollemache, *The Tollemaches of Helmingham and Ham* (Ipswich, 1949), pp. 76–7; Bod. Lib. Ballard MSS. 39, f. 87.

115 *Parliamentary Diary of Luttrell*, p. 97.

116 *Ibid.*, pp. 252–7; Grey, *Debates*, x. 253–66.

117 *HMC, Rutland MSS.*, ii. 138; Grey, *Debates*, x. 309.

118 *CJ*, xii. 635; *Letters of William III and Louis XIV and of their Ministers, 1697–1700*, ed. Paul Grimblot (London, 1848), ii. 225.

119 *HMC, House of Lords MSS.*, n.s. iii. 372–5.

III

Law and quarters

In the wake of the mutiny of the Royal Scots at Ipswich in March 1689, the House of Commons rushed through a bill which was to become the first Mutiny Act. It was to last for six months, from 12 April to 10 November 1689.[1] The Bill of Rights, later graduated into a statute, had created little or no new law except for clause six which declared that the maintenance of a standing army in time of peace without the consent of parliament was illegal. The Mutiny Act seemed to be the legal formalisation of that particular concept.[2] The sad experiences of the previous reign also suggested that a parliamentary control over the armed forces of the crown was long overdue. Unfortunately, it is very doubtful if either of these notions are really applicable to the Mutiny Act of 1689. In the first place, the statute was only passed in response to 'this time of danger', and made no mention of its being an amplification of the Declaration of Rights; in other words, it was an emergency measure, a mere temporary precaution. Secondly, although parliament felt it essential to have 'an exact discipline' during the uncertain spring of 1689 'and that soldiers who shall mutiny or stir up sedition or shall desert their majesties' service be brought to a more exemplary and speedy punishment than the usual forms of law will allow', that was the extent of its innovation. Effectively, the Mutiny Act of 28 March 1689 repealed clause sixty-four of the 1686 Articles of War which were to be reissued in 1692 to form the code of military law for the entirety of William's reign.

From the time of the Restoration in 1660, the army had run its own legal affairs. Being totally under the control of the monarch, the army possessed its own code of military law by which it governed its own internal affairs during peacetime. In wartime or during a domestic emergency, that code of military law automatically became the code of martial law which could extend to both soldiers and civilians. Naturally, military law in England could not be permitted to infringe the sacred common law and so there was a clause in the Articles of War which forbade any court-martial from inflicting a punishment which might endanger the life or limbs of an offender. Such punishments were the preserve of the common law. Provided that this was obeyed, and by and large it was, parliament seemed content to allow the army self-government through its own rules and regulations in much the same way as the House of Commons operated through its own standing orders and precedents.[3] Technically, all the 1689 Mutiny Act achieved was to allow the court-martial to take life or limb in cases of proven mutiny, sedition, and desertion. As James II had demonstrated, the common law was adequate and capable of dealing with soldiers charged with these offences but its procedure was necessarily slow and it could not insist upon a showpiece execution in front of the convicted man's comrades. Something sharper and more efficacious was required during the troubled winter of 1688–9 and this was the limited intent and achievement of the first Mutiny Act. It did not create military discipline as that was already in existence. Initially, the statute was only to endure for six months, a clear indication of its status as a reaction to a national emergency, and its continuation throughout most of the war years in William's reign merely reflected the continuing uncertainty about army loyalty and the fact that parliament came to use the act as a convenient vehicle for odds and ends of legislation relating to the military. The Mutiny Act did not give parliamentary sanction to a standing army in time of peace; quite the contrary as England was at war, the Act did not mention the concept of a permanent armed force, and the Act was not renewed during the short peace between 1697 and 1701. It did not make soldiers into a separate category before the law; soldiers remained subject to the common law and were still regarded as civilians except in cases of mutiny, sedition, and desertion. Despite their technical illegality, the army continued to govern itself by the Articles of War and the Mutiny Act gave no official approval of this code of discipline. The army was perfectly capable of both existing and of regulating itself without the Mutiny Act as was shown by the statute's lapse between 10 April 1698 and 20 February 1701.[4] The political acceptance by parliament of a standing army in time of peace was still below the horizon in 1689.

In many ways, the Mutiny Act was political rather than military in intent. It was parliament's way of enforcing the army's loyalty to the new regime by suppressing mutiny, sedition, and desertion, the fruits of its divided loyalty. Also, it only applied to troops in England. It had long been accepted practice that on foreign stations and on active service, all soldiers were subject to the rigours of martial law and the common law of England had no writ. The army had to be dragged from its allegiance to James II and the Mutiny Act was instrumental in bringing this rapidly to fruition.[5] The eventual passage of the Mutiny Act had been eased by Blathwayt's order to all officers and soldiers on 19 February 1689 obliging them 'to submit unto the Articles and Ordinances of War'. Although not overtly mentioned in the Mutiny Act, it was tacitly assumed that the court-martial would administer loss of life and limb according to the 1686 Articles of War. Pressure for a speedier form of military discipline than the common law was apparent in parliament well before the outbreak of mutiny at Ipswich. Hugh Boscawen, member for Cornwall, told the House that,

'tis not unknown that many soldiers disbanded, or who have disbanded themselves, have arms in their hands. I have letters that the soldiers in Cornwall are as bad as the rest; and when the magistrates rejoiced at the happy change, the soldiers killed a man. I would consider some regulation or discipline of the soldiers, and not have them proceeded against in Westminster Hall, and to make some temporary provision for the safety of the government.[6]

On 13 March, a committee of the House of Commons assembled to draw up a Mutiny Bill, the same day as the rebellion of some of Sir Charles Littleton's infantrymen at Brentford. The Royal Scots mutinied at Ipswich on 14 March, but William Harbord did not officially inform the House of either event until 15 March.[7] Clearly, the Mutiny Act had far deeper roots than the misbehaviour of one Scottish regiment.

The Mutiny Act did not affect the constitutional position of the army. It continued under the sole command of the king who had the right to appoint all officers, recruit soldiers, decide upon those aspects of its discipline which were not covered by the new statute, and order its distribution and deployment. Parliament had no role in the making of these decisions and when it grew concerned in 1692 over the appointment of foreign generals, many members reminded the House that they were dangerously close to trespassing upon a royal prerogative. The dispensability of the Mutiny Act can be seen in the fact that it was not in force for the whole of William's reign. There was no act on the statute book between November and December 1689, there was a gap of eight days in 1690, another of eighty-two days in 1692, and nearly three years between 1698 and 1701. The army could, and did, function perfectly smoothly without the Mutiny Act. When the Act was not in operation, courts-martial in England were forbidden to inflict capital punishments but those cases were all actionable under the common law before local assizes. A soldier was tried before the Court of Verge on 14 June 1698 for murdering his officer, two months after the expiry of the Mutiny Act on 10 April.[8] When it was in force, the Mutiny Act was a convenient 'christmas tree' on which the House of Commons could hang some additional clauses, from time to time. The first renewal in December 1689 included a comprehensive code against false musters and laid down ground rules about paying for and organising quarters. These basic regulations were further elaborated in later years and in 1692 some new orders were appended dealing with the requisitioning of waggons and horses.[9] There was, however, a result of the Mutiny Act which parliament had not intended. In effect, the Mutiny Act gave general courts-martial sanction to inflict corporal punishment and the death penalty as and when they saw fit as there were scarcely any military misdemeanours which a skilled advocate could not include under the heads of 'mutiny, sedition, and desertion'. This truth was officially recognised on 15 July 1690 when William III issued instructions that all court-martial verdicts which asked for the ultimate penalty had first to be submitted for his personal ratification. He reserved the absolute right to commute or confirm.[10] Without either intention or realisation, parliament had created through its mutiny legislation an army which was partially exempt from the common law. When this had occurred under James II in 1688, the omens were sinister, but the process in 1689 and during the 1690s remained within parliament's control and authorisation.

Inside England, the relationship between the common law and military law continued to be strained and tense. Civilian society gradually asserted its dominance over the military, a tendency which had been developing since 1660, but there were perpetual hiccups. Some of the king's messengers were searching for arms in the vicinity of Somerset House in November 1689 and they called upon some soldiers of the First Foot Guards for assistance. They helped rather too well and refused to hand over the weapons which they had found, which included a valuable case of pistols and a rather fine sword both of which were duly appropriated by Lieutenant Charles Gostwick and his sergeant. Lord Shrewsbury admonished Colonel Lord Sydney and reminded him to keep his men within the bounds of their duty when aiding the civil power.[11] Lionel Copley's activities in Hull demonstrated how easy it was for the military in a garrison town to abuse their might and muscle. Similarly, the inhabitants of Royston had much to complain of in 1695. The balance between the military and the civil remained hard to maintain although it was clearly enough defined. All citizens, whether soldiers or civilians, were subject to the common law with military law only applying to those cases where all concerned parties were members of the standing army. Any case which involved a soldier and a civilian had to be heard before a common law court. The trouble, as was so often the case in the seventeenth century, was the enforcement of this basic principle. It was all very well to issue complex orders concerning the taking and paying for quarters, or about requisitioning, or the behaviour of soldiers on the march, but who was to enforce them? Many of the offences committed by the soldiery emanated from a shortage of ready cash and arrears of pay, making blame hard to apportion and punishment often less than just. In practice, in order to gain any redress for misdemeanours committed against him by the military, a civilian had to petition the king, privy council, or parliament, an expensive business requiring lobbyists in London, and sympathetic lawyers and members of parliament. Even a large and relatively wealthy institution like the corporation of the city of Hull, had to work through expensive notaries, lawyers, and its member of parliament in order to have its case against the army properly heard.[12] Part of the trouble lay in the fact that the army was still very much the servant of the crown but it was not yet the servant of society. Society was the victim of the army and far from viewing the soldiers as its protectors and policemen, it saw the military threaten its law and assault its freedom. The anti-standing army sentiments expressed both in parliament and in the country at large, originated as much from a feeling of powerlessness before the effrontery and abusive behaviour of the quasi-independent army as it did from its fears for the survival of the constitution. Hatred of the standing army was local and real as well as national and theoretical.

The system for applying the dominance of the common law was fairly well established by the time of the Revolution. When Ensign Murray wounded a parish constable in Harwich, he was immediately placed in the custody of the civil magistrates as a matter of course even though Shrewsbury wrote to the mayor to make certain that the proper procedures had been carried out. Two days later, Blathwayt wrote again to Thomas Langley, the mayor of Harwich, instructing him to arrest the privates from the Scots Guards who had recently killed one of the townspeople, 'which is the usual and legal method of obtaining justice in such cases'. In similar vein, Lieutenant-Colonel Edward Mathews was sternly rebuked by Blathwayt on 11 June for allowing his men to requisition horses; this was a job which could only be carried out by civil magistrates.[13] By 1697 and 1698, it was unquestioned practice for soldiers guilty of offences against civilians to be apprehended by the civil power and tried before the common law, usually at the assizes.[14]

Inevitably, it was over billetting and quartering that the army and civilians most frequently and acrimoniously came into contact. Although the Earl of Ranelagh calmed the House of Commons by explaining that the king 'will keep no more soldiers in his dominions than what he shall judge absolutely necessary for their security, and the rest he will transport beyond seas', there remained a sizeable body of troops in England throughout the War of the Grand Alliance.[15] On average the garrisons in England numbered around 10,000 between 1689 and 1697. These were composed of ceremonial and guard units housed in and around London, the regular garrisons, regiments which were in the process of raising their initial levies, recruiting depots and companies for established formations, and troops either resting after service in Flanders or in transit between Ireland and the Low Countries. A proposal for a Jacobite invasion of England in 1695 gave the domestic garrison as a mere 9,000 men, 3,000 of whom were stationed in London, a further 3,000 in the permanent garrisons, leaving just 3,000 more available as a masse de manoeuvre. The garrison of England was not always so depleted. An additional 10,000 soldiers were held in England during the invasion scare in 1692 and were then retained to undertake the abortive descent on the French coast. Fifteen new regiments were raised during the winter of 1693–4 and the preparations for the Brest expedition in 1694 kept an extra 7,000 or 8,000 men in England. The invasion fears of 1696 also brought additional battalions back into England. However, for most of the time, the actual number of soldiers in England was roughly half that which it had been during James II's reign and was approximately equivalent to the size of the English army during the last three years of the time of Charles II.[16] These troops were constantly on the move; to and from seaports, from summer camps on Blackheath or Hounslow Heath back into winter billets, or taking part in the regular rotation of garrison units. There was a tendency for the principal seaports to see more soldiers than they had done during the previous two reigns because of the overseas campaigns in Ireland, Flanders, and the colonies but this did not alleviate a substantial burden for the remainder of England and Wales.

Considering that the number of soldiers in England at any one time was appreciably lower than between 1685 and 1688, there do seem to have been an inordinate number of complaints by civilians and instances proved against the soldiery. Perhaps it was because many of the officers and privates were new to the game and did not fully understand the rules, or perhaps the shortage of pay was the real villain. The confusion of 1689 created especial difficulties but even after this had ebbed away, general, blanket complaints about the army surfaced from time to time in addition to very real and specific problems experienced by particular communities. Gilbert Burnet took his pastoral duties as bishop of Salisbury very seriously and informed the Earl of Nottingham on 3 September 1692 that,

there are great complaints over all the country of the quartering of soldiers and their breaking into private houses. I hear of a very long list will be sent up to the House of Commons for it is said that though complaints were made to the cabinet council some redress was indeed ordered for the future but nobody was punished. I hope you forgive the liberty I take to tell you what meets me almost in every corner and company.

Narcissus Luttrell hinted at similar, widespread problems in 1693.[17]

Despite the great cornucopia of regulations tirelessly penned by Blathwayt in an effort to govern the quartering of troops, there are a number of indications that William did not much care about supporting and backing-up his secretary at war. It was most unusual to find either an officer or a soldier brought before the common law courts for a breach of billetting regulations, even though the majority of these had been enshrined in the first renewal of the Mutiny Act. Courts-martial were not concerned with billetting offences because they were not technically covered by military law and as they concerned civil–military business they belonged to the competence of the common law. Of course, if soldiers or officers committed criminal acts – robbery, murder, assault, rape – whilst in their quarters then they were usually proceeded against by the local magistrates, but the mere breaking of quartering regulations was infrequently punished by either the military or the civil authorities. The army command seemed to turn a blind eye. Part of the problem was that regiments were generally quartered in very small units whilst on the march, often with only a non-commissioned officer in charge of each little party. Commissioned officers were absent, more often than not, and it was exceedingly rare to find an officer with a rank higher than captain actually marching with the troops. Field officers invariably travelled separately from their men. There was often simply no officer of sufficient seniority, maturity, or responsibility to take charge. Absent officers should have been present with their commands and much of the blame lies squarely on the shoulders of company officers, but there was another factor. Most of the units which refused to pay for their quarters or extorted money from civilians could, with some justification, plead shortage, or total lack of pay. When trying to point an accusing finger, it was hard to find the right target. Despite his attempts to enforce the regulations, Blathwayt was inconsistent and seems to have left the task of allocating quarters and arranging the necessary marches to his most junior clerks and was not, himself, routinely involved. There really should not have been any problem. Blathwayt's survey of all available beds and stables in public houses in England and Wales had been completed in 1686 to cater for 20,000 soldiers in England, not 10,000.[18] Again, as with so much else in the Williamite army, the impression is left that poor relations between the military and the citizenry did not affect the operational efficiency of the army in Flanders and so William was not unduly bothered. It was just something which the unmilitary and pernickety English would have to get used to. After all, it was nothing compared with the burdens placed upon the peasantry in the Spanish Netherlands, or the United Provinces, or France, or in parts of Germany.[19]

As early as 8 January 1689, the Prince of Orange issued a proclamation forbidding soldiers to quarter on private landlords without their consent and making magistrates responsible for apportioning quarters in public houses. No officer or soldier was to select billets for himself. This seems to have produced little result and so Blathwayt repeated the message on 23 January. Similar instructions were issued for the use of the Scottish army by the privy council in Edinburgh on 17 September and, on 20 December 1689, the first twelve month renewal of the Mutiny Act laid down the new rules governing quarters.[20] All soldiers had to lodge in public houses under the orders and directions of the local 'tithingmen, headboroughs, and other chief officers and magistrates', and if a magistrate did quarter a soldier upon a private householder then the victim could seek full remedy at law for all the damage caused. Local justices of the peace were charged to set rates for quarters 'from time to time' at quarter sessions. For troops marching through, the justices had to fix the rate for the first night's stay and for all subsequent nights, but for troops going into garrison in their area, the justices fixed the rate for the initial night and it was then left to the officers and the innkeepers to reach a contract. Any officer or soldier who took money for excusing quarters was to be cashiered. Middlesex was quickly off the mark ordering all petty and chief constables to bring lists of all innkeepers liable to billet troops under the terms of the Mutiny Act to the next sessions with an account of the number of men and horses each house could accommodate. Constables, to whom fell the lion's share of allocating quarters, were enjoined that it was to be done 'fairly'. In other words, that the burden was to be evenly distributed and that the poorest innkeepers were not to receive an undue proportion of the load.[21] The Nottinghamshire justices decided to charge each captain and lieutenant one shilling a night, eightpence to ensigns and cornets, sixpence to troopers, fivepence to foot soldiers, and sixpence for each horse.[22] Clearly, rates must have varied from county to county and from town to town, as the renewal of the Mutiny Act in 1690 fixed the rates for the whole of England and abolished the discretion of the local magistrates. Subaltern officers were still charged one shilling a night with sixpence for every one of their horses, but the infantryman's rate was reduced to fourpence. In an effort to make sure that the soldiers actually paid for their quarters at the legal rate, all agents, company clerks, captains and regimental paymasters who received the soldiers' subsistence money had to inform all innkeepers in their area when they received cash with which to pay their men. Within four days of this announcement, the innkeepers who had billetted soldiers had to bring their written accounts to a pre-determined location and the regimental officers undertook to meet these accounts in full before any money was handed over to the troops. The balance of subsistence pay could then be released to the men. If a unit was due to leave its quarters but had received no funds from the paymaster-general, a not infrequent state of affairs, then one officer had to stay behind to make up an account of what was due to the local innkeepers and tradespeople. This account was then forwarded to the paymaster-general who met the amount owed from the regiment's arrears of pay. If a formation left its quarters without either meeting its demands in full or without deputing an officer to make up an account, claimants could bring their cases before the next quarter sessions provided that they could produce two witnesses. A certificate would then be produced from the quarter sessions which would be posted to the paymaster-general. He was then obliged to pay the account from the regiment's arrears or from its next full pay.[23]

In spite of all these precautions, the old practices continued. Blathwayt issued a proclamation on 3 December 1691 to remind soldiers returning to England from Ireland of the rules governing quarters, but this had to be repeated on 23 June 1692. The Mutiny Act of 1692 forbade military men from lodging their 'wives, children, and maid-servants' in their billets without the consent of their landlord.[24] The Royston episode of 1695 brought yet more reminders and new orders. When soldiers arrived in a town or village to take quarters, a trumpet had to be blown or a drum beaten to herald a public harangue that no credit was to be allowed to any soldier above the rates allowed for quarters under the Mutiny Act. The implication here was that unscrupulous landlords were responsible for luring the unwary soldier into debt. If, however, the boot was on the other foot and any officers or soldiers tried to extort money from innkeepers to excuse them from having to offer billets, then a complaint had to be entered with a justice within five days. The magistrate could then order the responsible officer to appear before him and enter into a recognizance of up to £40 to answer the charges before King's Bench. If the higher court found for the plaintiff then he stood to benefit from double damages and double costs, whilst the unfortunate officer would be cashiered and rendered incapable of further serving the king. If the court found for the defendant then the plaintiff had to pay the costs of the case. To make absolutely certain that everyone knew of the regulations, all mayors, bailiffs, headboroughs, tithingmen, constables, and magistrates had to provide themselves, at the cost of one penny, with a specially printed edition of the 1695 Mutiny Act which had marginal notes 'to explain the clauses therein', and reimburse themselves out of the parish chest.[25]

The burden of quartering fell squarely upon innkeepers and it was bitterly resented. Local constables were bribed into sending soldiers into neighbouring parishes, and publicans off-loaded their unwanted guests onto private householders, usually helpless and vulnerable widows.[26] The licensed victualling lobby must have been intensive as the 1697 Mutiny Act admitted defeat and allowed what amounted to a serious erosion of the quartering regulations. So many innkeepers had lost trade through having nasty, dirty soldiers billetted on them that, after 10 April 1697, they were permitted to buy off their military guests by giving the foot soldiers fourpence and the cavalry sixpence to buy their own food and provisions. The soldiers still had to live in the public house but, at least, they could be kept out of the public rooms. In effect, the military were now legally permitted to extort money from innkeepers to excuse them from quarters.[27] It was the thin end of the wedge and an admission of the failure of the previous regulations

which had been applied to billetting. Partly, this can be explained by
the fact that Blathwayt's 'Book' of 1686 was out of date by 1697.
Throughout the course of the war, the secretary at war had been glad
to receive petitions, complaints, and observations by officers indicat-
ing the increase or decline in a town or village's quartering facilities.
Units were deputed to lodge in a certain village only to find that the
number of beds had decreased sharply from the figures given in
Blathwayt's book. Embarrassment, buying off landlords, or taking
quarters with private householders tended to result. Indeed, so
inaccurate had Blathwayt's book become by 1697, that George
Clarke, the judge-advocate general and Blathwayt's deputy in
England, proposed to undertake a new survey of the quarters in
London and the home counties in readiness for the troops which were
about to return from Flanders, most of whom would have to billet
near London in the first instance. This scheme was endorsed by the
Lords Justices.[28]

Many of the problems with quarters might have been alleviated if
more barracks had been constructed. Ireland undoubtedly led the way
in this respect but Ireland was virtually a colonial territory occupied
by an English army and the barracks took on the role of control posts,
police stations and blockhouses. The same was true in Scotland.
Schemes to build barracks in Limerick in 1693 came to fruition in the
following year but they then stood empty for want of beds and
furniture.[29] As troops flooded into Ireland after the Peace of Rijkswijk
in 1697, a sum of £77,000 was earmarked for new barracks in
Limerick, Waterford, Cork, Dublin, Athlone, and other Irish towns
but the plans were cancelled on 18 November 1701 as nearly all the
regiments in Ireland had returned to Holland.[30] Barracks did exist in
England but, generally, they were grossly inadequate. Major-General
François du Cambon inspected Portsmouth barracks in 1689 and
found them in a wretched state and positively dangerous to the health
of the garrison. Barracks had been built for the Hull garrison in 1688
but they were far too small to accommodate all the soldiers. The 'old
barracks' at Sheerness were so 'rotten' that they caused sickness
amongst the troops. Overall, by 1697, there were sufficient barrack-
beds in England for 5,000 men but most of them were in such a
disgusting state of repair that they were uninhabitable. The only
barracks in regular use were those in the Tower of London and in the
Savoy.[31]

Relationships between the citizenry which loathed soldiers and
regarded the provision of quarters as one of their most irksome civic

duties, and an army which was irregularly paid and frequently con-
temptuous of civilian values, were bound to be strained. Official policy
exacerbated this rift. In the early years of the reign, there was clearly an
unwritten policy of quartering troops upon known or suspected Jacobites, an intention which was virtually a license for the soldiers to
misbehave. This billetting policy was still in operation as late as
1694.[32] Formations which had served in Ireland were not accustomed
to the delicate conduct required in English billets, whilst the regiments
in Flanders were at liberty to select their own quarters and negotiate
their own rates with their landlords. It was small wonder that the
British soldiers found difficulty in adjusting to English conditions and
even less surprising that the townspeople much preferred to lodge
Dutch or Danish soldiers who were far better mannered and disciplined.[33] No doubt, the soldiers themselves were adversely affected by
the quality of their billets and the general atmosphere displayed
towards the heroes of the foreign wars. Wakefield was 'one of the best
towns for quarters' John Barrett had ever seen, but as Captain Henry
Boyle slogged across Lancashire he had to stay in Hoggshead, 'which
is worse than any part of the world I ever saw, neither man's meat nor
horse meat. I could not imagine any part of Lancashire could be so
barbarous.'[34] Kendal was always a delight and, consequently, the
troops were usually 'very civil'. On the occasions when the civil
authorities broke the law and refused to quarter soldiers, forcing them
to camp in sheds and outhouses, the fragile bonds between soldier and
civilian came under stress.[35] Some lucky institutions and individuals
were exempt from having to provide quarters. London and Edinburgh
enjoyed this freedom, postmasters and deputy-postmasters were
technically exempt, and scarcely any peers or gentry suffered. The
burden fell squarely upon the keepers of public houses and private
householders in the towns, cities, and larger villages.[36]

To provide a catalogue of disputes between the civil and the military
over quarters would be tedious in the extreme. One or two of the
juicier stories will suffice. Portsmouth, a regular garrison town, found
itself under considerable pressure during the first half of 1689 being
encumbered by the Irish en route for the Isle of Wight, a larger than
average garrison to protect the naval dockyards, and the general
confusion as the reform of the army gathered pace. The soldiers
billeted upon private householders without their consent and left
behind not only unpaid bills but their wives and children as well who
then became a burden on the parish poor rates. The mayor argued that
the soldiers should lodge in the barracks first of all and any overflow

should be accommodated in the public houses. If there were still soldiers without a roof over their heads when all these places were full, then the town undertook to find some lodgings. Alderman Nicholas Hedge's pet scheme was to shovel any surplus into Gosport and let the authorities there deal with the issue. The major in command of the garrison understandably refused to put his men into the barracks as they would probably have contracted something quite unprintable, and flew into a rage at the mayor's lack of co-operation. The mayor and the major both petitioned the Prince of Orange who replied that the regulations must be obeyed and the barracks must be used. The business was temporarily papered over but it was not the last of Portsmouth's troubles. So bad had matters become by 1698, that the governor, Colonel John Gibson, removed all his soldiers from public houses and ordered them to lie three-in-a-bed in their barracks. This raised an interesting question relating to public houses; not all seventeenth century licensed premises had rooms available but the quartering regulations made no distinction between a simple bar and a large inn with dozens of guest rooms. A naval gunner in Portsmouth took out a license to sell liquor in 1692 because he had a wife and family to support and his pay was in arrears. He had neither accommodation nor kitchen facilities and the bar was his downstairs room. Yet he still had to quarter two soldiers and when he complained to Colonel John Gibson that this was unreasonable, the mayor sent round two constables who duly beat him up.[37]

Another regular garrison town, Hull, experienced difficulties over quartering in 1691, just after it had rid itself of Lieutenant-Governor Lionel Copley. Hull had some barracks, but not enough, and sufficient public house beds for only 300 out of its 500 strong garrison. These additional men were usually lodged with private householders at an agreed local rate of eightpence a day. Then came the Mutiny Act which stipulated a daily rate of fourpence for infantrymen. The mayor and corporation of Hull enlisted the support of their member of parliament, Charles Osborne, petitioned the privy council, took legal opinion from Serjeant Sir Cresswell Levinz, engaged a lawyer, Nicholas Baker, to draw up their petitions, and all to no avail. The new rate was fourpence and at fourpence it stayed. Colonel Sir George St George ordered some more beds to be made available in the Hull barracks but that was the extent of the corporation's achievement. Soldiers in Hull remained quartered with private householders but paid only half the previous allowance.[38] During the currency crisis in 1696 and 1697, serious difficulties occurred in many garrison towns. The 300 troops in Berwick were 'subsisted' by the town for over thirty-two weeks. When the burghers could no longer afford this on account of their poverty and the 'decay' of their trade, sixty soldiers were turned out onto the streets, forty of whom promptly deserted. They petitioned the government for relief but the lords of the Treasury replied that they knew how bad things were in Berwick but they were no better elsewhere. Two or three hundred London landlords had pulled down their signs and the Dutch Blue Guards had been turned out onto the streets; it might prove 'extremely clamorous' to favour Berwick's plight at the expense of London and other towns. The solution was to send some money to a private person in Berwick who then distributed the cash amongst the householders to subsist the soldiers for a little longer until the Treasury could lay its hands on some coin. Berwick was a special case as it was the only garrison town in England where most of the soldiers had to be quartered with private houseowners because of a shortage of barracks and public houses and Berwick fulfilled a vital police function along the Scottish border. Portsmouth was also 'subsisting' soldiers in 1697 and had to endure the sight of Colonel Gibson's regiment sailing off to Newfoundland leaving behind twelve months' unpaid bills. Carlisle was in a similar condition.[39]

The publicans of Canterbury petitioned for compensation of £1,400 for trade lost through having to billet soldiers; troops lodging in Harwich after their return from Flanders in 1692 did enormous damage to farm buildings and livestock; Market Harborough was simply too small for the number of troops allocated to it in 1692; and discipline totally collapsed amongst the units quartered in Sittingbourne in 1693. A troop of Colonel Edward Leigh's dragoons marched out of Staines owing £24 13s 2d to twelve different landlords.[40] Grievances were deep and long-lasting, caused mainly by the inability of the state to meet its commitments. Barracks were not properly maintained and so soldiers had to lodge in public houses; there were never enough places in public houses and so troops had to be billetted on private householders. When soldiers came to leave their quarters and settle their accounts they were often unable to do so because they had not been paid. Although machinery was created whereby civilians could reclaim military debts from the paymaster-general, it was a cumbersome procedure and broke down completely during the currency crisis of 1696–7. In these two years, the state virtually expected its civilian population in certain key towns and cities to pay, support, and feed its army, gratis. It is perhaps an indication of the tolerance and patience of the inhabitants of Berwick,

Portsmouth, Carlisle, Hull, and London that there was not more trouble and that they were prepared to dig deep into their own pockets. For many there was no choice as their trade and commerce depended absolutely on the market of the soldiers but considering the national hatred of the standing army their forbearance was remarkable. However, this merely emphasised the distinction between the institution of the army and the soldiers as individuals. Common humanity towards the underpaid and starving soldiery, as well as economic necessity, probably lay at the root of the goodwill shown in 1696 and 1697, sheer charity towards men whose lot was amongst the worst of any in the late seventeenth century.

There remained one final bone of contention between the civilians and the soldiers – the requisitioning of transport. The army possessed no transport of its own, and every cart, waggon, and horse, including the waggons which carried the company and troop baggage, had to be hired or requisitioned from civilians. Only in Flanders, where all carts and draught horses were supplied by specialist contractors, was the army assured of a regular provision of transport. In 1689 and 1690, there were complaints from the inhabitants of Leicester and Nottingham that pack-horses had been seized by soldiers and not returned, and in 1693 some regulations governing the requisitioning of horses and waggons were included in the renewal of the Mutiny Act.[41] Well in advance of a proposed march, the responsible officers were obliged to give notice to the local justices of the peace of the number of waggons and horses required. The justices then had to inform the local constables to provide the actual vehicles. Waggons cost eightpence a day if they were pulled by more than five horses, and sixpence if fewer than five horses were involved, the money to be paid by the army officers to the constables. Transport could only be requisitioned for one day, on penalty of a five pound fine, to ensure that precious carts and even more valuable horses did not begin a journey in Exeter and finish up in Carlisle. It was a severe imposition on both rural and urban communities. Refusing a requisitioning order was an offence and malefactors could be presented before quarter sessions, but very often the army met with a complete lack of co-operation from all levels of the county hierarchy. Captain John Hutchinson's company from Viscount Charlemont's regiment of foot, was en route from Macclesfield to Westbury. At Worcester, a number of his men fell sick and the weather became very bad so he asked the mayor and constables for a waggon and two or three horses. He met with deliberate obstruction and had to leave without any assistance. At other places, Hutchinson did manage to secure some horses although he had to wait ages for them to be delivered – two hours in Tewkesbury, three in Gloucester, four at Hampton, two in Malmesbury, and four in Cheppenham. All of this put Hutchinson's marches out of schedule.[42] As with quartering, the requisitioning of horses and waggons was a further evil visited by the army upon the countryside.

Notes

1 *SR*, vi. 55–6, 1 William & Mary, c. 5.
2 L. G. Schwoerer, *The Declaration of Rights, 1689* (Baltimore, 1981), pp. 71–4.
3 Childs, *Army of Charles II*, pp. 75–89; Childs, *The Army, James II, and the Glorious Revolution*, pp. 91–5; Walton, p. 818; *RPCS 1691*, pp. 554–69.
4 M. A. Thomson, *A Constitutional History of England, 1642–1801* (London, 1938), pp. 292–7; R. E. Scouller, 'The Mutiny Acts', *JSAHR*, l. (1972), p. 44; D. L. Keir, *The Constitutional History of Modern Britain, 1485–1937* (London, 1948), p. 268; F. H. Dean, 'The history of military and martial law', in, *A Guide to the Sources of British Military History*, ed. Robin Higham (London, 1972), p. 617.
5 R. E. Scouller, *The Armies of Queen Anne* (Oxford, 1966), pp. 255–7; C. M. Clode, *The Administration of Justice under Military and Martial Law* (London, 1872), pp. 10, 39, 43.
6 WO 5/5, f. 73; Grey, *Debates*, ix. 131.
7 Chandler, *Debates*, ii. 284.
8 Luttrell, iv. 391.
9 *SR*, vi. 146–8, 393–8.
10 Clode, *Military Law*, p. 65.
11 *CSPD 1689–90*, p. 329.
12 See the references under footnote 38 below.
13 *CSPD 1689–90*, pp. 52, 144; WO 4/1, f. 65.
14 HCRO, L. 1170, 24 Nov. 1697, Edward Barnard to Mayor of Hull; L. 1177, 5 Mar. 1698, Charles Osborne to Mayor of Hull.
15 Grey, *Debates*, x. 167, 9 Nov. 1691.
16 Macpherson, *Original Papers*, i. 520, June 1695; BL, Add. MSS. 15,897, ff. 88, 90; *Portledge Papers*, pp. 198, 264; *CJ*, x. 557; BL, Stowe MSS. 481, f. 24.
17 *Lyme Letters, 1660–1760*, ed. E. C. Legh, Baroness Newton (London, 1925), p. 164; HMC, *Finch MSS.*, iv. 442–3; Luttrell, iii. 95.
18 WO 30/48; HMC, *Frankland–Russell–Astley MSS.*, p. 92.
19 see, M. P. Gutmann, *War and Rural Life in the Early Modern Low Countries* (Princeton, 1980).
20 Steele, i. 475; ii. 435; WO 5/5, f. 51; *SR*, vi. 146–8, 1 William & Mary, session 2, c. 4.
21 *Middlesex County Records, Calendar of the Sessions Books,*

1689–1709, ed. W. J. Hardy (London, 1905), p. 4, Jan. 1690.

22   *Nottinghamshire County Records: Notes and Extracts from the Nottinghamshire County Records of the 17th Century*, ed. H. Hampton Copnall (Nottingham, 1915), pp. 97–8, 11 Feb. 1690.

23   *SR*, vi. 227–30, 2 William & Mary, session 2, c. 6; LCA, Temple Newsam MSS., TN/PO2/2A/II/21 & 23; *CSPD 1689–90*, p. 493; *Bucks. Sessions Records*, i. 380–1.

24   Davis, *Second Queen's Royal Regiment*, ii. 186; *LG*, nos. 2722, 2778; Steele, i. 491; *SR*, vi. 398, 4 William & Mary, c. 13; *Parliamentary Diary of Luttrell*, p. 418.

25   Steele, i. 497; *SR*, vi. 586–9, 6 & 7 William & Mary, c. 8; Luttrell, iii. 432.

26   *Hertford Sessions Rolls*, i. 424.

27   *SR*, vii. 203–5, 8 & 9 William III, c. 13.

28   BL, Add. MSS. 9,727, ff. 185, 213; BL, Add. MSS. 22,231, f. 11; *CSPD 1697*, p. 405; Scouller, *Armies of Queen Anne*, pp. 163–4.

29   *CSPD 1695*, pp. 59, 146, 227–8.

30   *CTP 1697–1702*, p. 138; *Vernon Correspondence*, ii. 230–1; *Council Books of the Corporation of Waterford, 1662–1700*, ed. S. Pender (Dublin, Irish Manuscripts Commission, 1964), p. 347; Steele, ii. 173; *CSPD 1700–1702*, pp. 57, 183, 449.

31   *CSPD 1689–90*, pp. 180–1; HCRO, L. 1145; WO 4/1, f. 73; *CSPD 1690–1*, pp. 101–2; Scouller, *Armies of Queen Anne*, pp. 163–4; *CTP 1697–1702*, p. 510.

32   *CSPD 1689–90*, p. 32, 20 Mar. 1689; Luttrell, iii. 393.

33   BL, Add. MSS. 9,723, f. 56; Burnet, *History*, iv. 152–3.

34   BL, Add. MSS. 22,231, f. 11; *Orrery Papers*, p. 374.

35   WO 72/1, bundle 1; *CSPD 1697*, p. 318; HMC, *Westmoreland & Other MSS.*, p. 331.

36   *Extracts from the Records of the Burgh of Edinburgh, 1689–1701*, ed. Helen Armet (Edinburgh, 1962), p. 9; *CSPD 1697*, p. 405; HCRO, L. 1162; WO 72/1, bundle 1.

37   Max Beloff, *Public Order and Popular Disturbances, 1660–1714* (London, 1963), p. 112; *CSPD 1689–90*, pp. 108–9; PCRO, Portsmouth Corporation MSS., S3/B/47 & R/1/10; *Extracts from the Records in the possession of the Municipal Corporation of the Borough of Portsmouth*, ed. Robert East (Portsmouth, 1891), pp. 190–1; BL, Add. MSS. 9,727, ff. 50–1; BL, Add. MSS. 9,755, f. 11.

38   Petre, *Norfolk Regiment*, i. 5; HCRO, L. 1137, L. 1144–49, L. 1151, L. 1156; Childs, *The Army, James II, and the Glorious Revolution*, p. 186.

39   BL, Add. MSS. 9,727, f. 157; *CSPD 1697*, pp. 190, 192, 289; BL, Add. MSS. 33,278, f. 69; BTRO, Guild Book GM 14, ff. 159–273.

40   *CTP 1557–1696*, p. 225; BL, Add. MSS. 9,727, ff. 60, 98, 117; *Middlesex Quarter Sessions*, p. 127. For other incidents over quarters, see *Edinburgh Records*, pp. 126, 287; *The Journal of James Yonge, 1647–1721*, ed. F. N. L. Poynter (London, 1963), p. 205; *CSPD 1694–5*, p. 253; Luttrell, iii. 249, 515; *CSPD 1696*, pp. 200, 246;

GCRO, Blathwayt MSS. D. 1799/4, 7 Aug. 1696; *CSPD 1697*, pp. 192, 210, 289, 334, 360; BL, Add. MSS. 9,755, f. 36; *CSPD 1698*, p. 414; *Acts of the Parls. of Scotland*, x. 151; *The Correspondence of Sir John Lowther of Whitehaven, 1693–1698*, ed. D. R. Hainsworth (London, British Academy, 1983), p. 518; *SR*, vi. 230, 2 William & Mary, session 2, c. 6; *HMC, Finch MSS.*, ii. 227–8; *The Complaint of the Inhabitants of the Island of Guernsey, 1690*, ed. J. Stevens Cox (St. Peter Port, 1970), pp. 2–4; *Records of the Borough of Northampton*, ed. C. A. Markham & J. C. Cox (Northampton, 1898), ii. 480–1.

41 *Records of the Borough of Leicester, Judicial and Allied Records, 1689–1835*, ed. G. A. Chinnery (Leicester, 1974), p. 22; *Nottingham Borough Records*, v. 362; *SR*, vi. 397–8, 4 William & Mary, c. 13.

42 *Hertford Sessions Rolls*, i. 405, 407, anno. 1693; BL, Add. MSS. 9,727, f. 189, 21 Dec. 1696.

IV

The soldiers

England had a population of around five and a half million people during the 1690s, 1,310,000 of whom were male and fell within the age bracket of from sixteen to sixty. As the army drew its recruits, officially, from males between the ages of sixteen and forty, this left a 'recruiting pool' of about one million men. This is obviously too high. Once the lame, the sick, the exempt, the rich, the powerful, the well-connected, the insane and the undesirable had been removed, the reservoir sank appreciably. An abstract of the 'General musters taken throughout the whole realm of England and Wales' for the purposes of militia recruitment at some time during the reign of William III, gave a total of 462,253 available fighting men.[1] Impossible though it is to prove, this 'feels' a more accurate assessment of the men in England eligible for service in the ranks of the army. The demands made upon this resource during the War of the Grand Alliance were high.[2]

James II had raised his army to around 40,000 by early November 1688 and although this slumped dramatically during late November and in December, the paper establishment of the British army on 1 April 1689 called for 58,914 soldiers excluding a Dutch corps of 14,788 already in England.[3] In the same year, the Dutch army numbered 84,650 of which 55,642 were native Dutchmen and the rest 'subsidie troepen'; the United Provinces possessed a total population of just under two million.[4] When the Earl of Ranelagh presented the military estimates for 1690 to the House of Commons on 9 October 1689, he called for 49,238 British subjects to be assisted by 14,788 Dutchmen and 5,610 Danish mercenaries.[5] This figure remained static for 1691 but fell very slightly to 48,828 during the following year.[6] In 1693, the total British forces dropped to 40,763 men and this weakening establishment was exacerbated by the losses incurred during the unsuccessful campaign in Flanders and the growing pressures for a diversionary attack on the French coast.[7] Accordingly, the establishment for 1694 was augmented to 93,635, of whom 68,725 were to be raised from within the British Isles.[8] This total fell slightly to 66,148 for 1695 and then remained at that level until the end of the war.[9] The great disbandment between 1697 and 1699 whittled away this grand army leaving a mere 7,000 men in England and 12,000 in Ireland by 1700, but the coming of the War of the Spanish Succession brought the British army back to a strength of 48,379 British troops and 21,672 foreign mercenaries by the middle of 1702.[10] If the assumptions are correct, then one man in every seven within the legal recruiting age and fitness range was actually summoned to the colours to serve in the army during the War of the Grand Alliance. This figure is only a suggestion and is scarcely based upon reliable statistics but it does seem to point towards a relatively high level of military participation, particularly when both the militia and the navy called for able bodies from within the same social grouping.

Recruiting was a constant and never-ending business. Huge recruiting drives went on in 1689 and in the winter of 1693–4 to raise new regiments, but every winter recruiting parties from Flanders spent three or four months gathering new men against the coming campaigning season. For the regiments based in England, recruiting was a year-round concern. The numbers of replacements required annually were huge. Officers from Ferdinando Hastings's foot, which had been commanded by the Earl of Huntingdon during James II's time, were sent off to Stafford and Belfast in the early spring of 1689 to raise over 500 recruits. The battalions of the British corps which arrived in Flanders in March and April 1689 were woefully short of men and, despite drafts from formations in England, it was still 775 men short of its establishment strength in June. In the following year, Sir David Colyear's battalion was 200 men short of its proper strength of 600; Lieutenant-General James Douglas's needed 500 new men; and Colonel Francis Fergus O'Farrell's had to raise 100. Colonel John Hill's regiment at Fort William was fifty-eight below its establishment in 1696, a factor which the commander blamed upon the prevalent sickness in that station. When Hastings's battalion sailed into Portsmouth from Ireland in June 1692, it mustered 460 out of a paper strength of 600. Of the ten battalions which took part in the Brest expedition in 1694, only three could parade eighty per cent of their establishments in August and the other seven were a great deal worse. The 'weekly lists' from the army in Flanders for September 1696, show that the majority of the regiments were between ten and twenty per cent under their establishments. The two regiments of marines, which should have numbered 3,000 men, were a mere 1,940 below this figure in January 1696.[11] Naturally, when the war ended and the constant demand for recruits evaporated, the few surviving regiments were able to keep their muster strengths roughly up to establishment and Sir David Colyear's foot could account for nearly all its soldiers in 1698. During the war years, the majority of infantry battalions were permanently between ten and twenty per cent understrength, a deficiency caused by sickness, battle casualties, poor recruiting conditions, shortage of recruits, and desertion. In addition, the company officers frequently indulged in false musters and the entire mustering procedure for the troops in Flanders was nothing short of farcical. The enormous disparity between the paper and effective strengths of the British regiments had been a constant cause of concern to Schomberg at the Dundalk camp in Ireland during the winter of 1689–90 and although not everyone went as far as William Harbord with his non-existent troop of horse, there can be no doubt that William III's British army must have hovered constantly at about seventy per cent of its assumed strength.[12]

Recruits were supposed to be volunteers. Unlikely though it may seem, some genuine volunteers did come forward although they were usually to be found in the cavalry and dragoon regiments which enjoyed a greater social status to the infantry and received much higher rates of pay. The Cameronians were a wholly volunteer infantry battalion, at least in the first instance, whipped up and inspired by the covenanting preachers.

Curse ye Meroz, said the angel of the Lord, curse ye bitterly the inhabitants thereof; because they came not to the help of the Lord, to the help of the Lord against the mighty. [Judges, v. 23][13]

However, the Cameronians were unique and the remainder of the army had to be 'raised'. A recruiting party usually consisted of a junior commissioned officer – a lieutenant or an ensign – and two or three non-commissioned officers. They set up in a likely town or large village, beat their drum, and then sat in an alehouse and waited for customers to come forward. Once a decent-sized body of men had been gathered, the non-commissioned officers escorted them to the depot, if the regiment was based in England, or to the port of embarkation if the formation was serving overseas. Should a new company be raised, as soon as the first twenty-five men had been collected the captain had to inform the commissary-general of the musters who then arranged for a deputy commissary to muster the infant unit. Pay for both officers and men dated from this first muster.[14] Recruiting officers were under some pressure to achieve results. Regiments in Flanders sent home at least one-third of their officers every winter to make recruits in England, Ireland, or Scotland and each officer was given a quota which he was obliged to fulfil. Recruiters who were tardy in bringing their victims to the agreed rendezvous in the appropriate numbers were threatened with dismissal. The French employed similar, draconian measures, which was probably the source of Blathwayt's scheme. Smart and fashionable units, particularly the cavalry and the dragoons, advertised in the *London Gazette* telling potential volunteers when and where to enlist.[15] Justices of the peace were instructed to give recruiting officers every assistance and the secretary at war did his best to inform local magistrates in advance that a recruiting party would be operating in their area. However, no quotas were given to individual parishes or counties.[16]

In Scotland, though, quotas were employed. For raising the new regiments in the winter of 1693–4, the Scottish Privy Council laid down quotas for every city, town, and shire and gave the responsibility of collection to the local magistrates. Edinburgh had to raise 119 men, with a further fifteen from Leith and another fifteen from Cannongate. Quotas were again used to raise 1,000 recruits in Scotland during the winter of 1696–7, with shires being assessed for between eighty and fifteen men. Failure to produce sufficient men was only excused on the payment of £24 Scots for each absentee. Such a system, although it took some of the pressure off the army, allowed local communities to rid themselves of unpopular and undesirable individuals. As far as the records show, the quota system was only used in Scotland for raising these two large levies and established regiments had to recruit their own replacements by beat of drum, as in England. However, the Scottish system was a trifle more civilised than its English counterpart; the men enlisted through the quotas were only engaged for three years, whereas men raised by beat of drum served for life or until disbandment. In Scotland, with its semi-feudal society, most of the colonels were aristocrats or substantial gentry, enabling their territorial interests to guarantee a steady flow of suitable men.[17]

Reciting orders from the king, Sir John Dalrymple blithely informed the Duke of Hamilton that, although army officers must not force anyone to enlist, it was essential once a man had agreed to sign on that he should not be given the opportunity to change his mind and renounce his decision. The best way to prevent this was to keep recruits in gaol until the time came to ship them over to Flanders. Similar tactics were employed in England, where recruits were 'lodged' in the Tower of London until embarkation at Tower Wharf.[18] To assist in raising a new regiment or in replacing the losses of an existing formation, the government paid 'levy money'. Levy money was not bounty. Levy money was issued to a unit when its new recruits had been first mustered and it was intended to reimburse recruiting officers for their expenses, to pay for the immediate 'necessaries' of the new soldiers, to provide a bounty should one be paid, and to buy a horse for a cavalry or dragoon volunteer. The standard levy money in England was either forty or twenty shillings for each infantryman 'over and above the pay due unto them'. In 1696, in order to replace battle casualties, a sum of £3 was allowed to the colonels of the First and Coldstream Guards for each guardsman who had died and £1 for each man who had been wounded and discharged. The discrepancy between the cost of replacing a dead man and replacing one who had been severely wounded was caused by the assumed loss of the accoutrements of the former whereas the injured man's equipment could be inherited by his replacement. Most regiments operated a 'bank' in order to fund recruiting. By making a small stoppage against the subsistence pay of all soldiers and non-commissioned officers, a fund was accumulated within the regiment which was used to meet the initial expenses of recruiting. In turn, the bank was periodically topped-up with levy money. In Flanders, William allowed all British regiments to 'muster complete' regardless of how many men actually were with the colours, and the difference between the full pay of the formation and its actual strength represented an additional fund with which to defray the costs of recruiting. Temptation sometimes overcame an officer's sense of duty. Lieutenant James Corbet was sent to the Midlands with £200 worth of levy money to recruit Colonel John Gibson's new regiment of foot but he produced no volunteers and absconded with the proceeds.[19]

During the War of the Grand Alliance, some regiments developed an unofficial 'depot system' in England. It took two forms. When a unit was posted to Flanders, some of its junior officers were left behind to act as permanent recruiters for the inevitably needed replacements. This small recruiting depot operated throughout the summer and was reinforced by additional recruiting officers from Flanders during the winter months. James Stanley's regiment operated this system and so did the Royal Horse Guards which always had one or two troops in England acting as recruiting bases for the remaining troops serving with the field army across the North Sea. Infantry regiments which consisted of two battalions – the First Foot Guards, the Coldstream Guards, the Royal Scots, the Duke of Bolton's, and Thomas Erle's – retained one battalion permanently in England to act as a recruiting and training depot. The Royal Marines went one stage further in 1695 and formed fixed local headquarters. A commissioned officer and a sergeant were sent to Plymouth, Deal, Portsmouth, and Chatham to form a base to look after sick marines, arrange for quarters, receive deserters, and recruit.[20] An embryonic depot system also grew up around the dubious practice of drafting. The drafting of trained men from one unit to fill gaps in another has never enjoyed much favour with the military as it tends to break up *esprit de corps* and internal cohesion in both affected formations and it relegates the drafting regiment to the status of a mere training battalion. In the seventeenth century there was the additional disadvantage that the men were recruited, clothed and equipped at the expense of the officers of the regiment, and when the soldiers were drafted into another unit the officers of the parent formation were left with a mountain of debt and little chance of satisfaction. There was, of course, a system by which the officers of the receiving regiment paid compensation to their colleagues in the donating battalion but it was never enough and the scheme frequently failed to function amid the complexities of contemporary book-keeping. Despite all these problems, the drafting system was regularly employed during William's reign as it was quick, effective, and to the government at least, cheap. From William and Blathwayt's point-of-view, there were further good points in drafting. Recruits could be attracted into regiments in England on the mistaken assumption that they were volunteering for home instead of foreign service. Not only did this ease recruiting, but trained men and not raw levies were available as replacements for the army in Flanders. However, they were not necessarily the best soldiers as drafting regiments tended to push out their worst and most troublesome individuals. In an attempt to acquire better men through drafting, Blathwayt introduced a new system in 1692. Regiments were paraded, the drafting orders were read, and then a bounty of twenty shillings was offered to all who would volunteer for overseas service.[21] In Scotland in 1694, the privy council tried to encourage soldiers to volunteer for drafts for Flanders by granting an automatic discharge after three campaigns.[22] When the drafts arrived at the army in Flanders they were divided 'by lot' amongst those regiments most in need of replacements; only drafts from the Guards went straight into their own battalions in Flanders.[23] Regiments in England thus served as recruiting and training battalions for the formations serving with the army in Flanders and in the colonies. There was no official linking or pairing but there was a tendency for regiments on the home establishment to remain there and little exchange occurred between battalions in Flanders and battalions in England. This fitted in with William's wish to have as few formations as possible in his British army, as this eked out the available supply of officers and allowed him to concentrate experience and competence. This practice was illustrated in Ireland between 1697 and 1701. Many officers qualified for half-pay but they were not preferred for commissions when vacancies occurred as they had no field experience having spent the entirety of the war serving with recruiting and training battalions.[24] The fact that the almost permanent resident regiments in England – John Gibson's, William Northcote's, Sir Richard Atkins's, Edward Leigh's, Thomas Windsor's – were usually composed of new levies may partially have accounted for the high incidence of ill-behaviour in quarters.

Recruiting was never easy. Whenever possible, officers used local or family connections to persuade men to join and when this was successfully achieved it added a certain *esprit de corps* to a unit and created some genuine bonds between officers and men. Ensign Michael Fleming raised his initial twenty men from around Rydal in Westmoreland and he recruited in that region every winter.[25] Generally it was an up-hill struggle to find volunteers. 'I went to Charlbury to church', wrote the Earl of Clarendon. 'There was a lieutenant and a sergeant beating up for men for my Lord Drogheda for the service of Ireland. They got but one man here.' The situation had not altered by 1691 when very few officers were optimistic about raising enough soldiers for Ireland and recruits were merely 'trickling' into Bristol. The Duke of Bolton's regiment, which was destined for the West Indies, could only be filled by drafting, as could the 300 vacancies in the ranks of the First Foot Guards after the Battle of Steenkirk in 1692. Recruiting in Edinburgh in 1694 and 1695 resulted in serious rioting, and few men came forward in Cheshire during the same period.[26] When recruits did wander in from off the streets they were not like Alcibiades. Some of the mopped-up odds and ends from James II's army were 'very promising men', but this supply was rapidly exhausted on the fields of the Boyne, Limerick, Cork, Aughrim, and Walcourt. Clarendon was as unimpressed with the quality of the new recruits as he was with their quantity. He took his dinner at Benson on 5 April 1689,

where I found my Lord Drogheda's new-raised men. One Fitzmaurice, an ensign, was the only officer with them. He told me they were marching to Brecknock, the place for their general rendezvous. The men seemed very ordinary, most of them very boys.

Daniel Dering's foot had to be filled up with native Irish recruits during the winter of 1690–1, 'little men' whom the colonel was anxious to exchange for decent sized recruits from England. The Royal Marines attracted some low forms of human life in 1695 and the colonels rather optimistically hoped that an improvement in the quality of the uniforms might attract a better sort of man. Morale amongst such soldiers was understandably poor. Contemporary social attitudes tended to regard the army as a dumping-ground for misfits and John Locke suggested to the Board of Trade in 1697 that the solution to the plague of 'begging drones' was to conscript them into the armed forces.[27]

Faced with the difficulty of finding sufficient men within a limited time, officers all too often resorted to illegal methods. In England, during William's reign, there was no legal sanction for the use of the press, but matters were different in Scotland. In 1696, the Scottish Parliament passed a statute permitting the king to levy 1,000 men annually by quotas demanded from every parish. The parishes of Strabock and Ecclishmachen were asked to provide one recruit between them, but they chose instead to pay the forfeit of £24 Scots in order to leave their inhabitants in peace. To make up the quotas, sheriffs were empowered first to seize 'all idle, loose, and vagabond persons . . . who have not wife or children'; then 'all young fencible men of the bounds, not having wife or children, and who are not menial or domestic servants to any . . . but earn their living by daily wages or by termly hire.' The recruits were to be gathered at a predetermined place and then, in good French style, they had to throw dice to decide who would be unlucky enough to go across the water to Flanders.[28] Although there was an element of lottery and communities could buy their way out of the system, it was nothing short of conscription by the press.[29] In England, despite its illegality, the press was used extensively. 'There is much pressing both sea and land men', wrote Charles Osborne to the mayor of Hull in 1691 and, in the following year, the Duke of Bolton's regiment 'forced away sixty to seventy householders to complete the regiment' before it set sail for Flanders.[30] So widespread had the use of the press become by early 1693 that a royal proclamation was issued on 9 February forbidding the practice absolutely and the renewal of the Mutiny Act on 1 March contained the outlines of the Attestation Procedure. The latter was sparked off by the untimely pressing of a London bricklayer by Captain Thomas Cooke, who then kept his victim in custody in the Tower of London in spite of the man's friends having obtained a writ of habeus corpus.[31] Such a blatant infringement of the common law spurred parliament in action. From 1 March 1693, all recruits had to appear before a justice of the peace or a high or petty constable to 'declare his free consent to be listed or mustered as a soldier before he shall be listed or mustered or inserted in any muster roll'. The justice or constable had then to give a certificate 'gratis' to the recruit's officer stating that he had been attested and this certificate had to be produced for the perusal of the deputy commissary at the next muster as proof of legal enlistment. Attestation of all recruits became the normal procedure. Recruiting officers usually brought their volunteers before the local justice in large groups so that there was not a separate certificate for each individual but a small number of certificates with a large number of names on each, fifty-two in one case.[32] With justices anxious to 'assist' and officers desperate for men, attestation was not treated too seriously and recruits were given little or no opportunity to raise objections to their own enlistments.

Recruiters amused themselves with all manner of devious tactics to lure the unwary and the simple into the army. George Venables was sitting quietly by the fire in the George Inn at Hatfield when in walked John White, a soldier. He went straight up to Venables and said, 'here is all the money I have left of the king's, here is a round O. Look on it'. Unwisely, Venables took the coin, inspected it, and was about to return it when White burst out, 'you are a soldier now', and would not receive back the shilling. Venables flung it down on the floor and refused to be tricked.[33] Another favourite device was to pretend that a man was a deserter from the army thus making impressment look like legitimate arrest. In December 1692, a number of complaints had been made to the House of Commons against some army officers for causing 'with the help of the press masters of the navy', several hundred men to be kidnapped, transported to Holland and Flanders, and then forced to enlist. A servant of a member of parliament suffered this fate and Sir Edward Seymour was asked to bring the matter to the attention of the king. On 9 February 1693, William replied that army officers had been ordered not to accept recruits who had been pressed and all offenders would be punished. Not completely satisfied, the House added this to the list of complaints which led to the adoption of the Attestation Procedure.[34]

However, all of this paled into insignificance beside the activities of Michael Tooley, the provost-marshal of the Coldstream Guards. Tooley was in a class by himself, a crimper extraordinaire. Lord Coningsby reported from a committee of the whole House on 24 February 1694 about a complaint which had been laid before the Commons twelve days before 'touching persons having been pressed for land service, and carried to a house near Turn Stile in Holborn.' This was the house of Michael Tooley, known as the Marshalsea house, which he had rented on the orders of General Thomas Talmash, the colonel of the Coldstream Guards. Tooley kept prisoner in his house over 100 men whom he had lured inside to drink, to play cards, to be hired as servants or simply kidnapped off the streets. Once through the door, no one bothered about attestation, and the unfortunate victims were sold at a handsome profit to the company captains from Tooley's own regiment and to officers from other formations. As Tooley's enterprise saved recruiting officers the bother and expense of finding their own volunteers, his business was much in demand. The army knew all about Tooley and Robert Davis and John Bright, the provost-marshals of the First Foot Guards who ran a similar establishment just round the corner, as they employed sergeants to kidnap potential recruits and official sentries stood outside their front doors. Henry Goodall, unemployed and looking for work, was hired by an officer. The gentleman gave him a shilling for carrying his cloak to the Tower of London and Goodall was then taken 'to a place where there were several others'. A colonel came to inspect them and the unfit were dismissed but Goodall was bundled along to Tooley's house where he was detained against his will and twenty-five shillings was demanded for his release. Tooley and Davis appeared before the bar of the House of Commons on 27 February 1694 and the sergeant-at-arms was ordered to take them into custody. Nothing happened. Tooley and Davis had been released from prison within a few weeks and they were back in business before the end of the year, but this time the London mob took matters into its own hands. The Middlesex Quarter Sessions had ordered Tooley to free Richard Lumbley, a man who had been forcibly recruited by Captain Edward Taylor, and a sheriff appeared before Tooley's house to see the writ executed. A guard of foot was posted outside the front door and prepared to resist the efforts of the sheriff. Close-by, in Lincoln's Inn Fields, a crowd was watching a wrestling match and it took little to persuade them to leave their recreation and 'assist' the civil authorities. Their assistance amounted to stripping the house of all its 'moveables' and burning them in the street, setting free some 200 prisoners who were found inside Tooley's commodious residence, and finally causing £2,240 worth of damage to the structure. Having dealt with Tooley, the mob moved on to the house of Robert Davis in Drury Lane but he had been forewarned and had moved his prisoners to another location. However, despite the guard of horse and foot, Davis's furniture and effects were thrown into the street and his house was thoroughly looted before the rioters proceeded to the Marshalsea, a small prison in Finsbury, and another provost-marshal's house, all of which contained illegally enlisted men. Faced with the prospects of massive riots, the troops were called into London's streets with orders to fire with powder and ball. This quelled the ardour of the mob and the disturbances subsided, but not before Tooley had been committed to Newgate. Needless to say, he was tried and acquitted in July, but he was dismissed from his position and was reduced to petitioning for relief in October 1696, seemingly unable to provide for his wife and six children.[35]

Tooley's case raises a number of points. In the first place, gaols were universally used to house recruits for the regiments in Flanders which says a great deal about the popularity of that service and the methods of recruitment. Secondly, at any one time, Tooley, Davis, Bright, and other provost-marshals were detaining between 400 and 500 recruits, all of whom had been tricked into enlistment. Taking money from an officer or a soldier for anything whatsoever carried with it the risk of immediate enlistment. Thirdly, Tooley and his associates operated with the full knowledge and blessing of the army at all levels, from the humble privates and non-commissioned officers who kidnapped innocents off the streets, to commissioned officers who forced shillings into the pockets of passers-by, to the colonels who inspected the volunteers, up to Lieutenant-General Thomas Talmash who had authorised Tooley to rent the house in the first instance. The whole business stank. In London at least, attestation was a poor joke and the enlistment of men for service in Flanders was a sordid and criminal racket, connived at by some very senior officers, yet parliament took no effective action. The full horror of Tooley and Davis's activities – and they were only the more conspicuous because they were provosts of the foot guards and so were permanently resident in London and had large regiments to supply – was revealed to the House of

Commons who, effectively, heard all the evidence and then did nothing. Tooley and Davis escaped scot-free both from the common law courts and parliament. Did no one care that the armies in Flanders were recruited by kidnapping, except for the victims and their families? Probably not. To the House of Commons the army was a disgusting eyesore which was undertaking a socially useful task in mopping up the unemployed, vagrants, the homeless, the near-criminal and general riff-raff from the streets. These types were better off in the army with a suit of clothes, some pay and food, and the opportunity to do service for their king and country. It was preferable for the army to be filled with such persons than to recruit from amongst honest, hard-working artisans and labourers. The trouble was that Tooley and his colleagues made no such subtle distinctions between the employed and the unemployed, or the artisan and the vagrant; they seized anyone. Exactly the same recruiting methods had been used in Scotland and England during the 1670s, only on a greatly reduced scale, and in March 1695 there was a nearly identical case in Paris. Several soldiers, including two from the bodyguard of Louis XIV, were arrested for kidnapping likely men in and around Paris and then selling them to recruiting officers. Like Tooley, they held their victims in special houses called 'fours', of which Paris boasted of more than eight.[36]

This cynicism was reflected in the increasing tendency to recruit directly from amongst criminals. The first suggestion that the enlistment of convicted criminals offered a convenient and cheap means of recruiting the army occurred in Scotland in January 1691, when the privy council ordered all magistrates to deliver 'burdensome and expensive' prisoners to Colonel George Ramsey, the officer commanding the Scottish forces to be sent to Flanders. At about the same time, Jonathan Rose was committed to Hertford gaol without having been accused of any particular crime and the assizes offered to release him provided that he enlisted in the army. He took ten months to consider this gracious offer and finally, realising that it was his only hope, accepted and enlisted in the Earl of Danby's dragoons.[37] By June 1693, it had become quite regular for prisoners convicted of relatively minor offences at the Old Bailey to be sentenced to obligatory enlistment in the king's forces: nine were enlisted from the June sessions, four from the July hearings, and three in September.[38] John Sweetingham was committed to the Warwick House of Correction as a 'sturdy beggar', having travelled illegally on a counterfeit pass and beaten up a parish constable. He was sentenced to be put to work and scourged but this punishment was later remitted on condition that he enlisted in the army. For stealing a sheep worth ten pence, John Harris, a labourer from Kenilworth, was ordered to be flogged but his sentence was commuted to enlistment in the army.[39]

This sentencing of minor criminals to be enlisted in the army was partially formalised by the Act for the Relief of Poor Prisoners for Debt or Damages, passed in 1695, which allowed men under forty years of age who had been imprisoned for debt to be freed provided that they took service in either the army or the navy for the duration of the war with France. Seven such men received their discharges for debt from Newcastle gaol in 1696 and duly entered Sir John Jacobs's foot.[40] In Scotland, in the same year, poachers of salmon and 'black fish may be delivered to serve as recruits'. The Middlesex justices sent Robert Dale to stand in the pillory for three hours in Bloomsbury 'for a trespass and false imprisonment' but he was given the option of serving in the army instead. Blathwayt authorised Captain Joseph Bennett of Richard Ingoldsby's foot to call at Warwick gaol to collect all the prisoners who had been convicted of 'small crimes' and were fit for service with the armed forces. Two circuit judges, Sir John Powell and Sir Nicholas Lechmere, were politely requested to assist Captain Bennett by recommending any of the inmates of the prison who might be 'proper objects of mercy and fit for service in the army'.[41] Many may have thought this a contradiction in terms.

If volunteeers, legal recruiting, kidnapping, and enlisting criminals failed to produce sufficient soldiers for the king's service, then there were always deserters from other armies in Flanders. On 15 June 1694, William III received intelligence that between 400 and 500 Swiss deserters from the French army had arrived in Maastricht. Luckily these Swiss were protestants and so an officer from every British regiment in Flanders which was in need of replacements was dispatched to Maastricht to take his pick. The two marine regiments which served in the Mediterranean with Edward Russell's fleet in 1695, collected any number of deserters from the French corps in Catalonia.[42] If foreign deserters failed to provide enough men, then domestic deserters could be re-enlisted. In order to raise the new regiments in the winter of 1693–4, the Scottish privy council was content to enlist deserters from other, established regiments with no questions asked provided that they had fled from their previous units before 1 November 1693. All this indiscriminate recruiting allowed a certain number of catholics back into the rank and file and one of the first movements towards a general disbandment after the signing of the Peace of Rijkswijk on 10 September 1697 was for officers to tender the oaths to their soldiers and to cashier any revealed catholics immediately.[43] To the modern reader, all of this leaves an unpleasant taste in the mouth and it must also have added fuel to the fire of the anti-standing army faction between 1697 and 1700. During the war, politicians, members of parliament, the king, and the armed services had connived at crimping, kidnapping, and the enlisting of criminals as these had seemed the only means by which to collect sufficient men but once the war was over pious constitutionalism was allowed free rein. The army resembled a giant sponge which had soaked up much of the dross and dirt from English society for nine, glorious years and this horrible social mess was suddenly suspended, dripping over peacetime England.

Yet, this institution which enjoyed the distinction of social ostracism and national regard simultaneously, was composed of human beings and it is possible to gain an impressionistic picture of the rank and file of William III's army. According to Gregory King, the 35,000 soldier families in England in 1688 were not the worst-off in the land. Their annual income was £14, just a little lower than that of labouring and 'out-servant' families, but well ahead of the £6 10s earned by the 400,000 cottagers and paupers. Soldiers, though, earned £6 less than common seamen.[44] All of this is very vague and generalised and King took no account of such complications as subsistence money, off-reckonings, and arrears. He also made the fatal error of assuming that a common soldier took home his full pay and calculated the foot soldier's daily wage as 10d when, in fact, only the guards received this sum and all other infantrymen were paid 8d.

Many soldiers in the army were foreign. As Andrew Fletcher pointed out, Scotland had provided twenty battalions of foot and six squadrons of horse for William III's war effort 'and every fifth man in the English forces was either of this nation or Scots-Irish, who are a people of the same blood with us'.[45] German troopers were to be found in the Earl of Macclesfield's horse and of the four 'hautbois' with the Earl of Argyll's foot, one was a Frenchman and the other three came from Liége. The Earl of Bath's hautbois was also French and there were Dutchmen in the ranks of the Coldstream Guards and in the marine regiments, and Brandenburgers in the Duke of Bolton's foot. One hundred and ten gentleman privates of the Life Guard were foreigners and had to be naturalised rather hastily in 1699 to comply with the stipulations of the Disbanding Act.[46] This cosmopolitan profile fitted in perfectly with an army which took anyone from anywhere by any method but it did not prevent the foreign soldiers from being as unpopular as Dutch and German generals.

The bi-weekly government newspaper, the *London Gazette*, frequently carried advertisements from company and regimental officers giving physical descriptions of men who had deserted from their commands, and offering modest rewards for information. Although these descriptions present useful cameos of contemporary army life and provide some information on the actual appearance and physical characteristics of the common soldiers, they are fraught with difficulties for the historian. In the first place, the advertisements record only desertions which took place in England and were only issued when the colonel or captain decided that it was worth his while to spend money on publicity. Secondly, the men who deserted may well have been the more enterprising and were thus atypical of their comrades who were content to endure hardship and remain with the colours. Thirdly, these descriptions say nothing of the types of men who were kidnapped and crimped into serving in Flanders, Ireland, or the colonies; they represent either new recruits still in their prime in England or soldiers from those battalions which lived a soft existence in England throughout the duration of the war.[47] Bearing in mind all these caveats, the overwhelming proportion of those deserters whose ages were recorded fell between twenty and thirty, with the next highest group falling between thirty and forty. This was followed by men in their forties, then teenagers, and, finally, old men over fifty. It was an army of young men in their twenties, not a formation of boys in their teens or decrepit veterans, although one private from the First Foot Guards was well over half a century old. As one might expect, a large number of them bore the ravages of small-pox and a surprisingly high number had physical defects which must have seriously affected their performances as soldiers: missing eyes, knock-knees, one leg shorter than the other, cleft palettes, and short-sight. Where a soldier had been attached to a trade before his enlistment, nearly all artisan callings were represented from barber-surgeons, to strolling players, to pipe-makers, millers, blacksmiths, wheelwrights, gardeners, butchers, joiners, carpenters, scriveners, and glovers. The most frequently mentioned trades were tailoring, weaving, and shoemaking. Other snippets of contemporary evidence bear out these conclusions. Private Daniel Arnold was a joiner before his enlistment.[48] Narcissus Luttrell mentioned great numbers of weavers, shoemakers, and butchers enlisting in March 1689, presumably because of a temporary slump in those occupations. James Sawyer, aged over sixty and a veteran from

Sir John Guise's foot, had been a tailor before he took to soldiering. Edward Billington had been a labourer.[49]

In the descriptions of deserters less than twenty-five per cent of those listed have trades entered against their names. The majority of the deserters, and perhaps one can extrapolate from this the majority of the rank and file of the army, did not have trades but had drifted into the service from failed apprenticeships, idleness, unemployment, and the fringes of the criminal underworld. If occupations had been noted by the company clerk they would have read labourer, servant, or farm-hand. Thomas May was probably fairly typical, 'a wandering pedlar, who never was settled in any place from his birth, but removed from one town to another' until he joined the army leaving his wife and five children on the parish. Gregory King classified soldiers and seamen as 'transitory' people numbering about 140,000, of whom 60,000 had no recognised home or abode.[50] Given the methods of recruitment and the way in which recruiting parties from Flanders operated in the winter months when casual and agricultural employment was at a low ebb, these impressions of the social origins of the common soldiers are probably reasonably accurate. The majority of the rank and file were footloose and possibly even half glad of the army for some pay, decent clothes, and some order and routine in their lives. For those with trades, their skills were readily appreciated in the army, as well as giving those men the chance to earn some extra money by casual work. No evidence from during William's reign has been found to support the notion that soldiers worked at civilian trades during their off-duty hours in order to supplement their meagre pay, but it seems almost inconceivable that the Guards regiments in London and the garrison companies in Hull, Chester, Carlisle, Berwick, Portsmouth, Plymouth, and Sheerness did not hire out their services as labourers or servants. After all, they had little else to do during their copious spare time and as they were billetted in small groups with inadequate supervision, such moonlighting must have been the norm rather than the exception.

Such casual work by soldiers possibly helped to bridge the huge rift between the military and civilian worlds. With so many soldiers having been tricked into the army by crimpers and kidnappers or 'volunteered' by their local communities, a majority of soldiers must have nursed a burning resentment against all things civilian. Pulling on the red coat rapidly brought with it the adoption of military values and mores, and gaining revenge on the civilians in general was probably a major factor in the strained relations between the army and its parent society.

Colonel [Edward] Fitzpatrick's regiment came to Witney on Saturday and design to march towards London tomorrow. They were very disorderly and broke open people's houses, as Mr Shorter told me, and forced men's horses from them to carry the officers.[51]

'These Dutch dragoons', wrote Thomas Piddocke, the bailiff of Ashby-de-la-Zouch, to the Earl of Huntingdon, 'have a way of poisoning fish in pools, and I have complained to the chief officer and he hath promised redress. If not, I am resolved to take some lusty fellows and club them.'[52] Poor Benjamin Browne, the junior proctor of Brasenose, ventured into the Mitre Tavern in Oxford at ten o'clock in the evening on Tuesday 15 November 1692 to seek out scholars who were illicitly drinking. Instead of undergraduates he found four troopers who locked him in a sideroom until midnight and then forced him to pay their bill of 4s 6d.[53] There was a 'great affray' at Oakham in Rutland between some butchers and soldiers in which many were killed and seriously injured on both sides. Five or six people died in Salisbury during 'great scuffles' between townsmen and soldiers in the same year, and two were fatally wounded in skirmishes at Newport on the Isle of Wight. Bulk purchasing of grain by army provision contractors forced up prices and created a local scarcity in Northampton in 1695 leading to the inevitable outbreak of riot.[54]

Soldiers were not encouraged to marry and recruiters were certainly not allowed to enlist married men. Dr Waddell has traced eleven wills from ordinary soldiers during William III's reign, and only two recorded the fact of marriage. On the other hand, out of thirty soldiers who died between 1694 and 1700 and who had their last testaments listed in the archdiocese of Canterbury, only four wills specifically mentioned that the deceased had been bachelors. Although the evidence is admittedly thin, there is a suggestion here that quite a number of soldiers were married and the indiscriminate recruiting methods employed during the war might support such a conclusion. In the Scottish army, no minister was allowed to marry a soldier unless the banns had been read three times, both in the woman's parish church and in the parish church of the bridegroom's quarters. Even then, the lucky man had to produce a certificate from his captain stating that he was not already in a condition of matrimony.[55] The Earl of Macclesfield reputedly admitted no trooper into his cavalry regiment who had a family, but then a lot of things were attributed to the Earl of Macclesfield's regiment very few of which were true. Undoubtedly, it was difficult for a serving soldier to marry but that does not rule out the possibility that a number of privates were married before their enlistment. During the massive demobilisation at the end of the war, every effort was made to rid the army of married men and retain only bachelors. Frequently, says Colonel Walton, the umarried were retained and the married discharged and the bachelors were then moved around from corps to corps to fill up vacancies.[56] It is easy enough to understand why marriage was discouraged.

A soldier's pay was pitifully inadequate to support even the soldier let alone a wife and family, there was no fixed family home, and there was only a remote chance of a pension should the breadwinner die or be disabled. It was better for privates and non-commissioned officers to remain single. Not all army wives became a drain on the community – the spouses of Sergeants Henry Fletcher and John Hirst both kept alehouses – but the vast majority slipped rapidly into extreme poverty as soon as their menfolk died or went away on active service.[57] John Lawrence was killed in Ireland leaving his wife Martha and a small child in Hertford, the objects of charity and the parish poor rate. The inhabitants of the village of Hunsdon petitioned the local justices to move the children of Private Thomas Ingold back to the parish of Matching in Essex where they had been born. Margery Roberts turned to picking pockets following the enlistment of her husband for service in Ireland, whilst Elizabeth Newton could only beg for relief from the parish of St Margaret's in Leicester after her husband 'had gone for a soldier' leaving her with six small children and 'in extreme want'.[58] Undoubtedly, the military had to face the fact that some soldiers were married and in 1694 each company of the Royal Marines was allowed to take three women onto its strength. Obviously they could not have gone to sea but must have stayed ashore to assist in the regimental depots. Most regiments seem to have adopted a similar practice by allowing a small number of soldiers' wives to travel with a formation as camp followers and more military spouses probably attached themselves to the sutlers' train. They seem to have been a rough bunch of females. Whilst Sir Henry Ingoldsby's infantry battalion was waiting in Preston before travelling to Whitehaven for embarkation for Ireland, 'a woman of them almost killed another in the cart with a grenadier's hatchet'. On 16 May 1698, William III gave the royal assent to a bill which naturalised all children who had been born to British soldiers overseas between 13 February 1688 and 25 March 1698.[59]

A discharge was like gold-dust. Only in Scotland in 1696 was a fixed

term placed upon enlistment; elsewhere service was for life or until
disbandment. The only effective method of achieving a discharge was
to fall seriously ill or suffer debilitating wounds. The Duke of Württemberg gave Thomas Talmash a list of sixty-seven 'disabled' and
eighty 'unfit' soldiers, all of them old, who should be discharged on 14
May 1693 and they were each to be allowed £3 from the paymaster to
meet their expenses in travelling from Flanders to England. Another
forty invalids were discharged on 31 May 1696. Discharges were so
uncommon that Sir John Trenchard, the secretary of state, brought the
matter of the discharge of Private William Gaunt from Ferdinando
Hastings's regiment before the privy council in London.[60] In the
regiments of the Scots Brigade in the Dutch service there appeared to
be a vague policy of granting discharges after twenty-four years'
service in the ranks but this was never committed to paper as a
regulation.[61] Most soldiers served for the duration of the war and then
faced destitution after the general disbandments between 1697 and
1700. The spate of highway robbery and the overall increase in the
crime rate which affected England during the decade of the 1690s
partially resulted from the numbers of soldiers cast onto the streets in
1688–9 and 1697–1700, as well as from the host of wounded and
maimed soldiers who returned each year from Flanders. One religious
crank advocated presenting each disbanded soldier with a free copy of
the *Christian Monitor* before putting them on a ship bound for the
colonies. It might not have been such an outlandish idea as the colonies
were short of labour and the soldiers had little else to occupy their
time.[62]

We have every day some disbanded soldiers with passes from the mayors of
Liverpool, Chester, etc. directed for passage to Ireland from Whitehaven
who, wanting money, are burdensome. I must make bold sometime to return
to the mayor of Liverpool some of his passengers by the constables.

'Begging, disbanded soldiers' were hovering in and around Waterford
in April 1698 and one Murray, a disbanded trooper, was so fed up that
he was convicted at the Westminster Quarter Sessions 'for speaking
reflecting words on Duke Schomberg: his wife was also convicted for
speaking seditious words against his Majesty'. Not every ex-soldier
took to crime and vagrancy. William Wey, who had been a private in
Colonel John Hales's foot, had settled back into life as a blacksmith in
Tolpuddle by 1701. For most the aimlessness of disbandment did not
last for long and the great sea of old soldiers began to be soaked up by
the army as it expanded for war during the late spring and early

summer of 1701.[63]

Unable to obtain a discharge and provided that the soldier did not drown whilst bathing in the River Dee at Chester, the most obvious way of escaping from the army was by desertion.[64] Desertion was not a peculiarly military phenomenon. Desertion was endemic in the army, navy, and in civilian life; servants ran from their employers, apprentices fled from their masters, sailors escaped from the navy, and soldiers left their colours. The penal servitude of many of these lower class occupations must have induced a despair and claustrophobia which could only be assuaged by desertion but the prevalence of desertion was also a symptom of an under-legislated society. The *London Gazette* for the reign of William III contained far more advertisements for the return of servants who had run away from their employers than for soldiers who had left their units, although there were rather more servants and menials in England than soldiers. Soldiers were customarily recruited from amongst vagrants, petty criminals, and casual labourers, men who were permanently itinerant and probably experienced the greatest difficulty in settling down to a relatively fixed occupation. Also, the forcible methods of enlistment must have caused many soldiers to regard the legal ties which bound them to the army to be exceedingly thin. Desertion was also very easy to accomplish. In England, units were frequently marching from one billet to another offering ample opportunity for stragglers to slip away and the quartering arrangements themselves presented every conceivable inducement to desert. Men were lodged together in very small groups – a single company of foot containing fifty men might be accommodated in the public houses of four or five separate villages – with minimal supervision from their officers. A private soldier could disappear and his sergeant might not even discover his absence until the time came for drill or duty. This problem was exacerbated for those formations which were perpetually domiciled in the capital. The horse and foot guards were quartered all over Westminster, Southwark, Holborn, and the 'out-parishes' in taverns and public houses in ones and twos. Many were frequently engaged on part-time jobs during their off-duty hours making some money to supplement their pay, and it often took many days to find out that a private had actually deserted and had not simply changed his quarters or gone out to work. As if these circumstances were not sufficient to tempt soldiers into running from their colours, the punishments for the unfortunate few who were recaptured were not excessively severe for the first offence.

Desertion was largely a crime of the foot soldiery. Few dragoons or cavalrymen deserted partly because horse troopers were principally recruited from genuine volunteers with minimal use of the press. Also, the pay of the horse soldiers was far higher than that of the infantry and offered a fairly respectable wage. Sheer poverty must have caused the foot soldiers to desert. Twopence out of their daily eightpence went straight to their company officers as 'off-reckonings' and the remaining 'subsistence money' of sixpence was further eaten into by the paymaster-general's 'poundage', the 'agent's man', and illegal stoppages by the captain. The fourpence or fivepence which actually reached the private soldier was often hopelessly in arrears, and only sufficient to cover the legal cost of his quarters in England. The common soldier had literally nothing left from his army pay with which to supplement his diet, buy drink, or feed and clothe his wife and children and he was dependent for both the quality and quantity of his food upon what his civilian landlord saw fit to give him. It was no wonder that soldiers rioted against civilians. Casual work was essential to the soldier if he was to have sufficient meat and drink and not live on ammunition bread and water. This was another reason for the unpopularity of service in Flanders as fighting with the field army offered no chance of taking on casual work and earning a few extra pence. Unfortunately for the historian no soldier from this period has left a written statement of what motivated him to desert and no court-martial investigated the reasons behind desertion, but the circumstantial evidence leaves the overwhelming impression that desertion was principally a financial business made worse by the illegal recruiting procedures.

Much desertion was not really desertion, in the sense that the soldier ran away from the army, but is best described as 'bounty jumping' where a man left one regiment without permission to join another. There was real desertion where a soldier just wanted to escape from the army altogether and the Mutiny Act of 1695 expressly forbade anyone to buy or exchange a soldier's clothes and arms on pain of a penalty of a £5 fine. When a man enlisted he received one shilling and whatever bounty was on offer from that regiment, sometimes as much as twenty shillings. This was a goldmine to the underpaid soldiery and many deserted from their regiment simply to re-enlist in another and enjoy a temporary alleviation of their plight. The officers frequently connived at this as deserters arrived complete with training, uniform, arms, and accoutrements. During William's reign, most of the uniforms of the infantry battalions were basically identical and differed only in the colour of the linings of the coat. A quick visit to the regimental tailor rapidly translated a deserter into an invisible member of his new battalion. One of the reasons for the gradual complication and decoration of military uniforms during the eighteenth century was to make this absurdly simple business less easy. Lieutenant William O'Brien of Edward Dutton Colt's foot was found guilty by a court-martial of entertaining men in his company knowing that they really belonged to the regiment of Colonel Henry Rowe.[65] Sergeant Edward Holland received a discharge from Richard Brewer's foot and then re-enlisted in another company of the same regiment only to desert 'taking several things of the captain'.[66] Once in Flanders, desertion became even easier. The nature of the campaigning in the Low Countries meant that all the opposing armies were in close contact with each other in a geographically restricted theatre. Also, the army in which the British troops served was a confederate force composed of Dutch, Brandenburg, Hessian, Württemberg, Bavarian, Danish, and Hanoverian contingents all living cheek-by-jowl in the same camp. Desertion, or hopping from one regiment to join another in order to gather the bounty, was desperately straightforward and most company officers were so short of men that they took anybody who walked in with no questions asked. One or two sartorial alterations to the uniform and that, by and large, was that. The non-existent mustering arrangements in the British corps in Flanders was also of great assistance both to the deserters and to the officers who received them into their units. French agents were busy spreading pro-Jacobite propaganda amongst the British and German troops in Waldeck's army in 1689 and Talmash reported that twelve men had gone over to the French in two days. Sixteen Scottish soldiers deserted as soon as they stepped ashore at Ostend in 1691 and when Lord George Hamilton's foot assembled in Cork to embark for Flanders, 450 out of its complement of 700 men mutinied and deserted. During the Duke of Württemberg's short voyage to England in April 1696 to render assistance in the event of a French invasion, 100 men from Sir Henry Bellasise's and Thomas Erle's battalions ran away. Two hundred of Colonel John Foulkes's foot deserted when they disembarked from the fleet onto the sands of the Isle of Wight in 1692.[67]

Finding deserters was difficult, time-consuming, and expensive. Bounty jumpers were usually almost impossible to detect but soldiers who had run from the army altogether were worthy of pursuit. Rewards were the order of the day. If, as usually happened, a soldier deserted with his uniform and equipment then his company captain stood to make a financial loss. Should a soldier desert shortly after a 'new clothing' then the captain's potential loss was considerable but if the man went off when his clothing was old and due for replacement then the captain's embarrassment was greatly reduced. The level of rewards offered reflected this. Fairly high rewards of two or three guineas were offered for information about the former but usually just one guinea for the latter.[68] When a deserter was apprehended, a fairly rare event as most seem to have escaped, then a file of men under one or two non-commissioned officers had to be sent to escort the recalcitrant back to the regiment, a costly exercise which had to be funded from the regimental 'bank'.[69] It was very difficult to trace deserters. Very few regiments kept detailed records of their recruits and most of the advertisements offered the vaguest of descriptions – 'a currier, about thirty, short black hair, and a long face with a mournful look', or, 'short, brown hair and a smooth face'. Some formations, the First Foot Guards and the Marine regiments in particular, appear to have kept fairly close notes on their recruits and were able to present descriptions which mentioned height, age, colour of hair, complexion, trade, and any curious physical characteristics. Whether these records were made at the time of enlistment and were then used to verify muster rolls as well as serving as useful identification in the event of desertion, or whether they relied upon the memory of an officer or a non-commissioned officer is unclear. Many deserters absconded wearing civilian clothes, a fact which indicates desertion whilst marching from their point of enlistment to the regimental depot. In some cases, soldiers may have possessed some civilian clothes purchased with the fruits of their part-time labours. The offering of rewards for the apprehension of deserters did have its dangers and one Mr Hoyle of Leeds was fined forty marks for 'forcing people away on pretence of being deserters'.[70] This was an interesting variant on crimping.

The army's disciplinary code was harsh. During William III's reign, military punishments became tougher and less yielding and it was at this time that flogging became established as the principal mode of correction. However, most of the fierce, physical punishments were only inflicted on soldiers when in Flanders as there was still a marked reticence about exacting punishments affecting life and limb in England despite the limited authority of the Mutiny Act. Memories were long and caution prevailed. When set beside the contemporary civilian criminal code and its range of punishments, the military discipline was not out of place or unreasonable. Nor was the court-martial unduly arbitrary in its proceedings when compared with the justice usually meted out by the common law courts to the lower social orders. The judge-advocate general was the chief legal official in the army, an office held by Dr George Clarke throughout William's reign, whilst Sir John Topham officiated in a similar capacity in Ireland.[71] General courts-martial in England could try any offence provided that it fell within the Articles of War and did not involve a civilian. They had liberty to impose their own punishments although these could only extend to life and limb in cases of mutiny, sedition, and desertion. In all other cases, the courts-martial had to remain within the parameters of the common law and apart from when dealing with these three offences mentioned in the Mutiny Act, it sat as the army's internal disciplinary body and not as a known and legal court of law. The general court-martial consisted of a president and twelve officers above the rank of captain and was competent to hear cases involving any rank within the army. Regimental courts-martial composed a president and twelve other officers but they could only judge cases involving soldiers and non-commissioned officers and were not allowed to inflict the death penalty. General courts-martial, the only courts for which records survive, were held in the Great Room at the Horse Guards in Whitehall and all the administrative arrangements were undertaken by the judge-advocate general. The Mutiny Act of 1690 stated that no court-martial was to sit other than between the hours of eight o'clock in the morning and one o'clock in the afternoon, presumably to ensure that all business was conducted with clear heads before dinner. Until 1695, a separate warrant was issued by the king or the lords justices for each court-martial in England but, in that year, William issued a blanket warrant and authorised courts-martial to be held as and when required with Brigadier William Selwyn as permanent president.[72] In Flanders and all other active service stations overseas, the common law was unknown and courts-martial reigned supreme administering the martial law contained within the Articles of War.

The maintenance of discipline in the regiment and the apprehension of offenders was the duty of the provost, a post customarily executed by the regimental quartermaster. Both in Flanders and in Ireland, 'a troop of provost' was formed to assist the provost-marshall general in keeping order and discipline within the field army.[73] The regimental provost was also responsible for executing any punishments laid-down by the court-martial: imprisonment, running the gauntlet, death, or flogging. To begin with, floggings were not of excessive length being limited to thirty-nine strokes, the maximum allowed under old Jewish law, but, in 1695 there was a case of 100 lashes with a cat-of-nine-tails being ordered for the fairly trivial offence of 'creating a disturbance'.[74] Discipline deteriorated when the army in Flanders went into winter quarters or endured a long stay in one particular camp, as at Cockelberg in 1697.[75] Boredom and drink caused most of the problems. Soldiers quarrelled, duelled, assaulted each other and civilians, murdered, robbed, and disobeyed their officers. With that same lack of a sense of social responsibility which allowed so much desertion and witnessed the frequent breaching of elementary trust and contract in contemporary society, Private William Smith of the First Foot Guards just 'went off his post at the gate entering into Duchy Lane in the Savoy and left his musket there'. It was the action of a child, not of a man.[76] Yet, considering the size of the army, the number of general courts-martial and cases involving the military which came before common law courts was not excessive. William's army was not ill-disciplined by the standards of the later seventeenth century and operational efficiency was never threatened by a general lack of order in the ranks.

Thomas Bellingham observed that as the troops assembled around Preston in 1689 ready to be shipped for Ireland, the soldiers drank at every available opportunity. One man died from excess and several others were 'very ill with drinking'. The assaults on villagers near Ghent by Colonel Charles Ross's Irish dragoons were caused directly by drink. Drink was also the reason behind the riots in Edinburgh in November 1690.[77] Two grenadiers of Thomas Erle's foot indulged in the popular pastime of 'clipping coins'; Sergeant John Archer stole a silver spoon and scraped off the owner's name for which offence he was reduced to the ranks.[78] A sergeant and three privates 'gilded' milled shillings and tried to pass them off as guineas. Others shot game and poached.[79] A Dutch trooper murdered George Doddell, 'a poor man', in Leeds in 1693, but more often soldiers brawled and fought amongst themselves.[80] When soldiers did disobey their officers or mutiny, the reasons were usually lack of pay or the prospect of being sent to fight overseas. Brigadier William Stewart's foot mutinied when ordered to board the fleet at Portsmouth and sail for Catalonia and three dragoon regiments rebelled in Southwark through arrears of pay in April 1694.[81] The discipline of the Dutch formations stationed in England during William's reign was no better, despite claims to the contrary, and there were, proportionately, as many cases involving Dutch soldiers as British.[82]

Much of the indiscipline was of the mindless, childish variety. John Barrett was absent without leave because he had forgotten his linen and had returned to his quarters without permission. A Dutch soldier shot his corporal because he ordered him to a sentry post in London which he did not like. Two privates had to run the gauntlet because they had spent one night out of their quarters without seeking prior approval.[83] These cases and hundreds like them did not constitute serious indiscipline but merely a lack of social responsibility and maturity which could scarcely have been otherwise given the reservoir from which the army recruited. In defence of the private soldiers, their officers set extremely poor examples in many cases and in drinking, duelling, and brawling, the rankers merely emulated their superiors. A military discipline similar to that of a modern army was impossible to achieve. Twentieth century military conduct has only become possible through the social pressures imposed on individuals by factory hours, the Industrial Revolution, and adequate personal incomes. All of these factors were unknown in the seventeenth century. It was an age of the individual not of corporate identity and although the behaviour of both officers and soldiers might seem infantile to the modern reader, it was the norm for all classes and social orders. Given the artificiality of a military discipline to seventeenth century society, the conduct of William III's British army was remarkably good.

Notes

1   Gregory King, p. 40; Bod. Lib. MSS. Bod. 981, ff. 21–4.
2   William Blathwayt calculated infantry battalions at six hundred men and cavalry squadrons at one hundred and thirty (BL, Add. MSS. 9,724, f. 169).
3   BL, Add. MSS. 15,897, ff. 88–9. All troop totals are for non-commissioned officers and men only. Officers were in addition.
4   ARA, Raad van State, 1932/2, f. 143. The Dutch consistently raised far more men than the British from a population that was less than half the size:
    1688 64,979
    1689 84,650 (including 29,005 'subsidie troepen')
    1690 64,596 (ditto)
    1691 64,044 (ditto)
    1692 63,267 (ditto)
    1693 63,267 (ditto)
    1694 87,978 (ditto)
    1695 100,796 (ditto)
    1696 101,880 (ditto)
    1697 101,680 (ditto)

1698 46,009

5   *CJ*, x. 430–2.

6   *RPCS 1691*, pp. 10–13; *Portledge Papers*, p. 87; *CJ*, x. 547, 557; *Parliamentary Diary of Luttrell*, pp. 28–9.

7   *CJ*, x. 712–13; Dalton, *Army Lists*, iii. 289–90; *HMC, Westmoreland and Other MSS.*, p. 355.

8   Bl, Harl. MSS. 1,898, ff. 40–1; Leopold von Ranke, *A History of England, principally in the seventeenth century* (London, 1875), vi. 227; *CJ*, xi. 18–20; Chandler, *Debates*, ii. 421, 428–9.

9   *CJ*, xi. 176–8, 345–7, 569–71; *HMC, House of Lords MSS.*, n.s. ii. 131–5; Chandler, *Debates*, iii. 28; Davies, 'Reduction', pp. 15–16; PRO, SP 8/16, f. 53.

10 BL, Add. MSS. 28,082, ff. 121–3; *CJ*, xiii. 695–6.

11 Everett, *Somerset Light Infantry*, p. 14; Knight, *The Buffs*, i. 285–6; *RPCS 1690*, pp. 11, 168, 205, 583–4; *HMC, Hope-Johnstone MSS.*, p. 170; BL, Add. MSS. 9,727, f. 36; *HMC, Buccleuch (Montagu) MSS.*, ii. 110; Edye, *Royal Marines*, i. 480–3; *CSPD 1697*, p. 55; Erle–Drax MSS., 4/18, ff. 3–5; Johnston, 'Scots chaplain', pp. 3–5.

12 SRO, E. 100/8/28–52, Muster Rolls, 1698; Sir J. W. Fortescue, *A History of the British Army* (London, 1910–30), i. 342–8.

13 Luttrell, iii. 59; *The Life and Diary of Lieut. Col. J. Blackader*, ed. Andrew Crichton (Edinburgh, 1824), pp. 33–4, 107; Johnston, 'Scots Chaplain', p. 3, quoting Chaplain Alexander Shields.

14 WO 5/5, ff. 61–2; Wood, *Life and Times*, iii. 321; SRO, Shairp of Houston Muniments, GD. 30/51/2084; Luttrell, ii. 604.

15 Davis, *Second Queen's Royal Regiment*, ii. 227; *CSPD 1695*, p. 249; *LG*, no. 3133.

16 *Bucks. Sessions Records*, i. 381; *CSPD 1690–1*, pp. 260–1.

17 *Edinburgh Records*, pp. 140–1; Steele, ii. 456, 462, 466; *A Selection from the Papers of the Earls of Marchmont*, ed. G. H. Rose (London, 1831), iii. 111; *Carstares*, pp. 160, 168, 172.

18 *HMC, Hamilton (Supplementary) MSS.*, p. 122, 24 Oct. 1691; Luttrell, iii. 42.

19 Walton, pp. 489–91, 795, 843; Guy, *Oeconomy and Discipline*, pp. 63–4; *HMC, Finch MSS.*, iii. 156; Edye, *Royal Marines*, i. 305; Waddell, pp. 349–50; Williams, *Stanhope*, p. 15.

20 *HMC, Le Fleming MSS.*, p. 320; Luttrell, iii. 432; Edye, *Royal Marines*, i. 462–3; Hamilton, *Grenadier Guards*, i. 353.

21 *CSPC 1689–92*, no. 768; BL, Add. MSS. 9,727, ff. 107, 111.

22 Steele, ii. 456; *CSPD 1695*, p. 298.

23 Edward D'Auvergne, *The History of the Last Campaign in the Spanish Netherlands, 1693* (London, 1693), p. 115; Luttrell, iii. 413.

24 WO 5/5 & WO 5/6, passim; *HMC, Buccleuch (Montagu) MSS.*, ii. 113, 121.

25 *HMC, Le Fleming MSS.*, pp. 331–7.

26 Clarendon, *Diary*, ii. 333, 28 Mar. 1689; Japikse, iii. 205–6; *CSPD 1691*, pp. 252–3; BL, Add. MSS. 9,724, ff. 73–4; *Edinburgh Records*,

pp. 143, 185; *HMC, Le Fleming MSS.*, p. 357.

27 *Diary of Thomas Bellingham*, p. 46; Clarendon, *Diary*, ii. 334; Atkinson, *South Wales Borderers*, p. 15; *HMC, Buccleuch (Montagu) MSS.*, ii. 241; *HMC, Portland MSS.*, iii. 440; Maurice Cranston, *John Locke* (Oxford, 1985), pp. 424–5.

28 *Acts of the Parls. of Scotland*, x. 61, 1696 c. 23; SRO, GD. 30/51/2095 & 2096; Walton, pp. 482–3.

29 S. H. F. Johnston, 'The Scots Army in the Reign of Anne', *TRHS*, 5th series, iii. (1953), pp. 12–13. Mr Johnston fails to take the 1696 Act into account.

30 HCRO, L. 1145; *HMC, Finch MSS.*, iv. 91.

31 *LG*, no. 2844; *SR*, vi. 479–80, 5 & 6 William & Mary, c. 15; Luttrell, iii. 26.

32 *Hertford Sessions Rolls*, i. 417, 429.

33 *Ibid.*, i. 394, 1691.

34 Lediard, iii. 429, Dec. 1692.

35 Luttrell, iii. 435, 460–1, 494; BCRO, Trumbull Add. MSS. 116; *Middlesex Quarter Sessions*, p. 128; *Lexington Papers*, pp. 75–6; *CSPD 1696*, pp. 421, 464; *Hatton Correspondence*, ii. 216; *Portledge Papers*, pp. 199–200; *HMC, Le Fleming MSS.*, p. 335; *CJ*, xi. 108–10, 185, 187.

36 Childs, *Army of Charles II*, pp. 174–7; John Childs, 'The British Brigade in France, 1672–1678', *History*, lxix. (1984), pp. 387–9; *Memoirs of the Court of France, 1684 to 1720, from the Diary of the Marquis de Dangeau*, ed. John Davenport (London, 1825), p. 278.

37 *RPCS 1691*, p. 7; *Hertford Sessions Rolls*, i. 403, 1691–2.

38 Luttrell, iii. 118, 141, 189; iv. 28, 51, 66; v. 120.

39 *Warwick County Records, Quarter Sessions Records, Easter 1690 to Michaelmas 1696*, ed. H. C. Johnson & N. J. Williams (Warwick, 1964), pp. 95, 98.

40 *SR*, vii. 75–7, 7 & 8 William III, c. 12; Everett, *Somerset Light Infantry*, pp. 38–9.

41 *Acts of the Parls. of Scotland*, x. 77, 1696, c. 35; *Middlesex Quarter Sessions*, p. 151; WO 5/8, f. 367, 27 Mar. 1697.

42 Edward D'Auvergne, *The History of the Campaign in the Spanish Netherlands, 1694* (London, 1694), pp. 24–5; Edye, *Royal Marines*, i. 464; *LG*, nos. 3093, 3095.

43 Steele, ii. 453–4; Luttrell, iv. 282.

44 Gregory King, pp. 48–9.

45 Andrew Fletcher, *First Discourse on the Affairs of Scotland* (Edinburgh, 1698), quoted in, Johnston, 'Scots Army', pp. 1–2; see also, John Robertson, *The Scottish Enlightenment and the Militia Issue* (Edinburgh, 1985), pp. 22–59, for a discussion of Fletcher and the standing army controversy.

46 *CSPD 1696*, p. 81; *LG*, nos. 2490, 2582, 2601, 2626, 2650, 2725; *LJ*, xvi. 402.

47 *LG*, anno. 1688–1702.

48 *Index to the Wills proved in the Prerogative Court of Canterbury,*

1694–1700, ed. Marc Fitch (London, 1960), p. 12.

49 Luttrell, i. 515; *CSPD 1693*, p. 199; *Bucks. Sessions Records*, ii. 75.

50 *Hertford Sessions Rolls*, i. 378; Gregory King, p. 36.

51 Clarendon, *Diary*, ii. 333, 1 Apr. 1689.

52 *HMC, Hastings MSS.*, ii. 214, 31 Mar. 1690.

53 Wood, *Life and Times*, iii. 407, 15 Nov. 1692.

54 Luttrell, iii. 63, 78, 114; *CSPD 1695*, pp. 262–3.

55 Waddell, pp. 325–9; Steele, ii. 447, 16 Sept. 1692; *Canterbury Wills*, passim.

56 Luttrell, iii. 280; Walton, pp. 492–3.

57 WO 72/1, Bundle 1.

58 *Hertford Sessions Rolls*, i. 397, 398; *Bucks. Sessions Records*, i. 366, 392–3; ii. 73; *Leicester Records*, pp. 29–30.

59 Edye, *Royal Marines*, i. 479; *SR*, vii. 380–1, 9 William III c. 20; *Diary of Thomas Bellingham*, p. 75, 25 July 1689.

60 BL, Add. MSS. 9,724, f. 141; BL, Add. MSS. 9,725, f. 29; WO 5/10, f. 5; DCRO, D60/X4, 1 Oct. 1693, Cabinet Memoranda of Sir John Trenchard.

61 *CSPD 1698*, pp. 69–70.

62 *HMC, Downshire MSS.*, i. 767.

63 *Lowther Correspondence*, p. 509; *Council Books of Waterford*, p. 344; Luttrell, iv. 569; *CSPD 1700–2*, p. 413.

64 CCRO, QCO/1/16/24, 23 May 1693, QCO/1/16/31, 14 July 1694, Coroners' Inquisitions for the City of Chester.

65 *SR*, vii. 1078, 7 & 8 William III, c. 23; WO 5/5, f. 106; WO 71/3, f. 9, 5 Nov. 1694; G. A. Steppler, 'The common soldier in the reign of George III', (Doctoral Dissertation, University of Oxford, 1985), p. 223.

66 *LG*, no. 2855, 20–23 Mar. 1693.

67 Müller, ii. 163–4, 23 July/2 Aug. 1689, Camp at Mellay; Luttrell, ii. 218; Davis, *Second Queen's Royal Regiment*, ii. 189–90; BL, Add. MSS. 9730, f. 53; BL, Add. MSS. 9,727, f. 70; WO 89/1, ff. 238–42.

68 *LG*, anno. 1688–1702.

69 WO 5/8, ff. 278, 336, 342, 1696–7.

70 Luttrell, iv. 401.

71 Luttrell, i. 559; Dalton, *Army Lists*, iii. 99.

72 *SR*, vi. 227–30, 2 William & Mary, Session 2, c. 6; Clode, *Military Law*, p. 65; *CSPD 1696*, p. 459.

73 Walton, p. 553; WO 5/6, f. 293; Bod. Lib. Rawlinson MSS. A. 349; BL, Add. MSS. 9,724, f. 50.

74 Walton, pp. 559–63; WO 71/13, f. 14.

75 WO 89/1–2, passim.

76 *LG*, no. 2561, 26–29 May 1690.

77 *Diary of Thomas Bellingham*, p. 60; WO 89/1, ff. 197–201; *HMC, Le Fleming MSS.*, p. 304.

78 *CSPD 1695*, pp. 311–12; WO 71/13, f. 35, 2 Dec. 1695, St Iago de la Vega.

79 BL, Add. MSS. 9,731, ff. 9–10; Steele, ii. 168; *SR*, vi. 398, 4 William &

Mary, c. 13.

80 *The Diary of Ralph Thoresby, F.R.S.*, ed. Joseph Hunter (London, 1830), i. 233, 3 May 1693; CCRO, QCO/1/16/45, 16 July 1698.

81 Luttrell, iii. 288, 300, 452.

82 Burnet, *History*, iv. 153.

83 WO 71/13, ff. 29, 42–3; Luttrell, iv. 186; *Portledge Papers*, p. 253.

V

The Huguenots

Danes, Brandenburgers, Swedes, Dutchmen, Württembergers, Hanoverians, Luneburgers, and Bavarians all fought as auxiliaries in British pay during the War of the Grand Alliance but only the Huguenots actually formed a part of the British establishment. French Huguenots did not suddenly appear in the English, Scottish, and Irish armies in 1689. The Earl of Feversham, James II's commander-in-chief, originated from Huguenot stock, as did William III's right-hand man in 1688, the old Duke of Schomberg. The Marquis de Miremont had raised a regiment of horse for James II in the autumn of 1688 and any number of subaltern officers under both Charles II and his brother had been Huguenot refugees – Henry Foubert, Charles St Clair, and Anthony Penetière. After the Glorious Revolution, the Huguenots came to form a separate enclave within the British armed forces possessing their own, distinct regiments as well as contributing a considerable number of officers to other formations. Five Huguenot regiments were created during William's reign.

The first unit to be recruited, in March 1689, was a regiment of horse designed to serve as a life guard for the aged Duke of Schomberg and it was officered by Huguenot reformadoes from the Dutch Blue and Red Dragoons. Following Schomberg's death at the Boyne in 1690, Lord Galway took over this formation and under him it fought in Ireland and Flanders before serving in Piedmont from 1694 until 1697. Between March and June 1689, three Huguenot battalions of foot were raised. Isaac de Monceau de la Melonière had been the colonel of the regiment of Anjou in Louis XIV's army but in 1686 he was committed to the Bastille for his refusal to disavow his faith. Melonière contrived to escape to the United Provinces where William of Orange made him a colonel in the Dutch army and his personal aide-de-camp. In 1689, he transferred into the British army as the colonel of one of the new Huguenot battalions and Melonière commanded his unit throughout the war in Ireland and Flanders. François du Cambon had been a French engineer officer until 1685 when the Revocation of the Edict of Nantes obliged him to seek employment overseas. After service with the Dutch army, du Cambon was commissioned colonel of one of the new Huguenot regiments in England in 1689 and he fought his battalion through the Jacobite Wars in Ireland before leaving for service in Flanders. Du Cambon was killed at the Battle of Landen in 1693 and he was succeeded by Frederick William de Roy de Rochefoucauld, Comte de Marton, later created Earl of Lifford, who had entered the English army under James II as a guidon in the Life Guards. In April 1689, Galway's brother, Pierre Massue, Comte de la Caillemotte, raised the third Huguenot foot battalion but he was killed at the Boyne and was replaced by his lieutenant-colonel, Pierre, Marquis de Belcastel. The fifth and last Huguenot corps was a dragoon regiment which the Marquis de Miremont raised on the Irish establishment in 1695. Two additional Huguenot regiments were raised by Galway after he had assumed duties as envoy extraordinaire to the Court of Savoy in 1694 but they were largely raised from amongst Huguenot refugees in Switzerland and were paid by the treasury of Victor Amadeus and not that of William III.[1]

Tracing the precise origins of Huguenot officers is not an easy task. Some were already in England at the time of the Dutch invasion in 1688 having fled from France during the peak years of emigration between 1686 and 1687. Others came over with the invasion force of William of Orange in November 1688, still more probably travelled over to England early in 1689 from the United Provinces and Brandenburg searching for military employment. Of one fact the historian can be certain; there were large numbers of refugee Huguenot officers anxious for work. William III had fifty-four Huguenot supernumary officers, or reformadoes, attached to his Blue Dragoons in 1688 with a further thirty-four in his Life Guards. Schomberg's regiment of horse and the three battalions of foot possessed a total, official officer corps of 170 but a host of 'incorporated officers' were attached to each regiment. Schomberg's and Galway's horse had an additional major and two reformadoe captains, three lieutenants and three cornets with each individual troop, all enjoying half-pay. The foot battalions were not so lavishly provided for and they had to make do with just one reformadoe captain, one lieutenant and one ensign per company. By 1694, five hundred and ten Huguenot supernumaries were serving with the Huguenot regiments on half-pay.[2] As vacancies became available in other regiments in the British army, this pool of 'incorporés' was used to find trained, professional officers to plug the gaps.[3] Having fought with the premier army in Europe, these Huguenot officers met with the approval of William III and he infinitely preferred giving a commission to a committed and trained French protestant than to an ignorant Englishman. As far as William was concerned, the Huguenot refugees provided a reservoir of potential officers who were proven and trustworthy and they fulfilled a similar function to the Anglo-Dutch Brigade. The Marquis de Puissar's foot, raised in 1695, had an entirely Huguenot officer complement and Colonel Edward Fox's infantry possessed a considerable number of French officers. Six officers in the Royal Dragoons were French, as were nine in the Earl of Macclesfield's horse.[4]

Quite how many Huguenot officers fought with the British army between 1689 and 1697 is impossible to estimate with any degree of confidence. In the first place, it is beyond the ability of any historian to calculate how many officers of all nationalities served with the British forces during this period. Although the peak number of commissions available in the British army was 5,000 in 1694, this does not represent the total number of officers employed during the reign. When retirements, deaths, casualties, and disablements are taken into consideration, the number of gentlemen who held commissions at some time in the war was probably in the region of 8,000 to 10,000. Of these, well over 1,000 were probably Huguenot. The established officers of the five Huguenot regiments and the 'incorporés' numbered nearly 700 and there were at least another 200 or 300 scattered amongst the rest of the army, if not more. The suggestion that between ten and fifteen per cent of William III's British officer corps was actually French protestant would not seem unduly wide of the mark, a figure made more tolerable by the estimation of one historian that as many as 3,000 French Huguenot officers quitted the army of Louis XIV after 1685.[5] If these estimates are anywhere near correct, then they go a long way to helping to explain how William III was able to find sufficient officers in 1689 and 1690 to command his expanding army in the face of the disloyalty and lack of professionalism displayed by so many of the native English. The 'incorporés' presented the king with an immediate reserve of replacement officers.

Hazy though our knowledge of the Huguenot officers is, it is vast when compared with our information about the lower ranks. In all probability, the Huguenot regiments were only worthy of that nomenclature because of their officer corps. In the first place, relatively few Huguenots from the social orders from which soldiers were traditionally drawn succeeded in escaping from France and the huge majority had to remain as reluctant nouveaux convertis. Secondly, in October 1689, 140 roman catholics were discovered in the regiments of du Cambon and Caillemotte.

most of these [the roman catholics] had deserted the French service this summer, and passing to Holland, and thence to England upon the report that three French regiments were levying there, had listed themselves in the same, the officers raising their companies in so much haste that they had not time to examine them very strictly.[6]

This does not read like a clarion call for the purity of the rank and file, especially as one of the catholics had been a captain in Louis XIV's army and had been forced to flee after committing a murder. Matters did not improve. Once in Flanders, the three Huguenot battalions and Galway's horse were natural magnets for French deserters, whether catholic or protestant. When the Huguenot colonels dismissed their catholic soldiers as part of their preparations for the voyage from Flanders to Ireland in November 1697, their ranks were 'decimated' by the evictions and as many as 700 roman catholics had to leave the regiments. However, there was another side to the coin. Some Huguenot refugees were glad to join the ranks of the British army without commissions. Eleven Huguenots volunteered as troopers in Major Charles de la Tour's and the Comte de Paulin's troops in the Earl of Macclesfield's cavalry regiment in July 1694, but there is no record of any Huguenot refugees joining any of the British foot battalions.[7] The Huguenot regiments were basically French, although far from exclusively protestant, and resembled all the other corps in the British army in that they recruited whoever they could whenever they could. The officers were Huguenot but their men were distinctly cosmopolitan.

William had a very high regard for the Huguenot formations. They were well trained and professional and they fought with that personal hatred of Louis XIV which he knew and understood so well. This admiration did not extend from the native British officers and men. They were favoured foreigners and there was a good deal of jealousy between the British and the French as illustrated by the fact that the Huguenot units were pushed to the very back of the pay queue and their arrears were far larger than for any other section of the army.[8] There was no sense of gratitude expressed in the Disbanding Act of 1699 which insisted upon the discharge of all foreigners from all regiments on the English, Irish, and Scottish establishments by 26 March.[9] Between 9 April and 6 July 1699, two hundred and eleven disbanded Huguenot officers were given permission to sail from Ireland for the United Provinces, most of them in a 'destitute' condition.[10] William wanted to retain the Huguenot officers and soldiers in some sort of community from where they could be easily remobilised when war was renewed with Louis XIV. His solution was discovered in Ireland where the soldiers and their families were settled upon sections of the forfeited Jacobite estates. Lord Galway had been given Sir Patrick Trant's lands by William in 1696 and he established a Huguenot military community at Portartlington.[11] The three Huguenot foot battalions were shipped directly from Flanders to Ireland and there disbanded. Five hundred and ninety Huguenot officers and non-commissioned officers took pensions on the Irish establishment and settled down at Portarlington and on some other estates which had been given to refugee Huguenot noblemen, like the Marquis de Puissar.[12] However, when the trumpets sounded and the drums beat again in 1701 and 1702, the Huguenot regiments were not re-raised. There had been a good deal of dissatisfaction with the élitism of the Huguenot corps within the British army and they had also suffered from the growing unpopularity of all foreigners in the British service which had first manifested itself with the objections to the Dutch and German generals in 1691 and 1692. The Huguenots were very closely associated with William III's protestant crusade against Louis XIV, and anything or anyone which had supported the continental schemes of King William was bound to be odious to parliament in the aftermath of the war. Perhaps too, parliament felt beholden to the Huguenots for their contribution in defeating the Jacobite armies in Ireland and in providing the backbone of the British officer corps throughout the Nine Years' War. Between 1697 and 1699, the House of Commons was in no mood to acknowledge debts and its demand was for a native army commanded by native or naturalised officers; the unfortunate Huguenots had become an anachronistic embarrassment. Many Huguenot officers rapidly took naturalisation before 26 March 1699 enabling them either to retain their existing commissions or giving themselves the chance of rejoining the army at some time in the future. Captain Isaac St Eloy had been in Sir Bevil Grenville's foot for ten years and the only method by which he could continue to support his large family was to seek naturalisation.[13] The foundation of the military settlement at Portarlington went against the pattern of assimilation by which England has traditionally, and successfully incorporated foreigners within its society. Portarlington placed the Huguenot pensioners in a dangerously contrived position.

During the War of the Spanish Succession, many Huguenot officers and soldiers served in the British army but as individuals and not as a separate corps. Belcastel raised a regiment for the Dutch service from amongst the Huguenot veterans in Ireland in April 1701, and the Dutch raised more Huguenot battalions in the same year, but the heyday of the French protestant refugees was really over. Much of the impetus behind the formation of the Huguenot regiments in the United Provinces after 1686 and in England after 1689 had been the common sympathy with their plight displayed by their co-religionists in western Europe. They were the most obvious victims of Louis XIV's intolerance and their very presence in England seemed to give a physical justification to the Glorious Revolution, but all of that enthusiasm had passed and soured by 1697 and the Huguenots were no longer the living symbol of the international alliance against catholic France. The pressures were now upon the Huguenots to adapt themselves to fit into their new homes as unobtrusively as possible.[14]

Notes

1 C. E. Lart, 'The Huguenot regiments', *PHSL*, ix. (1911), pp. 482–98; *Dublin and Portarlington Veterans: King William III's Huguenot Army*, eds. T. P. Le Fanu & W. H. Manchée (Publications of the Huguenot Society of London, 1946), p. 3; DCRO, D60/X42, 27 Feb. 1694, Sir John Trenchard to Lord Galway; Geoffrey Symcox, *Victor Amadeus II: Absolutism in the Savoyard State, 1675–1730* (London, 1983), pp. 114–17. For some modern introductory remarks about the Huguenot regiments and the part played by Huguenot refugees in the defeat of Louis XIV's France, see, Robin Gwynn, *Huguenot Heritage* (London, 1985), pp. 144–50.

2 BL, Harl. MSS. 7,439, ff. 15–16; Dalton, *Army Lists*, iii. 118–20; DCRO, Ilchester MSS., D. 124, Box 278, Establishment 1694; Robin Gwynn, 'The arrival of the Huguenot refugees in England, 1680–1705', *PHSL*, xxi. (1966–70), pp. 366–73; BL, Add. MSS. 38,698, ff. 156–61, 177–8; BL, Add. MSS. 38,699, ff. 58–61.

3 SP 63/340, f. 179.

4 Atkinson, *Royal Dragoons*, pp. 50, 69n.; HMC, *House of Lords MSS.*, n.s. iv. 367; Dalton, *Army Lists*, iii. 354.

5 Lart, 'Huguenot regiments', pp. 480–2.

6 LG, no. 2496; Dalton, *Army Lists*, iii. 118–20; *Diary of Thomas*

Bellingham, p. 86.

7 BL, Add. MSS. 9,731, f. 31, 3 Nov. 1697, Sir Henry Bellasise to Blathwayt; *Hertford Sessions Rolls*, i. 417.

8 DCRO, Ilchester MSS., D. 124, Box 276, Accounts of Charles Fox and Thomas, Lord Coningsby, Paymasters-General of the Forces in Ireland, Jan.–Oct. 1698.

9 10 William III, c. 1.

10 W. H. Manchée, 'Huguenot soldiers and their conditions of service in the English Army', *PHSL*, xvi. (1938–41), pp. 263–5.

11 J. G. Simms, *The Williamite Confiscation in Ireland, 1690–1703* (London, 1956), pp. 88–9; Grimblot, i. 129, 8 Oct. 1697, William III to Galway; Agnew, *Galway*, pp. 79–80.

12 W. A. Shaw, 'The Irish pensioners of William III's Huguenot regiments, 1702', *PHSL*, vi. (1902), pp. 295–326.

13 *CJ*, xii. 525, 612.

14 W. H. Manchée, 'Huguenot regiments in Holland', *PHSL*, xiv. (1930–33), pp. 96–8.

VI

Pay and pensions

The paymaster-general in England was the principal financial official of the army. Richard Jones, Earl of Ranelagh, had assumed this office on 1 January 1686 and he continued in his post throughout the reign of William III. He was assisted by a number of deputy-paymasters. Edward Pauncefoot officiated until 1695 when Mordecai Abbot succeeded him, whilst Richard Hill, a protégé of Ranelagh's, acted for him with the army in Flanders. Charles Fox and Thomas, Lord Coningsby shared the paymaster-generalship of the forces in Ireland until 1698 when the latter assumed duties by himself.[1] Ranelagh operated from a house in St James's Park adjacent to the Horse Guards, whilst the Irish paymasters had premises 'over against the gate of Scotland Yard'.[2]

The salary of the paymaster-general was generated from the 'poundage', or the right to extract one shilling in every pound from all army pay passing through his hands. Eightpence out of each shilling was used as a central fund to finance the Royal Hospital at Chelsea, the salary of £1,000 per annum for the secretary-at-war, and the 'contingencies'. From the remaining fourpence, Ranelagh had to pay his fees to the exchequer, his clerks and officials, the running costs of his department, and his own official salary of £2,000 a year. Any balance was supposed to be paid to the king to dispose of as he saw fit but, in reality, the paymaster's salary was entirely flexible and consisted of the balances remaining in his hands after all commitments had been met. In 1685, Sir Stephen Fox, Ranelagh's predecessor, admitted that he paid himself an annual wage of £3,613 18s 4d from the poundage on £283,000, so one can only imagine what fantastic sums Ranelagh awarded himself from the poundage on over two million pounds a year.[3] The paymaster for Ireland enjoyed even richer pickings as his poundage was completely reserved to his own discretion to be spent 'in such manner as we shall from time to time direct'.[4] Beneath the paymasters-general and their immediate deputies, there may have existed unofficial regimental and company paymasters. Regimental paymasters are mentioned in the first renewal of the Mutiny Act in 1689 and a George Campbell was described by Major-General George Ramsey as 'his own and his regiment's paymaster' in 1697.[5] However, these regimental paymasters were almost certainly the regimental agents referred to by a different title. At company and troop level there is a reference to a sergeant acting as company paymaster with the responsibility of receiving the subsistence money from his captain and of distributing it amongst the men. Almost certainly, this paymaster-sergeant would have been obliged to keep accounts.[6]

Agents were the lynchpins of the army's pay system and although a number of agents came in for a bad press, most were competent and some were exceptionally efficient. 'Mr Wilson', the agent of Sir John Reresby's garrison company at York in 1687, was described by the deputy-commissary-general of the musters, David Crawford, as 'a very honest, civil man'. During 1697, the Earl of Argyll's troop of the Scottish Life Guard was kept afloat for ten months on the personal credit of its agent in the absence of any funds from Whitehall. The First Foot Guards and the Coldstream Guards were allowed to carry 'solicitors' on their establishments from as early as 1680, and these 'solicitors' were undoubtedly agents rather than the baggage-masters suggested by Colonel Walton. However, these two regiments were the sole corps permitted to enter their agents onto their establishments and thus these fortunate gentlemen were the only agents in the army who enjoyed the luxury of an official salary. All other agents were the personal employees of the regimental colonels and possessed no military rank or status. Most regiments and garrisons adopted agents during the decade of the 1680s until all formations were so equipped by 1689. Even so, the Commissioners for Public Accounts commented in 1691 that 'the agency to regiments is a thing lately brought into practice' and they continued with the observation that 'many of the agents giving great sums of money for their places, make their profits by deductions from the soldiers'.[7] There was no particular skill in being an agent. All the job required was the ability to handle simple book-keeping, patience, and personal credit-worthiness. It was not especially profitable. Most agents received an annual salary of around £190 and to make a reasonable living a man had either to serve as agent to a number of regiments or treat the post as strictly a part-time employment. Adam Cardonnel, Richard Povey, and John Thurston all held regimental agencies as well as full-time posts in the War Office; David Crawford was also deputy-commissary-general of the musters; Edward Pauncefoot and Mordecai Abbot were deputy-paymasters; James Bridgeman was a clerk to the privy council; Hugh Chudleigh, Nathaniel Hornby, and James St John were all employed in the Treasury and Henry Cornish was a stamp duty commissioner and a director of the Bank of England. Leading financiers like Gilbert Heathcote, John Ward, Valentine Duncomb, James Wood, and Richard Beauvoir took on agencies for a time as did two clergymen, James Deanes and Richard Topham. Dr John Bateman was a medical practitioner. Others like Arthur Slingsby, Henry St George, John Ward and nine others were serving officers.[8] Robert Curtis was agent to ten regiments which must have brought him an income of about £1,900 a year, William Wallis looked after the affairs of nine units, William Hamilton had seven, and Alexander Gawne, five. Any number of agents were responsible for two or three formations. Robert Curtis also acted for six battalions in Ireland which gave him a total of sixteen regiments and an annual salary of over £3,000. This was nothing when compared with Mr Calcraft of Channel Row, Westminster, who was agent to thirty-six regiments in 1759, practically half the English army.[9]

Many agents based themselves at Mann's coffee house in Charing Cross which was run by Mr and Mrs Mann who were both army sutlers, and from there they spun their financial webs.[10] The standard picture of a regimental agent was of a dishonest trickster who assiduously swindled both the officers and the men but, like most caricatures, this was largely inaccurate. The agent was appointed by the colonel as his personal servant; he was not a commissioned officer and had no legal responsibility to the regiment itself. Strangely, he was subject to military discipline when on foreign service stations in the same way as both sutlers and camp followers. One Mr Downes, agent to the Duke of Ormonde's troop of the Life Guard, absconded with £2,000 of the troop's money in 1694 and nineteen agents failed to make their returns in 1693.[11] It was not until the Royston Petition of 1695 that the abuses committed by some regimental agents came to light. Tracy Pauncefoot, brother of fellow agent and deputy-paymaster Edward, was taken into custody for failing to pay subsistence to the officers and soldiers billetted in Royston when he had the cash in his hands, and Richard Roberts, agent to Colonel Francis Langston's horse and Colonel Richard Ingoldsby's foot, and William Wallis, agent to nine regiments, were also arrested for refusing to appear before the Commissioners for the Public Accounts.[12] In the wake of this scandal, the House of Commons appointed a committee to investigate the operations of the agents but its report later in 1695 revealed not a sea of festering corruption but disorganisation and poor management. According to the committee, no standard method of accounting existed leaving the paymaster-general's office with the task of deciphering the individual patois of each agent. If an agent sold his position, there was no machinery for assuring continuity of practice between himself and his successor and the out-going incumbent was only responsible for his term in office. Usually, he closed his accounts on leaving his position and with arrears of pay running often into months and years new agents were simply unable to trace the true financial condition of their regiment. Not all moneys due to a formation passed through the hands of the agent. Colonels and captains received certain allowances, levy money and cash to cover contingencies, direct from the paymaster-general and this resulted in endless confusion with each regiment possessing three or four separate accounts. Although colonels enjoyed the undisputed right to appoint and dismiss their agents, the committee was in no doubt that the more unscupulous commanding officers had done this as frequently as possible in order to confuse and muddy the regimental accounts and disguise their own peculations. Ferdinando Hastings was a prominent member of this fraternity. The committee recommended that each formation should have one, continuous account book recording all moneys received and disbursed with the obvious corollary that all cash for whatever purpose should pass through the agency. In addition, the agent should keep separate account books with each troop and company within the regiment and all ledgers should be open for inspection on demand by all interested parties and auditors. Finally, the committee sought to regularise the position of the agent by suggesting that he become a commissioned rank.[13]

Such a reform implied a radical revision of the organisation of army finances by changing the colonel's personal servant into a commissioned, crown appointee in charge of all regimental moneys. The agent would have become a snooper for the central government into the private world of the captain and the colonel. The lobby against these proposals was far too strong for the king to weather even though their implemention would have saved money and placed regimental finances on a more honest and controllable basis. Instead, the

Commons left matters as they were but insisted that each agent produce bonds of surety from two or more guarantors before the paymaster-general advanced him one penny of public money. These guarantors were to remain liable until three years after the agent's dismissal or death.[14] Although no evidence exists for William's time, agents were accounting separately with each troop and company within their regiments by the second half of the reign of Queen Anne, perhaps suggesting that not all of the committee's recommendations were ignored. However, the complaints against agents and colonels continued. Objections that agents were witholding regimental moneys were still being voiced in 1697, sufficient to keep Mordecai Abbot and William Robinson busy on a series of special audits.[15]

Between 5 November 1688 and 29 September 1702, £19,518,452 4s 1d of public money passed through the office of the Earl of Ranelagh. Like his predecessor, Sir Stephen Fox, Ranelagh made a fortune out of the army but unlike Fox, much of Ranelagh's gain was probably garnered through illegal practices. However, a considerable degree of care and caution must be exercised. Ranelagh was only the biggest fish in a pond full of other predators all feeding off the juicy body of the public funds; the dividing line between official salary, fees, douceurs, and criminal fraud was none too clear in the later seventeenth century and Ranelagh merely executed on a grand scale what was done by countless hundreds of other major and minor government employees. Fox became a millionaire from the post of paymaster-general of the army and so did James Brydges, Duke of Chandos. A short spell in the office did the financial position of Robert Walpole no harm, and the position helped to pay for the extravagant life style of Henry St John, Viscount Bolingbroke. No holder of the office could avoid making huge sums of money from the poundage and other legitimate perquisites but Ranelagh went much further by taking open advantage of a slack system of financial control caused by the plunge into international war. Ranelagh's activities bordered on the criminal, and the fact that he escaped virtually without penalty comments eloquently upon the immature state of central government. However, some defence can be offered. By the mid-1690s, Ranelagh's personal proportion of the annual poundage was well in excess of thirty thousand pounds out of which he awarded himself a salary of over ten thousand. From each regiment he had to decipher three or four separate sets of accounts, all drawn up differently, some very full in detail some exceedingly sparse, all of which must have rendered the task of consolidating accurate central accounts almost impossible. The regiments with the field army in Flanders were allowed to 'muster complete' and their accounts and muster rolls bore no resemblance whatever to the actual numbers of men to be paid. Confusion and muddle must have been the order of the day in Ranelagh's office but when the Commissioners for the Public Accounts began to investigate the financial empire of the Earl of Ranelagh on 15 May 1702, they came to the conclusion that much of this confusion and muddle had been deliberately created in order to cover the paymaster-general's tracks. Out of fairness to Ranelagh, it must be emphasised that his affairs were only subjected to parliamentary scrutiny after William's death as part of the general hounding of those court politicians who could be easily associated with William's war effort and his pro-Dutch foreign policy. Ranelagh was more of a political scapegoat than a victim of outraged public morality. Indeed, he seems to have been something of a favourite in the House of Commons with his ready wit and convivial demeanour. Likewise, the fall of Henry Guy from his secretaryship to the Treasury in 1695 in the wake of the Royston affair had more to do with the attack on Guy's patron, the hated Earl of Sunderland, than with parliament's desire to cleanse the army's Augean stables.

Ranelagh's cash books and ledgers were certainly kept in a highly idiosyncratic manner. His personal style of entry was extremely general and vague with no attempt made to give dates or to itemize particular warrants. In fact, Ranelagh's ledgers did not constitute accounts in the accepted sense of the word, but were really no more than lists of cash received and payments made. It would have been impossible to construct accurate and detailed accounts from these records and this was precisely Ranelagh's objective. By contrast, the accounts of Charles Fox and Lord Coningsby for the forces in Ireland in 1698 were a mine of information with all payments precisely entered against the relevant warrants. The Commissioners for the Public Accounts wrote to Ranelagh on 15 May 1702 asking him to appear before them on 25 June bringing with him his accounts and balances. He turned up on the appointed day armed only with 'general abstracts of accounts with gross items of his payments, and such as were in no respect conformable to the method prescribed.' When questioned about his, Ranelagh merely shrugged and informed the commissioners that it was impossible to acquire any more detailed accounts, to which they quickly responded that he must possess more detailed accounts otherwise he would not have been able to prepare his abstracts. Rather weakly, Ranelagh admitted the logic of this statement and then fell back on the defence of querying the legal competence of the commissioners. On 2 July one commissioner and an auditor called at Ranelagh's office but he refused to let them see his accounts and then spent the next seven weeks consulting with legal counsel, at the end of which time he promised to send two ledgers but his clerks began to fall ill with curious frequency and another three weeks slipped by. When pressed again, Ranelagh disappeared to his house at Cranborne and the Commissioners were left frustrated and dissatisfied. From the little information that they did succeed in squeezing from the slippery paymaster, they brought twelve accusations against Ranelagh on 14 November 1702. The commissioners found that Ranelagh's assignment of interest on tallies was fraudulent and that several regiments of James II's army which had been denuded of troops in December 1688 were paid in full until April 1689. Even worse, these payments to non-existent regiments had been made one or two years after the event. The muster rolls, when available, did not tally with the accounts of pay; Ranelagh forged signatures on warrants; he repaid himself for raising two regiments which had been levied and paid by the States-General; and his records and accounts were so vague that checking was impossible. Payments made bore little relationship to the agreed establishments and the commissioners proved that he had actually stolen £172,340 in 1689 which should have been paid to 'other persons'. They also discovered that Ranelagh had carried forward a balance favourable to himself which was a mere £39,543 1s 11d more than it should have been. Typical entries in the paymaster's account ran:

Paid to several persons for special services and for sundry disbursements for special services relating to the forces	£27,150 16s 3d
Paid to several persons for contingencies of divers natures	£50,929 17s 3½d

Still, Ranelagh could not be caught. Nothing could be actually proved against him because regimental accounts were usually in a complete mess and so no 'back bearings' could be taken to show up the fraudulent nature of Ranelagh's figures. Also, the muster rolls had mysteriously disappeared. Obviously, the deputy-commissary-general of the musters, David Crawford, worked hand-in-glove with Ranelagh and probably shared in the profits. Certainly, the commissioners found that the garrisons in England had not been regularly mustered between 1687 and 1692. On 22 January 1703, the commissioners reported to the House of Commons and explained that they had experienced the gravest problems in bringing any sort of accounts before the House.

That though the accountant did at last bring us regimental accounts, yet having delivered up, as he pretended, all his partial vouchers and producing only general vouchers, which are commonly nothing more than names endorsed on the pay warrants, and several colonels and agents being since this time dead, or their papers and accounts lost, we had no other way to check the same than by the muster rolls, and they are very defective, many wanting; very plain gross erasures in the doquets of others; and the parchment rolls frequently differ from the paper rolls in the commissary's office; for which neither paymaster nor commissary has given us any satisfaction.

Ranelagh had first fallen under suspicion in January 1699, great exception having been taken by the House of Commons to one item in Ranelagh's estimates for disbanding the army. He had allowed £100,000 for the pay of the general officers in 1697 and 1698, when £30,000 per annum had proved sufficient to pay all the generals when the army was at full strength during the war. The virtuoso of evasion admitted that as some general officers had since been dismissed, it might be possible to lower the estimate by £5,000 but the House could penetrate no further. Similarly, in 1702 and 1703, nothing definite could be proved against Ranelagh although the commissioners were fairly certain that he had misappropriated at least £72,000 of public money. Without corroboration, Ranelagh could not be prosecuted but was merely expelled from the House of Commons on 1 February 1704.[16]

Foot soldiers in the guards received 10*d* a day, and all other infantrymen were given 8*d*; dragoon troopers took home 1*s* 6*d*, out of which they had to care for their horses, and cavalrymen were paid 2*s* 6*d*, again for both man and beast. Foot soldiers in Ireland had their wages lowered to 6*d* a day, rising to 8*d* when they were quartered in the more expensive environment of Dublin. This full pay was never actually issued as all rankers and non-commissioned officers were subject to 'off-reckonings'. Every soldier bought his uniform and accoutrements, excluding his firearm which was supplied gratis by the Ordnance Office but including his sword, on hire purchase from his colonel and that money was collected through the off-reckonings which were deducted from the full pay before it was given to the men. These off-reckonings amounted to 2*d* a day for infantrymen, 4½*d* a day for dragoons, and 6*d* a day for horsemen. The balance was paid out as 'subsistence money' and it was supposedly inviolate and could not be eaten into by further deductions on the grounds that it was from this residue of pay that the soldier provided himself with food and lodging and cared for his mount. Unfortunately, the off-reckonings were never sufficient to meet all the demands made upon the soldier's full pay. In addition to meeting the cost of his clothing, there was the poundage to the paymaster-general, one day's full pay per annum to the Chelsea Hospital, a fee to the clerk of the pells, 1s 5d a year to the regimental agent, and 6d per annum to the commissary-general of the musters. These total deductions were known as the 'gross off-reckonings' and were meant to be accommodated within the stoppage of 2d a day. The 'net off-reckonings' was the balance remaining from that 2d a day once all other deductions apart from the clothing contribution had been subtracted; in effect, the 'net off-reckonings' represented the clothing fund available to the colonel. Any surplus from the regimental clothing fund was retained by the colonel and became the 'bank', designed to meet contingency charges and the expenses of recruiting.[17]

Many contemporary memorials and notes on army pay blithely assumed that the soldiers received their full subsistence moneys and that the gross off-reckonings covered all the necessary deductions.[18] Nothing could have been further from reality. According to the notes kept on his company's pay by Ensign William Crammond in Flanders in 1689 and in Ireland during the following year, the subsistence money of the foot was seriously eroded by illegal deductions extracted by the colonel. Drummers' coats, drum-heads, the escorting of recruits, offerings for the judge-advocate general, special pay for the drum-major, exchange rate commission, and discounts on debentures were all met from the soldiers' subsistence money. Crammond's men actually received about 4d a day in subsistence money which meant that half of their full pay was taken from them, twenty-five per cent in legal stoppages and the remainder at the whim of the colonel. Clearly Crammond's battalion, Sir David Colyear's foot, was not exceptional as the Earl of Nottingham asked the Duke of Leinster on 10 June 1692 to make a report to the queen about how much subsistence money the soldiers under his command really received from their captains. A further memorandum on army pay gives an actual subsistence payment to infantrymen of 5d per diem, and a royal proclamation of 26 July 1697 in Ireland allowed captains to stop 6d a week from each of their soldier's subsistence money when billetted in Dublin and 4d a week when quartered in rural areas to buy their 'necessaries – shoes, linen . . . as shall be wanting between each general clothing'.[19] None of the surviving records suggest that the foot soldiers ever received their legal entitlement to 6d subsistence money every day. Their actual daily wage was between 4d and 5d which, with a basic daily quartering rate of 4*d*, left them with no money unless they undertook work in their spare time or hopped around the army deserting and picking up new enlistment bounties. Dragoon and cavalry troopers received a daily subsistence of 9*d* and 1*s* 6*d* respectively and, no doubt, this was also worn away by illegal, regimental deductions, but at least they were not reduced to the bread-line in the same way as the infantryman. The horse soldiers had a degree of financial cushioning, however slight. Replacement mounts were the main problem for cavalry captains. In dragoon and cavalry regiments, horses were the common property of the troop and only when a unit was completely disbanded was each man allowed to take his mount home. In 1697, a new set of orders allowed each troop commander to stop four shillings a month from each dragoon and seven shillings from each cavalryman during the six 'grass months', 1 May to 31 October the period when horses could graze, and this fund was used to purchase remounts. No stoppage was made during the other six months of year as the trooper had to buy fodder for his mount out of his subsistence money.[20]

Subsistence money was paid in full by the paymaster-general to the regimental agent as soon as the muster rolls had been returned to the Horse Guards, duly signed. The agent then subtracted the regimental stoppages – for the judge-advocate general, drums, the commissary-general of the musters, and the agent himself – and then apportioned the balance to the company and troop commanders. They then made further deductions from the subsistence money in order to form a fund with which to buy 'necessaries' for the men. The little that remained was finally handed to the paymaster-sergeant or the ensign for distribution amongst the privates. If few 'necessaries' were required by the troop or company, then the captain pocketed the cash referring to it euphemistically as his 'dividend', a sum which could amount to £60 in twelve months.[21] The paymaster-general in Whitehall retained the gross off-reckonings until he had made the appropriate deductions and then advanced the net off-reckonings to the colonel's agent to meet the cost of clothing and to build up the regimental 'bank'. Although the subsistence money was pathetically inadequate, it was at least issued fairly regularly. In Ensign Crammond's company in Flanders, the subsistence money was paid out every week during 1689, but when the battalion served in Ireland in 1690 this altered to a monthly arrangement. Sir Albert Cunningham's dragoons were paid once a fortnight when in Ireland between 1689 and 1690. Every attention had to be given to the provision of subsistence as an unpaid army was mutinous and rebellious and memories of the impecunious New Model Army in 1646 and 1647 were still reasonably vivid.[22] Arrears of pay built up in the issue of the net off-reckonings, better known as the 'clearings', from the paymaster-general to the colonels. Often, these were paid in debentures and not in cash which meant that their value was seriously eroded by the necessary discounting procedure rendering the regimental clothing fund desperately short of money. Officers' pay was also frequently not met in full and, again, was often in the form of debentures rather than cash. Out of the £1,200,000 owed to the army at the time of the Peace of Rijkswijk in 1697, over £1,000,000 was due to the officers in arrears of pay and clearings. Amongst the regiments which were still on foot in England in 1698, £115,000 was owed in subsistence to the officers and soldiers, the clearings were in arrears to the tune of £482,000, and the debt on general officers' salaries amounted to £100,00.[23]

Pay began to fall into arrears very early in the reign. Lieutenant-Colonel Francis Russell moaned that the Royal Dragoons had received not one penny in pay for three months between January and March 1689. His officers had dipped into their pockets to buy horses and to recruit their troops and Russell was obliged to beg a loan of £150 from his brother to pay for his regiment's quarters between Bedford and Morpeth. The gunners in the Hull garrison petitioned for their arrears of pay in November 1690, and Colonel Francis Luttrell asked the Treasury for his clearings of £1,500 in March 1691 to meet the debt due on his regiment's clothing. An officer of Du Cambon's Huguenot foot petitioned for fifteen months' pay in August 1691, having received just seventy days' wages during the previous eighteen months; officers of the Prince of Hesse's foot were eight months in arrears.[24] Captain Samuel Foxton of the First Foot Guards was placed in temporary command of a battalion of the Prince of Hesse's foot in the spring of 1692 and marched the men to Breda. They received no subsistence for a fortnight and the officers had to pay their men from their own pockets forcing Foxton to pawn all his 'equipage' for £120 in order to assist. General Schulenburg had previously lent Foxton £200, but £120 of this sum had already been spent to cover immediate debts and the regiment could not subsist on £80.[25] During 1691 and 1692 the army muddled through and by April 1692, the paymaster-general could report that all units had been cleared to the end of December 1691. However, the delivery of pay began to slip badly in 1693 and 1694 and as the currency crisis developed in 1696, the arrears of pay in the field army in Flanders became critical.

Complaints do come from Williamstadt for want of payments. I can tell you, sir, that I have every day and every hour of every day complaints of the same nature from every garrison in Flanders and Brabant, and I have neither agent, nor clerk, nor money to send to Williamstadt to prevent those complaints.[26]

On 16 March 1696, Richard Hill, the paymaster to the army in Flanders, reported to Blathwayt that he had received no funds from Ranelagh since 28 January and although he had eked out what little he had to make sure that each regiment received something, he feared the onset of serious trouble amongst the commands of Richard Ingoldsby, Sir Mathew Bridges, and Emmanuel Scrope Howe which were all out of cash. By 12 October, the whole of the British corps in the Low Countries was ten weeks in arrear and Hill encountered infantry officers selling their horses whilst the army victualling firm of Machado and Pereira refused to supply any more provisions until they had been paid.[27] Lord Galway had no money with which to pay the British troops in Piedmont in August 1696; three colonels waited on the king to beg for money to buy boots so that their men could march; and Lord Jedburgh's dragoons had been financed entirely by its officers.[28] The king sent Lord Portland to England to represent the seriousness of the situation in Flanders to the Lords Justices. Portland's description of the troops on the verge of mutiny and wholesale desertion with the corollary that such a disaster would have upon the condition of the alliance and the prosecution of the war with France, was sufficient to produce a loan of £200,000 from the Bank of England.[29] Gradually, the army recovered its financial foundations during the winter of 1696–7 as the recurrency and loans from the Bank of England eased the situation but a moutain of debt had emerged which was to dog the army long after the coming of peace. Unsettled arrears of £200,000 were still in dispute in 1711.

As most contemporaries fully realised, the arrears of pay which bedevilled the disbandment in 1697 and 1698 were basically clothing debts brought about by the delayed payment of clearings. The chief sufferers were the officers. A report in 1698 advocated the establishment of a commission to look into the arrears due to the army and to call for accounts from all officers, living or dead, starting with those from the oldest regiments. When the accounts had been passed, then the colonels could draw their money from a 'bank' which would be established by act of parliament.[30] Not until 6 April 1700 was such a commission set up and only then because the popular clamour for the payment of the arrears had grown so shrill. Samuel Atkins, Thomas Morris, William Farrer, George Langton, and Thomas Leister sat down together on 29 April and they were still busy clearing accounts on 26 September.[31]

The government was desperately short of ready cash throughout the reign, but particularly in 1696 and 1697. Payment by debentures was a regular feature. In August and September 1689, debentures were used to pay the clearings of sixteen battalions of foot and, occasionally, subsistence to the troops in Flanders was paid by debentures although these had to be redeemed for cash by the officers before being distributed to the men. In 1690, debentures were being discounted in London by forty per cent and in October 1694 officers were obliged to dispose of their 'tallies' at a loss of between twenty-five and thirty per cent. Brigadier William Selwyn's foot had its arrears from service in Ireland paid in tallies on the customs but these could only be realised for hard money at a discount of between twenty and twenty-two per cent. Major-General Thomas Erle received both his own pay and the clearings of his two foot battalions for 1695 and 1696 in a mixture of 'malt tickets' and 'salt tallies', all of which his agent, Thomas Pain, kindly volunteered to discount. The great financiers of the age must have thought that all their birthdays had come at once. Sir Stephen Fox is supposed to have sold land in order to raise cash and then to have employed a goldsmith near Hungerford Market to act as his broker in buying army debentures at a heavy discount in order to redeem them later at their par value, a charge hotly denied by his biographer.[32] Sir John Germaine and Stephen Evans were active in the same business. During the principal disbandments between 1697 and 1699, most officers were given their arrears in a combination of one-third cash and two-thirds debentures.[33] On 9 September 1697, some innkeepers in Westminster petitioned the Lords Justices that men from the Royal Horse Guards had paid for their quarters in malt tickets, redeemable from the malt tax in twenty months time. Naturally, the publicans objected to having to wait this long for repayment or, even worse, be reduced to having to accept far less than the face value for their paper from a discount broker, but what is clear from this episode is that the troopers had obviously been paid their subsistence in debentures. Also deep in the currency crisis in 1696, there was some talk of paying the men of the Plymouth garrison their subsistence in provisions rather than in coin and English cavalry in Ghent in June 1696 refused to accept bread in lieu of their subsistence money.[34]

Army debentures were issued in anticipation of the customs revenues and salt duty, as tickets in the 1697 million pound lottery which was secured on a malt tax, or on the estates in Ireland which had been confiscated from the Jacobites in 1690 and 1691. The latter were the most widely used during the disbandments following the War of the Grand Alliance. William had initially agreed to fund the army arrears from the forfeited Irish lands in February 1691, provided that a proportion of the estates were reserved for his own disposal to favourites and supporters. Unfortunately, William badly overstepped the mark and the lands which were supposed to fund the army arrears were given away in ever-increasing acreages – Talmash, Galway, Elizabeth Villiers, Henry Sydney, Henry Luttrell, the Earl of Albemarle, Portland, Zuylestein and Athlone all received handsome grants of Irish land. As the confiscated lands were steadily given away during the 1690s, army debentures resting upon their security were sold for higher and higher discounts to the detriment of both officers and soldiers. By the Act of Resumption in 1699, parliament took the forfeited lands away from William's grantees and put them into the hands of commissioners who were enjoined to raise money to meet 'the officers' arrears, debts for transport service and clothing, debts and interest on tallies, orders, tickets, and exchange bills and no other use whatever.' The Act of Resumption was a major political defeat and humiliation for William but it achieved its object in creating a fund from which at least some of the army debentures could be paid. Sir William Scawen, the London merchant and army clothier, bought estates in Galway with the debentures which he had received for equipping Colonel Charles Churchill's regiment. The Irish lands could not possibly have raised enough to satisfy all the military demands made upon the them and the residue of the army arrears was translated into £987,000 worth of South Sea stock in 1711.[35]

The payment of the troops in Flanders was a complex operation. First and foremost it depended upon good communications between England and the Low Countries and on one occasion when five weeks of persistent easterly winds prevented the delivery of money and letters of credit, Richard Hill had to put the army on half-pay for a fortnight. Roger Tizer acted as Ranelagh's deputy in Flanders until April 1692 when he was replaced by Hill who enjoyed a daily wage of one pound which was increased by one hundred per cent in 1694. Hill based himself in Antwerp where he ran an office with two clerks and a cashier, Thomas Janssen. All payments were made in specie with regimental quartermasters ferrying tons of coin back to their regiments by waggon. Naturally, these were the frequent targets of French *ambuscades*. As the troops in Flanders were paid in local currencies, the fulcrum of Hill's operation was to ensure a constant and favourable rate of exchange between the pound sterling and the Dutch guilder. As government credit began to weaken in 1693 and 1694, the exchange rate started to slip and Godolphin opened negotiations with the Bank of England to establish a branch in Antwerp to undertake the payment of the army at a fixed and agreed rate of exchange. The Antwerp branch functioned from 1695 until the end of the war and although it cost the Bank a loss of £130,000, it was invaluable to William's government and enabled it to weather the financial storm.[36]

The cost of the army to William's government was vast. Charles II's little army had cost £283,000 per annum during 1684 and James II's forces had drained his Treasury at an annual rate of £620,322. Between 5 November 1688 and 29 September 1691, the army alone cost William £3,481,585.[37] The shock to the political and financial system was seismic. Few English politicians had the remotest conception of what involvement in a modern war meant in financial terms and whereas the first two years of the war were spent running round in a panic, the last seven were consumed by grumbling. Godolphin was in despair when he received the king's order on 28 June 1692

to provide for the subsistence of the Hanover troops in our weekly returns. All I can say to that matter is that this being still another extraordinary and the funds for the public service of this year falling extremely short of the necessary charge of the ordinary estimates given to the parliament, we must endeavour, and with no small difficulty, to run the king in debt as far as we can and anticipate his whole revenue anew. . . . And also we must be forced to leave everything unpaid and run on in arrear to the king's household and family and all other charges to the civil government.[38]

Costs rose relentlessly, from £1,895,942 in 1691–2,[39] to £2,345,548 in 1692–3, to £2,709,713 in 1695–6.[40] With the coming of peace, army expenditure dropped to acceptable levels, a mere £331,466 in 1701.[41] Between 1689 and 1699, parliament raised a total of £22,000,000 for the use of the army, and when the navy, the ordnance, and all other incidental military charges were added, the grand cost of the British war effort was in excess of £60,000,000.[42]

It hardly needs to be said, but it was a great deal easier for an officer to acquire a pension at the end of his service career than it was for a common soldier or a non-commissioned officer. The first port of call for a soldier who had been 'disabled by wounds in a fight or other accidents in the service of the crown' was the newly finished Royal Hospital at Chelsea, financed from the poundage and a levy of one day's pay from all ranks in the army. By 4 March 1690, the 472 places in the Hospital were full and 107 'out-pensioners' were drawing allowances from the Royal Hospital's funds but were living in their own lodgings. In planning and constructing the Hospital, no one had taken account of the fact that the small armies of Charles II and James II might, one day, be augmented, go to war, and send home numerous casualties. The whole enterprise had been designed on a small scale to suit just the domestic army. Faced with a new Hospital which was filled to overflowing before it was properly finished, Ranelagh suggested a revision of the pensions' list with the object of weeding out the pensioners who were elderly but still hale and hearty and sending them off to man the garrisons.[43] Four 'invalid companies' were accordingly organised from amongst the out-pensioners, each numbering twenty-five in 1690 but increasing to one hundred and fifty by 1697. Every man was paid 5*d* a day and was given a new set of clothes every two years. They were stationed at Tynemouth, Windsor Castle, Chester, and Hampton Court and undertook simple and routine garrison duties. Some of the more robust of the 'in-pensioners' at Chelsea found themselves drafted into invalid companies from time to time to make room for wounded veterans returning from Flanders, especially after the Battles of Steenkirk and Landen.[44] Even if a pensioner avoided service with the invalid companies, he might have been detailed to labour in the gardens of Kensington Palace under the watchful eye of the housekeeper.[45]

If an old soldier who had been wounded or who had served for twenty years was unable to acquire a place at Chelsea, and the majority did not, then he could petition the king and privy council for the grant of a pension. After twenty-seven years service to the restoration monarchs, including the British Brigade in Portugal and the corps in France during the 1670s, Captain Adam Bolton prayed for half-pay and was given a pension of £40 per annum. Thomas Price of Worcester, an old soldier under both Charles I and Charles II who been shot through the left hand whilst serving with the fleet in 1673, was granted the next vacant almsman's place at Worcester Cathedral. Having lost his right arm in the service of Charles II, David Ellis still had a wife and four children to maintain. He was given an almsman's place in Christ Church Cathedral, Oxford. Veteran James Sayer, late of Sir John Guise's foot and aged sixty, was admitted to the next almsman's vacancy in Gloucester Cathedral. Joseph Gally was given a pension of five shillings a day from the Irish establishment after he had been wounded and disabled. Private Anthony Head of Henry Mordaunt's foot was seriously injured by falling timber whilst helping to fight a blaze at Winchester Cathedral, so much so that he had to be invalided out of the regiment. The dean and prebendaries of Winchester recommended him for an almsman's place.[46] However, the majority of military veterans did not bother to petition the privy council or were unsuccessful in their quests. For these unfortunates there remained one final fount of possible charity: the local justices of the peace and the organisation of the county.

Each county in England and Wales levied a rate of between 2*d* and 10*d* a week on every parish with the express purpose of providing a fund for the 'maimed soldiers', and this rate was collected by the churchwardens and parish constables ten days before a quarter sessions. Depending upon the size of the shire, there were one or two treasurers for the maimed soldiers who held office for twelve months. An applicant had to produce a certificate from his late commanding officer testifying as to his service and disability and, at the hearing, the justices quizzed the applicant fairly thoroughly about his injuries, his circumstances, and his loyalty. A pension could only be granted or amended by the justices at quarter sessions. On average, a successful applicant received an annual pension of £2, although it could go as high as £4 or even £10, but the pension was only granted and continued upon evidence of good behaviour. Pressed men had to apply to the counties from where they had been enlisted and volunteers had to apply to the shires where they had been born or lived for at least three years. The justices of the North Riding of Yorkshire would not, as a matter of policy, pension a man who had volunteered but only showed charity to those who had been coerced into the forces. There was a limited amount of money available in any one year for pensions and some applicants had to be given a lump sum to tide them over until a pension became vacant through the death of an incumbent. Every effort was made to prevent fraud and 'playing the old soldier'. Most county sessions moved around from town to town to make it easier for poor petitioners to present their cases and the majority of the seekers of military pensions were able to approach the justices in towns near to their homes.[47] Certificates from commanding officers had to be produced, and justices were apt to refuse petitions until this document had appeared. Even in cases where the commanding officer of an old soldier had long since been dead, the onus was still upon the petitioner to scratch around to discover some surviving officer who could vouch for him. William Burrall in 1697 managed to find a retired cornet with a memory long enough to recall that Burrall had served under Prince Rupert in Charles II's time.[48] Some sad cases had to be rejected.

Richard Warner had been a soldier for forty years and had been wounded so often that he was forced into retirement but the justices of Hertford could not give him a pension because 'nobody was dead nor no money in treasury handy to pay it'.[49]

In the early stages of the War of the Grand Alliance, in 1690, the Middlesex bench was informed by one of its number, Thomas Hariott, that there were not many maimed soldiers enjoying pensions in the county at that time and so there was 'sufficient in the treasurers' hands to pay them their full pensions'. Needless to say, this healthy situation rapidly deteriorated as casualties returned from Ireland and Flanders. Edward Billington, of Cubblington, a labourer, lost his right arm at the siege of Namur in 1695 and had to be invalided out of Colonel John Courthope's foot. He was given a pension of £2 a year and the justices were especially sympathetic as he had been pressed into service.[50] However, when all was said and done, a pension of between £2 and £4 was a miserable pittance. It was better than nothing but it only provided 1½d a day, 2½d less than the actual take-home pay of an infantryman. For a very lucky few, there was one other route to a pension. Henry Wood, an old trooper of the Royal Horse Guards, was retained on the muster rolls of that regiment even though he was far too ancient to do any duty. James II had initiated this arrangement and William III had sanctioned its continuation.[51] There may well have been others like Wood who were kept on their regimental strengths as reformado privates.

An officer stood a much better chance of securing a pension than a common soldier. Wounded and disabled officers could petition the privy council and were usually rewarded with considerable bounties. Captain Edward Thorneycroft was awarded £100 after being wounded at Brest in 1694, a Captain Bettsworth lost a leg at Landen in 1693 for which he received £146, and Captain Philip Armstrong was given £150 for his wounds received in the same action.[52] For officers who were simply old but otherwise fit, there was every chance of being retained in the regiment as a reformado, effectively a half pay officer who did no line duty but was responsible for drill, training, and extraneous tasks. During the War of the Grand Alliance, it seems probable that the regimental recruiting depots and bases were run by reformado officers in order to save the full pay and younger officers for service in the field.[53] Officers' widows were also treated relatively generously. Nine-nine officers' 'relicts' drew pensions from the establishment in 1697, ranging from £40 per annum for the wife of a lieutenant-colonel down to £20 for the spouse of a deceased ensign or quartermaster. When Colonel Anthony Heyford died, his wife was allocated a pension out of the secret service fund. Inevitably the system was partial and inconsistent and favoured the dependents of higher ranking and influential officers at the expense of regimental subalterns from unfashionable line battalions. Charles Gourney served for thirty years, rose to the dizzy heights of lieutenant, and was killed at Landen leaving his wife Anne with nothing. She applied to the privy council for a pension but no result was recorded.[54]

The widows of common soldiers fared badly both from the central and from local government. William III, according to the Earl of Shrewsbury, was well disposed towards a scheme to provide pensions for the widows and orphans of ordinary soldiers and non-commissioned officers but nothing ever materialised, even though he was inundated with petitions during 1689 and 1690. Widows of deceased rankers were obliged to apply to the quarter sessions and the justices were far less generous to these applicants than they were towards the old soldiers themselves. Margaret Hatcher, who was both antique and blind and whose husband had been killed in Ireland during the Jacobite Wars, was allowed the sum of one shilling a week from the overseers of the poor in Wendover in 1692. Elizabeth Ransome, the widow of Robert, a poor and maimed soldier who had recently died, was allowed to collect the ten shillings due on her husband's county pension but no more. Ransome's pension died with him and there was nothing for his widow except the parish.[55] For both officers and soldiers, only the most obviously deserving cases secured pensions; the majority of ex-soldiers slipped back into civilian life to make do as best they could. The attitude of the authorities was well illustrated in a royal warrant to the commissioners of the Scottish Treasury. Their lordships were enjoined to ensure that the 'stock' from which the Scottish military pensioners were paid grew and was well managed, but they were to be equally careful to restrict the number of invalids who received its benefit.[56]

Pensions were much needed as the medical facilities for the troops both in Flanders and in England were abysmal. In defence of the government it can be offered that seventeenth century medicine, in any form, was more of a hindrance than a help, but the Dutch army's medical arrangements were infinitely superior to those of the British corps in the Low Countries. Dutch sick and wounded were taken straight from the army to one of two field hospitals which accompanied the troops on campaign and from here, after immediate treatment, they were transferred to the 'Grootlegerhospitael' in

Brussels. Again, the Brussels military hospital only served as a clearing station and the sick and wounded soldiers were quickly moved on to permanent military hospitals at Maastricht, 's-Hertogenbosch, which was the largest, Namur, Breda, Delft, Gouda, Rotterdam, Dordrecht, Gorinchem, and Bergen-op-Zoom. The Dutch even had a special waggon for the surgeon of each regiment. One of the reasons for the relative excellence of the Dutch medical organisation was that they had learned during the Franco-Dutch War of 1672 to 1678 that the catholic nuns of Flanders cared only for their co-religionists and they refused to look after nasty protestants from Holland, Germany, or England.[57] The English had taken part in the latter stages of that war but no one seemed to have remembered this fundamental lesson.[58]

Sickness was endemic in the seventeenth century armies – dysentery, typhus, typhoid, small-pox, food-poisoning – and in July 1689, Waldeck reported to William that 200 of the British corps in Flanders were sick. However, it was in the aftermath of major battles that the true nature of the pathetic medical service provided for the British soldiers was revealed. During the Jacobite Wars in Ireland, an under-populated country with few towns of any size, the Williamite army established a base hospital at Dublin and organised a 'marching hospital' to travel with the army. Additional surgeons' mates were appointed to many of the regiments serving in Ireland.[59] No such refinements were to be found in Flanders. There was an abundance of towns in which to lodge sick and injured men obviating the need to pay for an organised network of field and base hospitals. After the Battle of Steenkirk in 1692, British wounded 'were lying with their wounds up and down the streets' of Brussels, as the base hospital was filled with Dutch casualties. Luckily there was a Florence Nightingale in the form of the Princess de Vaudemont, the wife of William's general, who went in her coach with the assistance of link-boys and had the wounded soldiers moved into the great hall of her palace before calling in her own, personal surgeons and physicians. The Princess and her ladies acted as nurses. It was just as well that this angel was on hand as Blathwayt described the British hospitals at Malines, Ghent, and Bruges as 'miserable', under-funded, and badly in debt. French surgeons and apothecaries who were practising in Brussels had to be drafted to look after the British casualties and, needless to add, they were never properly remunerated. When Blathwayt referred to these hospitals, he did not mean hospitals in the sense of the Dutch institutions – proper buildings with organised staffs and equipment – but a few, reserved beds in private houses in a town under the vague supervision of an army or local surgeon. From Brussels, most of the British wounded from Steenkirk were shipped by canal to Bruges and Nieuport before being sent across the North Sea to the Tower of London which served as a giant repository for injured soldiers. It also served as a prison to prevent the convalescent soldiers from deserting. Even this progress of repatriating the wounded could be painfully slow and British sick and injured from Steenkirk were still housed in billets in Flanders as late as April 1693.[60] The situation was no better following the Battle of Landen in 1693, but in 1694 a fundamental change was made in army medicine. Admitting defeat, the army medical service handed over the organising, supplying, staffing, and equipping of its hospitals in Flanders to a private contractor, Patrick Lambe. By September 1694, Lambe had created reasonably sized hospitals at Ghent, Mechlin, and Brussels, and a new station was established at Dixmuyde after its capture late in that same campaigning season. Unfortunately for Lambe, the surrender of Dixmuyde to the French in July 1695 lost him £472 9s 6d worth of equipment. Lambe was also responsible for setting up a British hospital at Liége in the summer of 1695 to which the British wounded from the siege of Namur were shipped down the Maas by boat.[61] The care of the sick and wounded certainly improved under Lambe's supervision and the number of British soldiers admitted to the army hospitals in Flanders who ultimately succumbed showed a marked decline after the summer of 1694.[62]

In England there was nothing. Sick men remained in their quarters until death or recovery. In 1692, Jonathan Leigh, Robert Gower, Edward Harle and James Anderson, apothecaries, contracted to supply all British army surgeons with drugs and Sir Christopher Wren fitted out three rooms in the Savoy for the use of this first 'army drug service'. In Ireland on 21 October 1700, a house was rented by the army at St Auden's Arch in Dublin to act as a military hospital. It was very small, only a surgeon's mate was actually in permanent residence although army surgeons and chaplains made daily visits, and there was a sinister article in the charter which allowed an inmate's regiment the sum of four shillings in the event of a subsequent funeral, but it was a start in the right direction.[63]

Notes

1   Horwitz, *Parliament, Policy, and Politics,* pp. 146–7; *CSPD 1700–1702,* p. 206; P. G. M. Dickson, *The Financial Revolution in England* (London, 1967), pp. 52, 366; *CSPD 1698,* p. 35; Luttrell, iv.

410; Christopher Clay, *Public Finance and Private Wealth: the career of Sir Stephen Fox, 1627–1716* (Oxford, 1978), pp. 266–75.

2 GCRO, Blathwayt MSS. D. 1799/4/2; *LG*, no. 2462.

3 *HMC, House of Lords MSS.*, iii. 407, 12 Dec. 1691, 'Observations made by the Commissioners for the Public Accounts'.

4 WO 24/10, f. 12, 29 July 1689; BL, Harl. MSS. 7,437, ff. 13, 14.

5 *SR*, vi. 147, 1 William & Mary, Session 2, c. 4; WO 89/2, f. 95, 5–6 Feb. 1697.

6 BL, Add. MSS. 29,878, Ensign William Crammond's Diary, 1689–90.

7 LCA, Mexborough MSS., Reresby Correspondence, 50/34; *CTP 1697–1702*, p. 107; Walton, p. 441; *HMC, House of Lords MSS*, iii. 407.

8 Waddell, pp. 259–64; BL, Harl. MSS. 7,018, ff. 116–17.

9 BL, Harl. MSS. 7,018, ff. 110, 112; *CTrB 1693–6*, pp. 1045–6; Edward Hughes, 'The professions in the Eighteenth Century', *Durham University Journal*, xliv. (1951–2), p. 51. For the later history of regimental agency see: Alan Guy, 'Regimental agency in the British Standing Army, 1715–1763; a study in Georgian military administration', *Bulletin of the John Rylands University Library of Manchester*, lxii. (1979–80), pp. 423–53; lxiii. (1980–81), pp. 31–57; 'Minions of fortune; the regimental agents in early Georgian England, 1714–63', *Army Museum '85* (London, 1986), pp. 31–42.

10 This coffee house is not to be confused with Jenny Mann's, which was in the Tilt Yard and was habituated by whig army officers. See; David Green, *Queen Anne* (London, 1970), p. 308; G. S. Holmes, *British Politics in the Age of Queen Anne* (London, 1967), p. 23; Bryan Lillywhite, *London Coffee Houses* (London, 1963), p. 352.

11 Luttrell, iii. 292; BL, Harl. MSS. 7,018, f. 107.

12 *CJ*, xi. 217, 230, 236.

13 BL, Harl. MSS. 7,018, f. 222, 'Concerning agents of the army'.

14 *SR*, vi. 586–9, 6 & 7 William & Mary, c. 8; BL, Add. MSS. 23,642, ff. 3–4, 17 June 1695.

15 Luttrell, iv. 198; *CTP 1697–1702*, p. 78; *CSPD 1697*, p. 345; *CTP 1557–1696*, pp. 187, 309–10, 327, 436; Preston Papers, Netherby Hall, Cumbria, consulted at Sothey's, London, prior to their sale to the British Library on 10 July 1986, Muster Rolls, ff. 3–18.

16 Walton, pp. 686–7; DRCO, Ilchester MSS., D. 124, Box 278, Ranelagh's Ledger 1688–1692 & Ranelagh's Cash Book, 1688–1690; Box 276, Accounts of Charles Fox and Lord Coningsby in Ireland, 1698; *HMC, House of Lords MSS.*, n.s. v. 58–64, 379; 'Debates in the House of Commons, 1697–1699; William Cowper's Narrative', ed. D. W. Hayton (to be published by Camden Society), 11 January 1699.

17 Walton, pp. 844–5; DCRO, Ilchester MSS., D. 124, Box 278, Army Establishments.

18 Bod. Lib. Rawlinson MSS. A. 245, f. 98, 'Memorial of the pay to the army'.

19 BL, Add. MSS. 29,878; *HMC, Finch MSS.*, iv. 217; BL, Add. MSS.

15,897, f. 104; Walton, pp. 844–5.

20 Walton, p. 845, 13 Aug. & 2 Sept. 1697, Dublin.

21 BL, Add. MSS. 29,878.

22 BL, Add. MSS. 29,879, ff. 1–21; BL, Harl. MSS. 7,439, f. 8.

23 Davies, 'Reduction', pp. 22–3; Rawlinson MSS. A. 245, f. 92, 'Arrears of the Army', 1 Feb. 1698; Erle–Drax MSS., 2/47, f. 1.

24 *CSPD 1689–90*, p. 47; HCRO, L. 1128; *CTP 1557–1696*, p. 168; *CSPD 1690–1*, p. 493, 18 Aug. 1691.

25 BL, Add. MSS. 9,723, f. 26, 11 Mar. 1692, Breda.

26 BL, Add. MSS. 9,723, f. 70; BL, Add. MSS. 9,730, f. 37, 1 Mar. 1696, Antwerp, Richard Hill to Blathwayt.

27 BL, Add. MSS. 9,730, ff. 43, 76.

28 *CSPD 1696*, p. 360; *HMC, Hastings MSS.*, ii. 273–4, 290; *Acts of the Parls. of Scotland*, x. 46–7.

29 *HMC, Buccleuch (Montagu) MSS.*, ii. 383; *Private and Original Correspondence of Charles Talbot, Duke of Shrewsbury*, ed. William Coxe (London, 1821), pp. 137–8.

30 Rawlinson MSS. A. 245, f. 102.

31 Luttrell, iv. 631, 639, 644, 684, 689, 690–1; *Vernon Correspondence*, ii. 315–16, 322; Horwitz, *Parliament, Policy, and Politics*, pp. 268–9.

32 BL, Add. MSS. 9,755, ff. 15–16; BL, Add. MSS. 29,878; *CTP 1557–1696*, pp. 397, 433; Ailesbury, *Memoirs*, i. 241–2; Clay, *Private Finance and Public Wealth*, p. 251; Erle–Drax MSS., 2/47, ff. 1, 4.

33 Walton, pp. 685–6; Steele, ii. 174.

34 *CSPD 1697*, p. 359; *CSPD 1696*, p. 277; *HMC, Buccleuch (Montagu) MSS.*, ii. 360.

35 Japikse, iii. 211–12; Simms, *Williamite Confiscation*, pp. 82–120, 148–9, 155.

36 Edward D'Auvergne, *The History of the Campaign in Flanders for the Year 1697* (London, 1698), p. 22; L. M. Waddell, 'The paymaster accounts of Richard Hill at Attingham Park', *JSAHR*, xlviii. (1970), pp. 50–9; *CSPD 1693*, p. 329; Luttrell, iii. 473; BCRO, Trumbull Add. MSS. 103.

37 Childs, *The Army, James II and the Glorious Revolution*, p. 5; *HMC, House of Lords MSS.*, iii. 357–8, Accounts of the Commissioners for the Public Accounts.

38 BL, Add. MSS. 9,735, f. 57, 28 June 1692, Godolphin to Blathwayt.

39 The accounting year for the Commissioners for the Public Accounts ran from 30 Sept. to 29 Sept. following.

40 *HMC, House of Lords MSS.*, iv. 163; n.s. i. 67; n.s. ii. 163; BL, Harl. MSS. 7,018, ff. 169, 173–4.

41 *CTrB 1695–1702*, pp. dlii–dlv.

42 Rawlinson MSS. A. 245, f. 30b.

43 BL, Harl. MSS. 7,437, f. 14; Walton, p. 604; *CSPD 1689–90*, p. 494; WO 24/10, ff. 13, 14.

44 *CJ*, xii. 357; DRCO, Ilchester MSS., D. 124, Box 278; Scouller, *Armies of Queen Anne*, pp. 330–2.

45 WO 5/6, f. 88.
46 *CSPD 1690–1*, pp. 126–7, 192, 440, 449; *CSPD 1693*, p. 199; *CSPD 1697*, p. 360; *CSPD 1698*, p. 436.
47 *Minutes of Proceedings in Quarter Sessions held for the parts of Kesteven in the County of Lincoln, 1674–1695*, ed. S. A. Peyton (Lincoln, 1931), i. pp. lxxxi–lxxxiii; *Bucks. Sessions Records*, ii. 55, 215; *Middlesex Quarter Sessions*, pp. 8, 10, 27, 48, 68, 109, 114.
48 *Bucks. Sessions Records*, ii. 55, 66, 86, 113, 215.
49 *Hertford Sessions Rolls*, i. 429, 1697.
50 *Middlesex Quarter Sessions*, p. 3, Jan. 1690; *Warwick Quarter Sessions*, p. 57; *Bucks. Sessions Records*, ii. 75, 248.
51 WO 4/1, f. 74, 21 Aug. 1689.
52 *CTrB 1693–6*, pp. 773, 904, 1155.
53 BL, Stowe MSS. 315, ff. 17–18.
54 Dalton, *Army Lists*, iii. 403–4; iv. 289–90; HMC, *Buccleuch (Montagu) MSS.*, ii. 97, 104; *CSPD 1694–5*, p. 331.
55 *CSPD 1689–90*, p. 318, 12 Nov. 1689; *Middlesex Quarter Sessions*, p. 10; *Bucks. Sessions Records*, i. 424.
56 *CSPD 1700–1702*, pp. 2–3.
57 ARA, Raad van State, 489, ff. 88, 267–71; BL, Add. MSS. 9,723, f. 100; Baxter, *William III*, p. 282.
58 Childs, *Army of Charles II*, pp. 72–4, 191–2.
59 *CSPD 1690–1*, pp. 356–7; Walton p. 849; WO 24/10, f. 14; Müller, ii. 165; Erle–Drax MSS., 4/18, f. 6; DCRO, Ilchester MSS., D. 124, Establishment 1690.
60 Edward D'Auvergne, *A Relation of the Most Remarkable Transactions in the last Campaign of the Confederate Army . . . in the Spanish Netherlands, 1692* (London, 1693), pp. 48–9; BL, Add. MSS. 9,722, f. 30; BL, Add. MSS. 9,724, f. 54; Japikse (Welbeck), ii. 202; BL, Add. MSS. 9,731, f. 7; Luttrell, iii. 189.
61 HMC, *Bath MSS.*, iii. 14; Parker, *Memoirs*, p. 58; BCRO, Trumbull Add. MSS. 103; BL, Add. MSS. 38,698, f. 173; BL, Add. MSS. 38,699, ff. 23, 88; BL, Add. MSS. 38,700, f. 213.
62 BL, Add. MSS. 9,731, f. 19.
63 *CTrB 1689–1692*, p. 1441; Steele, ii. 176.

VII

Home service

'The Earl of Devonshire's regiment of horse came here. They are indifferently well mounted', observed Thomas Bellingham on 11 July 1689. Colonel John Cunningham's battalion in Ireland in February 1692 should have possessed 711 effective men. It actually contained 411 soldiers in a vertical condition, the remaining 300 having permanently or temporarily succumbed to the horizontal. Even the entirely bogus musters of the British corps in Flanders in 1689 reckoned that the field strength was twenty per cent below the establishment and the reality was probably a great deal worse. Waldeck sent some of the British regiments into premature winter quarters in August 1689 because they were seriously understrength and riddled with sickness. In addition, he found the men to be lazy, unmotivated, and poorly equipped. In Ireland at Schomberg's camp at Dundalk, British soldiers died in their hundreds through neglecting the simplest sanitary arrangements whilst their Danish and Huguenot comrades survived the Irish winter without undue difficulty.[1]

William III was faced with the task of creating a command system and a method of bureaucratic control over his army, sufficiently effective to remedy its manifold defects and to achieve operational efficiency and uniformity of practice. His success was only partial. He divided the army into two distinct sections: the army in England and the forces in Flanders. Over the latter he took personal command and treated it as simply one corps amongst many in the confederate army under his own leadership. After the campaigns of 1689 and 1690, when the British forces had fought under the direction of Marlborough, William did not appoint a commander-in-chief of the British troops in Flanders but simply commissioned a lieutenant-general of foot and a lieutenant-general of horse but these were general appointments relating to the entire allied army. As neither the British foot nor horse fought together as a corps in battle, there was no need for a separate, national command structure. The British formations were brigaded under brigadier-generals and then deployed where required. Sir John Lanier was lieutenant-general of the British horse in Flanders until his death in 1692, and Thomas Talmash commanded the infantry from 1691 to 1693.

The British corps in Flanders consisted of separate regiments and battalions each looking after its own, internal affairs. Each unit drew its pay from Richard Hill in Antwerp; each regiment provided its own quarters and victuals; and each formation clothed and equipped itself. On the rare occasions when an overall and centralised command was required, it was executed through William Blathwayt who travelled with William to the Netherlands for every campaign serving both as secretary of state and secretary-at-war. Blathwayt issued orders for courts-martial and acted as a general clearing house for correspondence with regimental colonels. Both British and confederate general officers were only commanders of ad hoc battlefied groupings and they did not have a specific administrative role to play. There were surgeons-general, apothecaries-general, chaplains-general, and waggon-masters-general but, these few functions apart, William allowed his British regiments in Flanders to control and run themselves under the vague direction of Blathwayt as chief-of-staff, assisted by Richard Hill. Only for tactical purposes were regiments brigaded and general officers appointed, but these structures were only temporary having no lasting status. General officers had to remain as regimental colonels in order to retain their financial and power base within the army.

In England, the army staff was equally small. William Blathwayt acted as secretary-at-war during the winter months and then handed over to the judge-advocate general, George Clarke, when he went to Flanders for the summer season. With David Crawford in the office of commissary-general of the musters and Ranelagh in the pay office, this tiny nucleus of civilian officials relayed the king's orders to all the regiments and garrisons in England, made known new regulations, oversaw the clothing and payment of the troops, and controlled the routine rotation of units between various garrisons. With the exception of the king, the administration and thus the general direction of the army in England was firmly in the grip of civilians. However, a civilian staff could not be responsible for inspection and tactical efficiency – that duty had to be undertaken by professional soldiers.

William needed a body of senior army officers to direct these aspects of the army in England in close liaison with Blathwayt, Crawford, Ranelagh, and the lords justices. The solution was the foundation of the Board of General Officers.

The Board came into existence in 1689 as a direct successor to the weekly court-martial which had met every Friday at the Horse Guards since 11 March 1688 to hear all cases concerning military personnel and complaints against the army by civilians. The Board had a quorum of three and was responsible for approving clothing patterns, hearing complaints concerning quarters, ordering the strategic distribution of forces within the British Isles, approving recommendations for subalterns' commissions whilst the king was away on campaign, and generally advising Queen Mary and the lords justices on military matters. All general officers in England were eligible to serve on the Board but the more usual attenders were the Duke of Schomberg and Leinster, Thomas Erle, the Earl of Macclesfield, the Earl of Scarborough, Major-General William Stewart, the Duke of Ormonde, the Earl Rivers, William Selwyn, and Charles Trelawney. They held very limited executive authority mostly confining themselves to offering advice, but they did form a court-martial and thus enjoyed some legal weight. The Board was also entrusted with adjudicating in disputes about regimental precedence and between officers over seniority. They also had the right to object to any military order made by the lords justices during the absence of the king.[2] The Board of General Officers provided the essential military expertise to assist the civilian staff and it was furnished with sufficient independent legal powers to put some of its decisions into effect.

To support the work of the Board and the civilian staff, William reviewed his forces in both England and Flanders as often as he could. When that was impossible, the lords justices performed this function on his behalf.[3] In the wake of the Royston scandal in 1695, Lieutenant-General the 3rd Duke of Schomberg and Leinster, the eldest son of old Schomberg and commander-in-chief of the forces in England during William's absence in the Netherlands, was sent on a tour of inspection of all the regiments in England and Wales with the object of making a detailed report to the king. His brief was similar to that of the special commissioners of 1689 and he took two months to complete his investigations. His conclusions, delivered at the end of August, found matters in a reasonable condition although he did note the tendency of colonels to maintain their regiments below establishment strength and fill them up only on muster days. In other words, false musters were still widespread and Schomberg had a circular sent to all commanding officers reminding them of the existence of the regulations.[4] In March 1697, Major-General William Stewart was dispatched to Ireland to inspect all the regiments and to make a report with recommendations for 'improvement'. Two years later, Schomberg inspected all the English and Welsh garrisons in the company of David Crawford, the deputy commissary-general of the musters, and Colonel Henry Withers, the adjutant-general of the foot.[5] The precedent of periodic general inspections by senior officers, begun in 1689, coupled with the fairly frequent formal reviews and parades which were really inspections of clothing and equipment, did much to improve the standard of control over the army in England and did something to back-up the stream of orders and regulations which emanated from Blathwayt's desk in Whitehall. Blathwayt was an administrator and although he could issue instructions he could not, himself, enforce them and it was difficult to acquire information about their effectiveness. The Board of General Officers and the general inspections thus provided both teeth as well as eyes and ears for Blathwayt and the civilian staff. A Board of General Officers for Ireland was set up in January 1701 under Major-General Richard Ingoldsby, performing the same functions as its brother across the Celtic Sea.[6]

William actively encouraged the Board of General Officers to take a firm grip upon the administration and discipline of the formations in England, and he usually appointed Schomberg, one of the Board's members, as commander-in-chief during his periods of absence in the Low Countries. The idea of two militarily ignorant secretaries of state handling the major decisions relating to army administration and the equally ill-educated lords justices ordering troop deployments, quarters, and approving commissions, did not appeal to the king. The Board offered a solution to most of these difficulties and put some expertise where it was badly needed. His unease was increased during the Earl of Nottingham's tenure as secretary of state, with his Tory and 'blue water' bias. At the very centre of the military web sat William Blathwayt, a professional administrator who was utterly apolitical. Although 'the discharge of the office of secretary at war is not a difficult task', William could rely upon Blathwayt to issue the royal orders without political coloration or complaint and by taking him to Flanders to act as *pro tem* secretary of state during the campaigning seasons, even if he only served as an executive and lacked political influence, William successfully undermined the military duties and pretensions of the secretaries of state in England. He was unable to prevent Nottingham and Shrewsbury from offering advice about military matters and questions of strategy and neither could he stop the lord justices from trying to interfere, but Blathwayt's unique double-authority made certain that the secretaries of state in England were strictly limited in their responsibilities and influence. The Board of General Officers acted as a similar restraint upon the lords justices. Through the media of Blathwayt and the Board, whether in Flanders or in England, William commanded and controlled his own army and suffered a minimum of interference and nagging from English politicians. He had grown used to an absolute control over his armed forces in the United Provinces and he did his best to introduce a synonymous system into his new domain. Because of this, the political function and station of the secretary at war did not advance. He remained a mere functionary and administrator, issuing orders devised by the king, the Board of General Officers, the secretaries of state, and the lords justices. Blathwayt may have been highly acquisitive of material wealth but he was not, seemingly, ambitious for political power.[7] However, the unchanging constitutional status of the secretary at war was deceptive. William's employment of Blathwayt as the pivot of army administration gave the secretary enormous personal weight in matters of patronage, particularly over appointments.

One of the duties of the Board of General Officers was to approve the clothing patterns brought forward by regimental colonels. Regulations governing the uniform of the army were laid down on 30 May 1690. Each regiment was to have new clothes every two years but new 'necessaries' – shirts, stockings, personal linen – were to be provided annually, as appropriate. Together with the Board, the king was to lay down a standard of clothing which a colonel was forbidden to exceed.

That when the time of clothing shall draw near, the colonel shall be obliged to call together the several captains, who are to choose two or three of their own number to find out cloth, lining, and other necessaries for the clothing according to such patterns as shall be given them by the colonels. And to beat down the price as low as they can and to make their report to the colonel who, approving the rates, is to make a contract with the tradesmen and to sign it, together with all the captains.

The off-reckonings for each regiment were to be stopped in the hands of the paymaster-general and used to pay the tradesmen after the clothing contract had been satisfactorily completed. This clause was a dead-letter from the start, and the net off-reckonings were always given directly to the colonel who then paid the clothiers himself. A further set of clothing regulations, this time for Ireland on 26 July 1697, insisted that all clothing charges had to be met from the net off-reckonings without any stoppages from the subsistence money.[8] This struck at the heart of the issue. Colonels wanted their regiments to be as smart and attractive as possible and to outshine all other units on parade, but the net off-reckonings only amounted to thirty shillings a year per man, a mere three pounds over the two-year clothing cycle. The 'necessaries' which had to be bought every year were usually paid for from a company stoppage on the subsistence money, or less commonly out of the captain's 'dividend' or the regimental 'bank'. However, for the sartorially enthusiastic colonel, three pounds was not much with which to make one's men the talk of the barrack square.

Clothing had to be bought in England, even for troops stationed in the colonies. The New York garrison tried hard to argue that the sending of ready-made uniforms from England was time-consuming, expensive, and there were plenty of excellent tailors in Manhattan, but all to no avail.[9] When a clothing was due, the colonel invited several designers and manufacturers to tender their patterns and he and his captains then made their selection. Before Lord Cutts reclothed the Coldstream Guards in 1699, he paid a certain Mr Olifont £9 for several of his patterns, a further £1 10s to a Mr Lewis for his hat patterns, and Major Churchill received £12 for his designs. The colonel then proceeded to sign a contract with the manufacturer. The resulting agreement between Joseph Ashley and Lord Cutts in February 1699 for reclothing the Coldstreamers amounted to £7,702 15s 4d, to be paid from the net off-reckonings which would be given to Cutts by the paymaster-general and then forwarded to Ashley.[10] Naturally, this meant that Ashley would receive his money in instalments, as and when the paymaster-general issued the clearings to Cutts; during 1700, Ashley's repayments came at intervals of six months, four months, and two months. Clearly, clothing contractors had to be men of considerable credit as they had to wait a long time for their money.[11] Ashley, and many like him, did not undertake to make all the clothing themselves. Most of the work was subcontracted to specialist manufacturers. Hatters provided the headgear; swords and bayonets were forged by John Hawgood of St Martins-in-the-Fields; lace came from another source. In reality, the principal clothiers were brokers rather than manufacturers. During the War of the Grand Alliance, it was a profitable business and a list from 1695 names thirty-three individuals and partnerships with an interest in army clothing, four of whom were also involved in regimental agency. Joseph Ashley was in partnership with Samuel Hellyer for a while during the mid-1690s.[12] Sir William Scawen, Sir Joseph Herne, Richard Acton, Elkanah Downes, William Woollett, and John Hayes were all making money from providing uniforms.

The Commissioners for the Public Accounts noted on 12 December 1691 that 'many of the contracts for the clothing the army in Ireland have been at much greater rates than for which they might have been provided.' This was an understatement. Lord Castleton managed to beat down his supplier from a quoted price of £2 9s to clothe each private soldier to £1 19s 6d, and a sergeant's attire from £5 11s to £4 8s 6d. Colonel Frederick Hamilton clothed his soldiers for £2 19s 6d in 1696, a sum at the very limit of the total net off-reckonings for each man over the two-year period. Neither Castleton's nor Hamilton's contracts included swords, bandoliers, cartridge boxes, knapsacks, or bayonets, all of which were customarily renewed every third year.[13] Lord Raby, the colonel of the Royal Dragoons, was quoted a price of £14 a man by Thomas Hall in 1699, with gilt buttons adding an extra 6d per head. Again, this was at the very frontier of the net off-reckonings which amounted to £13 12s for a dragoon over two years.[14] Clothiers were driven to demand high prices as they had little security for their repayment. When their money did arrive it was usually well in arrear and often in the form of debentures rather than cash; it was scarcely surprising that the steady rise in uniform prices between 1689 and 1702 reflected this growing financial risk. By 1695, the whole army was in debt to the clothiers to the tune of £80,000 and this had to be anticipated from the estimates of the following year. In 1695, Colonel John Tidcomb signed a contract with James Moyer to clothe his infantry battalion for 1696. Their agreement stipulated that Moyer would be paid from the regiment's net off-reckonings but, unfortunately, Tidcomb's clothing fund was partially anticipated to meet the cost of the 'necessaries' for 1695 and so Moyer would have to wait until the latter part of 1696 and into 1697 before he could claim his share of the off-reckonings. Accordingly, Moyer increased his charges by ten per cent and Tidcomb had no option but to agree. There were no means of checking the nature of the contracts between colonels and clothiers and it was not unknown for contractors to be obliged to give colonels a ten per cent commission in order to secure a contract with a five per cent cut to the agent, but these douceurs were merely added to the total cost of the clothing to be met from the off-reckonings of the common soldiers. Because of the slow repayments, most clothiers had to borrow money to buy their materials and to pay their subcontractors, all of which added another unhealthy ten per cent to their charges. When the Commissioners for the Public Accounts looked briefly into the provision of army uniforms in 1695, they came up against a brick wall of non-co-operation from both colonels and clothiers. There was gross fraud. John Cardy contracted to clothe Colonel William Lloyd's dragoons for 1695, promising delivery in Flanders in March. In the event, the suits did not arrive until May and, on inspection, Lloyd found that the cloth used averaged three shillings a yard rather than the six shillings and sixpence stated in the contract. Cardy had made each suit for twenty-two shillings instead of the stipulated thirty. Quietly tucking his £700 profit into his back-pocket, Cardy, naturally, denied it all, safe in the knowledge that if he refused to reveal his accounts then he could not be exposed. An anonymous set of proposals suggested setting aside an annual sum of money equal to the total net off-reckonings for the army. This would deny the need for clothiers to purchase materials on credit and bring down their charges to the point where the two-year clothing cycle of a regiment of foot might average £3,335 instead of £5,244. If things went on as they were, said the author, the army clothing debt would be over £500,000 by the end of 1696. He was not far wrong, for it was approaching £1,000,000 by December 1697. Riddled with fraud and interest charges though the system was, its principal failing was in calculating net off-reckonings against a two-year clothing cycle. There was, in fact, annual reclothing with 'necessaries' having to be bought every year, full uniform every other year, and arms and accountrements every three years. With such a ramshackle and inadequate organisation, it was virtually impossible for the subsistence money to remain inviolate and all regiments were subject to an endless anticipation of their net off-reckonings. One of the reasons for stripping the dead on battlefields was to return the expensive uniforms for clothing recruits in a vain effort to keep down regimental costs.[15]

The majority of regiments in the British army wore red. The scarlet coats of the Coldstream Guards were lined with blue and edged with narrow, white lace. Their breeches and waistcoats were blue, their black hats were trimmed with broad lace, the shoes were black, the stockings white, and all belts, the cartridge box and the knapsack were covered in blue cloth. The Royal Horse Guards wore blue coats, as did Lord Castleton's foot, and the battalions of Lord Drogheda, Richard Ingoldsby, and the Duke of Bolton. Lord Galway's horsemen and the foot soldiers of the Earl of Monmouth and Peterborough were turned out in grey coats. This adoption of blue, the basic uniform colour in the Dutch army, may have been inspired by certain commanding officers wishing to ingratiate themselves with the new monarch. Richard Brewer's foot had red coats lined with white; the First Foot Guards sported blue breeches and facings; Ferdinando Hastings's battalion paraded in red coats with yellow linings and breeches, grey stockings and black hats; and Edward Howe's men had red coats lined with orange set off by blue breeches. The Life Guardsmen wore uniforms costing £40 each and they were so magnificent that they only came out of mothballs for ceremonial occasions and the Life Guard usually did duty in undress grey coats and breeches.[16] Increasingly, regiments provided an additional item of clothing for their men – 'surtouts' or great coats. Eighteen thousand were produced during the winter of 1689 and the Coldstream Guards were fully equipped by the end of that year.[17] Not every item of clothing was provided by a private contract between the colonel and the manufacturer. Israel Fielding, the commissary-general of the provisions, supplied 60,000 pairs of boots in 1691 and another 10,000 in 1692, together with 10,000 pairs of stockings and 10,000 shirts. These were purchased by colonels in Flanders to replenish their stocks as their men wore out their boots and shoes.[18] No doubt, these items would have been paid for from the 'necessaries' fund. Officers had to clothe themselves according to the agreed regimental pattern but it seems that some formations contracted for all their officers' uniforms with one supplier. Joseph Ashley made all the clothes for the officers of the Marquis de Rade's battalion.[19]

The fecundity of invention shown in developing new weapons of war – multiple grenade throwers, super-heavy mortars, long-range cannon – was not matched by the courage of the establishment. Most of these new wonder weapons were tested on Blackheath or at Hounslow and most seem to have performed satisfactorily but none were adopted by the army.[20] In 1689 there was a severe shortage of muskets for the expanding forces. Until that year, muskets for the army had been supplied by the Company of London Gunsmiths which had held a monopoly of gun manufacture for the Ordnance Office since 1657. The first orders for snaphance muskets were placed with Birmingham gunsmiths in 1689 and by 1692 they had a regular contract to deliver 200 guns per month. The London gunsmiths were slow in comparison as they often had a shortage of parts for assembly, but the Ordnance Office circumvented this by buying locks and barrels from Birmingham which it then distributed to the London gunsmiths for assembly and also to build-up a stock of spare parts for subsequent repairs, a function which the Ordnance Office carried out itself.[21] Muskets were imported from the United Provinces in 1689 and the two marine regiments were completely armed with Dutch handguns. Dutch muskets were of high quality having undergone rigorous batch-testing before being delivered into the Ordnance stores. British guns were frequently of rather poor quality, sometimes blowing up in a soldier's face, and those which were stocked in the Tower of London in 1689 were old and rusty and soon failed when employed in the field.[22] On active service in Flanders and Ireland, the guns of the foot, dragoons, and cavalry were maintained by the train of artillery which carried spare muskets, pistols, carbines, pikes, bayonets, flints, locks, and cartridge boxes.[23] Gradually, the number of flintlock and bayonet armed infantrymen in each regiment grew as the body of pikemen declined. Sir Edward Dering's foot in 1689 was equipped with two-thirds muskets and one-third pikes but all of the battalions which crossed from Ireland to Flanders in the summer of 1691 had only fourteen pikemen per company, less than a quarter of the establishment. By the middle of the 1690s, some foot regiments had changed completely to muskets and bayonets.[24]

Twenty-six fixed garrisons in England had first been manned in 1637. They had not been kept in good repair by Charles II, his brother was not long enough on the throne to effect many of his planned improvements at Hull and Portsmouth, whilst William III was not very interested and pumped every available penny from his military budget into the army in Flanders. Most of the fortifications of the English garrisons dated from the sixteenth century, Hull and Berwick being the most notable examples, some, like Pendennis, had been modified during the Civil Wars, and only a handful were modern and up to date. Tilbury and Portsmouth were the most progressive structures but they were scarcely up to the standard of fortress design in France, Italy, Holland, and the Spanish Netherlands. Despite the invasion scares of 1692 and 1696, the English fixed fortifications had fallen into miserable disrepair. Celia Fiennes found Carlisle surrounded by ancient towers and battlements with entry confined to a drawbridge but her principal memory was 'of a young, giddy landlady that could only dress fine and entertain the soldiers'. Chester was defended by nothing more substantial than its medieval walls.[25] So little had been done by the government to improve the fortifications of Waterford that the city council built four guard houses for the garrison from muncipal resources. Our intrepid female traveller found Dover Castle 'left much to decay and ruinated, only a small apartment for the governor of three or four rooms, else the whole is spoiled'. Despite the strategic importance of the Isle of Wight covering the main anchorage of the English battle fleet, the defences were in a deplorable condition by 1689, no more than £1,000 having been spent even though the Ordnance engineers had estimated that an outlay of £19,000 was required. Plymouth seemed to be in a decent state of repair but then that fortress was more remarkable for its lavish architecture than for its military efficacy.[26] Matters were not better in Scotland and Ireland. By 1696, the Scottish garrisons were short of equipment, supplies, and money. Fort William, the principal post in the Highlands, was falling down with cannon dismounted, buildings crumbling, and soldiers' beds and bedding rotting. The Irish garrisons were in a similiar, run-down condition. The most modern fort in the British Isles, Tilbury, had been designed by Sir Bernard de Gomme and built between 1670 and 1683. By 1691, it had a garrison of just two officers and fifteen men and, three years later, this key post guarding London and the Thames saw its gun-line slip into the river mud from neglect and decay. Defending the entrance to Harwich, Landguard Fort had its four bastions and sixty-three cannon in good, working order in 1699 but the barracks leaked like a sieve leading to serious sickness amongst the garrison.[27]

Throughout the war, the standing fortifications were manned by permanent garrison companies of foot, filled out by companies from the line regiments who moved from station to station on fixed patterns of rotation. This was in imitation of the French system of 'étapes', whereby every French regiment in garrison changed its station once a year. During the invasion scare in 1690, Captain Thomas Phillips was rushed to Portsmouth to try to do something to improve its fortifications. He turfed some breastworks, 'flung up' a few new works, and put up some palisades but Phillips thought that the main value of his modifications would be to prevent the theft of naval stores rather than deter the French. When the Duke of Leinster inspected the Portsmouth defences two years later, most of Phillips's temporary works had fallen into disrepair.[28] His Grace then crossed the water to the Isle of Wight only to find the fortifications 'totally ruined' with the walls of Cowes Castle 'rent from top to bottom and . . . in great danger of falling to the ground with every cannon's firing'. Sandown Castle was also

very much out of repair and of the forts that were formerly kept in repair upon the beach from Sandown to St Helens, where an army of forty thousand may land under the shelter of the cannon of a fleet, there is not so much as a stone left to see where they stood.[29]

Hull's defences were impressive but unfinished. On 23 February 1699, a select committee of the House of Commons heard a report by Sir Martin Beckman on the fortifications of Portsmouth. Beckman, who blamed most of the faults in the Portsmouth defences on the fact that both Charles II and James II had acted upon the advice of Sir Bernard de Gomme rather than that of Beckman himself, said that the main rampart was literally sliding into the ditch with the weight of the cannon. Gosport and Portsmouth dock were virtually undefended. All could be put right, said Beckman, at a cost of £112,614 16s 1d, whilst another £17,870 9s 1d was needed to repair the other fixed fortifications in England. Nothing was done. In the final year of William's reign, the inhabitants of North and South Shields pointed out that over 600 ships regularly used the port of the Tyne but the fortifications at Tynemouth Castle, Clifford's Fort, and the Spanish Battery were useless. Clifford's Fort had no parapet left and its cannon were buried in the sand, and yet the Tyne was within easy reach of the French-occupied ports in the Spanish Netherlands and was a prime target for privateering raids. It was small wonder that an English traveller, Robert Jennens, was bowled over when he first encountered Menno van Coehorn's new fortifications at Bergen-op-Zoom, but then the Dutch, Belgian and French fortresses were front-line posts whereas the English fortifications were simply designed to protect naval anchorages and prevent the French from raiding the coast. Even so, by 1702 hardly any of the English forts were in a condition to achieve that most modest aim.[30]

In company with the fixed fortifications, the army shared the basic duty of defending the country against foreign invasion. In the aftermath of the naval defeat off Beachy Head on 30 June 1690, the army in England was lamentably ill-prepared for this, its first and principal function. There were only 5,000 foot and 1,000 horse in England. Critics were quick to observe that 50,000 British troops were serving in Ireland, Scotland and Flanders, yet there were hardly any available to protect the homeland. Luckily the French failed to exploit their success and dithered about the Devon and Cornish coasts and only burned Teignmouth before sailing back across the Channel. At the time, though, England did appear naked and highly vulnerable to a major French invasion, possibly at Exeter or Plymouth, and every stop was pulled out to gather scratch forces into the west country.[31] Five battalions were hastened back from the British corps in Flanders and, together with some of the troops already in England, went into camp on Blackheath. Marines were landed from the fleet to reinforce Portsmouth, the Isle of Wight raised over 7,000 militia to assist the six companies of regulars which formed its garrison, and a whole army of over 40,000 gentry, volunteers, and militia hovered around Plymouth. The East India Company offered to raise a troop of horse, the City of London militia turned out, and the lord mayor and alderman promised the queen that they would create more regiments to assist the common cause. It all came to nothing, and the militias were stood down on 30 August.[32]

The next invasion panic, in 1692, found England better prepared. Louis XIV announced his plans on 20 February. The 12,000 Irish who had come to France after the Treaty of Limerick were to be billetted in Britanny and would lead the assault, supported by 12,000 French troops. In order to distract William and to stop forces being pulled out of Flanders to reinforce England, the invasion was to be timed to coincide with the opening of the siege of Namur.[33] Initially, the English thought that the French build-up was aimed at the capture of the Channel Islands but these ideas were rapidly dispelled by fresh intelligence and from 19 April the Earl of Nottingham and the king were in no doubt that the French intended a full-scale invasion. The Earl of Portland's and Thomas Langston's cavalry regiments, which had already embarked to sail for Flanders, were recalled into the Thames, three battalions were shipped at Leith and sent to the Isle of Wight, and William sent Selwyn's, Beveridge's, and Lloyd's battalions from Willemstadt back to England. The forces were centred on Portsmouth, so much so that four regiments were packed into Portsmouth town forcing the usual garrison to sleep three to a bed and spill over into private houses. Over 10,000 troops were concentrated within a forty mile radius of Portsmouth. The Duke of Schomberg and Leinster and Sir Henry Bellasise were put in command of the concentration area with Brigadier William Selwyn in charge of London, but the lords justices had little faith in any of these generals and asked the king to send over Thomas Talmash. William agreed to dispatch Talmash as soon as Hugh Mackay had arrived at the army in Flanders, and he placed another six battalions on stand-by to sail for England in case of dire emergency. Despite pleas from the lords justices for more soldiers, William was convinced that there were now enough men in England to resist a French landing and he refused further reinforcements. In the event, Edward Russell's fleet action off Cape La Hogue on 19 and 20

May ruined all the French plans.[34] Talmash returned to Flanders and Leinster retained the corps in England in order to undertake a 'descent' on the French coast.

After two previous dry-runs, preparations to meet the projected French invasion plans of 1696 and 1697 went comparatively smoothly. There were already 10,000 troops in England in February 1696, and the lords justices decided to concentrate these around London and along the coasts of Kent and Sussex. The Duke of Württemberg sailed over from Flanders with twenty battalions which he kept on board their transports in the Downs ready for deployment in any direction. The posts were stopped, the militia was embodied, and all roman catholics and suspected Jacobites were interned.[35] Similar measures were put in hand for the final invasion scare of the reign between December 1696 and January 1697, with fifteen battalions in Flanders being placed on instant alert for embarkation for England.[36] In between these major emergencies, persistent coastal raids by French privateers kept the army constantly employed on watching long stretches of coastline and responding to reports of French men-of-war cruising near vulnerable points. Sir Thomas Livingstone, the commander-in-chief of the Scottish army, deployed units along the beaches of Fife and Lothian in July 1692 in response to a false report that French troops had been plundering the Northumbrian coast.[37] Despite the fact that the formation of two regiments of marines provided 3,000 men for service with the fleet, the regular army had always to supply a limited number of infantry to supplement this force. The Royal Irish spent the summer of 1693 enjoying a summer cruise as did Samuel Venner's foot for two consecutive years. Colonel William Northcote's was summoned for sea service in 1695. In March of that same year, the battalions of Henry Rowe, Richard Coote, William Stewart, and the Marquis de Puizar embarked on transports to sail with Edward Russell's fleet to Cadiz and Catalonia.[38]

In England itself, the army acted as a ceremonial guard, the protector of the king and the royal family, and as a police force. The Life Guard defended the king whether he was in London or in Flanders, with a division from the three troops in constant attendance. The First Foot and the Coldstream Guards always retained one battalion in and around Westminster charged with guarding the Palace of Whitehall, Kensington House, Hampton Court, St James's Palace and Park, and the Royal Mews. Detachments of cavalry escorted William to Harwich when he left England and brought him back to London in the autumn of each year. The queen was similarly attended and when the

Prince and Princess of Denmark took a short holiday at Tunbridge Wells in June 1697, 200 men from the First Foot Guards made sure that no harm befell them. The Scottish Troop of the Life Guard watched over the person of the Lord Commissioner, as well as mounting guard at Holyrood Palace and other key sites in Edinburgh.[39] In addition to providing a spectacle at state occasions and enhancing the prestige of the court, the army was an important agent of the crown in the provinces and its active involvement in the celebration of coronations, royal births and marriages was an important function and helped to encourage loyalty. The ceremonies in Cambridge to rejoice in the proclamation of William and Mary as joint sovereigns marked a union of loyalty between the armed forces and the university, a not inconsiderable combination.[40]

Smuggling and Jacobitism were closely connected in the eyes of Williamite politicians. 'Owlers' operating from the coasts of Kent and Sussex, particularly the Romney Marshes, smuggled wool, spirits, tobacco, and French silks but they also took Jacobite plotters and agents to and fro across the English Channel. Patrols of dragoons and cavalry operated in and around the Isle of Thanet, from Canterbury, Ashford and Guildford, and in the Romney Marshes themselves in an effort to keep down both the illegal traffic in woollen exports and the flow of Jacobites. By 1698, the trade in Jacobites had declined to an insignificant trickle, and the main concern of the privy council was the smuggling of wool in return for French silks. Detachments of horse, usually between five and ten men, were placed under the command of the local riding officers of the customs with orders to patrol the highways and, occasionally, they actually intercepted some smugglers. On 20 December 1698, one troop from William Lloyd's dragoons was ordered from Canterbury to Ashford and to come under the command of Henry Baker, solicitor to the Treasury. Small patrols were then sent out from Ashford to Folkestone, Hythe, Dymchurch, New Romney, Lydd, and Guildford, to hunt for owlers. Operations against smugglers were best executed by mounted soldiers, but on 8 April 1696, one sergeant and a file of musketeers from Colonel John Tidcomb's battalion at Canterbury were directed to march with Joseph Beverton, a customs' officer, to Romney Marshes and to obey his instructions. Encounters with smugglers were rare. Some dragoons intercepted a gang with seven or eight horses carrying wool from Canterbury to the coast in March 1699 and although a smuggler was shot through the head only one pack-horse was seized. Later in the same year, two dragoons assisted in confiscating six packs of wool and two horses 'in the marsh near to the sea side'.[41] The army was also called upon to billet in towns suspected of Jacobite sympathies, Norwich and Exeter receiving visitations in 1693.[42] Such trivia as a reported cock-fight near Sherborne in Dorset at which a number of 'disaffected persons' had supposedly been spotted was enough for a company of foot to be marched into the area *pour encourager les autres*.[43]

Soldiers were expected to keep law and order by assisting the civil power. Some seamen were waiting outside the Navy Pay Office in London on 20 October 1692 and 'gave some jealousies of disorder amongst them'. Robert, Lord Lucas, the governor of the Tower of London, noticed this and drew out his garrison onto Tower Hill to do some drill thereby dropping a strong hint to the sailors to behave themselves. Whilst his men were going through the manual of arms, Lucas wandered across to the seamen and had a chat with them, effectively calming down any potential trouble.[44] Similar subtlety in dealing with public order was rare. Rumours of a cabal being held by seventeen 'disaffected' persons in an upstairs room of a tavern in the Strand, encouraged Lieutenant John Luppington to surround the place with a file of musketeers, march up the stairs and barge into the chamber threatening to shoot the first person who made a false move. Over 100 people were arrested when soldiers assisted the king's messengers in sweeping through the inns and coffee houses of Holborn in March 1691.[45] Soldiers escorted prisoners from county gaols to London, guarded the Savoy and the principal prisons in London and Edinburgh, protected the station of the royal messengers in the Haymarket, and patrolled St James's Park and Hyde Park. The sentries outside the Royal Hospital in Chelsea helped the Earl of Plymouth to beat off some footpads on 15 September 1696. In London, when the city trained bands could not control a situation, as during the Weavers' Riot in March 1697, the army came to their aid. Scottish troops had to escort itinerant justices, try to prevent outbreaks of clan warfare, and stop incursions into the Lowlands by the Highlanders.[46] All over England, Ireland, and Scotland, cavalry patrolled most of the major roads. Parties of horse soldiers guarded shipments of bullion from the Navy Pay Office to the dockyards at Chatham, Plymouth, and Portsmouth, they took waggonloads of money for army pay from Ranelagh's office to the various garrisons and quarters, and they rode with the mails and convoys of merchants' goods as they travelled the insecure highways.[47] These were lawless times and the roads were riddled with highwaymen and robbers. Disbanded soldiers and officers from James II's army, Jacobite ex-soldiers from Ireland, wounded veterans from Flanders, all contributed to the growing number of criminals who infested the countryside. Parties of cavalry were quartered in most of the major towns in England and they were expected to maintain constant patrols along the main roads in their areas searching for highwaymen. Six Dutch troopers took four highwaymen near Reading in September 1692 and three were seized by some soldiers in Chelsea in 1693. On the evening of Thursday 10 October 1693, two highwaymen committed a robbery near Hounslow. They had not ridden far when they met a patrol of four troopers from whom they escaped after a short fracas but they soon encountered another group of four cavalrymen further down the road. This time, only one of the criminals managed to get away and the other was arrested. Later, he admitted to having served in James II's army. Patrols of four troopers were operating in similar intensity in 1698.[48] The infantrymen who guarded the Royal Mint in the Tower of London were suspected of conniving at attempts to steal from the 'press room' in July 1697 so that 'the sentinels begin to be rather a grievance than security to us'. Soldiers fought fires, laboured in the naval dockyards for 6d a day, served as part-time gamekeepers to protect the royal deer in the Forest of Dean, and maintained public order outside the Theatre Royal in Drury Lane and the Queen's Theatre in Dorset Garden.[49]

In between these civic duties and when they were not out searching for part-time jobs, the soldiers had a few hours to spare for drill and training. The artillery, supervised by the Ordnance Office, was far better organised than the army in this respect. Before each campaign in Flanders, the master-gunner held a training course on Blackheath where all the gunners, mattrosses and firemasters in England practiced their art on cannon and mortars before a draft was selected to fill up the ranks of the train of artillery in the field in the Netherlands.[50] Army training took place during the winter months under the watchful eye of sergeants, corporals, and reformado officers with the aim of rendering the regiment's new recruits in a useful condition for the coming campaigning season. When the new regiments were raised in the winter of 1693–4, it was deliberate policy by Blathwayt and the Board of General Officers to send the older formations to Flanders and to retain the new units in England until they had been 'disciplined'. Some never achieved this condition. Colonel William Northcote's foot was still 'raw and unseasoned' in September 1695.[51] Modelled on the practice in the Dutch army and the example of James II, sections of the regiments in England held an annual training camp, either at

Blackheath or on Hounslow Heath. The camp of 1689 lasted for five weeks and contained ten battalions and six squadrons. After 1690 there seem to have been two types of summer training camp. Battalions and regiments which had been ordered to Flanders went into a camp near London to await embarkation and to undergo some drill and instruction, and there was a separate summer camp for the regiments which were to remain in England. The Scottish army also instituted a training camp with the first being held at Stirling in 1691.[52] These camps appear to have performed a valuable role. As well as company and battalions exercises, all the forces encamped usually took part in a mock battle towards the end of proceedings which gave instruction in large formation manoeuvres and in the co-ordination of infantry, cavalry, and artillery. In St James's Park in 1691, the army recreated the siege of Mons, mainly as a public spectable although it also served as a training exercise.[53] At ceremonial reviews, the formations under inspection were usually ordered to go through their drills and perform some regimental or battalion manoeuvres.[54] As the new and unseasoned regiments waited around Preston in the spring and summer of 1689 ready to embark with Schomberg's expeditionary force for Ireland, Thomas Bellingham noted the fairly frequent exercising of the men by their officers, both at company and battalion level, including live firing at the butts.[55] The impression, and it can only be an impression, is that training was taken rather more seriously under William III than it had been under Charles II and James II, but that was only to be expected with a solider–king leading the country into foreign war.

Notes

1 *Diary of Thomas Bellingham,* p. 72; Petre, *Norfolk Regiment,* i. 32; Knight, *The Buffs,* i. 295–6; Müller, ii. 178, 185; *LG,* no. 2493; Wouter Troost, 'William III and the Treaty of Limerick, 1691–1697', (Doctoral Dissertation, University of Leiden, 1983), p. 19; Maurice, *Scots Guards,* i. 56; J. G. Simms, *Jacobite Ireland, 1685–1691* (London, 1969), pp. 126–31; ARA, Heinsius Archive, 142, unfoliated, 6/16 July 1689, 7/17 Sept. 1689, 23 Sept./2 Oct. 1689, Waldeck to Heinsius.

2 Childs, *The Army, James II, and the Glorious Revolution,* p. 92; Clode, *Military Law,* pp. 59, 77; *CSPD 1697,* p. 139; Luttrell, iii. 547; Cowper, *King's Own,* i. 86.

3 Luttrell, iii. 454, 455, 552, 565; iv. 250, 646, 649, 712; BCRO, Trumbull Add. MSS. 103; *CSPD 1697,* p. 186.

4 BL, Add. MSS. 9,722, f. 70; BCRO, Trumbull Add. MSS. 118; Everett, *Somerset Light Infantry,* p. 37.

5   BCRO, Trumbull Add. MSS. 118; Luttrell, iv. 533.
6   *CSPD 1700–1702*, pp. 193, 208–9, 216.
7   *Hatton Correspondence*, ii. 133; Olive Anderson, 'The constitutional position of the secretary at war, 1742–1855', *JSAHR*, xxxvi. (1958), p. 166; Scouller, *Armies of Queen Anne*, pp. 15–18; WO 5/7; WO 5/8; *CSPD 1698*, p. 120; GCRO, Blathwayt MSS. D. 1799/4/1.
8   *LG*, no. 2564; Walton, pp. 844–5.
9   *SR*, vi. 393–8, 4 William & Mary, c. 13; Bod. Lib. Rawlinson MSS. A. 238, ff. 109–10, 16 Dec. 1701.
10 NRO, Ashley of Ashby St Ledger Collection, ASL 235, ff. 4, 236.
11 NRO, ASL 232–5.
12 BL, Harl. MSS. 7,018, ff. 228–9; NRO, ASL 237.
13 *HMC, House of Lords MSS.*, iii. 407; Walton, p. 388; NRO, ASL 231–2, 243.
14 BL, Add. MSS. 22,231, f. 1.
15 BL, Harl. MSS. 7,018, ff. 175–6, 189–90, 195; Erle–Drax MSS., 4/13, f. 6; Brian Lyndon, 'Military dress and uniformity, 1660–1720', *JSAHR*, liv. (1976), p. 109; *HMC, House of Lords MSS.*, n.s. iv. 173–4; Chandler, *Debates*, ii. 450; BL, Add. MSS. 38,700, ff. 5–6, 107.
16 NRO, ASL 231, 244; *LG*, nos. 2474, 2767, 2827; Lyndon, 'Military dress', p. 119.
17 Luttrell, i. 602; NRO, ASL 247; *LG*, no. 2509.
18 *CTrB 1689–92*, p. 1039; *HMC, Finch MSS.*, iv. 82.
19 NRO, ASL 253, 254; Walton, pp. 844–5.
20 Luttrell, ii. 372; iii. 93, 310; iv. 59; *HMC, Le Fleming MSS.*, p. 267.
21 H. C. Tomlinson, *Guns and Government: the Ordnance Office under the Later Stuarts* (London, 1979), pp. 109–11.
22 Edye, *Royal Marines*, i. 314; Waddell, p. 34; BL, Add. MSS. 9,731, ff. 7–8; WO 4/1, ff. 70–1; ARA, Raad van State, 1545, ff. 44–5; Atkinson, *South Wales Borderers*, pp. 7–8; *Bucks. Sessions Records*, i. 482–3, 1693.
23 Bod. Lib. Rawlinson MSS. A. 349.
24 Hamilton, *Grenadier Guards*, i. 349; Atkinson, *South Wales Borderers*, p. 6.
25 *The Illustrated Journeys of Celia Fiennes, 1685–c.1712*, ed. Christopher Morris (London, 1982), p. 172; CCRO, Assembly Books, AB/3/59v–61v.
26 *Council Books of Waterford*, p. 334; *Celia Fiennes*, pp. 122–3, 201–2; *HMC, Frankland–Russell–Astley MSS.*, pp. 76–7; *HMC, House of Lords MSS.*, ii. 134–6; Luttrell, iii. 78.
27 *Carstares*, p. 276; *CSPD 1698*, p. 175; *Seafield Correspondence*, pp. 229–31; *HMC, Buccleuch (Montagu) MSS.*, ii. 432–3; BL, Add. MSS. 9,727, f. 28; V. T. C. Smith, 'The artillery defences at Gravesend', *Archaeologia Cantiana*, lxxxix. (1974), pp. 152–6; A. D. Saunders, 'Tilbury Fort and the development of artillery fortifications in the Thames estuary', *The Antiquaries Journal*, xl. (1960), pp. 152–64; R. B. Doyle, 'The notebook of a marine officer, 1693–1699', *JSAHR*, xlii.

(1964), pp. 153–4; *The Correspondence of Richard Steele*, ed. Rae Blanchard (Oxford, 1968), p. 12.

28 *HMC, Finch MSS.*, ii. 386; iv. 180; Luttrell, ii. 77; C. C. Sturgill, 'Changing garrisons: the French system of Étapes', *Canadian Journal of History*, xx. (1985), pp. 193–201.

29 *HMC, Finch MSS.*, iv. 166.

30 *Celia Fiennes*, p. 99; *HMC, House of Lords MSS.*, iii. 303–6; *CSPD 1700–1702*, pp. 495–6; *HMC, Cowper MSS.*, ii. 404.

31 *Memoirs of Mary, Queen of England, 1689–1693*, ed. R. Doebner (London, 1886), p. 30; *HMC, Finch MSS.*, ii. 360.

32 *HMC, Le Fleming MSS.*, pp. 277, 279, 282, 285; *HMC, Finch MSS.*, ii. 353–4; Evelyn, *Diary*, v. 29–31; *Portledge Papers*, pp. 78–80; *HMC, Hastings MSS.*, ii. 215–16.

33 Symcox, *Crisis of French Sea Power*, pp. 117–21; Philip Aubrey, *The Defeat of James Stuart's Armada, 1692* (Leicester, 1979).

34 *HMC, Finch MSS.*, iv. 63–181.

35 BCRO Trumbull Add. MSS. 116, 23 Feb. 1696, Minutes of the Council; *Portledge Papers*, p. 223; *Lexington Papers*, pp. 163–89.

36 *Archives ou Correspondence inédite de la Maison d'Orange-Nassau*, 3rd series, ed. F. J. L. Kramer (Leiden, 1907–9), i. 511, 15/25 Dec. 1696, William III to Heinsius: *Vernon Correspondence*, i. 79–80, 158; *HMC, Buccleuch (Montagu) MSS.*, ii. 431–2.

37 *RPCS 1696*, p. 434, 22 July 1691.

38 NLI, Diary of Brigadier Robert Stearne, MSS. 4166, p. 22; Parker, *Memoirs*, pp. 40–1; Atkinson, *South Wales Borderers*, pp. 19–20; *HMC, Buccleuch (Montagu) MSS.*, ii. 224; *HMC, Frankland–Russell–Astley MSS.*, p. 81.

39 *HMC, Le Fleming MSS.*, p. 321; Luttrell, iv. 241; *CSPD 1697*, p. 441; *CSPD 1698*, pp. 320–1; WO 5/6, f. 227.

40 Newton, *Diary*, pp. 99–101.

41 Ailesbury, *Memoirs*, i. 339; *CSPD 1690–1*, p. 483; WO 5/6, f. 209; Luttrell, iii. 402; WO 5/8, f. 117; *CSPD 1697*, p. 439; *CTP 1697–1702*, pp. 173–4; WO 5/10, f. 276; *CSPD 1693*, p. 175; Paul Muskett, 'Military operations against smuggling in Kent and Sussex, 1698–1750', *JSAHR*, lii. (1974), pp. 94–6.

42 Luttrell, iii. 194, 198.

43 *CSPD 1696*, p. 242.

44 *HMC, Portland MSS.*, iii. 505, 23 Oct. 1692.

45 *HMC, Le Fleming MSS.*, p. 261; Luttrell, ii. 189.

46 *HMC, Kenyon MSS.*, pp. 361–3; Luttrell, iii. 403, 426, 478; iv. 82, 112; *CSPD 1695*, p. 330; *HMC, Marchmont MSS.*, pp. 136–40; *Portledge Papers*, pp. 254–5; *CSPD 1700–1702*, pp. 339–45, 376; *The History and Proceedings of the House of Lords from the Restoration in 1660 to the Present Time* (London, 1742), i. 388–9.

47 WO 5/5, f. 56; WO 5/6, ff. 206, 254; Atkinson, *Royal Dragoons*, pp. 75–6.

48 Luttrell, ii. 576, 616; iii. 7, 336, 341, 537; WO 5/9, 16 Aug. 1698; *CTP*

1697–1702, p. 222.

49   *CSPD 1698*, p. 436; Edye, *Royal Marines*, i. 353–5; Pomeroy, *5th Dragoon Guards*, i. 6; *CSPD 1689–90*, pp. 321–2; Luttrell, ii. 313, 315; *The Correspondence of Isaac Newton*, eds. A. R. Hall, L. Tilling, & H. W. Turnbull (Cambridge, 1959–76), iv. 243–4.

50   Luttrell, ii. 351–2, 380, 392–3; iv. 11.

51   Luttrell, iii. 259; *HMC, Buccleuch (Montagu) MSS.*, ii. 224.

52   *HMC, Cowper MSS.*, ii. 391, 401–2; Hamilton, *Grenadier Guards*, i. 339; Luttrell, i. 568; ii. 72; iii. 85, 353, 359, 479, 485; *CSPD 1697*, pp. 174–6, 207; *HMC, Le Fleming MSS.*, p. 323; BL, Add. MSS. 38,700, f. 1.

53   Luttrell, ii. 242; iii. 129, iv. 255.

54   GCRO, Blathwayt MSS. D. 1799/c. 6.

55   *Diary of Thomas Bellingham*, pp. 57–74.

VIII

The great disbandment

Colonel-General Hans von Seeckt was directing a staff ride in East Prussia in 1922. One of his juniors noticed how the great man persistently assumed, without bothering to offer any explanation, that the Russians would be the future opponents of Germany. 'How do you know that the Russians will be the enemy?', asked the young man, full of innocence. Von Seeckt turned in his saddle to face the author of such juvenile effrontery, twisted his monocle and replied with the wisdom of centuries, 'Sir, you must have an enemy'.[1]

The enemy of the English politicians in the latter half of the seventeenth century was the standing army, or rather armies in general. They were the traditional bogey of the landed classes in much the same way that the Russians were the ancient menace of the Prussian aristocracy. Armies were the founts of all evil responsible for arbitrary government, absolutism, and aggressive catholicism. They were the wreckers of parliaments and representative institutions, the destroyers of individual liberty, and a threat to the vested interests and political franchises of the English landed classes. Armies were a danger to 'balanced government'; with an army at his back, a monarch could oppress the people and overthrow the delicate authority of the lords and commons. There was some merit in these arguments, especially in the immediate aftermath of the reign of James II, but the anti-standing army ideology had become dogmatic by the 1690s and out of touch with political reality. Certainly, many of the politicians of William's reign had lived through the memorable experiences of the 1640s and 1650s and all had witnessed James II throw his army into the political arena but there was an inconsistency in nearly all the arguments put forward to oppose the retention of a standing army in peacetime.

Armies were necessary. The standing army controversy expressed between 1697 and 1700 might have been 'perhaps the most thorough single debate on forms of military organisation to occur in early modern Europe', but it avoided the obvious conclusion that there was no adequate or realistic alternative military organisation for a large and populous state other than a standing army. The disbandments of the army which parliament insisted upon between 1697 and 1699 reduced the forces to the size which they had been in 1679, to the basic 'guards and garrisons', the irreducible minimum if roads were to be swept clear of highwaymen, the king protected, property guarded, rioters restrained, and the civil power supported. A fairly sophisticated society like England, with its increasing urban population, had to have a legalised means of coercion, there was no option. The Marquis of Halifax, employing his famed intellectual amalgam of scepticism and brillant moderation, suggested that the English political system in the later seventeenth century required the omnipresent bogey of arbitrary government and militarised absolutism to keep it vigilant and on its toes. 'Though perhaps at bottom there is no true reason in it', he mused, 'yet there is charm in the music.'[2]

For the country elements in the House of Commons, the anti-standing army issue had an appeal all of its own. It was a rag-bag into which could be shoved all the customary gripes and grumbles nursed by backwoods members of parliament against the secretive government at Whitehall. Armies represented centralising power, their officers formed a political interest group of placemen, they cost a great deal of money and necessitated heavy taxation, they reduced the power and importance of the sacred militia, and they weakened the independence of the provinces. By arguing against the retention of a standing army in time of peace, politicians wielded a multi-edged sword with which to strike the government. That William III was a foreigner and used the British army to fight wars which seemed only to benefit the economic interests of the United Provinces merely added fuel to the fire. Onto this could be tacked the campaign against the foreign general officers and the simple notion that standing armies were a nasty, foreign invention and were demonstrably un-English. Finally, armies were an unpleasant reminder of the Civil Wars and the resulting aberration in England's constitutional development. By 1697, nearly all the arguments for and against a standing army had been repeated many times over and had become received wisdom. The level of debate and information witnessed between 1697 and 1700 was deplorably low. Although some words of sense and thought were uttered on the subject and, occasionally, an original idea crept into the debate, most of the points and the general ignorance of detail had already been well aired before the arguments recommenced in earnest at the end of the war.

William Harbord pointed out to the Convention parliament that all laws and declarations melted into nothing without 'the sword of a king must protect you'.[3] In other words, every political system had to have some coercive base, some point beyond which opposition could not pass. On 2 November 1689, the House of Commons turned to debating the size of the army for the campaigns of the succeeding year. Sir Thomas Clarges was utterly against the proposed establishment of 70,000 men as it was far too expensive. In 1678, when England had last fought France, 25,000 had proved quite sufficient and this would be enough for the future. Cromwell had conquered Ireland with less than 40,000 soldiers, Clarges's inference being that if Charles II and Oliver Cromwell could make do with this scale of force then so could William III. Jumping onto this promising bandwagon, William Garraway demanded the encouragement of the fleet and the retrenchment of the number of soldiers for 'England knows no need of them'. Rising to this line of attack, Sir Edward Seymour declared himself in favour of withdrawing the British corps from the confederate army in Flanders but he was rapidly put in his place by Sir Thomas Lee's acid rejoinder that the Dutch might then decide to withdraw their ships from the allied fleet. Sir Robert Howard finally introduced some sanity into these ridiculous proceedings by pointing out that the removal of 10,000 men from the Williamite army in Ireland would present James II with game, set, and match, and Sir John Trevor drew this Alice in Wonderland debate to a much-needed conclusion by delicately suggesting that the honourable members were pig-ignorant of military affairs and that the king should be left to make up his mind about the size of his armed forces with the help and advice of his general officers. 'We are not a council of war', said Trevor, 'but representative of the people, to assist him. We are but to supply, according to the numbers of men.'[4] This debate had revealed that the opponents of the army and of the land war were unaware of the realities and costs of international war and seemed determined to live in the past rather than face up to unpleasant truths. This dog-in-a-manger attitude was to persist throughout the reign. No matter how often William tried to persuade his Commons that the enemy, France, would not go away, the country members preferred to look backwards into their own insular history rather than consider the contemporary situation.

The next target for the anti-standing army brigade was more

legitimate – the Earl of Ranelagh. How was it that the paymaster presented estimates to the House of Commons for 10,000 men in the corps in Flanders and yet the muster rolls showed only 4,000 present? What had happened to the public's money? Secondly, Ranelagh had presented accounts for taking over the pay of 50,000 men from James II's army and yet, on his own admission, 22,000 had run away. Fortunately, regimental finance was so impenetrably complicated that Ranelagh was able to fudge his answers and wriggle out of a tight corner. To have admitted the truth, that the regiments in Flanders had been allowed to muster complete both to keep the officers loyal and to provide the units with some cash for recruitment and 'necessaries', would have been massively damaging to William's prestige and to the future of the war effort.[5] Again, on 30 November 1691, the Commons thought that the estimates for 1692 were too high and referred the matter to a committee. Sir Christopher Musgrave reported from this body on 15 December with the recommendation that the army should not be decreased in size but could be made more cost-effective by increasing the number of men in a foot company from fifty to eighty thereby saving on the pay of officers. To this not unreasonable suggestion, Colonel Charles Godfrey replied that the French had recently changed their method of fighting by operating in smaller companies with two captains and two lieutenants in each. The British ought to follow suit. This really was the most dreadful rubbish as the French had increased their company officers to soak up their huge pool of unemployed aristocrats, not to give their units any greater tactical flexibility.[6] In the debate over the estimates for 1694, Sir Thomas Clarges returned to the idea that British troops were not needed in Flanders basing his argument on the entirely specious and untruthful point that Ireland had been reconquered by British soldiers without help from the confederates. He had forgotten the enormous contribution of the Dutch, the Danes, the Württembergers, and the Huguenots to the success in Ireland. To the likes of Clarges, if there had to be an English army then its sole purpose was to protect the British Isles and not fight wars in Europe.[7] The 93,635 men asked for by William in the winter of 1693 came as a great shock to the Commons. Clarges, Sir Christopher Musgrave, Sir Francis Winnington, Sir John Thompson, Nicholas Barbon, and Sir John Dorrell all spoke of the danger which an enlarged army posed to liberties and the constitution. It was left to Sir Charles Sedley to point out that the augmented army was intended for the defeat of France and popery, and not to defeat the House of Commons. Understandably, the army officers in the House, particularly Henry Cornwall and Lord Colchester, were all in favour of the increase. As the first attack waned, Clarges turned his focus to the large number of foreign troops paid for from the English Treasury but Sir John Lowther and Sir Christopher Musgrave both saw that the confederacy would be hugely discouraged if English funding was reduced or withdrawn. The nail was finally driven into the country coffin by Lieutenant-General Thomas Talmash in a telling speech. After presenting some facts – that the French paraded 115,000 men in Flanders every year and that the king had done very well to contain them with his much smaller forces – Talmash persuaded the House that the king had to be provided with equal numbers otherwise he would be forced into a premature peace on bad terms and another war would break out before the debts incurred during the current conflict had been paid off.

It may be thought that I, having no estate, am ready to put the nation to a great charge; but I do declare I am as weary of war as any person and as desirous to have an end of it. And although I cannot answer for the success of the war, yet if the House will enable the king to come into the field with a good army, they may be able to preserve Flanders. And therefore I conclude to move the committee to augment the forces for 1694.[8]

The assumption has to be made that the members knew of and understood the basis of Talmash's arguments, although it was very clear that a number of members had no real appreciation of the fact that both the French and the Dutch regarded the Spanish Netherlands as an essential buffer state and that the fall of the Spanish Netherlands to the French would probably equal the political demise of the United Provinces.

Between 1694 and the end of the war in 1697, the debates in parliament over the army died down, but the signature of the Peace of Rijkswijk on 10 September 1697 brought the issue to the forefront of politics. It was not restricted to parliament for on the streets of London a great pamphleteering campaign started which lasted until 1700. John Trenchard, Walter Moyle, Andrew Fletcher, Samuel Johnson, and John Toland were the principal antagonists for the retention of the standing army, whilst John Somers, Daniel Defoe, Mathew Prior, and Richard Kingston did their best to defend the unpopular institution. Amidst the sea of pamphlets and broadsheets, there was a scarcity of original arguments. There were now more writers and stronger emotions, but the war in the press retrod much of the familiar, muddy ground which had been constantly trampled since 1660. Defoe tried to alter the core of the debate by arguing that the actual existence of a standing army in time of peace was no longer the main issue as that army was now firmly under the control of parliament. It had become legal and constitutional, solving the age-old problem, and what mattered now was the physical size of the armed forces. There was also the simple point that the Peace of Rijkswijk was no more than an armed truce and Louis XIV had disbanded none of his troops; with this sword of Damocles hanging over England's head a major demobilisation would have been most inadvisable. This view was not universally shared. Both the Earl of Sunderland and Henry Guy considered that France had been so drained by the previous war that the peace was bound to endure. Samuel Johnson and John Toland reactivated the arguments in favour of a strong navy and a reformed militia, but those who advocated the supremacy of the militia lived in a fantasy world and those who were solely for the navy forgot that men-of-war had difficulty operating in Derbyshire. The invasion scares of 1690, 1692, 1696, and 1697 were all ignored in the paper debates. England would not be invaded, they cried, and if it was then the reformed militia composed of honest yeomen and farmers fighting in defence of their lands, family, and country would be a match for any invader. Standing armies did not have the attachment to the people which was the hallmark of the militia. All a standing army could do was oppress the population, smother representative government, and abuse the law. Many of the standard views of John Trenchard and the anti-standing army faction were not based on English experience at all, but upon those of Denmark which had recently been publicised by Robert Molesworth in his *Account of Denmark*. Molesworth's remark that King Christian's domain resembled 'a monster that is all head and no body, all soldiers and no subjects', was music to the ears of the opponents of the army, but this exaggerated interpretation of the Danish situation was of dubious relevance to England. Quite how much all this affected the views of parliamentarians is hard to assess. Popular feeling at the end of the war was markedly anti-military, particularly in London, but this attitude was fairly normal although heightened by the peculiar circumstances of 1697. Lying at the back of all this was the sense that many of the opponents and proponents of the standing army were using the pamphleteers to make political points in readiness for the coming general election, the first to be held under the Triennial Act of 1694. Aware of the public hatred of the army, a number of members of parliament were prepared to alter their customary political stances in order to curry favour with the electorate.[9]

In military terms, the whole affair was monumentally irrelevant. England had expanded her army rapidly for war in 1678, the army had been augmented to deal with Monmouth's Rebellion in 1685 and to face William's invasion three years later, and it had been hugely expanded in 1689 and again in 1693–4. A vast amount of martial expertise had been built-up and a considerable number of men from all walks and stations in life had gained military experience and learned the soldierly trade. The anti-standing army lobby could do nothing to de-militarise the gentry and aristocracy, they could not wipe out the military expertise accumulated, and they could not erase the precedent of the mass armies of the 1690s. The entire debate, both inside and outside parliament, was a giant red herring. Nobody – neither king nor officers nor parliament – assumed that the army would be retained at full wartime strength after 1697, and all that was at issue was to decide the actual size of the peacetime establishment. How large a cadre should be retained? Not one of the pamphleteers argued for the total abolition of the army but all assumed that the base-line was to be the establishment of 1680, before the return of the Tangier garrison in 1684 but after the disbandment in 1679 of the forces which had been raised for the projected French war. What was the debate all about? It was certainly not about the existence of a standing army; it was about numbers, troop levels, and what the country was prepared to afford. All armies dropped to cadre strength in peacetime and the debates between 1697 and 1699 were concerned with the size of that skeleton. Between 1697 and 1700, England did not endure a debate about the standing army but about the size and shape of that army. Whatever Trenchard and his cronies might have written, a regular army was already a permanent feature of the English political scene, controlled through parliament's monopoly of national finances. The battle over standing armies, about their direction, political deployment and exist-ence, had been one of the major themes during the reign of Charles II and throughout the tenure of James II, but it had been convincingly won by 1697. Although the Mutiny Act and the Declaration of Rights had not effectively altered the constitutional status and position of the standing army, the parliamentary dominance over finance which had grown during the course of the war ensured that the lords and commons held the whip hand over future military developments. William was not so blind that he was unable to appreciate the major errors of James II, and between 1697 and 1699 he made no attempt to force a larger army upon parliament. He moaned and groaned in private but he had more sense than to challenge his parliament over this most sensitive issue. Throughout the war, parliament had enjoyed the right to agree to raise funds for the army; William had decided upon the requisite number of soldiers but parliament had to vote sufficient money for their recruitment or retention. The so-called anti-standing army debates of 1697–1699 were simply an extension of the annual debates about the army estimates which had taken place in parliament during the War of the Grand Alliance, only this time it was the level of the peacetime establishment that was under debate. It was a debate about details rather than principles.

Strong and pressing practical reasons demanded a major disbandment of the army in 1697. Already, there was enough trouble over quarters for the 10,000 men of the garrison of England without having to cater for another 50,000 returning from Flanders. Most politicians with a nodding acquaintance of international affairs and of the attitudes of Louis XIV were aware that some land forces had to be kept on foot in order to oblige the Frenchman to honour his agreements but they were equally conscious of the enormous popular clamour in England for a wholesale demobilisation. Edmund Bohun, who hovered on the brink of public life, wrote in August 1694, that 'if he [William] can settle his affairs abroad, he will return with an army hardened in the field and made so acquainted with war that nothing in England can resist it'.[10] To be fair, although these fears that William might possibly have created some variety of militarised absolutism at the conclusion of the war can be seen as absurd, there was some method in contemporary madness. William was not recognised in the United Provinces as a constitutional angel and the decade of the 1690s in England had been wracked by political insecurity and threatened instability. James II lurked across the Channel enjoying the active military and political support of Louis XIV, real or imagined Jacobitism helped to destabilise the regime of the Glorious Revolution, and the succession to the English throne remained a constant problem. What contemporaries failed to realise, or publicly to admit, was that the army and the navy by fighting the War of the Grand Alliance had kept James II and the Jacobites at bay and had protected the fragile bloom of the Revolution Settlement. The success of the new regime of the last decade of the seventeenth century depended, ultimately, upon the military stalemate which had been forced upon France. Yet, memories were so short and selective that the paper concession by the French monarch that he would recognise William III as the legitimate sovereign of England and would cease to uphold James's claim, was taken at face value and the international aspect of the army problem was washed from the political consciousness. Disband, disband, disband, was the only cry which reached the ears of the king. With that basic premise William did not disagree, but by how much? Enough to reduce the English army to the political police force of Charles II, or just enough to reduce costs and yet retain a sufficient corps with which to frighten Louis XIV into abiding by the Peace of Rijkswijk? In the end, by insisting upon the evisceration of the army, parliament virtually invited Louis XIV to disregard his commitments in the Peace of Rijkswijk relating to the English throne. Without a sizeable military establishment in the British Isles, the French sovereign was placed under no coercive obligation to abide by the terms of the treaty. Similarly, the cavalier acceptance by Louis of the will of Carlos II of Spain in preference to the conditions of the Second Partition Treaty, was greatly influenced by the obvious emasculation and unprepared-ness of the British armed forces.

William tried hard to mitigate the worse effects of a general disbandment but his endeavours were always private and clandestine, never public. As Anthonie Heinsius, the Raadspensionaris of Holland, pointed out, what mattered was not 10,000 men more or less in the British army but that parliament and the king should be seen to be working in harmony. That, emphasised the Dutchman, was the factor which added strength to England's international position; whether the army numbered 10,000 or 20,000 was scarcely relevant. With good relations between crown and commons, 10,000 could become 40,000 within a matter of weeks as the country was awash with disbanded soldiers and half-pay officers who could rapidly be re-enlisted.[11] This line of argument was intended to discourage William from picking a fight with parliament on disadvantageous ground and over an issue of intense sensitivity. Put simply, Heinsius was advising his master not to engage in battles he could not win, but to adopt a more subtle policy designed both to defuse the political crisis arising over the disband-ment and to place himself in the best possible political position to raise a mass army at short notice in the near future. William did not altogether agree. He was less than willing to see an army which had improved so much over the previous nine years disappear into the parish poor houses and the London coffee shops. He was deeply concerned and it was, for him, the most important issue in contempo-rary English politics.[12] The subtlety of Heinsius's point was lost on William. His whole adult life had been dominated by the need to contain French aggression and his experience told him that this could only be achieved by constant watchfulness and armed force. Any sign of weakness would be instantly exploited by the French king. William also had his own prestige to consider; he had not led the alliance against Louis between 1672 and 1678 and again from 1688 to 1697 because he was some wilting violet but through his personality and through Dutch economic power. The conquest of the English throne had greatly enhanced his personal position and authority within the European alliance and he thought, probably correctly, that a massive disbandment of the English army would make him look ridiculous in the eyes of Europe and render his alliance next to worthless when dealing with the militarised monarchies in Germany and Scandinavia. 'I see no likelihood of bringing the parliament to give money sufficient to keep so considerable a body of troops in the Spanish Netherlands as I had the last war', he wrote to Heinsius on 1 April 1698, 'and without that I see no possibility of defending them.'[13] William was also seriously worried that the disbandment in England would be misread by his continental allies – the United Provinces, Spain, the German princes, and the Holy Roman Emperor – for it was vital that they should remain fully armed, the same as Louis XIV.[14] 'I am so chagrined at what passes in the lower house with regard to the troops that I can scarce turn my thoughts to any other matter', wailed William to the Grand Pensionary on 20 December 1698, and Tallard, the French ambassador in London, certainly thought that the House of Commons had acted intemperately 'as in a fury'.[15] The only gleam of light that William could detect was the Commons' decision to provide half-pay, 'so that, if we can afford it, we should have the means of forming again a considerable army'.[16] But many contemporaries argued that William had only himself to blame for suffering this assault on his dignity and international standing. He briefed his ministers and managers in the House of Commons about the international situation and explained his own concern about the disbandment, but he refused to tell them how many men he actually wanted. He would not commit himself to a precise number. As a result, the court interest in the Commons floundered about in vague arguments of principle lacking the rallying point of a specific target and without that there was nothing with which to offer Paul Foley, Robert Harley and the 'New Country Party' in negotiation.[17] This was especially disadvantageous to William's interest as the central ground of the whole debate was about numbers and not about principle. The king endeavoured to gain support for the retention of a decent-sized army. He made himself less remote and more sociable and he closetted members of parliament and peers who might prove sympathetic to his point of view but he was labouring against many practical difficulties. The whig junto was in a weakened state having broken with Sunderland, Shrewsbury, and Godolphin and the most effective government campaigner for the army, John Somers, had just been elevated to the House of Lords. The whigs in the Commons were divided amongst themselves into court and country, leaving the government interest with no clear focus for support. William's efforts were often ill-directed and half-hearted like a man who, whatever his own belief in the justice of his cause, knew that he could never persuade others. His weak-kneed attitude is well illustrated by the pathetic and transparent piece of propaganda which purported to show that Louis XIV had 8,365 Irish catholic soldiers in his army ready to invade England.[18]

Knowing that some level of disbandment was inevitable, William's first instinct was to revert to Charles II's policy of 'losing troops in Ireland'. He wrote to Galway on 8 October 1697 approving of a plan to disband most of the depot regiments and battalions then in Ireland and replace them with twenty battalions of infantry, four regiments of dragoons, and eighteen troops of horse from the army in Flanders. No one else was to know of the project, except Lord Portland. As a rider, William confided in Galway his scheme to hide the three Huguenot infantry regiments in Ireland as well.[19] At that time, William was guessing that parliament would allow a peacetime establishment of 30,000 men in England, with additional forces in Scotland and Ireland. William's policy of disbanding those regiments which had spent most of the war in the British Isles learning how to misbehave in their quarters and replacing them with experienced formations from Flanders, started in Scotland at the end of October 1697 when two newly-raised battalions were broken to make room for the Scottish Foot Guards and Henry Rowe's fusiliers.[20] Whilst William, Lord Galway, and Portland were hatching their own, private arrangements, the lords of the Treasury and the lords justices in England had come up with the idea of retaining as many regiments as possible but only at cadre strength. All officers were to be retained and most of the non-commissioned officers but the ranks would be thinned to skeletal levels. Although the prime motive was financial in that it delayed having to meet the officers' arrears of pay but could dispose of the men to whom practically nothing was owing, it did have the military merit of enabling regiments to be expanded rapidly in the event of a future war. Their lordships were aware though, that their proposals would encounter vociferous opposition in parliament.[21] William ignored this compromise suggestion and stuck to his private guns throughout the winter of 1697 and into the summer of 1698. Eppinger's Dutch dragoons were retained in England and two battalions of foot were sent to Ireland in their stead, simply because the cost of two infantry regiments was equivalent to one of dragoons and William thus preserved two formations for the price of one. Similar considerations reformed the two marine regiments into four on 18 July 1698; the same number of men were kept but the number of officers and non-commissioned officers was doubled.[22] William was still hard at work secreting regiments away from parliament's stare in January 1699, ordering Galway to break nine regiments of foot in Ireland and Brigadier William Wolseley's horse to make way for eight battalions from Flanders and Galway's own regiment of Huguenot cavalry.

I design also, when parliament rises, to send you your regiment of horse, and the three French regiments, and perhaps Miremont's dragoons, but that must be very secret, although I much fear my design is already suspected here. . . . All this together would amount to eighteen battalions of foot, three regiments of horse, and five of dragoons . . . and this would be in a manner agreeable to your project and, according to my calculation, the expense no greater. . . . You will easily perceive how necessary it is that all this be kept secret. . . . There is a spirit of ignorance and malice prevailing here beyond conception.[23]

On 8 April 1698, William even toyed with the idea of sending four or five regiments into the West Indies using the excuse that they would be ready to capture any islands belonging to Spain should the French try a pre-emptive move in Europe over the Spanish Succession.[24] William seemed in the mood to attempt any device to save a few soldiers. If the king had put as much energy into informing his ministers and parliamentary managers of exactly what he wanted – 30,000 men or 20,000 – and into stating his case judiciously in the press as he did into dreaming up underhand schemes with which to outwit the Commons in collaboration with his old cronies, Galway and Portland, then he might well have entered the year 1700 with an army of a respectable size. In the event, all that his devious tricks achieved was to make parliament even more angry and even less rational when the truth was unmasked. Quite why William acted like an overgrown schoolboy is unclear. Perhaps he fully comprehended the spirit of Heinsius's advice that the maintenance of amicable relations between king and parliament was essential to the international climate and saw no means by which to preserve that friendship if there was to be a blazing row over troops numbers. Provided that the Commons did not discover what was actually going on then William could have allowed parliament its head over disbandment whilst safe in the knowledge that he had secretly prevented and limited the potential damage. Perhaps, after correctly assessing the truculent mood of parliament, William, who was much less forceful and more mellow in these, his declining years, simply could not find the personal resources for a protracted political battle. Perhaps sheer anger and pique at the blinkered attitudes of parliament got the better of his judgement. Whatever was the real reason, the king displayed an uncharacteristic lassitude which was unfortunate as there was every indication that if he had made a stand and stated the number of troops that he wanted then a negotiated settlement might well have been reached. As it was, his inaction and uncertainty allowed a wilful Commons to march all over him with scarcely any opposition. There was a majority in favour of a sensible peacetime establishment in the House of Lords, but this was nullified by the Commons' clever tactic of 'tacking' the second Disbanding Bill to a Money Bill. Their lordships could not delay a money bill and they had no wish to foment a division between the two houses. The bloody-mindedness of the parliament coupled with the vacillating and deceitful conduct of the king created the situation that everyone had sought to avoid. To France, England appeared war weary and incapable of significant intervention in European affairs. Safe in that assumption, Louis XIV invaded the Dutch barrier fortresses in 1701, comfortable in the thought that England would not fight to uphold the Spanish Succession.

Whilst William pottered around saving a battalion here and a dragoon regiment there, writing to Galway in vanishing ink, parliament had a field day. It was like Exclusion come again; the king was down and they hammered him unmercifully. At the opening of the session on 2 December 1697, William brusquely informed the lords and commons that the maintenance of a standing force was a necessity and the tone of his speech was taken as a great affront to parliamentary dignity. On 10 December, the House of Commons went into Grand Committee and resolved to disband all land forces which had been raised since 29 September 1680, and John Conyers reported the resolution of the Committee to the full House on the following day. Ominously, the king found that he had been deserted by three of his customary supporters: Sir Herbert Crofts, Sir Richard Onslow, and Sir William Strickland. Despite a last minute attempt to advance the cut-off date to the accession of James II, a manoeuvre which would have preserved another two battalions of foot, one regiment of horse and one of dragoons, the original motion was carried by 185 votes to 148. Fifty-two English regiments plus a number of Dutch and Huguenot formations in English pay would have to go. Robert Harley and Jack Howe had proposed and seconded the motion in the Grand Committee, with additional support from Sir Edward Seymour, Grenville Norris, Sir William Strickland, Sir Herbert Crofts, and Sir Francis Winnington. Christopher Montagu, Lord Coningsby, Goodwin Wharton, Lord Ranelagh, Sir Thomas Littleton, and Sir Robert Rich, placemen all, did their best to stem the tide basing their arguments around the need for defence against the dangers from abroad and insecurities at home, but their contributions were inconclusive and they had to make do with asking for a stay of execution rather than proposing a specific size of establishment. William's lack of leadership was glaringly obvious. The one light to emerge from this debate was the common consensus that the disbanded officers ought to be offered half-pay, and Grenville Norris thought that this should be funded from compensation paid by war profiteers. Robert Harley informed James Vernon that half-pay should be for three years although the fate of Scottish and Dutch officers on the English establishment had still to be clarified.[25] According to a report by the placeman, James Sloane, the court managers had hoped for an army of around thirty-five thousand including the Dutch regiments and the Huguenot formations in Ireland.[26] The corollary of reducing the army to the three troops of the Life Guard, the Royal Horse Guards, the Royal Dragoons, the First Foot Guards, the Coldstream Guards, the Royal Scots, and seven line battalions, in addition to the independent companies stationed in the garrisons, was a remodelling of the militia and Sir Richard Onslow was deputed to draft and bring in a bill for this purpose. It was introduced to lie on the table on 26 February 1698 and a committee considered its provisions on 24 March but it was ultimately lost in a great sea of indifference about who was to pay. Anything which smacked of military expenditure in 1698 was immediately unpopular.[27]

After their vote to limit the army to 10,000 men, the Commons waited until the new year before proceeding to work out the details of how to finance the necessary disbandments. Despite the earlier resolution of the Commons, there was still a remote hope that they would eventually settle for an army of 15,000, particularly if the country members were presented with the scalp of the hated Sunderland as a sweetener. Sir Thomas Littleton moved for a grant of £500,000 to support the new establishment, an obvious indicator that a larger army was thought desirable, but despite the efforts of Sir Charles

Sedley, John Pulteney, John Jeffreys, Sir Thomas Dyke, Charles Montagu, Sir Christopher Musgrave, and Sir William Williams who all urged the House to be cautious and think again, these optimistic expectations were dashed by twenty-four votes. It was noticeable that a number of government employees, Paul Methuen and Robert Molesworth among them, deserted their proper allegiance in this division. On 11 January 1698, the Commons debated the level of supply for the armed forces and after rejecting proposals for £500,000, £400,000, and £300,000, they settled upon Sir Christopher Musgrave's compromise of £350,000, sufficient for 10,000 men, and this was adopted unanimously.[28] Six days later, on 17 January, the Commons proceeded to the much more congenial task of voting funds for the disbandment of the existing forces. They decided to raise the money to meet the total army debt of £2,348,102 in instalments, starting with £250,000 with which to pay off the common soldiers. This was a relatively cheap exercise as little money was owing to the rank and file. The disbanded officers who enjoyed the privilege of being natural-born Englishmen were to have half-pay until they had been fully paid off or 'otherwise provided for'. This clause, 'otherwise provided for', resulted in a protracted debate which ended with Sir Edward Seymour asking whether the officers of the army were any the worse for their service and experience. To this, Sir John Hotham replied that the officers had been more honourably employed during the late war than Sir Edward. Quickly, the Speaker intervened to prevent a duel but it was more generally observed that this kind of personal remark had lately become more frequent in the House. Although half-pay was thus introduced as a purely financial expedient to buy the government sufficient time to raise enough cash to pay off the officers in full, William was quick to appreciate its military advantages.[29]

It is fortunate, however, that they [parliament] have resolved to give half-pay to all the officers who shall be disbanded. I estimate their number at 1,500, or nearly so; so that if we could afford it, we should have the means of forming again a considerable army; and many persons think that another parliament will be more disposed to do so.[30]

Throughout the Commons' debates and into the summer of 1698, William, Galway and Portland shipped veteran regiments into Ireland and there disbanded depot regiments to make room for them. Although the Civil List Act had made it virtually impossible for the king to top-up the money voted by parliament for the new establishment, William did secure a minor victory on 3 March 1698 when the Commons voted to retain the two marine regiments at an annual charge of £55,000 to the naval establishment.[31] In June, William ordered all half-pay officers to do duty with the standing regiments, 'by which they will be doubly officered', and in September a special 'Royal Company' composed of forty half-pay captains, thirty lieutenants, and thirty ensigns was attached to the First Foot Guards. As the disbandments continued during the spring and summer of 1698 gradually reducing the army to its target of 10,000, regiments became top-heavy with officers until, by March 1698, there was one commissioned rank for every eleven men.[32] In spite of William's pessimism about the disbandment, parliament's straitened purse and his own manoeuvreing had produced something positive for the army. Most of the officers, the vital and professional core of the army, were being retained either on half or full pay, and they were continuing to serve and do duty.

The procedure for disbandment was modelled upon that which had been used in 1679. Regiments were paraded before a general officer, usually a brigadier, with a deputy commissary of the musters in attendance. Foot soldiers were permitted to take away with them all clothing which had been purchased out of their net off-reckonings but they had to surrender their swords for which they received three shillings in exchange. Horsemen and dragoons were allowed to keep their horses and saddlery, neatly equipping them for instant careers as highwaymen. In 1679, each private soldier had been presented with 10s as a free gift to enable him to travel home, but in 1698 the men were given just ten days' subsistence money – 3s 4d for a foot private, 5s 6d for a drummer, and 7s for a sergeant. This parsimony aroused an immediate furore to which the War Office quickly capitulated and allowed fourteen days' subsistence to all disbanded men. Broken soldiers were ordered to return home in groups of not more than three, in an effort to preserve the public peace and prevent the rapid formation of criminal gangs.[33] Generally, the reduction of the army went smoothly and calmly. Brigadier George Cholmondeley served as a disbanding officer, as did Brigadier William Selwyn and Sir Charles O'Hara. Where possible, regiments which had been principally recruited in one particular locality were marched there and so disbanded as close to their homes as possible. Thomas Erle's foot was broken by O'Hara at Exeter, having been raised in Devon and Somerset. Occasionally, complications arose. When William Selwyn came to Lincoln to disband Colonel Thomas Saunderson's foot he found chaos. The men were nearly in open mutiny and beyond the control of their officers, refusing to hand in their arms until their demands had been satisfied. They were owed money by their officers, most of whom had already left the regiment, the colonel was absent as indeed was 'Lord Ranelagh's man', there had been irregular stoppages from pay in Flanders, and the agent had barely enough cash to pay the subsistence and the disbandment bounty. Somehow, deploying all his tact and diplomacy, Selwyn sorted out the mess and had succeeded in breaking the formation by the end of week.[34]

By 19 March 1698, eight battalions, two dragoon formations, and two horse regiments remained in England, with a further fifteen battalions, three dragoon units, and two cavalry regiments in Ireland. To meet the target of the 1680 establishment and to stay within the budget of £350,000, a further ten regiments needed to be demobilised.[35] It was at this point that the money ran out. Between the end of May 1698 and the meeting of parliament in December, no more regiments were reduced. Although the king's speech was well enough received, the Commons suspected that they were being duped over the progress of the disbandment in much the same way as Charles II had deceived parliament in 1678. In readiness for the debate on 16 December, the English and Irish paymasters were asked to lay lists of the current forces on the table; James Vernon timorously hoped that the news that Carlos II of Spain had nominated the Electoral Prince of Bavaria to be his successor would cause the Commons to stop and think before acting too hastily over the army. Ranelagh's list showed the embarrassing total of 14,834 men still in England, with a further 1,258 in the colonies, and 600 men in the invalid companies. Coningsby revealing in his paper that 15,488 men were still on foot in Ireland. William's deceptions had been uncovered. With John Conyers in the chair, the House went into Grand Committee on 16 December and debated the issue for seven and a half hours before resolving, without a division, to reduce the English establishment to 7,000 men, including officers, servants, and non-commissioned officers. On the following day, another Grand Committee took the Irish establishment down to 12,000, again including officers, servants, and non-commissioned officers. James Vernon put the blame fairly and squarely on William for refusing to give a lead to his ministers and managers. Instead of seeking a negotiable establishment, he sulked, stamped his foot, and adopted the attitude that if 10,000 was already too few what did it matter if the figure fell yet further. Ranelagh was also to blame. It was his intemperate suggestion that 3,000 men would be sufficient for the garrisons and 4,000 would be enough for the guards which had led the House to settle upon 7,000 as the total establishment, when, in reality, this figure hardly allowed for a token garrison in the Channel Islands let alone in the Americas and the West Indies. Vernon's implication was that surely Ranelagh, so adept at pulling the wool over the eyes of the Commons to mask his massive peculations, could have dressed-up the troop estimates a little better. 'The king is very uneasy at yesterday's resolution and thinks it ruinous.'[36] Of especial chagrin to William was the Commons' decision that the British army must be composed solely of native-born troops; the Dutch Red Dragoons and the Blue Guards would have to return to the United Provinces. As well as being a personal insult to William, it posed additional problems as there was no room on the Dutch establishment for these regiments and William had to disband three out of the six regiments of the Scottish Brigade and a number of Swiss mercenary formations in order to create the necessary vacancies. Desperately, the king's managers tried to claw back the lost ground during the second reading and in the Grand Committee before the final reading, concentrating particularly on gaining a concession over 'foreign troops' which might have enabled the king to retain his precious Blue Guards. However, William's cause was doomed. No politicians wanted to appear to befriend the interest of the unpopular army when there was every prospect that the smooth passage of the Disbandment Bill might result in a more amicable and harmonious session of parliament. William did his best to gain 'converts' over the Christmas period but the Commons viewed the army and the question of its disbandment in domestic, not in international terms. The perspectives of William and his parliament were diametrically opposed and neither even pretended to appreciate the deeply held convictions of the other.

During the Grand Committee on the second Disbandment Bill on 4 January 1699, the placemen and government managers in the Commons tried to stage a rearguard action and regain a little of the lost ground. Despite William's efforts during the Christmas recess, John Smith and Thomas Pelham of the Treasury both spoke against the army, and the king's cause was only supported by those who had 'great places in the court and the army [and] some few country gentlemen of small fortunes and consideration'. Lord Hartington and Sir Richard Onslow also deserted the court but the major error of the day was committed by William Blathwayt. After Ranelagh's inept performance on 16 December, the secretary-at-war was briefed for the Grand Committee and entrusted with the task of presenting convincing figures and statistics to the House to show that 7,000 men were simply inadequate. He badly bungled his case and left the House with the impression that 7,000 men were ample for the guards and garrisons, especially when the 1,500 soldiers in the Royal Marines were taken into account to do duty in naval garrisons. At this, the government benches threw in the towel.[37] The resultant Disbandment Act asked for 7,000 men in England by 26 March 1699 and for 12,000 in Ireland by 10 April, including officers, non-commissioned officers and servants, and all personnel were to be natural-born Englishmen. Naturalised subjects were excluded. To fund these further disbandments, £800,000 was borrowed at seven per cent. The court had based its opposition to the second Disbandment Bill upon the dangers from France but they had been countered by Harley, Simon Harcourt, Sir Christopher Musgrave and Sir John Packington with the point that William's claim to the throne was no longer precarious but was legal and secure. England was an island, said Sir Charles Sedley, surrounded only by water. It did not really matter whether France had an army of 20,000 or 200,000; the Spanish Armada had been beaten at sea and William of Orange would have been defeated in 1688 if he had not been opposed by 'an infatuated prince'. The experience of the Brest expedition of 1694 had shown how easy it was for a small force to prevent an armed landing. 'If we are true to ourselves', he concluded, 'ten thousand men are enough, and, if not, one hundred thousand are too few.' The Bill passed its third reading by 221 votes to 154.[38] This final debate on 18 January lasted for five hours and was dominated by the court's manoeuvres to pass an amendment to preserve the king's Blue Guards. Success seemed possible until Lord Coningsby, who led for the government, over-stepped his brief and began to re-debate the whole issue of the army and its numbers. The officers of the court and the army then trudged through all the old arguments but were ignored by the country members, who were content to rely upon their massive majority, until Sir William Blackett, 'of great estate in the north', Sir John Mainwaring, and a few others attacked the bill as leaving the nation naked, insecure, and 'dissatisfactory to people of the kingdom in the parts represented by them'. This dragged in other speakers and the proceedings became more protracted than had been expected. On 31 January, the bill passed the Lords for the third and final time, very few peers opposing it as they did not wish to go against the decisions of the Commons and damage relations between the two Houses. Even before the bill became law, William had accepted the inevitable and had issued orders for the disbandment of the necessary units to bring both the Irish and the English establishments down to their required level. William was left with 7,000 men in England, 12,000 in Ireland, 4,000 in Scotland, 600 invalids, and 1,000 in the colonies, making a total of 24,600 men.[39] The Lords offered a sop to William on 1 February by declaring themselves 'ready and willing to enter into any expedient' for retaining William's Blue Guards. Ranelagh told the House of Commons that the king 'would take it kindly' if they would allow the Guards to stay but the suggestion was politely rejected and on 25 March 1699, Overkirk embarked the last of the 2,500 Dutch troops in England ready to sail for the United Provinces. William had lost on all fronts and had been able to salvage nothing from the wreck.[40] Whilst the English parliament was busy hacking back the army to 10,000 and then to 7,000, the Council of State in the United Provinces agreed to maintain the Dutch army at 4,100 cavalry and 41,440 infantry, and the States-General levied a tax of Fl.800,000 on all seven provinces for the improvement of the fortifications in the Generality.[41]

Just as in 1679, the Great Disbandment of 1697–1699 took place against a highly unfavourable background. Hordes of troops flooded back from the Low Countries and the sheer weight of soldiery in England heightened the tension and gave illusory substance to the more lurid fantasies of the anti-standing army brigade. The great bulk of the British forces in Flanders were concentrated, initially, around Ostend, Ghent, and Bruges and shipped across the North Sea between the end of October 1697 and the middle of February 1698. Most of the infantry were ferried from the quayside at Ostend, Nieuport, and Blankenburg on a variety of strange craft – bilanders, canal boats, and fishing smacks – out to the waiting transports and men-of-war. The majority of the cavalry horses were shipped from Rotterdam and Willemstadt, an operation which had to be temporarily halted in mid-December when ice closed the ports. Sir Henry Bellasise masterminded the evacuation of the British corps from Flanders with efficiency and attention to detail.[42] Irish and Scottish regiments sailed directly to their home countries, to Cork and Leith, whilst the English troops came ashore at Hull, Newcastle, Harwich, Ipswich, Deal, Dover, Gravesend and Dartford. With so many soldiers arriving in East Anglia and the Thames estuary, London and the home counties were inundated. George Clarke, David Crawford, and the Middlesex justices of the peace reviewed all the quarters available in the London area in October 1697 in an effort to uncover every spare bed and stable, but whatever their success, there remained a superfluity of under-paid soldiers loitering in and around London during the time of the disbandment debates.[43]

Needless to say, the disbandment was highly unpopular with most grades of military personnel. The commissioned officers had been under the impression that the war had been fought to preserve liberty, the protestant religion, and to secure the inheritance of William III, yet everywhere in London they read pamphlets in which they saw themselves described as traitors and enemies of freedom. Immdoerate language in parliament, initiated by the likes of Jack Howe, increased the smouldering rage of the half-pay officers. They swore vengeance on the Grub Street hacks and country politicians, and Howe found it prudent to retire from the town and one writer went about with a loaded pistol in his pocket.[44] So rapid was the disbandment that it created enormous problems of law and order. An Act of Parliament came into effect on 1 May 1699 which allowed all disbanded officers and soldiers, who had not deserted, to set up in their trades regardless of whether they had actually finished an apprenticeship. To gain benefit from this statute, a certificate of service was required signed by an officer. As an additional incentive, all those who took advantage of the provisions of the act were exempted from arrest for debt for a period of three years as well as for any debts which they may have had at the time of their enlistment. A group of Scottish soldiers settled down at Chesham with their families to begin trading under the terms of the Act, but this only brought forth a stream of complaints from the local inhabitants who feared that their businesses might fail and the Scots would then become a charge on the parish.[45] The future for many was certainly bleak. A riotous mob surrounded the Houses of Parliament on 27 February 1700, baying for their arrears of pay. Brigadier Francis Langston was thrown into the Gatehouse prison on the suit of his ex-regimental officers who considered that he owed them huge sums in arrears of pay and clothing charges, whilst Captain Robert Swift killed his colonel, Edward Colt, in a duel which originated in a disagreement over arrears of pay.[46] Many old soldiers simply turned to crime. Highwaymen attacked travellers on Hounslow Heath, in the Thames Valley, and even in Hyde Park. A string of guard houses had to be built along the road from London to Kensington to protect the public from insult. Five out of a gang of seven robbers who operated in the region around Henley-on-Thames were disbanded soldiers, probably ex-cavalrymen or dragoons all of whom had been allowed to keep their horses at their demobilisation.[47] The problem did not go away. The roads were still unsafe in 1701 and stragglers from the army in Flanders trickled back into England, penniless, throughout 1700.[48] The only solution was war. As the mass levies began in the summer of 1701, the unemployed soldiers and half-pay officers were taken back into the army and the question of what to do with disbanded soldiers was put into abeyance for another thirteen years.

At root, the disbandment furore revolved around differing perceptions of England's foreign policy and of her place in the contemporary international scene. William clearly viewed his new acquisition as a part of continental Europe with a duty and responsibility to help uphold the interests of the balance of power and resist French aggression. English politicians, in general, had grown up in a country where isolation and a conscious reticence to become involved in European affairs was a strong and engrained tradition. Both whigs and tories had been obliged to bow to the logic of the Dutch invasion and the Glorious Revolution and enter the War of the Grand Alliance but once Louis XIV had agreed to recognise William as the legal sovereign of England and renounced his support for James II, then the English purpose had been served. After 1697, the House of Commons wanted nothing more than to withdraw back into its traditional island fastness and concentrate upon colonies, navies, and trade. Accordingly, if an army had to be maintained then it was to be used for the physical defence of the British Isles from foreign invasion and to garrison overseas territories; it had no further role in Flanders. William, the expedient exploiter of England's human and financial resources, continued to see his second domain as a magazine to supply his lifelong war with Louis XIV and he was unable to sympathise with the attitudes which were current in parliament and the country at large. Perhaps then, the great debate over disbandment was no more than a vehicle for an argument over foreign policy, a stage in the gradual maturation of England's relationship with continental Europe. The debate was concerned with the size of the future establishment; size depended upon the perceived role of the army; and that role could only be decided by England's foreign policy. England was eventually persuaded of the necessity to become an active participant in the War of the Spanish Succession through Louis XIV's recognition of James III as the legitimate monarch of England and Scotland. Effectively, this made the conflict over the throne of Spain into a continuation of the Nine Years' struggle, even though the issue of the preservation of the Glorious Revolution seemed more remote. Throughout William's reign, in peace and in war, decisions over foreign policy and strategy were dominated by the supporters of

William's notion of the 'continental commitment', and the majority of 'country' opinion which favoured the 'blue water' school of thought.[49]

Notes

1 Loosely based on, W. Görlitz, *The German General Staff* (London, 1953), p. 236.

2 Foxcroft, *Halifax,* ii. 139, Draft of a speech to the Lords, 1690; Z. S. Fink, *The Classical Republicans: an essay in the recovery of a pattern of thought in seventeenth century England* (Evanston, 1962), p. 185; Robertson, *Scottish Enlightenment and the Militia Issue,* p. 15.

3 *Miscellaneous State Papers, from 1501 to 1726,* ed. Philip Yorke, 2nd Earl of Hardwicke (London, 1778), ii. 421, 29 Jan. 1689, 'Notes of what passed in the Convention'.

4 Grey, *Debates,* ix. 388–93.

5 Grey, *Debates,* ix. 427–39, 16–23 Nov. 1689.

6 *Parliamentary Diary of Luttrell,* pp. 51–3, 80–2.

7 Burnet, *History,* iv. 151–2; Grey, *Debates,* x. 332–3, 28 Nov. 1693.

8 Grey, *Debates,* x. 339–44, 358–64, 5–11 Dec. 1693.

9 Burnet, *History,* iv. 375–6; *Marchmont Papers,* iii. 146–7; *CSPD 1698,* p. 414; L. G. Schwoerer, 'The literature of the standing army controversy, 1697–1699', *Huntingdon Library Quarterly,* xxvii. (1965), pp. 188–203; E. A. Miller, 'Some arguments used by English pamphleteers, 1697–1700, concerning a standing army', *JMH,* xviii. (1946), pp. 307–13; Caroline Robbins, *The Eighteenth-Century Commonwealth Man* (Cambridge, Mass., 1959), pp. 103–9; Dennis Rubini, *Court and Country, 1688–1702* (London, 1968), pp. 132–7. For a more succinct statement of her views, see L. G. Schwoerer, *No Standing Armies!: the anti-army ideology in seventeenth century England* (Baltimore, 1974), pp. 155–87.

10 Japikse (Welbeck), ii. 100–1, 13 Sept. 1698, James Vernon to Portland; *The Diary and Autobiography of Edmund Bohun Esq.,* ed. S. Wilton Rix (Beccles, 1853); pp. 122–3.

11 Baxter, *William III,* p. 362.

12 Schwoerer, 'Controversy', p. 189; W. L. Sachse, *Lord Somers, a political portrait* (Manchester, 1975), p. 130.

13 Harwicke, *State Papers,* ii. 342; Burnet, *History,* iv. 377.

14 Grimblot, i. 438–9, 23 April 1698, William III to Portland.

15 Ibid., ii. 216–17, 219–30.

16 Ibid., i. 150–1, 21 Jan. 1698, William III to Heinsius.

17 Burnet, *History,* iv. 374–5; *Vernon Correspondence,* ii. 241–2.

18 *A Collection of Scarce and Valuable Tracts,* ed. Sir Walter Scott (London, 1809–15), xi. 473; L. G. Schwoerer, 'The role of King William III of England in the standing army controversy – 1697–1699', *JBS,* v. (1966), pp. 76–93.

19 Agnew, *Galway,* pp. 79–80; Grimblot, i. 127–9.

20   HMC, *Hope Johnstone MSS.*, pp. 100, 102; Grimblot, i. 133.

21   *CSPD 1697*, pp. 478–9, 19 Nov. 1697.

22   *CSPD 1698*, p. 359; Grimblot, ii. 85–6.

23   Grimblot, ii. 248–9, 27 Jan. 1699, William III to Galway.

24   Hardwicke, *State Papers*, ii. 340–1, 8 April 1698, William III to Heinsius.

25   *CSPD 1697*, pp. 505–6; *Vernon Correspondence*, i. 441–2; HMC, *Cowper MSS.*, ii. 372; Burnet, *History*, iv. 376–7; *CJ*, xii. 5; Luttrell, iv. 317; Schwoerer, 'Role of King William III', p. 83.

26   *CSPD 1697*, pp. 511–12, 14 Dec. 1697, to Sir Joseph Williamson.

27   *CSPD 1697*, p. 518; *CSPD 1698*, pp. 114–15, 154, 160.

28   HMC, *Lonsdale MSS.*, p. 108, 1 Jan. 1698, Duke of Leeds to Lord Lonsdale; *CSPD 1698*, pp. 23–4; *Vernon Correspondence*, i. 460–1, 11 Jan. 1698, Vernon to Shrewsbury; Chandler, *Debates*, iii. 79; Hayton, 'Salway Winnington's Notes, 10 Dec. 1697 – 8 Jan. 1698'.

29   *CSPD 1698*, pp. 33–4; *Vernon Correspondence*, i. 464.

30   Grimblot, i. 150–1, 21 Jan. 1698, William III to Heinsius.

31   *CSPD 1698*, pp. 128–9, 3 Mar. 1698, Report on the proceedings of the House Commons; Arthur Trevor, *The Life and Times of William the Third* (London, 1835–6), ii. 334–5.

32   Luttrell, iv. 392, 424; Walton, p. 820; BL, Add. MSS. 9,755, ff. 57–8; Petre, *Norfolk Regiment*, i. 40.

33   Childs, *Army of Charles II*, pp. 194–5; Walton, pp. 492–3; *LG*, 14 Feb. 1698.

34   WO 5/10, f. 29; BL, Add. MSS. 9,755, ff. 13–18; Doyle, 'Notebook', p. 154.

35   Bod. Lib. Rawlinson MSS. A. 245, f. 24a.

36   *Vernon Correspondence*, ii. 230–7; Luttrell, iv. 462–3; *CSPD 1698*, pp. 427–8; *CJ*, xii. 359–60; Hayton, 'William Cowper's Narrative and Salway Winnington's Notes'.

37   HMC, *Portland MSS.*, iii. 600–1; Horwitz, *Parliament, Policy, and Politics*, p. 250; Hayton, 'William Cowper's Narrative'; *CJ*, xii. 387; *Vernon Correspondence*, ii. 239–47.

38   *SR*, vii. 452–3, 10 William III, c. 1; *Hatton Correspondence*, ii. 238–9; Chandler, *Debates*, iii. 190–1.

39   Grimblot, ii. 243–5, 248–9, 252; *Hatton Correspondence*, ii. 238–9; Davies, 'Reduction', pp. 23–4; Hayton, 'William Cowper's Narrative'.

40   HMC, *House of Lords MSS.*, n.s. iii. 284–5; *CJ*, xii. 601–4.

41   N. Japikse, *Prins Willem III, de Stadhouder-Koning* (Amsterdam, 1930–33), ii. 398–9; *Briefwisseling tussen Simon van Slingelandt en Sicco van Goslinga, 1697–1731*, ed. W. A. van Rappard (The Hague, 1978), pp. 1–4.

42   See: Parker, *Memoirs*, pp. 65–6; NLI, MSS. 4166, p. 40; BL, Add. MSS. 9,731, ff. 27–97; WO 5/10, ff. 4–6, 133.

43   *CSPD 1697*, p. 405; *Middlesex Quarter Sessions*, p. 175.

44   *Carstares*, pp. 356–63; T. B. Macaulay, *The History of England*, ed. C. H. Firth (London, 1913), vi. 2747–8.

45   *SR*, vii. 528–9, 10 William III, c. 17; *Bucks. Sessions Records*, ii. pp.

xiii–xiv.
46 *CJ,* xiii. 230–1; Luttrell, iv. 679, 683–4, 715.
47 Luttrell, iv. 285, 394, 412, 587; v. 106; Macaulay, *History of England,* vi. 2828–9; Knight, *The Buffs,* i. 397; *Verney Letters of the Eighteenth Century from the MSS. at Claydon House,* ed. M. M. Verney (London, 1930), i. 31–2.
48 BL, Add. MSS. 9,728, f. 90.
49 See, T. J. Denman, 'The debates over war strategy, 1689 to 1714' (Doctoral Dissertation, University of Cambridge, 1984).

IX

An English operation

Intellectually, strategy is simple. It consists of the options available for the fighting of a war and the establishment of priorities within those options. In conducting the War of the Grand Alliance, England had few choices. It was a conflict into which she had been dragged through the clandestine activities of a few of her politicians and it was the political price which she had to pay for accepting William III as monarch in place of James II. It was a penance, nine long 'Hail Marys' imposed by the great father confessor of international relations. William had only one objective; to beat back the forces of Louis XIV and return the frontiers of the United Provinces to their position before the French invasion of 1672. There was also the small matter of securing his new throne but that would be achieved through attention to his main objective and, to all intents and purposes, the English throne was only a means to the one end. 'He hath such a mind to France', observed the Marquis of Halifax on 2 June 1689, 'that it would incline one to think he took England only in his way.' Unlike most seventeenth century monarchs, William could not found a dynasty, and he was the last of the Dutch freedom fighters provided by the House of Orange-Nassau.

English politicians had three strategic options. They could have agreed to fight on William's terms and have made a massive commitment of troops and money to the defeat of Louis XIV on land. Secondly, they could have ignored the land war and sought to ruin France through a series of naval campaigns designed to weaken her overseas' trade and capture her colonies. Thirdly, they could have thrown in the sponge and sought an early peace on the xenophobic grounds that it was a Dutch war, fought for Dutch gain and England was merely being exploited for Dutch interests. The latter option was never available as James II lurked across the water in France waiting to be pushed into an attempted invasion and, more importantly, the political success of the Glorious Revolution depended upon forcing Louis XIV to come to terms with the new situation in England. Seeking a premature peace was tantamount to inviting James II to return. The effective choice of strategies rested between fighting a land war in Flanders and Germany, or conducting a war against French trade and colonies.

Life, invariably, is not that simple. France could not have been defeated by the strangulation of her trade. She was an enormous country with a population in excess of twenty million people, and self-sufficient in most commodities. Her overseas trade was miniscule and French Canada and a few West Indian islands counted as nothing in her war effort. She could, however, as William III fully realised, be contained if not defeated by co-ordinated opposition to her aggressive designs along the Rhine and in the Spanish Netherlands. Unfortunately, English politicians distrusted this entire concept of strategy. Fighting wars on continental Europe involved large, standing armies which might be employed to threaten the liberties of England if they were misused. Above all, standing armies were hugely expensive and the burden of their cost would have to be shouldered by the English country gentry through a land tax. English landed society much preferred the naval or 'blue water' option, even though it was strategic nonsense in terms of winning the war and involved throwing good money after bad. However, it was an admirable strategy if the aim was not to win the war in European terms but to squeeze every possible commercial and economic advantage out of a necessary evil. Here, the impossibility of compromise between William III and the landed gentry was revealed. The king wanted to wage and win a war against France in order to prevent the further erosion of Dutch territory and security whilst the English country politicians merely wished to favour England's traditional interests in maritime trade and the development of colonies. Sadly, the supporters of the blue-water strategy conveniently forgot that fighting navies were as expensive as armies; throughout the war years between 1691 and 1697, the army and the navy each cost an annual average of two and a half million pounds. What was needed was a compromise between the continental school and the blue-water battalions, a truly English strategy of half-measures and total ineffectiveness. It was found in the notion of the 'descent', the forerunner of 'breaking French windows with guineas'.

The genesis of 'descents' was political rather than military. Descents attracted those back-bench members of parliament who were terrified of the costs of a long land war, as well as mercantile pressure groups who could see some commercial benefit in supporting a naval war effort, if only to protect English trade rather than to attack that of their opponents. Naval officers liked descents as they gave their service a more glamorous role to play, and senior army officers were similarly beguiled by the prospect of starring in some British military enterprise where the limelight was not going to be seized by a Solms or a Waldeck or an Overkirk. William, professional and realistic as he was, regarded all this as ridiculously amateur but he had to go along with it, to some extent, in order to humour the country elements in the House of Commons and ensure a regularity of financial supply for the main military commitment in Flanders. The 'English strategy', or the 'soft underbelly of Europe', or 'descents' bore about as much relevance to winning the War of the Grand Alliance as the Dutch occupation of Rockall, but it was supported by the majority of country members of parliament and it was at least a negotiable option which could be argued with some degree of coherence and authority.

As early as 1689, William had come to regard Ireland as a sideshow and viewed every British, Dutch, Danish, or German soldier sent into the bogs as a man denied to his main armies in Flanders. In his opinion, an effective naval blockade of Ireland to cut off French supplies and reinforcements would have brought the Jacobite armies to their knees within a few weeks, but William was unable to convince his English listeners with his strategic arguments for two, simple reasons. In the first place, he could not dispel the fact that a continental war was bound to favour the Dutch long-term interests rather than the English and, secondly, William's land wars were remarkably unsuccessful. William III was not a great general. He was a good organiser and administrator and a skilful and resourceful politician, but he rarely possessed enough soldiers in the army in Flanders to gain the upper hand over Luxembourg and the French generals. It was not that William was a poor soldier. He was competent enough and he did win some battles – St Dennis, the invasion of England, the Boyne, Ath, and Namur – but most major actions in the later seventeenth century were gigantic slugging matches in which weight of numbers was usually decisive. Luxembourg only won at Landen in 1693 because he so outnumbered William that he was able to batter the allied defences until they finally cracked. If anything, William was a rather unlucky soldier, but what mattered in the context of English politics was that his campaigns did not bring negotiable results. He hammered away from year to year, losing town upon town and battle after battle, demanding ever more men and money, and all to no visible effect. Both William and the English parliament had unwittingly become involved in a war of attrition, a war which would be decided by wealth and resources. In order to be victorious, or to prevent French territorial advance and to stop James II reclaiming his throne, there was no alternative but to pour more and more money into the melting pot until the French could be dominated by superior numbers and then whipped towards the peace conference. However, such a domination was unlikely to occur if the British military effort was dissipated by raids on the French coast and ill-judged assaults upon Brest. It was an escalating spiral but it was to prove ultimately unavoidable. As Sir John Lowther told the House of Commons on 19 November 1691, there seemed only one escape route from this vicious circle of spiralling costs for minimum results; 'there is no way left' but to attack Louis XIV 'in his own country with a force sufficient. The only way is to land an army upon him.'[1]

William had toyed with the idea of a landing on the French coast in the depression of 1689, as a possible means of saving Ireland, but he had rapidly lost interest. Certainly, in the early years of the war it was difficult to support a purely naval war with any conviction. Bantry Bay and Beachy Head did not inspire confidence and although Russell's success at La Hogue restored some credibility to the Royal Navy, there was still the debacle of the Smyrna convoy to weather in 1693. The Brest expedition of 1694 may well have been an attempt to atone for the loss of the Dutch Smyrna fleet in the previous year.[2] The whole ethos of the English strategy of descents was summed up by Admiral Lord Berkeley on 2 July 1696 in a letter to Lord Shrewsbury.

We hope by appearing in the Bay [Bertheaume Bay, near Brest] with the whole fleet, to alarm the enemy so much as not only to make them raise their rear-ban [arrière-ban], but to march them to and again, which will injure much the country now the corn is upon the ground, for the horses must have forage. Besides, it may hinder them from increasing their forces in Flanders.[3]

There was one area of France where a descent might have produced all the expected prizes, the Cevennes. Miremont wrote a memorandum to William III on 25 May 1689 urging that some army officers and a sum of money be sent to the Cevennes to help the numerous Huguenots in that region to foment a rising. Nothing came of his proposal yet when such a rising did occur in the Cevennes during the War of the Spanish

Succession, it proved to be a substantial drain upon French military and financial resources. A good opportunity to assist the main war effort at minimum cost was passed by to be replaced by expensive and utterly useless schemes dreamt up to satisfy political opinion in England and not strategic necessities abroad.[4]

By themselves, seventeenth century navies were blunt weapons.[5] Ship building and marine architecture, gunnery, tactics, and the short campaigning season all combined to render naval warfare indecisive and strategically limited. No naval action during the War of the Grand Alliance was properly exploited. The sole strategic intervention of any real significance by a navy was Edward Russell's expedition to the western Mediterranean in 1694 and 1695 which locked the French fleet into Toulon and did something to keep Savoy in the war and to restrain French operations in Catalonia. It must be wondered why the British placed so much money and faith in their navy. Partly, it emanated from the necessity of their island situation but mostly because the navy helped to guarantee the smooth running of trade. However, pure blue-water strategists made their prejudices more palatable to William and more effective in terms of the European land-theatre by devising descents, or joint naval and military raids on the French coast. Central to this thinking was the belief that the Huguenots would rise. Largely because so much of their intelligence about France came from Huguenot sources, the British believed that there were considerable numbers of Huguenots and nouveaux convertis in the coastal regions of France, all awaiting the catalyst of an invasion force. In fact, this was quite misguided. Most of the remaining Huguenots were concentrated in the Massif Central and towards the Swiss and Italian borders, although a few were gathered along the Channel and Atlantic coasts waiting for an opportunity to escape.

Louis XIV recognised the weakness of his long Atlantic and Channel coastline. As early as 1691, Pontchartrain had been given as his first priority the deployment of the fleet to defend French ports and the shoreline as there were no regular troops to spare from Flanders, Germany, or Savoy. Coastal defence had to be left in the hands of a few garrison companies consisting of poor quality soldiers, the militia, and the arrière ban. The best defence was for the French fleet to scare the English away from making any attempt but after the defeat off Cape La Hogue in 1692, that means of defence evaporated and the English Channel became temporarily clear for a major English operation with combined arms against a principal French port. The attempt,

supposedly against St Malo, failed through inefficiency and irresolution but that did not invalidate the strategy. In the following year,
the French navy recovered much of its strength and effectiveness and
proved that its teeth still bit by the destruction of the ill-guarded
Smyrna convoy but that proved to be the last French fleet operation of
the war. The harvest of 1693 failed disastrously and many of the
northern and central regions of France were faced with the prospects
of famine. The fragile French economy, which had been steadily
undermined by years of high war taxation, all but collapsed. In
addition to the human misery and the expense of the importation of
grain from the Baltic, French war priorities had to be revised; the
money no longer existed for an equal effort by both land and sea. As
the tax yields fell so the government had to retrench and it was the
navy which bore the brunt of the swingeing economies losing a quarter
of its budget. Just before the crisis struck with its full vigour, Louis
launched an all-out land offensive in an effort to force the confederates
to an early peace before the shortage of money and supplies wrecked
his war machine. It failed. Landen was an indecisive and phyrric
victory; the capture of Charleroi was not enough to oblige William to
sue for peace; and neither did the battle of Marsaglia, the capture of
Heidelberg, nor the small advance into Catalonia amount to mortal
blows to the confederate cause. This offensive was Louis's last throw
until the defection of Savoy from the Grand Alliance in 1696 allowed
him to concentrate overwhelming numbers of troops in Flanders for
the campaign of 1697 and drive the allies into a peace by threatening
Brussels. The English currency crisis of 1696 was another vital factor
in bringing the war to a conclusion in 1697. For the campaign of 1694,
Louis was on the defensive, fighting everywhere with reduced numbers
and equipment. Faced, for the first time, with equal rather than
superior numbers of men, William captured Huy and this marked the
turning-point in the war in the Low Countries, allowing the confederate leader to besiege and take Namur in the following year. The French
fleet was laid-up and naval strategy was altered to commerce raiding
and privateering, the 'guerre de course'. Harrassing and effective
though the privateers of Dunkirk and Calais became, their tactics
could not be decisive. Bart and Forbin chalked up some remarkable
successes in capturing and interrupting English and Dutch trade but
their efforts were only irritants and could not compensate for the lack
of a battle fleet in the English Channel. For the enthusiasts who
favoured descents on the French coast, the disappearance of the enemy
war fleet into a squadron based in the Mediterranean and small units

for the 'guerre de course' gave added validity and opportunity for the propagation of their schemes. Yet the French themselves had demonstrated the weakness of such a strategy. After their victory off Beachy Head in 1690 which gave them unchallenged command of the Channel for the better part of two months, they only managed to burn parts of the village of Teignmouth. To make any effective showing on the French coast sufficient to draw in and distract significant numbers of French regulars from Flanders meant landing a large army and supporting it from the sea. If descents were to make any strategic sense then they had to ensure that the French were obliged to draw men from their field armies in Flanders, Germany, Italy, and Spain in order to defend their coastline against damaging raids.

The whole coast of France is alarmed with our fleet's being at sea, and as I am informed are removing from St Malo and other places their more considerable goods. But barely to burn a French Teignmouth is too mean a project for such a fleet, and that, you know, the king scorned to do.[6]

The Marquis of Carmarthen expressed support from a descent on the French coast in 1691, using the troops recently freed from operations in Ireland by the conclusion of the Treaty of Limerick. He gave as his reasons the standard response about obliging the French to withdraw some troops from their armies in the Low Countries to protect their coasts, but he also laid great stress on the view that parliament would appreciate such a strategy as they were tired of paying for large armies in Flanders which appeared to do nothing except lose ground to the French. The advice of the Duke of Leinster was sought and he and some other general officers suggested a landing near Bordeaux at the estuary of the Gironde, largely on the grounds that the now redundant forces in Ireland could sail there directly without having to come into England. This was not a reasoned argument but the application of Parkinson's Law of Armies: the number of operations expands to occupy the troops available. To have landed at the mouth of the Gironde would have achieved nothing more than the French immolation of Teignmouth and all at vast expense and some risk to the fleet. As an alternative, Leinster thought that a descent into Normandy with 10,000 foot and 2,500 horse to burn and lay waste the countryside might succeed in diverting some French soldiers from Flanders. Earlier in the year, a raid on Dunkirk to destroy the port facilities had come under scrutiny but had been rejected on the technical grounds that fireships would have been unable to put the twin piers which guarded the harbour entrance out of action.[7] All of these schemes and suggestions were based upon an unhealthy and false premise. To an extent the strategy of descents had a long tradition which stretched back into the previous century. Drake's raid on Cadiz stuck in the contemporary mind, as did Charles I's expedition against the Isle de Rhé. These attacks had allowed England to become involved in continental wars at minimal expense and, it must be admitted, with minimal effectiveness. However, the examples to which nearly all soldiers and politicians instinctively referred during the War of the Grand Alliance had occurred in the reign of James II. In 1685, the Duke of Monmouth had successfully invaded England through Lyme Regis and in 1688, William of Orange had landed 14,000 infantry and cavalry on an open beach in Torbay in early November, had marched on London, overthrown a king and seized a kingdom almost without a hitch or a hiccup. Nearly all the soldiers and sailors who fought for William III had been involved in that campaign on one side or the other and had witnessed how very easy it had proved to undertake amphibious operations. If William had achieved all this in November what could not be accomplished in the height of summer? What everyone conveniently forgot was that William's first sailing had very nearly sunk the entire expedition at the bottom of the North Sea and the amount of luck which he had enjoyed during his second attempt would have kept the entire population of London happy for a hundred lifetimes. William's enormous gamble, because of its ultimate victory, was rapidly translated in the public mind into a strategic and political master-stroke. It was, but that did not bear the corollary that every other amphibious operation would automatically be a walk-over. The idea that all one had to do in order to conduct a combined operation was to place a few soldiers in a ship, cross the Channel, put them into rowing boats and then run up the beach, seems to have imbued even the most sensible military minds in England. Neither the St Malo expedition of 1692 nor the descent on Brest in 1694 was properly planned. No one had the faintest clue as to how the soldiers were actually to be landed and even less idea of what they were supposed to do once they had reached the shore. Supply, evacuation, and the horrible possibility that the landings might be opposed in force, were simply ignored. The descent operations of the 1690s were poorly conceived and ill-prepared and were entered into with the spirit that 'it will be alright on the night' because everything had worked to perfection in 1688. The descents did not deserve to be successful. Descents were political operations of war and showed all the symptoms of their political origins at every stage in their growth, including the conduct of the military aspects. Descents were invented to prove a political point but they only succeeded in proving that William had been right all along in treating them with the height of suspicion.

Once faced with the increasing political strength of the descent lobby in the House of Commons, William had to pay reluctant lip service to the idea. Even though he would have liked every available man in Flanders, he tried to make the best of the situation by making sure that the descents were organised in combination with operations in Flanders and, if possible, to their advantage. The descent of 1692 was devised against the background of the grinding siege of Namur by the French which was a relatively close-run affair. If Leinster had been able to launch a significant raid on the French coast and diverted some troops from the Duke of Luxembourg's covering army in Flanders, then William may possibly have been able to force the battle which was his sole hope of saving Namur. There was the added possibility that if the descent had been made at the appointed time and not two months late, then Louis may have been so worried about the security of his ports and coasts in the aftermath of the defeat off Cape La Hogue that he would not have felt strong enough to have attempted Namur in the first place. All of this helps to explain why William was so angry at the repeated delays which dogged the organisation of the 1692 descent. Instructions were given to the Duke of Leinster in May telling him to assemble the troops freed from Ireland and then sail for France with the intention of landing as far as possible from the known concentrations of French troops. Apart from that vague order, he was to capture a town or a fort or simply to subsist as long as possible in France without being cut-off and without undertaking any rash offensives. In other words, Leinster was to be a nuisance, a thorn in the French side.[8] As William well knew, the chances of Leinster making a significant difference to the troop balance in Flanders was slight; the only real hope of lessening French pressure in Flanders was if Prince Eugene of Savoy with the Imperial army acted offensively in northern Italy.[9] Endless hold-ups and administrative muddles prevented the descent from being launched in May. The bomb-vessels were late in being fitted-out, insufficient transport ships were available to move the troops from Ireland, when they did sail the men were landed in Bristol and Milford Haven rather than Portsmouth or Plymouth. Then the beer supplies failed. By 16 June 1692, William had lost faith in the enterprise and told Portland that he had come down firmly in favour of a Flanders-based strategy for 1692 and he ordered five cavalry regiments to be released from Leinster's corps and shipped to Willemstadt.

To add insult to injury, William instructed some of Leinster's transports to convey these troops across the North Sea. Four days later,
probably having reached his decision at a meeting with Portland, the
Earl of Nottingham received William's letter which stated that Leinster's original instructions were no longer appropriate and that only a
limited action against Brest or St Malo should now be attempted. By
28 June, Leinster possessed firm orders to bombard St Malo[10] only to
be followed by another month of delay until the whole sad business
was called off.[11] Descents do not seem to have figured in William's
planning conferences which preceded the majority of his campaigns in
Flanders. The whole philosophy rested upon the twin notions that it
was better to do something than nothing and that any landings would
be unopposed. The latter point was vital. Seventeenth century linear
tactics were particularly ill-suited to making landings on open beaches
in the face of opposition as the infantry had to debuss, form-up, dress
its ranks, and advance in line. Foot soldiers were not trained in
individual fire and movement. To disembark from open boats and get
into line required flat beaches, no cliffs, no marshes, and, above all
else, a complete absence of harassing fire.

Brest was only a minor fishing village in 1660, but it possessed
enormous natural advantages as a future naval base. It had one of the
finest deep-water harbours in northern Europe, complete with shel-
tered flanking anchorages. In addition, it was close to the English
Channel and in an ideal position to threaten the major trade routes of
both the English and the Dutch. Colbert developed Marseilles as the
French galley base, Toulon for the Mediterranean fleet, and Rochefort
and Brest for the Channel and Atlantic squadrons. To begin with,
Rochefort was the favoured site but it was soon found to be too far up
the River Charente and too distant from the English Channel. After
1674, all attention was turned to the development of Brest. The
dockyards had the capacity to handle thirty men-of-war in 1670, but
this had increased to sixty in 1694, the majority of the French battle
fleet. There was just one major disadvantage in Brest's geographical
location which partially negated its strategic value. To leave Brest,
ships had to come out on an easterly wind but that same wind brought
English vessels down the Channel towards Ushant. The French then
had to wait for a westerly breeze before they could enter the Channel
itself and although a wind from this direction put the French to the
windward of the British, the latter were likely to be close enough to the
French to limit their freedom of manoeuvre.[12] Brest was always a
probable target for English raids, and three frigates were damaged by

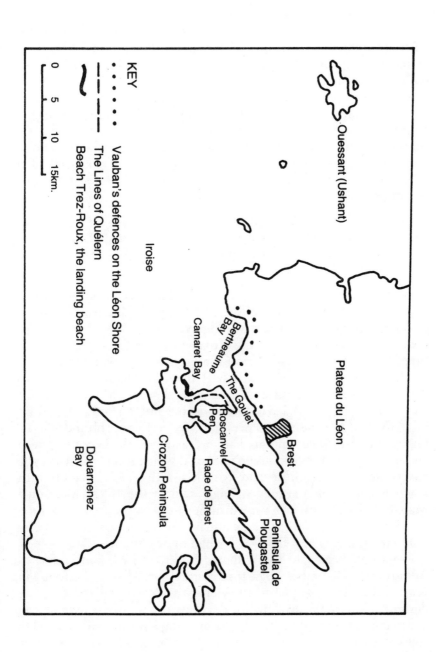

KEY

• • • • • Vauban's defences on the Léon Shore

– – – The Lines of Quélern

—— Beach Trez-Roux, the landing beach

0   5   10   15km.

Ouessant (Ushant)

Iroise

Plateau du Léon

Bertheaume Bay

Camaret Bay

The Goulet

Roscanvel Pen

Brest

Peninsula de Plougastel

Rade de Brest

Crozon Peninsula

Douarnenez Bay

allied warships in Camaret Bay in July 1691. The emphasis of British naval officers at this time was on attacking Brest with the object of putting the ships or the dockyards, or both, out of action. The concept of blockading Brest, which was to become standard British naval policy by the middle of the eighteenth century, was vetoed by Edward Russell who was scared of losing his ships on a lee shore. However, after the failure of the Brest expedition in 1694, Russell began to realise the tactical advantages in a blockade, even though he could not suppress all his concerns about being exposed to the Atlantic weather and blown onto Ushant and Cape Finisterre. Russell wrote to the Earl of Shrewsbury on 15 December 1696, stating that the ideal method of preventing a French invasion of England was to have,

a squadron of ships sent to cruise off the French coast, and off Brest. For my own part I dread their being disabled by storm, and England left naked, and if they should not go, and the French should land, I do not know who can answer for their lying at Spithead.

This, though, was in the future, and in 1694 naval strategists favoured physical attacks on Brest itself.[13] Obviously, any destruction which could be wrought upon Brest would have been of great benefit to the British and the Dutch, but the Royal navy had other reasons for supporting a major assault upon the French base. The navy cost as much to run as the army and, apart from La Hogue in 1692, had nothing to show for it. Indeed, the abortive descent on St Malo in 1692 and the bungling which led to the loss of the Smyrna fleet in Lagos Bay in 1693, had left the navy's prestige at a very low ebb indeed. The English mercantile community had lost heavily in the Lagos Bay fiasco and it was the London commercial world which raised the money for government loans. Brest had to succeed in 1694. Significantly, whereas Russell had argued strongly against the 1692 attack on St Malo because 10,000 men were insufficient, he supported the planned attack on Brest two years later, a much tougher proposition, with just 7,000 troops. He knew that a show had to be put on.[14]

Plans had been laid by William III, his inner cabinet, and the Admiralty in December 1692 for an attack on Brest in the following year as the logical sequel to the victory at La Hogue and the failed descent on St Malo. In April, the troops for the Brest assault were ordered into camps along the coasts of Hampshire and Sussex and the transport commissioners had spent £33,000 on various preparations by the end of the month. At this point, the scheme was abandoned because the bulk of the navy was needed to escort the Smyrna fleet into the Mediterranean.[15] The plans, though, had been roughly drafted and when the pressures for a renewal of the Brest scheme began again in the spring of 1694, it was merely a matter of blowing the dust off the existing blueprints. The drive to renew the Brest operation came from the whigs and senior army officers of a whiggish persuasion. John, Lord Cutts, had long been an advocate of an armed diversion on the French coast, and the Earl of Macclesfield and Lieutenant-Colonel Goodwin Wharton were also strongly in favour. Thomas Talmash, the eventual commander of the land forces engaged on the expedition, had been one of the first to broach the subject of an assault on Brest as a means of reducing the attacks on English shipping in the western approaches and in the Bay of Biscay. Thomas Erle, Richard Coote, Samuel Venner, and Henry Rowe, all colonels whose battalions took part in the Brest expedition, were whiggish in their politics. It made perfect sense for the whigs to support a raid on Brest as they had close connections with the mercantile and moneyed interests in the City of London, and William was content to offer the scheme his blessing both to placate the London commercial interest groups after Lagos Bay and to throw a crumb of compensation to the country elements in parliament. His approval of the Brest excursion also marked his acceptance that the days of trying to govern with a mixed and balanced administration had come to an end; from now on, William had to work in co-operation with the whigs if he was to secure sufficient funding for his war in Europe. The Brest expedition was a political hybrid. It was a compromise between blue-water strategy, supported by the tories and the country interests in parliament, and the commitment to a full-scale war in the Low Countries, which was the preferred strategy of the whigs and the king. There were more sinister and partial interests at work. The navy badly needed to improve its public image and the senior army officers had an axe to grind. A number of colonels and generals were still smarting from William's preference for Dutchmen and Germans. What the British officers needed was a British project commanded by British senior officers to show William what they could do. Brest was the perfect solution. There was not to be a Dutch senior officer involved, and only the Marquis de Rade, a rough, tough, and abrasive Huguenot and two Huguenot engineering officers spoiled the overall effect. Brest was to be the showpiece of the abilities of the British officers corps and demonstrate publicly how well they could manage without the cheese, herring, and sauerkraut eaters. To lead them in this massive public relations and propaganda coup came the doyen of the British army, Lieutenant-General Thomas Talmash.[16]

Born in 1651, the son of Elizabeth Murray, Countess of Dysart and later Duchess of Lauderdale, and of her first husband, Sir Lionel Tollemache, Thomas Talmash was destined for distinction but he was only a second son and not the first. With just under £1,000 from his father's will, he purchased a captaincy in the Coldstream Guards in 1678 but he was deprived of his place following a duel in 1682 with Captain John Parker, the future Jacobite plotter. Talmash's known whiggery would not have been in his favour in 1682. After a short spell in Paris, he travelled to Tangier and served as a volunteer until the evacuation in 1684. He did not have to wait long for another employment and James II commissioned him as lieutenant-colonel of the Royal Fusiliers in 1685 but he resigned in April 1686 'as soon as he saw that the army was to be used to set up an arbitrary power'. Crossing the North Sea to the United Provinces, he was accepted into the Anglo-Dutch Brigade achieving a colonelcy in March 1688. During 1688, Talmash worked closely with the whiggish conspirators against James II and he was rewarded by William III for his support and constancy with the colonelcy of the Coldstream Guards in 1689. After service in Ireland and Flanders, Talmash was promoted to major-general and then to lieutenant-general in 1692, distinguishing himself in the withdrawal of the infantry after the defeat at Landen in 1693. Talmash was packing his bags ready to return to Flanders in April 1694, when he was ordered to remain in England and assume command of the land forces assembling for the raid on Brest.[17] Talmash had been one of the leaders of the movement against the foreign general officers in 1691 and 1692 and it was ironic that his elevation to lieutenant-general in 1692 had been to replace that other outspoken critic of the Dutch generals, the Earl of Marlborough. Talmash, though, had been more diplomatic than Marlborough and was less nakedly ambitious and avaricious. Above all else, William knew Talmash as an old trustee from the Anglo-Dutch Brigade and his politics were consistently whig and pro-Orange. Perhaps he was a better soldier than Marlborough – Ginckel thought highly of him – although his performance at Brest makes this judgement rather questionable. Perhaps there was a rivalry between Talmash and Marlborough for the premier position in the British army occasioned by their changes of fortune in 1692. Perhaps Marlborough thought that Talmash was wearing the uniform that rightly belonged to him. Certainly there was something about Talmash's involvement with the Brest expedition which made Marlborough act in a most peculiar fashion.

Just as the whigs supported the Brest scheme with the help of the senior army officers and the navy, so there were doubters. Sidney, Lord Godolphin, was antagonistic to the proposals largely on the grounds of expense. He thought that little or nothing would be achieved, even if it was superficially successful, and the whole enterprise was tantamount to pouring good money down the drain. Edward Russell, who was to command-in-chief the battle fleet in 1694, was more doubtful than optimstic even though he expressed general support in public. On 3 May 1694, he confided to Shrewsbury that the proposed splitting of the fleet to provide a squadron to attack Brest and a squadron to proceed into the Mediterranean to assist in the defence of Catalonia and to protect Anglo-Dutch trade through the Straits of Gibraltar, would fatally weaken both operations. He also considered that the number of soldiers was too small to tackle a town like Brest and, as if this catalogue of uncertainties was not enough to emanate from the pen of the senior officer involved, it would take a long time to launch the Brest expedition as the store ships, transports, and bomb vessels were still in the Thames estuary and not at Spithead. Shrewsbury replied to Russell's epistle in equally gloomy style. Both operations, launched simultaneously, were too much, he agreed, but orders were orders. If Russell came before Brest and the French fleet was still in harbour, then Russell was to 'dally' for a while to see if he could do anything positive against the enemy shipping but after a respectable interval he was to proceed to the Mediterranean in order to execute his major task which was to prevent Marshal Noailles's drive along the Catalonian coast from reaching Barcelona. However, if the Brest squadron had already flown south by the time of Russell's arrival, then he was to leave Lord Berkeley with his squadron to tackle Brest and take the main battle squadron post haste to the south and the Spanish coast. The inference behind Shrewsbury's orders to Russell was that the commitment of the majority of the fleet to the Mediterranean was the priority and that Brest was a mere sideshow in stategic terms. Four days later, Shrewsbury repeated his arguments before the privy council, and on 19 May Russell received a direct order from William, via Shrewsbury, to take the bulk of the battle fleet straight to the Mediterranean to interrupt the French who were advancing through Catalonia with the support of their Toulon squadron. Palmos was in danger and Barcelona looked to be the next target. Russell, William, Shrewsbury, and Berkeley were all champing at the bit by 22 May, fearful lest more delays jeopardise both sections of the operation. The blame lay at the door of 'that driveller, the general of the

Ordnance', otherwise known as Lord Sydney, for it was his bomb vessels and store ships which were keeping everyone waiting. Russell felt certain that the French would have used the interval to reinforce Brest and he informed Sir John Trenchard, the secretary of state, that it was essential for Talmash to receive flexible orders to enable him to attack another port if Brest proved to be too strong. So great an investment in time, money, resources, politics, and reputations had been made in the project that something worthwhile had to be achieved.[18]

There remains the remote possibility that the decision to attack Brest in 1694 can be defended as sound strategy. Unfortunately, the case is not strong. The transfer of the main allied fleet from home to Mediterranean waters in 1694 left the English Channel and the southern North Sea but weakly defended against privateers from Dunkirk and Calais and the remnants of the French battle fleet in Brest. Although it is now clear that the campaign of 1693 was the last to be conducted by a full-strength French navy, the change of French naval strategy from fleet action to the 'guerre de course' which commenced in the spring of 1694 was only partially appreciated in England at the time. French battleships in Brest continued to be an imagined danger. In these circumstances, the concept of dividing the fleet in 1694 and sending a portion to protect the home waters and the communications of the fleet sailing towards Spain by raiding Brest, can be represented as sound tactics. This argument breaks down on a number of details. In the first place, the plan for the attack on Brest in 1694 was a replica of the design for 1693 when no commitment to the Mediterranean was envisaged, and it was principally an army rather than a naval operation. Secondly, Talmash's orders were exceptionally vague about what he was to attempt before Brest: to destroy the dockyards, to sink ships, or make a bridgehead in order to attract French regulars from other theatres? Thirdly, hardly anyone involved with the expedition expected to find any French ships in Brest. Given the endless delays, all the senior commanders felt certain that the squadron in Brest would already have sailed to the Mediterranean to link-up with the Toulon ships.

Louis XIV knew all about the plans to attack Brest long before Talmash tried to come ashore on 8 June. Lord Macaulay accused the Earl of Marlborough of treason in telling the French monarch that an attack was to be made on Brest and in giving fairly precise details of the timing and probable strength.

It is only today I have learned the news I now write to you; which is, that the bomb-ketches and the twelve regiments encamped at Portsmouth, with the two regiments of marines, all commanded by Talmash, are destined for burning the harbour of Brest, and destroying all the men-of-war which are there. This will be a great advantage to England.

Since this letter was written, John Paget, Arthur Parnell, Godfrey Davies, E. M. Lloyd, Sir Winston Churchill, and David Chandler have debated the pros and cons, with each version depending upon the author's perceived notion of Marlborough's character. Those trying to exonerate their hero have not enjoyed an easy task. Although the manuscript evidence rests upon a copy of Marlborough's letter transcribed by Thomas Carte, which now resides amongst the Carte Papers in the Bodleian Library, the case against Marlborough is circumstantially strong. On 1 May 1694, Louis XIV wrote to Vauban at St Malo, where he was inspecting and improving the fortifications, summoning him to Brest because he had just received intelligence of a prospective attack on that port by 7,000 men. Louis's information emanated from David Floyd, or Lloyd, an agent of the Earl of Middleton who operated in England, and had come into Louis's hands on 1 May. This communication prompted Louis's immediate missive to Vauban in St Malo. Marlborough's letter announcing the imminence of the Brest expedition was not forwarded to France until 3 May by Colonel Edward Sackville. Marlborough's defenders have therefore been able to convince themselves that it was not his letter which gave the game away; Marlborough had only contacted St Germains after he already knew that Louis had received identical information from another source, possibly Lord Godolphin. By this line of argument, Marlborough was not technically a traitor but merely an extremely astute politician who took advantage of a unique occasion to keep his image shining brightly before the exiled king. Marlborough's crime was not the perpetration but the corroboration of treason. To understate the case grossly, this is an exceptionally flimsy defence and although it may possess an element of legal nicety it has no moral substance whatever. The honour of a soldier is entirely absent.

More solid reasoning is called for. The letter from Marlborough to Louis was discovered in a collection known as the Nairne Papers, named after David Nairne, a clerk to and a relative of the Earl of Middleton. Perhaps they were all forged. Perhaps Sir James Macpherson, the eighteenth century antiquary who published them, fabricated many of the key documents in the collection. Had not Macpherson invented the poems of Ossian? This seems a more realistic approach for those who wish to protect Marlborough's reputation but it fails to provide a satisfactory or conclusive solution.[19] In the long run it does not matter unduly except to students of Marlborough's character and motives. Was he playing a game of gigantic double bluff? Suspecting that the French already knew about the coming of Talmash's force, did he give away the information in order to draw French soldiers into Brest in the hope that the British general would then act upon his discretionary orders and assault another, undefended target? Such a convoluted explanation assumes an impossibly high level of sophistication. It seems more likely that Marlborough spilled the beans about Brest in order to effect the downfall of his rival, Talmash. It may not be insignificant that Marlborough approached William through the good offices of Shrewsbury immediately after Talmash's demise, offering his services. To be fair, Marlborough was only one of many English politicians who were in contact with St Germains for the purposes of political reinsurance, although his sin was a great deal more harmful than most of the bland and non-committal letters which reached the desk of James II. Not that it mattered. English political circles were riddled with Jacobite spies and agents making security an impossible goal. Sir Henry Goodricke had announced in the House of Commons on 28 November 1691 that the king had resolved to make a descent on the French coast in the following year, which gave Louis plenty of warning. Similarly, hard and fairly accurate rumours of a raid on the shores of France and its probable destination were circulating in English newsletters in April and May 1694. Louis XIV would have been the owner of an appalling intelligence service if he had not discovered all the details of the Brest expedition well before it set sail from England. One correspondent wrote to William that, in his view, the delays had been so great and the security so bad that the whole expedition ought to be cancelled and Berkeley's squadron redeployed to attack the mole at Dunkirk.[20]

The inner harbour and the town and dockyards of Brest were separated from the outer anchorages in Camaret Bay by a narrow strait, the Goulet. In the very centre of this passage jutted three large rocks, which were submerged only at spring tides. The Goulet could be swept by fire from the fifty cannon in the 'great fort' on the north, or Léon shore, and by the ten guns in the 'little fort' on the southern shore at the head of the Roscanvel peninsula.[21] Brest itself was fortified in the modern style and the whole of the inner harbour was virtually impervious to naval assault. A later commentator was of the opinion that the Goulet could only be forced at night with the benefit of total surprise by troops paddling through in flat-bottomed boats.[22] Following Leinster's abortive raid on St Malo in 1692, Louis XIV had appointed Sebastien le Prestre de Vauban, marshal of France and the world expert on all matters to do with fortification and fixed defences, to inspect the coastal protections of Brittany and Normandy as far south as the mouth of the Loire. The necessary work of repairing earthworks and building fortified camps was well under way when Louis informed Vauban on 4 April 1694 that the British intended to stage a large-scale attack on Brest. Vauban set to work with his customary skill and energy. By the beginning of May, ninety mortars and three hundred additional cannon had been mounted, four thousand regular infantry and a regiment of dragoons had been moved into Brest, and Vauban was converting sailors into temporary soldiers and drilling the local militia and arrière ban into a semblance of martial efficiency. Vauban constructed his new defences in exactly the right positions, no doubt benefiting from information derived from Jacobite agents in England but, more probably, from using his own experience and eye for the ground. As well as digging trenches along the western fringes of the Roscanvel peninsula and reinforcing the batteries guarding the vital Goulet, Vauban erected a stone 'tower fortress' to cover the beaches along the southern edge of Camaret Bay and constructed a double line of trenches and parapets in support. There was the lesser possibility that the British would try to land in Bertheaume Bay, so Vauban erected forts and blockhouses between Cape St Mathieu and Minou Point. However, the most likely objective for the allied attack was bound to be the Roscanvel peninsula as it dominated the Goulet and the whole inner harbour of Brest. Possession of this neck of land would have allowed the British to set up cannon and mortars to bombard the ships, the dockyards, and the town itself, as well as enabling them to pass vessels through the Goulet. The classical method of capturing a salient, whether geographical or man-made, was to cut-off its base; the British would try to land at the south-western edge of the base of the Roscanvel peninsula and this was where Vauban had concentrated his strongest defences, the 'Lines of Quélern'.[23]

Intelligence of the French preparations was not lacking in England. Intimation that the French would not be as strong at sea as they had been in 1693 was received as early as 2 February 1694. The lords of the Admiralty passed on the fruits of their interrogation of a captured French master mariner to Sir John Trenchard on 30 March: the French army was in readiness along the Channel coast and twenty-four large men-of-war were in Brest harbour. On 5 April, the Duke of Württemberg interviewed two Danish officers who had recently been released by the French having spent the winter in Paris. They corroborated the previous intelligence that the French would be weak at sea in 1694 putting out no more than forty men-of-war, twenty-four of which were to serve in the Mediterranean leaving the rest to operate as cruisers against trade. They also said that the French had 14,000 men around their northern and western coasts and that they seemed very unconcerned about the danger of a descent. Throughout April, information came in that the ships in Brest were preparing for sea, and on 7 May they sailed south to join with the Toulon squadron in order to operate in conjunction with the army of Marshal Noailles to capture Rosas, Palmos, and Barcelona. Whatever else the Brest expedition was intended to do, it was not designed to bottle-up the French Channel squadron in the inner harbour and destroy it by fire and gunshot. It had departed for the south a full month before Talmash landed on the sandy beaches of Camaret Bay. Then, on 18 May, the ultimate stupidity was committed. Three English cruisers put into Camaret Bay and attacked a small convoy of French merchantmen which was en route for St Malo. This incident put the French on their guard, and Vauban thought that the English vessels had put into Camaret Bay in order to reconnoitre possible landing beaches. Sir John Trenchard passed this information to Edward Russell on 28 May, in a letter which should have reached him before the fleet sailed. For the final three weeks before the landing, Vauban redoubled his efforts to put Brest into the best posture for defence. All of this was known and understood in England, to the extent that the *London Gazette* published 'Letters from Brest' on 4 June telling of the new trenches and batteries, of the 400 cannon, and of the presence of between 8,000 and 9,000 regulars in the immediate area.[24] In spite of all this, no one saw fit to alter their plans or even to suggest amendments. Political, economic, and personal pressures were so great that the show had to go on regardless of good sense and in the face of all the available intelligence. There is just the faint possibility that the British had spies inside Brest and that their information on Brest's defences and the state of the garrison lulled them into a malaise of false security.[25]

Ten battalions assembled on Portsdown Hill near Portsmouth at the beginning of May 1694, and settled into a camp of 'French tents'. Especially for the Brest expedition, the infantry were armed solely with flintlock muskets and bayonets, leaving their pikes behind.[26] The force amounted to just 6,000 men. Talmash was in overall command with John, Lord Cutts and the Earl of Macclesfield as major-generals. Colonel François de la Motte, the Huguenot chief engineer in Ireland, and Sir Martin Beckman, the colonel of the train of artillery for sea service, represented the technical branches. John, Lord Berkeley, commanded the naval squadron. On 11 May, Sir Cloudisley Shovell was ordered to embark Talmash's men at Spithead whilst the lieutenant-general was instructed to 'advise with Admiral Russell how best to annoy the enemy'. Clearly, at this early stage, the operations were to be kept as flexible as possible. Most of the soldiers were taken aboard the men-of-war with the remainder travelling on the victualling ships which had to serve as temporary transports. According to Talmash, the expedition should have departed with Shovell's squadron on 10 May to link-up with Russell's fleet in Torbay before sailing south. Instead there was a series of delays. First the bomb vessels failed to arrive and then the provision and victualling ships fell behind schedule. In the end, Talmash put his men on board ship on 22 May without adequate provisions and with only five out of the promised sixteen bomb-ketches actually present with the squadron. To hurry things along, Russell brought his whole fleet back to St Helens from Torbay and, at last, on 31 May the entire fleet disappeared over the southern horizon, tiding down the Channel. Eight of the bomb-vessels had eventually materialised and joined-up with the expedition but the missing eight were not to come up until they met Berkeley's ships sailing back to Portsmouth after the failure of the attack on Brest.[27]

Thomas Talmash was in a curious state of mind. Just after arriving at Portsmouth to assume his command, he wrote to his brother, Lord Huntingtower.

Just upon leaving London I had the favour of your obliging letter. I did indeed all this winter believe I should not be in a condition to serve the campaign and with some other reasons I resolved to go live in the country the rest of my life, but my ill fortune will not let me alone and now I am engaged more than ever, I must say much against my will. I am commanded by the king to embark on the fleet with ten regiments of foot. I shall return from this service in a month and then go for Flanders, so that I am in a continual hurry this summer.[28]

Whilst waiting with his men on board the cramped men-of-war at Spithead, Talmash received a copy of the letter from Paris which was published in the *London Gazette* on 4 June,

giving an account of Monsieur Vauban being at Brest and raising several batteries about the shore expecting the coming of the English to invade that place and that several regiments, both of horse and foot, were daily marching towards Brest.

The General [Talmash], understanding how the posture of affairs stood, writ to court his intention to have landed in some other places and so to have done more mischief than he apprehended he could do against Brest, which would also have diverted the French forces. But, having no answer, could not do the same.[29]

This passage is taken from Talmash's own account of the expedition, probably written at his dictation by one of his aides-de-camp when the general was lying ill on board ship or at Plymouth, shortly before his death. It is not written in Talmash's own hand and could have been composed on his behalf after his death by a close associate who had been present at Brest. Whatever its origin, it attempts to portray Talmash's conduct in the best possible light.

Detailed orders for Lord Berkeley were not issued until 29 May. Berkeley was to take his squadron of three first-rates, four second-rates, twelve third-rates, one fourth-rate, two fifth-rates, ten fireships, three hospital ships, three brigantines, and two bomb-vessels towards Brest and then hold a council-of-war of the senior army and navy officers to review the situation and see where the soldiers could best be landed to do the maximum damage to the French. The council-of-war was entrusted with the decision of how the ships could assist the soldiers and also to arrange the 'proper time' for the ships to enter Brest Water 'to render them the most serviceable on the intended design against that place, and the enemy's ships there'. When the army had achieved all that was possible before Brest, Berkeley was instructed to hold a further council-of-war to see if raids could be made against other coastal targets. Only when the council-of-war had decided that nothing else could be achieved was Berkeley to sail for England. It was stressed in his orders that Berkeley was to consult his council-of-war at all times and whenever there was any uncertainty.[30] No tactical flexibility was granted either to Talmash or to Berkeley in these final orders. After the debacle, Trenchard tried to persuade Berkeley that the spirit of the orders had been to allow Talmash to raid some other port if Brest proved impossible to assault, but the orders did not say or imply this.[31] The instructions of 29 May tied Berkeley and Talmash to attempting Brest by means of a military landing. Only if this failed were the senior officers permitted to consider alternative objectives. In spite of all the intelligence about Vauban's defences and the garrison of French regulars, despite the knowledge that the French knew Talmash's destination, the expedition was given no option but to attack. This inflexibility reflected the prestige and reputation which the expedition carried. It could not fail. Another aborted descent and another year without a military success was unthinkable for the whigs. Besides, Talmash ought to pull it off, after all he was supposed to be England's premier soldier.

Dogged by contrary winds, the fleet was still pottering around Dartmouth Bay on 3 June. Four days earlier, on 31 May, a grand council-of-war had been held on board *HMS Britannia*, Russell's flagship, with the admiral in the chair. The meeting resolved to send Berkeley to Camaret Bay in order to disembark the soldiers on the beaches. After this, the Roscanvel peninsula was to be captured and the fleet passed through the Goulet into Brest Water in order to wreak as much havoc as possible amongst the French shipping and the dockyards. On 5 June, Berkeley and Russell parted company and on the following day the Brest squadron weathered Ushant. Anxious to abide by his orders, Berkeley summoned another council-of-war as his ships were rounding Cape Finisterre and it was agreed to send the *Monk* and a Dutch frigate to batter Vauban's tower fort whilst the troops rowed ashore and that each landing boat was to be commanded by a naval lieutenant. Six hundred grenadiers, drawn from all ten battalions, constituted the first wave, with a captain and fifty grenadiers to form an advanced guard and conduct a rapid reconnaissance of the beaches before signalling the main force of grenadiers to land. Lord Cutts recorded his opinion that the first wave should not land if the vanguard party of fifty men discovered French regulars manning the Lines of Quélern.[32] Talmash's confidence must have sunk on 5 June when a French prize was brought into Berkeley's squadron and its crew were interrogated. He heard again the stories of Vauban and the trenches and batteries and thousands of regulars, all waiting for the British.[33] At two o'clock in the afternoon on 7 June, the ships sailed into Camaret Bay and anchored. No sooner had they lost way than mortar batteries opened up from the Roscanvel peninsula, the shore of Bertheaume Bay and the southern beaches of Camaret Bay and although the vessels were beyond effective range, the French mortars were reaching two and a half miles out to sea and there was always the risk that a lucky shot might sink a capital ship. More ominously, the number of French batteries meant that the larger men-of-war would not be able to close with the shore to support the landings and that the soldiers would have to row for a considerable distance across French fields of fire. During the night, patrols of longboats and brigantines circled the silent ships forcing back small enemy raiding parties.

In the face of this hostile reception, Talmash, in company with the Marquis of Carmarthen and Colonel de la Motte, conducted a reconnaissance of the landing beach late on the afternoon of 7 June from a galley. Perhaps the fire from the French batteries prevented Talmash from sailing close enough to the shoreline or perhaps Vauban had concealed the Lines of Quélern in masterly fashion, but Talmash informed a council-of-war at four o'clock on the morning of 8 June that there was nothing to oppose the landing except for the tower fort to the western side of the landing beach. It could have been that Talmash had been blinded by wishful thinking when making his reconnaissance as his optimistic assessment was not shared by some of his senior officers. Carmarthen, who had accompanied the general in the reconnaissance galley, reported, admittedly after the event, that the French seemed well prepared with numbers of regulars obviously present. He also thought Camaret Fort, Vauban's tower fort enfilading the beach, very strong and recommended bombarding it with two sixty-gun ships in addition to sending more frigates to provide fire support for the landings. The second part of his advice was heeded but not the first, and instead of being occupied with the broadsides from one hundred cannon, the fort was to be faced with mere frigates freeing the majority of its guns to fire down the flank of the landing beaches from end-to-end. The morning of 8 June was foggy, but the sea mist had lifted by seven o'clock and the signal was given for the soldiers to embark in the landing craft. Major-General, the Lord Cutts was placed in command of the nine companies of grenadiers which formed the vanguard, with Colonel Samuel Venner's battalion acting as the second wave, and Lieutenant-Colonel Thomas Hussey commanding Brigadier William Stewart's battalion in immediate support. By all accounts, the landing forces should have been arranged in a series of echeloned and mutually supporting waves but, largely because the boats had a long passage from ship to shore, as they followed the seven frigates of the Marquis of Carmarthen into Camaret Bay they lost formation and became thoroughly confused. There was also a long delay. The soldiers had been sitting in their cramped rowing boats for four hours before Carmarthen's frigates made their way into Camaret Bay at eleven o'clock, presenting the defenders with ample opportunity to make any last minute preparations. With the sun high in the firmament, the French gunners had an excellent view of the British and Dutch frigates which suffered many hits as they worked their way inshore. Eventually, Carmarthen managed to place two frigates opposite Camaret Fort and deployed the remaining five as floating, fixed batteries to pour fire onto the trenches along the landing beach. The frigates took a terrible pounding from the shore batteries and when the time came to withdraw they had to be towed clear by oared longboats as all the ships had lost their major rigging. One Dutch frigate, the *Wesel*, was sunk.

At midday, Talmash ordered in his landing forces. Cutts set off with his grenadiers but, as he neared the shore, a hail of musket and cannon fire swept around his boats. The landing beach, only 300 metres long, was protected by three batteries and three lines of trenches, with 150 musketeers positioned in flanking trenches to provide cross-fire. In addition, Camaret Fort was firing into the frigates, at the landing craft, and along the beach. Enthusiasm suddenly evaporated. Cutts loitered in the middle of the boats of his grenadier battalion and seemed thoroughly uncertain about whether to order his men to land or to fall back. He could not have been feeling very confident as he had advised the council-of-war not to land if regulars were discovered and French regulars manifestly were present, in considerable numbers. Seeing the irresolution of his point commander, Talmash had his own boat rowed forward and he called to Cutts, 'My lord, is this following of orders? Do you see how the boats are in disorder? Pray, my lord, let us land in as good order as we can.' At this stage of the proceedings, Cutts had not even ordered in the advance guard of fifty grenadiers and one captain to make a reconnaissance. In response to the firm order of his commanding officer, Cutts ordered a few of his men ashore, prudently remaining afloat himself, but Talmash, in an effort to set an example, landed. He waded through the shallows with Colonel de la Motte, Lieutenant-Colonel Jean de Montargier, and Captain Nathaniel Green, his aide-de-camp. Accompanied by just nine grenadiers, the four officers sprinted for the cover of some rocks thirty yards from the water-line and waited for more support to follow them in. Surprisingly, another 200 grenadiers came ashore with three captains in command. Talmash tried to organise them for a charge up the beach but Captain de Benoise with a company of French marines sallied from the trenches, sword in hand, and drove the faltering and confused grenadiers back to their boats. Even then, Talmash might have tried again to rally the men but Nathaniel Green spotted some French cavalry approaching the beach and persuaded Talmash to withdraw. This was easier said than done. Many of the landing craft were stranded on the shore as the landing had been made at the ebb tide and at least forty-five grenadiers meekly surrendered to the French whilst sitting uselessly at their oars, unable to pull away from the beach. As he retreated from the cover of the rocks to the water, Talmash was hit in the thigh by a musket ball and Montargier and Green carried him through the shallows to a boat which was aground and had been deserted by its crew. A longboat from Lord Berkeley's flagship was close at hand and for the princely sum of £5, its crew agreed to tow Talmash's craft off the sand. They were only just in time, for when they were six or eight boat-lengths from the shore the French horse arrived to complete the fiasco. From a safe distance out to sea, the Earl of Macclesfield took the responsibility for calling-off the assault and ordered all the landing boats back to the squadron.

General Talmash was carried to the *Dreadnought* where his wound was dressed by a surgeon. Half an hour later, Berkeley and his officers visited Talmash and conducted an impromptu council-of-war at which it was decided to return to Spithead. The unfortunate general was sent on ahead and arrived in Plymouth on 11 June where the local doctors were of the opinion that he would soon recover but gangrene had already set in and he died during the night of Tuesday 12 June. The expeditionary force had lost 300 men killed during the assault and the recriminations began immediately. The *London Gazette* reported the defeat in rather small print on the back of its single sheet and William III voiced his obvious annoyance to Shrewsbury.

I did not suppose they would have made the attempt without having well reconnoitred the situation of the enemy to receive them. Since they were long apprised of our intended attack and made active preparations for defence; for what was practicable two months ago, was no longer so at present.

The king still wanted a descent on the French coast as any diversion was better than none.[34] There had been a number of mistakes made. Talmash's reconnaissance had clearly been inadequate and he ought really to have reconnoitred in force before attempting a major landing, especially in view of the known French preparations. Morale amongst both the soldiers and the sailors was obviously not good. Talmash had been reluctant to accept the command in the first instance, knowing that it would gain him little if he was successful but would cost him dearly if he failed, and both his soldiers and his officers showed little stomach for the fight. Cutts had disobeyed orders in dallying off the beach and not leading his men into the attack. Maybe it was the only sensible thing to do in the circumstances but it was disobedience and no army can operate on that basis. The facts that the seamen had to be bribed to carry their wounded general off the beach and that a special reward was given to Carmarthen's sailors who had actually stayed on deck during the action speak volumes for the low ebb of confidence and morale. Tactical confusion had sent in long before the landing craft came under concentrated fire from the beaches but that was hardly surprising as there had been no training, no exercising, and no special drills. However, in the end, everything revolved around the question of whether or not Talmash had fixed or flexible orders. The instructions of 29 May were the guidelines under which the attack was made. Talmash may well have written to Trenchard asking for discretion and the secretary of state may then have approached the queen or the king for such an allowance of discretion to be given to the general, but Talmash received no written notification of this before the landing took place. Talmash cannot be blamed for obeying his orders. He can, and should, be made highly culpable for the inept manner in which those orders were executed.

Details were overlooked: the state of the tides, the fact that many of the landing boats had different draughts, and the perfunctory reconnaissance. All of these factors suggest that Talmash acted rashly and seemed to be in a fearful hurry to get the whole business over with so that he could return to the glory of Flanders or to his estates in England. Cutts's reservation about exercising caution if French regulars should be discovered was utterly disregarded and when the presence of large numbers of French troops was pointed out to Talmash he dismissed them as being mere militia and arrière ban, rubbish which trained and disciplined troops could easily overcome. Talmash seemed to think that the landings would be virtually unopposed apart from the cannon in Camaret Fort but these would be masked by Carmarthen's frigates. A brave man and a fine leader Talmash certainly was, but he was not cut out for independent command on this scale. His metier was that of a senior subordinate, an excellent man to have around in a crisis or in the midst of battle, but he was not intellectually very bright and lacked the mental capacity to balance all the different factors involved in making tactical decisions. Stated quite simply, he was not up to the job. When Jack Howe suggested to the House of Commons on 23 November 1694 that a member of the House had been sacrificed on an impossible mission, Cutts replied that it had not been the mission that had been impossible but the orders. This was not quite the truth. Even if Talmash's orders categorically instructed him to attack Brest, he did not have to land in Camaret Bay and certainly not at the very spot which the French had most heavily fortified, and he did not have to act so hastily or pay so little attention to vital details. Perhaps, what Talmash lacked above all else was a little imagination.[35]

Brest finished the strategy of descents for the remainder of the war. As the Marquis of Carmarthen, Major-General the Earl of Macclesfield, and Lieutenant-Colonel Goodwin Wharton paraded before the privy council to give their reports on 20 June, they were relating the story of the first and last descent which actually landed British troops on French soil during the entire war. Talmash's death provided an immediate and attractive scapegoat and Goodwin Wharton was only too happy to blame the failure of the scheme, which he had so ardently advocated earlier in the year, on the general's 'headstrong and ill management'.[36] This, however, was but cold comfort for so much had been staked on Brest. The entire country war strategy of attacking French trade and colonies had found its practical expression in the compromise of the Brest expedition; the ambitions and futures of both the Royal Navy and senior British army officers were tied up with Talmash and Berkeley; and the whigs needed Brest to assuage Lagos Bay and launch their ministry on a sound and illustrious footing. They failed because political operations do not, generally, make good operations of war. The *London Gazette* devoted as little space as it decently could to the defeat and the death of Talmash. No questions were asked in the House of Commons and the Lords only interested themselves in the administrative muddle which had delayed the sailing of the expedition by five weeks. Most interested parties found it best to forget and concentrate for the remainder of the war upon the one strategy which might actually produce results – the vigorous prosecution of the war in Europe. It was a bitter pill to have to swallow but there was some sugar. The French had been on the defensive in Flanders during 1694 and William had been able to capture Huy and Dixmuyde thus seizing the initiative from the French and that, in strategic terms and in relation to the overall allied war effort, was far more significant than the loss of 500 men and one small ship before the beach of Trez Rouz in Camaret Bay. Yet, in England, it marked the termination of the country emphasis on descents and assisted the concentration of national resources and attention upon the conflict in Flanders which was to bear considerable fruit in 1695.

Berkeley's squadron bombarded Dieppe later in 1694 and frightened the inhabitants of Le Havre, St Malo, and Cherbourg. In 1695 and 1696, abortive naval attempts were made to bombard the privateering bases of Calais and Dunkirk but these were not descents, merely attempts to control the ravages which the French privateers were making into British and Dutch trade.[37] Firing a few shells into a

French town was not likely to distract French forces from Flanders and as the French superiority in numbers in the Low Countries diminished in 1694 and disappeared in 1695, the arguments for descents became less strong. These naval assaults in 1695 and 1696 were made without troops on board the vessels.

Never one to miss an opportunity for propaganda, Louis XIV had a special medal struck to commemorate 'Custos Orae Armoricae at exergue Batavis et Anglis ad littus Armoricum caesis'.[38] There was also an element of bravado in this bombastic gesture. The British assault on Brest had been so foolhardy and so stupid that Louis did not feel able to calculate future British operations on the basis of sound, military judgement. Just as a precaution, he retained Vauban's new fortifications around Brest and maintained a sizeable garrison throughout 1695. Thomas Talmash had not died entirely in vain.[39]

Notes

1   Foxcroft, *Halifax*, ii. 84, 219–20, 228; *Parliamentary Diary of Luttrell*, p. 29, 19 Nov. 1691.
2   W. T. Morgan, 'The British West Indies during King William's War, 1689–97', *JMH*, ii. (1930), pp. 398–9.
3   *HMC, Buccleuch (Montagu) MSS.*, ii. 361.
4   *CSPD 1689–90*, p. 119.
5   Symcox, *Crisis of French Sea Power*, pp. 67–8.
6   *HMC, Finch MSS.*, iii. 95–6, 4 June 1691, Nottingham to Russell.
7   *CSPD 1690–1*, pp. 450–1, 18 July 1691, Carmarthen to William III; *HMC, Finch MSS.*, iii. 97.
8   Japikse (Welbeck), ii. 32–3.
9   *HMC, Finch MSS.*, iv. 11.
10 *HMC, Finch MSS.*, iv. 240, 246–7; Japikse (Welbeck), ii. 33–5; *HMC, House of Lords MSS.*, iv. 198–202.
11 Josiah Burchett, *A Complete History of the Most Remarkable Transactions at Sea* (London, 1720), pp. 475–6; *HMC, Finch MSS.*, iv. passim.
12 Symcox, *Crisis of French Sea Power*, pp. 43–5.
13 A. N. Ryan, 'William III and the Brest Fleet in the Nine Years' War', in, *William III and Louis XIV: Essays, 1680–1720, by and for Mark A. Thomson*, eds. R. Hatton & J. S. Bromley (Liverpool, 1968), pp. 53–5; *Shrewsbury Correspondence*, p. 441.
14 Ryan, 'Brest Fleet', p. 64.
15 John Ehrman, 'William III and the emergence of a Mediterranean naval policy, 1692–4', *Cambridge Historical Journal*, ix. (1947–9), pp. 269–71; Stephen F. Gradish, 'The establishment of British seapower in the Mediterranean, 1689–1713', *Canadian Journal of History*, x. (1975), pp. 1–16.
16 *HMC, Frankland–Russell–Astley MSS.*, p. 79; Clark, *Wharton*, p. 289;

Tollemache, *The Tollemaches*, pp. 77–8; Ranke, *History of England*, vi. 212; BL. Add. MSS. 20,007, f. 87.

17 Tollemache Family Archives, Buckminster, Grantham, Lincs., 638–9, 693, 715, 3049, 3078, 3136–40; Bod. Lib. Rawlinson MSS. A. 306, f. 265; ARA, Raad van State, 1928, f. 347; *HP*, iii. 576; Tollemache, *The Tollemaches*, pp. 74–6.

18 Tresham Lever, *Godolphin, his life and times* (London, 1952), pp. 92–9; *Shrewsbury Correspondence*, pp. 33, 192–6; HMC, *Buccleuch (Montagu) MSS.*, ii. 65–6, 70–1.

19 Macaulay, *History of England*, v. 2442–50; John Paget, *The New Examen* (London, 1934), pp. 15–31; E. M. Lloyd, 'Marlborough and the Brest Expedition, 1694', *EHR*, ix. (1894), pp. 130–2; Arthur Parnell, 'James Macpherson and the Nairne Papers', *EHR*, xii. (1897), p. 267; G. Davies, 'Macpherson and the Nairne Papers', *EHR*, xxxv. (1920), pp. 367–76; W. S. Churchill, *Marlborough, his life and times* (London, 1933–8), i. 420–5; Dorothy Middleton, *The Life of Charles, 2nd Earl of Middleton, 1650–1719* (London, 1957), p. 150; David Chandler, *Marlborough, as military commander* (London, 1973), pp. 47–8; D. H. Somerville, *The King of Hearts: Charles Talbot, Duke of Shrewsbury* (London, 1962), p. 93.

20 *The Parliamentary Diary of Luttrell*, p. 47; Luttrell, iii. 299, 301–4; *Portledge Papers*, p. 177; *CSPD 1694–5*, pp. 152–3, 26 May 1694, Sir P. Leeds to William III.

21 BL, Egerton MSS. 3,359, f. 5, 'A draught of Brest and the harbour', by J. Baxter.

22 BL, King's MSS. 53, f. 4.

23 L.A. Le Moyne de la Borderie, *Histoire de Bretagne* (Rennes, 1905–14), v. 565–6; Yves le Gallo, *Histoire de Brest* (Toulouse, 1976), p. 130; Clark, *Wharton*, p. 290; Reginald Blomfield, *Sebastien le Prestre de Vauban* (London, 1938), pp. 135–6; Tollemache, *The Tollemaches*, p. 78; Symcox, *Crisis of French Sea Power*, pp. 152–6.

24 ARA, Heinsius, 2173, 2/12 Feb. 1694, Intelligence from Paris; *Het Archief van den Raadspensionaris Anthonie Heinsius*, ed. H. J. van der Heim (The Hague, 1867–80), ii. 80; *CSPD 1694–5*, pp. 79, 80, 118–19, 130, 137, 155–6; *LG*, no. 2983; *CSPD 1695*, p. 258.

25 Luttrell, iii. 315, 24 May 1694.

26 Hamilton, *Grenadier Guards*, i. 381–2; *CSPD 1694–5*, p. 119; Luttrell, iii. 320. The ten battalions were: 1st Foot Guards, John Cutts's, Richard Coote's, William Stewart's, Samuel Venner's, Marquis de Rade's, Sir David Colyear's, Thomas Erle's, Henry Rowe's, and Ferdinando Hastings's.

27 *CSPD 1694–5*, pp. 130–42; HMC, *Buccleuch (Montagu) MSS.*, ii. 69–70; *Portledge Papers*, pp. 177–8; Luttrell, iii. 309–20.

28 Tollemache, *The Tollemaches*, p. 81, 6 May 1694.

29 Tollemache Family Archives, 716, 'An Account of the Brest Expedition in vindication of General Thomas Talmash, 1694'.

30 HMC, *House of Lords MSS.*, n.s. i. 484–5; HMC, *Buccleuch (Montagu)*

MSS., ii. 75.

31 *CSPD 1694–5*, p. 175, 13 June 1694, Sir John Trenchard to Lord Berkeley.

32 *CSPD 1694–5*, pp. 169–70; Peregrine Osborne, Marquis of Carmarthen and Duke of Leeds, *Journal of the Brest Expedition* (London, 1694), pp. 1–11.

33 The following account of the Battle of Camaret Bay is based upon: Tollemache Family Archives, 716; Carmarthen, *Journal*, pp. 1–33; *CSPD 1694–5*, pp. 168–70, 8 June 1694, Berkeley to Trenchard; *CSPD 1694–5*, pp. 180–4, 15 June 1694, 'The relation of Captain Nathaniel Green'; *Shrewsbury Correspondence*, p. 45; *CSPD 1695*, p. 263; *LG.* no. 2983; Clark, *Wharton*, pp. 290–2; 'Extracts from a Commissioner's note book, 1691–1694', ed. J. K. Laughton, in, *The Naval Miscellany*, ii. (Navy Records Society, London, 1912), pp. 202–5; *HMC, Portland MSS.*, viii. 41–2; Lediard, iii. 442; Luttrell, iii. 327–9; Burchett, pp. 495–500; Heim, ii. 85–7, 17/27 June 1694, Vice-Admiral van Almonde to Heinsius.

34 *Shrewsbury Correspondence*, pp. 44–5.

35 Ranke, *History of England*, vi. 251; *A Supplement to Burnet's History of My Own Time*, ed. H. C. Foxcroft (Oxford, 1902), p. 398; Baxter, *William III*, p. 318; Burnet, *History*, iv. 232–3; Edye, *Royal Marines*, i. 412; Walton, p. 284; *CSPD 1694–5*, pp. 148–9; *Shrewsbury Correspondence*, pp. 44–6; *HMC, Buccleuch (Montagu) MSS.*, ii. 73, 81.

36 BL, Add. MSS. 20,007, f. 87v–88, May–June 1694.

37 G. N. Clark, *The Dutch Alliance and the War against French Trade, 1688–1697* (Manchester, 1923), pp. 120–9.

38 Gallo, *Brest*, p. 130. 'The massacre of the English and Dutch on the shores of Brittany.'

39 BL, Add. MSS. 38,700, ff. 104–5, 25 May/3 June 1695, News from Brest.

X

The British and the war in Flanders

Look'ee, Captain, give us but blood for our money, and you sha'n't want men. I remember that, for some years of the last war (the War of the Grand Alliance), we had no blood nor wounds, but in the officers' mouths; nothing for our millions but newspapers not worth a-reading. Our armies did nothing but to play at prison bars and hide-and-seek with the enemy. (Justice Balance in Act Two, Scene 1 of *The Recruiting Officer* by George Farquhar)

The War of the Grand Alliance was a deceptive contest. When viewed through the eyes of parliamentary politicians or payers of the land tax in England, nothing appeared to happen. Armies sat around all year in camps not seeming to move more than a few miles at a time, and often they remained stationary for weeks on end. Battles were scarce – Walcourt in 1689, Fleurus in 1690, Leuse in 1691, Steenkirk in 1692, and Landen in 1693 – supplemented by a number of formal sieges. This sterile, static, positional warfare seemed incapable of rendering significant political results, or at least political results which could have been exploited to secure an advantageous peace. The age of the wars of attrition had dawned.

The Nine Years' War came to the breakfast tables of the upper reaches of English society through the pages of the *London Gazette,* a biased and heavily censored publication in which gentlemen and ladies were able to enjoy tales of small parties of British and confederate cavalrymen hammering enormous bodies of incompetent Frenchmen. On the evidence contained in the *Gazette,* the French army appeared to be markedly inferior to that of Britain and her allies losing every minor encounter although, somehow, it managed to win most of the engagements that really mattered. Explanations of this curious anomaly were never offered. Instead, the sad events of Steenkirk and Brest were hidden, as far as was possible, in minute and smudged print on the back of the *Gazette's* single sheet and were brushed over with indecent haste. The reporting by the *Gazette* of the heavy defeat at Landen was sharply attacked as inaccurate, rhetorical, and distorted. It had attempted to falsify the intensity of the drubbing which the allies had received by masquerading the battle as a partial victory for King William. The number of casualties was grossly inflated in order to demonstrate that the king had done exceptionally well to inflict such shattering and severe losses upon the enemy.[1] Unless a reader was in the fortunate position of possessing either a friend or a relative serving with the forces in Flanders who could inform him of the true state of affairs, then he would have received a very unreal picture of the conduct and progress of operations. The *London Gazette* may have helped to polish the public image of William III but it also fostered a bitter impatience with the slow tread of the war. Where was the tangible military and political benefit which should have accrued if the glowing reports in the *Gazette* were to be believed? Much of this was due to English inexperience. By the 1690s, the French had come to recognise that the halcyon days of the blitzkrieg of 1672 lay well in the past and that warfare had grown into armed attrition. However, the British were new to the business of international hostilities. The British wanted quantifiable results – raids, descents, battles, and territory. Parliament paid the pipers but it demonstrably did not, and could not call the tune. That musical composition was the product of a number of factors, the greatest of which was the nature of late seventeenth century warfare whose character was utterly beyond the control and influence of any one institution or individual.

The War of the Grand Alliance was encased within a thin veneer of civilised manners and behaviour. French and Spanish delegates had met at the village of Deynze, just outside Ghent, between September 1676 and February 1678 to discuss a bilateral reduction in the burden of 'contributions' which conquering armies were in the habit of levying upon occupied populations. Neither treaty nor written concorde resulted from the Deynze Conference but, early in 1677, Louis XIV decided to abide by the spirit of the proceedings and the Spanish concurred in the following year. Total contributions from an affected area were not to exceed the peacetime taxation which had been levied in 1669. Occupying armies were enjoined to negotiate contributions over wide geographical regions rather than victimise individual villages and if an area could pay the required sums then there was to be no physical damage to property but an orderly exchange of hostages until the money was handed over. This last clause removed the demon of 'brandschatting', the burning of towns and villages which were slow in paying their contributions. Overall, Deynze was a brave attempt to regulate the collection and assessment of contributions in order to make foreign occupation only a little more onerous than the exactions of peacetime government and it excised, partially, some of the gratuitous violence practiced by soldiers against civilians.[2] This worthy effort at introducing some elements of international law into the conduct of war had some limited effect and began the slow shift amongst the military to the opinion that there was more to be gained from the systematic exploitation of an occupied territory than from the wanton razing of every building to the ground. Unfortunately for the inhabitants of the Spanish Netherlands, Luxembourg, Liége, the Rhineland, and north-eastern France, European high commands had not been universally converted to the new code by 1688. Even if the collection of forced contributions had been regularised, there was nothing to prevent armies from ravaging tracts of countryside for the purposes of tactical advantage or political terror, as Marlborough was to demonstrate in Bavaria in 1704. Despite this, a number of more limited agreements enhanced the progress of humanity in warfare during the 1690s. Louis XIV, the 'kreise' or circles of Swabia and Franconia in the Holy Roman Empire, and the Duchy of Württemberg signed a cartel on 2 May 1692 which banned the use of poisoned bullets and insisted that all projectiles thrown from hand guns and muskets had to be moulded from lead. It also laid down that contributions should only be collected by parties of more than nineteen infantrymen or fifteen cavalrymen with at least one officer in attendance; lesser groups could be treated as robbers and imprisoned for two months by either side. A sceptic might suggest that this particular clause was inspired more by the need to maintain discipline within the respective armies than with the advancement of international law. A cartel between England and France governing the exchange of prisoners captured at sea came into effect in 1692, and a similar agreement covering prisoners taken on land was negotiated during the winter of 1694–5. Thereafter, England's commissioners for the exchange of prisoners were kept busy for the remainder of the war.[3]

In reality, the War of the Grand Alliance was nasty, brutish, and long with countries fighting to their last gasp. England's economy virtually collapsed in 1696; the French finances fell apart after 1693; and both English and Dutch commerce was seriously weakened leading to an interruption in the steady expansion of overseas trade. The Peace of Rijkswijk was a truce between prize fighters who had become utterly exhausted by the middle rounds of the protracted contest.[4] As if the Deynze Conference had never existed, the French opened the War by ravaging the Palatinate, the Moselle Valley, and the middle Rhine in the winter of 1688–9, and during the later stages of the conflict the French armies inflicted considerable material damage in the Spanish Netherlands, Luxembourg, and the Bishopric of Liége. During the siege of Mons in March 1691, the French promised to excuse the inhabitants in the region around the city from paying contributions provided that they ploughed up all their green corn and pastures to deny forage and supplies to any allied army advancing to relieve the blockade. The Dutch occupation of Flanders was continuous throughout much of the war, and their contributions became a regular, annual tax upon the Flemish people. Each person had to pay a rate of between ten and thirty pfennigs to the governor of Sluys. By the winter of 1694, the peasants of Flanders and Brabant had become so demoralised by the constant tramping of armies through their fields with the consequent contributions and depredations that they 'neglected the tilling of the ground, being unwilling to work in vain'.[5] Contrary to popular opinion, the war did not grind to a halt each autumn with the armies departing into winter quarters. Operations, mostly small-scale raids, were kept up by both sides during the winter months in order to levy contributions and gather supplies. Eight hundred French troopers from Dinant raided the country around Namur in February 1696, and in the 'extreme cold' of January 1693, the French captured the towns of Furnes and Dixmuyde. Fagel captured Oostdunkirke in February 1696, demolishing its fortifications.[6] The war, both in winter and in summer, was a series of small raids, ambushes, limited actions between foragers and contribution parties, with attacks on supply and money convoys, interspersed by the occasional formal siege and four major battles and a rearguard engagement at Leuse. It was not a war designed for massive territorial gains or for military objectives; its purpose was strictly political.

Warfare in the late seventeenth century did not seek the destruction of the opponent's army as its first aim, not because such a result was necessarily undesirable but because, apart from a few exceptions like the Battle of Blenheim in 1704, it was unattainable by contemporary methods. The aim was to capture towns and territories which could be traded and negotiated at a peace conference, tracts of land which could be used to gather forage, supplies and contributions and sustain an army on an enemy's soil at reduced expense to its national treasury. For the United Provinces, their security rested upon the existence of the Spanish Netherlands as a buffer zone between their southern frontier and France. Territory was thus epitomised by the fortified town or city. Every road and water junction in the Low Countries was protected by fixed fortifications. They could not be by-passed because to leave an enemy garrison in the rear of an advance was to court disaster and run the risk of losing vital supply and provision convoys. The raid by the confederate garrison of Charleroi in 1692 to beat-up a French supply train en route to the field army was typical of the dangers faced by leaving enemy garrisons unsubdued.[7] Every fort, however large or small, had to be besieged and reduced, and because this was the trusted and accepted method of conducting military operations so it became the currency of diplomacy and foreign policy. The objective of armies was the siege and capture of significant towns and cities in order to retain them for diplomatic ransom. With such objectives, warfare was bound to be slow and limited in both scope and ambition. International politics could only follow where its principal weapon led. However, there were other strictures upon military mobility; armies had outgrown their administrative and command mechanisms. Armies of fifty or sixty thousand men without regular corps, divisional, or administrative sub-groupings and composed of a multitude of different nationalities often commanded by princes of royal blood were notoriously difficult to reduce to a unified command and direction. William III spent as much of his time acting as peace-maker and diplomatist amongst his own allies as he did in fighting the French. Marlborough was to find himself in a similar position during the War of the Spanish Succession. The Elector of Bavaria suggested setting up a central army staff office in The Hague in 1691, but nothing came of the idea. Constantijn Huygens drew up a 'Reglément touchant les cérémonies, gardes, et ce qui en dépend quand l'armée se trouve en campagne' on 3 April 1691 which outlined the duties of general officers both in camp and on the march in an effort to impose some uniformity upon different, national practices.[8] Language was another difficulty. Foreign general officers gave orders to British troops in Dutch, French or German, tongues which were not readily understood. Contrary to the commonly held belief that the English upper classes had a knowledge of French, the language of civilisation, when the Earl of Portland drew up a list of those peers and members of the

House of Commons who could speak French well enough to serve as plenipotentiaries to the Rijkswijk peace congress, he came up with just thirty-one lords and forty-seven gentlemen from the lower house. George Saunderson, 5th Viscount Castleton, colonel of a foot battalion, had been present on the field of Steenkirk when, 'orders were sent to me in French [a language], which I profess neither I nor any of my officers understood.'[9] Huge armies moving in a country with few good roads and dependent upon water transport for their heavy guns and baggage, tied down to endless sieges, frequently incapable of unanimous action, and with only the horseman and the runner for communication, were unable to move either rapidly or frequently. Neither did weapon technology assist the quest for decisive methods. Inaccurate and short-range muskets with slow rates of fire were unlikely to decimate opposing infantry, and unbroken infantry could not be charged by cavalry. Heavy cannon fired solid shot, not explosive shells, making the breaching of earthwork fortifications a long and laborious business. It also took such a time to array an army in its battle formation that it was quite possible for the enemy to refuse the invitation to fight and leave the field without a shot having been fired. Battle could only take place by common consent of both parties. Just two battles in Flanders were forced upon an opponent: William's surprise assault on the French camp at Steenkirk in 1692 and Marlborough's running attack on the French at Oudenarde in 1708.

Armies spent much of their lives in camp. In springtime, the component parts of the confederate army marched from their winter cantonments to a general rendezvous near Brussels and then they marched to their first operational camp. Thereafter, they occupied the campaigning season trudging from camp to camp blocking French attempts to besiege key fortresses; half of the skill of a seventeenth century general lay in spotting the towns liable to attack and making sure they had been adequately supplied and garrisoned. From their camps, William, Luxembourg, and Villeroi sought to gain an advantage over the other by consuming forage and supplies or by forcing the enemy to camp in a position from which foraging was difficult, so obliging him to move camp to a less advantageous location. In this way, an enemy could be unbalanced opening the path for a sudden advance to seize a key town or fortress. Armies tried, literally, to 'steal a march' on their opponents. These Flanders camps seem to have been virtually permanent fixtures in the landscape. Earthwork defences, with which nearly all camps in Flanders were protected, endured the ravages of weather and man for a considerable time unless they were deliberately demolished. In 1690, the entrenchments which the Swedes had built near Bichel on the Rhine fifty-six years before were still in existence, and the battery from which had been fired the shot which felled Turenne at Salzbach in 1675 'is still to be traced there'. Not every one of the camps occupied by the French or the confederate armies in Flanders was honoured with field fortifications, but many were. If an army was in residence for more than two or three nights or if the enemy was in close attendance, some simple defences were thrown-up. At Anderlecht, Hall, Lembeek, Mariekirke near Ghent, Seneffe, Mont St André, and many other sites, the camps were permanent, ready to be occupied by whichever side needed them. They formed standard, set positions, complete with rudimentary fortifications. Warfare resembled chess in that there were only a limited number of 'squares' or camps within the given theatre, but with an infinite variety of moves between them.[10] Old established camp sites were preferred to new ones. New camps had to be 'prepared' in advance and, if the roads traversed wooded country or marshland, then they had to be widened or strengthened before the march of the main army, revealing the next movement very clearly to the enemy long before it occurred. With well-established camp sites none of these preparations were required as both the roads and the camps had long been converted to military usage.[11] Few camps were more than ten miles apart, the most that an army could travel in daylight. March routes were worked out in precise detail before a movement, with the roads, starting times, and river crossings all exactly organised. Armies marched in two divisions – the left and right wing – and each was sub-divided into six or seven columns to make use of all the available tracks and roads. The intention was for one wing to arrive before the other, usually around midday, giving ample time for stragglers to come in and for fortifications to be repaired or dug before nightfall. Oddly enough, the artillery always led the march. Clearly attacks whilst on the road were not anticipated and, if they were, then by the very nature of 'camp warfare' marches were usually made away from the enemy or parallel to him so that any sudden attacks would fall on the infantry and cavalry in the rear of the columns and not on the artillery in the van. This was the sequence of events at Leuse in 1691, when Luxembourg surprised Waldeck's rearguard during a river crossing.[12] All of these limitations on speed and freedom of movement which allowed French officers in camp to rise at noon and Field-Marshal the Prince of Nassau-Saarbourg to travel to Spa to take the waters in the middle of the campaign of 1696 pale into insignificance beside the restrictions imposed by supply. Supply – the provision of food for men and horses – dwarfed all other factors in making late seventeenth century armies lethargic in movement and unimaginative in strategy. Put quite simply, a moving army could be provisioned with relative ease; a static army only with great difficulty.

Before each campaign began, the confederates built supply magazines in the principal fortress towns in the southern part of the United Provinces and in the northern cites of the Spanish Netherlands. Brussels was the main allied base stocking 1,260,000 bread rations and 2,700,000 rations of hay in March 1690. Away from Brussels, subsidiary magazines were developed at Namur, Maastricht, Ghent, Liége, Louvain, Ath, Nieuport, 's-Hertogenbosh, and Arnhem.[13] These vast store cupboards varied in capacity depending upon the probable direction of the coming campaign and whether or not there was a risk of a particular town being subjected to a siege. Ath, a prime target for French attack in 1696, although it was not in fact attacked until the following year, was stocked with enough grain meal and green fodder in February 1696 to feed 40,000 men for three weeks. In Flanders, the British army provided bread for its soldiers but nothing else. Meat, cheese, beer, vegetables, and any other foodstuffs had to be purchased by the soldiers from the regimental sutlers or from the civilian merchants in the innumerable towns and villages in the Spanish Netherlands. The paymaster in Flanders, Richard Hill, deducted 'bread money' from the daily subsistence money of every man and used it to meet the bills of the provision contractors. Bread money was extracted for every day of the year, regardless of whether the troops were in camp or in winter quarters, as the bread contractors were only prepared to take on the work if they were guaranteed a full year's business. This was most unsatifactory as the troops could, usually, provide themselves with much cheaper and better bread during the winter months than that supplied by the contractors, but the annual contracts made it impossible for the soldiers to avail themselves of local produce.[14] William's armies in Flanders, numbering nearly 100,000 men, needed around 250,000 lb. of bread per day, in addition to 120,000 lb. of other consumables, whilst the horses devoured 1,600,000 lb. of fodder. To provide this amount of bread, 270 windmills were required to supply flour to 120 field ovens which were fired by 2,800 waggonloads of wood and served by 480 bakers. It was a massive operation by contemporary standards and only certain parts of Europe possessed a sufficient density of urban and rural population to furnish the labour and financial capital for its execution. The

Spanish Netherlands, northern Italy, the Rhine Valley, and West-phalia were the principal regions where organised warfare between mass armies could be conducted.[15]

It was impossible to stock these tonnages in magazines. Magazines were for emergencies, to rush supplies forward to a threatened fortress or to enable an army to take the field before the grass had started to grow, or for when an army found itself stationary for a long period either in camp or undertaking a siege. The latter was the real problem. Whilst marching, an army could live off the land, foraging and requisitioning as it travelled, but the moment that it came to a halt, it devoured the available human and horse feed in its immediate vicinity very quickly indeed and was obliged either to move on again or draw from its magazines. Armies did not dare to stray far from the magazines – four day's march was considered the maximum safe distance – but this was not a problem in the Spanish Netherlands, a small and compact campaigning theatre, where both the French and the confederates were always within easy reach of their bases. It was a different matter for armies operating in Hungary or Spain or Russia. An army horse needed between forty and fifty pounds of green fodder per day during the summer and an equivalent weight of corn in the winter. Army provision contractors only undertook to supply horse feed during the cold months of the year and in the summer the army had to provide its own green fodder by foraging and allowing its horses to graze on standing crops. This latter course was devastating to the local agriculture and economy and was avoided whenever possible on the obvious grounds that if the local resources were ruined then that area would be unable to support an army in the future. Foraging, the gathering of hay for the horses, took place once every three or four days when an army was in camp or immobile during a siege, and most armies foraged to their flanks and to their front. The rear was retained for emergencies or to sustain a retreat. As enemy armies were usually encamped in very close proximity, foraging grounds were often in dispute and the foraging parties had to be covered by large formations of cavalry and dragoons to hold off opposing patrols. A 'grand forage' could involve virtually the entire army and it was upon such a forage that the allied army was supposed to be engaged when it advanced to take Luxembourg by surprise at Steenkirk. It was this endless requirement for fodder which limited the effective campaigning period to the agricultural growing season. Men could fight during the winter but the horses could not be fed for long away from their stables and that put an end to large-scale manoeuvres and restricted the war to raids and patrols.[16]

Whilst the horses were relatively well cared for, and the confederate army in Flanders possessed over 80,000 horses, the nutritional value of the men's bread ration was desperately low. Seventeenth century soldiers fought and marched on 1,700 calories and forty grammes of protein a day. In the 1930s, a soldier on garrison duty was reckoned to need between 3,200 and 3,500 calories per day, rising to 3,800 calories and 160 grammes of protein when in action. Our poor soldier was living on the equivalent of a modern slimmer's diet and it was small wonder that he never marched more than ten or twelve miles in twenty-four hours and had to rest every fourth day. Edward D'Auvergne noted how the quality of the rations improved when the Duke of Württemberg's corps penetrated the French lines in July 1693. Each battalion was given two cows a week, paid for out of the contributions levied on the local population, with two sheep for the company officers and 'corn brandy' in plenty. This was in stark contrast to the monotonous 'ammunition bread' endured in the camp, supplemented by expensive cheese and meat from the sutler's tent.[17]

The commissariat of the British army was non-existent. After the supposed peculation and incompetence of commissary-general John Shales during the first year of the war in Ireland and the debacle of the Dundalk camp, even though there is more than a hint that Shales was made the scapegoat for the fiasco, William put no more faith or trust in the ability of the British army to run its own supply system. A commissary-general of the provisions, òne Israel Fielding, did function but he was solely responsbile for provisioning the transport vessels which ferried troops back and forth across the North Sea and the English Channel, or between England and Ireland. Fielding was paid £1 10s a day, and his deputy, John Murray, received £1. Their department employed thirty-one storekeepers, bakers, clerks, bricklayers, and carpenters. Fielding and Murray worked closely with the commissioners for transportation, who supervised the requisitioning, hire, and deployment of merchant vessels for the use of the army and the Ordnance Office. In England a soldier paid for and provided his own food and lodging out of his subsistence money, but once a soldier set foot in Flanders his daily needs became the responsibility of the civilian contractors who supplied the entire confederate army.[18]

The business of army provisioning grew naturally out of the Amsterdam grain trade of the sixteenth and seventeenth centuries and had become the monopoly of the Portuguese Jewish community by 1650. Jews enjoyed the advantage of being treated as neutrals by both the French and Dutch enabling them to travel freely all over the Low Countries in search of supplies.[19] The doyen of all the army victuallers was the firm of Antonio Alvarez Machado and Isaac Pereira. From their office in the Lange Voorhout in The Hague, Machado and Pereira supplied bread to the Spanish and Dutch armies throughout the Franco-Dutch War of 1672 to 1678, as well as waggons for its transport and distribution. Antonio Alvarez Machado, better known as Moses Machado, was a personal friend of William III and frequently accompanied him on campaign, and this probably accounts for Machado and Pereira's first contract with the Dutch forces coinciding with William's rise to power in 1672.[20] After the Treaty of Nijmegen in 1678, Machado and Pereira continued to supply the Dutch army during peacetime and they also tendered for, and received, the contract to victual William's expedition to England in 1688.[21] By this time, the firm enjoyed the title of Providiteur-Generals to the Dutch army and their retention of the bread contract in 1689 was a mere formality.[22] They also undertook to feed the Williamite army in Ireland between 1689 and 1691, charging $1\frac{1}{4}d$ a day per man, a sum which the paymaster deducted from the men's subsistence pay as the 'bread money'. Each soldier was given a single one pound loaf in return for his $1\frac{1}{4}d$, or a pound of biscuit if no bread was available.[23] In Flanders, Machado and Pereira began their contract in 1689 by charging 5 sols per man per day but his rose to 5.125 sols in 1690, at which figure it remained until 1697.[24]

A complete service was provided. Magazines were stocked with fodder and 'biscuit' during the winter and, in the campaigning season, waggons, complete with drivers and horses, were laid on to take the bread from the field bakeries, or from the magazines, to the army in the field. They supplied the British, the Dutch, the Brandenburgers, and the Hanoverians, as well as the brigades from Celle, Hesse-Cassel, Munster, Holstein, and Liége.[25] Municipal magistrates of the towns which had been selected as magazines were ordered by the States-General to liaise closely with the agents of Machado and Pereira to arrange for warehouses and granaries. Much of their business was sub-contracted and the two partners acted as brokers, although they did not look beyond the Jewish community for suitable associates. David Losada Coopman looked after the supply of grain and horses in Brabant and Maastricht, whilst Francisco de Cordova supervised their affairs in England.[26] They did not have things all their own way. F. V. Mourik was granted the contract for feeding the artillery and transport horses on 8 December 1690, using Mechlen as a base, and on 17

August 1691, F. Castaigne won the right to provide rations for 1,000 horses at Namur during the winter. G. van den Biesheuvel contracted to supply hay and oats to the Dendermonde and Ghent garrisons in March 1692, but these were tiny operations when set against the four million rations of winter horse feed stocked in Brussels by Machado and Pereira in September 1691.[27] Army contracting between 1672 and 1697 was synonymous with the firm of Machado and Pereira. In the latter year, Moses Machado died and that seems to have been the end of the business, although Isaac Pereira had some limited interests in army contracting during the opening years of the War of the Spanish Succession. Machado's son, Jacob, showed no interest in his father's profitable enterprise.[28]

Payment of the contractors was a monthly concern, and it was recognised as the first priority which had to be met even if other accounts were left uncleared as a consequence. The British corps's share of the confederate army's bill for a year's supply of bread, waggons, horses, and fodder was £82,000, of which sum £33,600 was paid as an advance at the beginning of the year. However, in the disastrous year of 1696, even this sacred account fell into arrear. In March 1697, Machado and Pereira were owed £9,544 for the 1696 contract and had yet to be paid the £17,600 advance for the 1697 agreement. Overkirk was obliged to pledge his personal estates as security in order for the soldiers to be fed.[29] Fortunately, the shoulders of Machado and Pereira were very broad and they weathered the storm without undue hardship. Their business gave a stimulus to the English economy during the war years, a considerable benefit during a decade of generally poor harvests and straitened economic circumstances. Machado and Pereira made bulk purchases of grain in 1692 from England and Scotland and, in the following year, they discovered an even cheaper source of supply, Ireland, where wheat cost a mere two shillings a bushel. Irish beef, butter, and corn, were still flooding into Machado and Pereira's warehouses through Ostend in 1695.[30]

The conveyance of provisions and men from England, Scotland, and Ireland to Flanders was the task of the commissioners for transportation. Machado and Pereira did not, surprisingly, run a shipping line of their own but depended upon the services of the transport commissioners, or transport board. These officials requisitioned merchantmen, made sure that they were at the right port at the correct time, and paid for their hire. The board was funded jointly by contributions from the army and navy budgets, and liaised closely with Israel Fielding whose office supplied the provisions for the ships' crews and for any soldiers who were being ferried across the sea.[31] Once in Flanders, Machado and Pereira resumed their commercial dominance and provided transport for the food and fodder, complete with horses and civilian drivers, waggons for the artillery, again complete with civilian drivers and horses, and baggage waggons for the individual regiments. There was a waggon-master-general with the British forces in Flanders but he was responsible for the discipline within the waggon train and for supervising the distribution of bread and fodder from the civilian waggons to the various regiments. To supply the British corps in the field, Robert Barker had under his jurisdiction over 1,000 waggons, 239 to carry ammunition and weapons, and the remainder to convey bread and foodstuffs. There was a separate baggage-master, a post assumed by one Bill Pickett, who supervised the baggage train which contained the personal effects of the officers.[32]

The scale of the War of the Grand Alliance witnessed an acute surge in the size of national establishments throughout western Europe. Armies had been increasing in numbers since the latter part of the sixteenth century, but the War of the Grand Alliance and the War of the Spanish Succession marked a temporary high-point, after which armies decreased a little in average size until the French Revolutionary and Napoleonic Wars at the turn of the eighteenth century. In November 1688, Waldeck's army in Flanders consisted of 23,270 men, composed of contingents from the United Provinces, Brandenburg, Luneburg, Hesse-Cassel, and Württemberg.[33] William rapidly augmented his forces. A series of troop contracts with Brandenburg, Brunswick-Luneburg, Brunswick-Wolfenbuttel, Hesse-Cassel, Württemberg, Sweden, and Saxe-Gotha in the autumn and winter of 1688–9, produced an army of 71,000 for 1689, with the British corps of 10,000 linking-up in the spring. On 28 December 1688, long before he was offered the throne of England, Schomberg had assured the Elector of Brandenburg that William would put 8,000 British troops into Ireland and raise another 30,000 for service in Europe.[34] During 1689, Denmark contributed troops and, in the following year, the Palatinate and Liége joined the alliance.[35] Saxony contracted to provide troops in 1692, with Courland and Saxe-Menningen, Holstein-Ploen, and Slippenbach making contributions in 1693. Munster was the last to join in 1695, with the costs of her 4,000 men being shared equally between England and the States-General.[36] For the campaign of 1693, the confederacy had a total of 220,000 men available for service. Forty thousand operated in Piedmont, 58,000 fought on the Rhine, and 122,000 served in William's field army in Flanders. By the end of that year, the total had risen to 287,040 and the forces for 1694 reached 317,040.[37] A further jump in 1695 took the grand total to 334,000, of which the army in Flanders numbered 123,540,[38] and these levels remained constant until the end of the war.[39]

The British contingent in the Low Countries gradually increased as the war progressed, although this was the beginning of the eighteenth century Westminster government's habit of preferring to hire foreign auxiliaries and allies for campaigns in Europe, reserving native, British soldiers for colonial enterprises. From the initial commitment of 10,000 men in 1689, there was a reduction to just 5,360 in 1690 as the majority of the British forces was needed for the subjugation of Ireland. In the wake of the Treaty of Limerick, some of the British troops in Ireland were deployed into England to ward-off the threatened invasion and to take part in the abortive descent on St Malo, but enough soldiers were shipped to Flanders to boost the British corps to 11,144. By 1693, 21,720 British soldiers were fighting with the confederate army, although the national revenues were meeting the costs of a further 19,000 Danes and Germans. The augmentation of the army in the winter of 1693–4 raised the corps in Flanders to 29,100, with a further 27,000 Dutchmen, Germans, and Scandinavians drawing their pay directly from the Whitehall treasury. The British contingent in the Low Countries then remained at this size until the termination of hostilities.[40] For the last four years of the war, Britain was paying for forty-five per cent of William's confederate army although it contributed only twenty-five per cent of the actual manpower. Thus, between 1694 and 1697, about one half of the British regular army was employed in the fields of Flanders, with the other fifty per cent deployed in the British Isles, the colonies, and on board the fleet. Another political advantage of the growing dependence upon the power of the British public purse to rent foreign auxiliaries and mercenaries to fight in Europe, was that it permitted the British standing army to be kept within numerically acceptable bounds. It helped to dim the prospect that involvement in continental warfare automatically led to the dreadful corollary of a mass army such as that suffered by France or Denmark. Autocratic and militarised monarchy was pushed further towards the distant horizon, despite the presence of a European soldier–prince on the British throne.

The operations of the French and confederate armies in the Spanish Netherlands during 1694 adequately illustrate the slow, negative, and frustrating nature of large-scale warfare during the 1690s. Between January and April, intelligence reached the British and Dutch governments of the desperate plight of France where the whole country was filled with 'misery and desolation'. However, this did not noticeably retard their winter raiding and patrolling. A French concentration around Ypres brought fears of a sudden offensive in mid-January towards Nieuport, taking advantage of the ice and hard frosts, but the 2,000 French horse were only to be employed in levying contributions on the unfortunate local inhabitants. It was too cold. The garrison of Dendermonde had the daily task of breaking the ice to keep the moat open.[41] The theatre lapsed into inaction until the weather improved and in March Machado and Pereira were instructed to bake one million biscuit rations in readiness for operations along the Meuse. From the beginning of April, the French slowly drew their field army together but not until the middle of May was the Duke of Luxembourg ready to commence effective operations. Luxembourg was slow to bring his troops into the field because of the shortage of money and supplies, whilst William was equally dilatory having waited in England for the closing of the parliamentary session.[42]

In intense heat, the allied army concentrated at the Camp of Bethlehem near Louvain, but because of the shortage of forage the cavalry were not brought to join the main body and remained quartered in cantonments. William's 90,000 men faced 100,000 French, camped near the village of Ramillies, and both armies were in visual contact with each other. Although William nursed vague hopes of attacking Namur, which had been seized by the French in 1692, he was also fearful that Luxembourg might attempt the main Dutch base in Maastricht, but the French were seemingly content to remain on the defensive. Without his customary heavy numerical superiority, Luxembourg considered that decisive operations were impossible and he had determined to watch the movements of the confederates and react to their marches in order to protect French territory and fortresses. After the frantic attacks by the French in all major theatres in 1693, prudence and the husbanding of increasingly scarce resources was the order for the following year. William also recognised the impossibility of out-manoeuvreing Luxembourg whilst their armies were of comparable size and so he placed his emphasis upon forcing the Frenchman to give battle in the hope that a victory might provide political capital in England and open the way in Flanders for a decisive acquisition of territory. Accordingly, the armies observed one another, Luxembourg covering Namur and William occupying a well-known camp at Mont St André near Tirlemont, and there they stayed for much of June, all of July, and most of August. Towards the end of August, William attempted to pull Luxembourg away from his impregnable position by sending a large raiding party under the Elector of Bavaria into French territory to raise contributions, but the French intelligence system was working well and Marshal Boufflers intercepted Bavaria at Pont St Esperies and the German returned to the main allied camp. In September, the allies seized Dixmuyde in Flanders by a coup de main and then proceeded to besiege Huy which fell after a feeble defence of only a few days, and that concluded the campaign. William had, in strategic terms, ended the year on a high note and had taken the initiative from the French, an advantage which he was to exploit in 1695 with the great capture of Namur.[43] Throughout the campaigning season, diplomatic exchanges had been conducted between French, Dutch and Imperial envoys. They foundered on the French refusal to discuss the unconditional recognition of William as king of England, whilst Louis tried hard to detach Emperor Leopold from the Grand Alliance.[44] It was hardly surprising that army officers were accused of prolonging the war in order to line their own pockets and extend their careers.

This campaign must, one way or other, give a great stroke towards bringing it (the war) to an end, except the officers on both sides can play the tricks they use to do, alternatively in Flanders &c., to spin out a war because they live upon it.[45]

Even the most original and effective soldiers of the age – Turenne, Luxembourg, Villars, and Marlborough – achieved little within the compass of the Spanish Netherlands. Contemporary methods of waging war, when added to the geographical limitations of the Low Countries, reduced most campaigns to attrition and ultimate indecision.

We saw in England a bloody civil war where . . . fighting was the business. Encampments, intrenchments, batteries, counter-marchings, fortifying of camps, and cannonading were strange and almost unknown things, and whole campaigns were passed over and hardly any tents made use of. Battles, surprises, storming of towns, skirmishes, sieges, ambuscades, and beating up quarters was the news of every day. Now it is frequent to have armies of fifty thousand men of a side stand at bay within view of one another, and spend a whole campaign in dodging, or, as it is genteely called, observing one another, and then march off into winter quarters. The difference is in the maxims of war . . .
Never fight without a manifest advantage,
And always encamp so as not to be forced to it.
And if two opposite generals nicely observe both these rules it is impossible they should ever come to fight.
I grant that this way of making war spends generally more money and less

blood than former wars did; but then it spins wars out to a greater length . . . and I think it is plain in the present war that it is not he who has the longest sword, so much as he who has the longest purse, will hold the war out best.[46]

A cynical view perhaps, but only away from the confines of Flanders in the more open spaces of Russia, Poland, Hungary, Germany, and Spain was more decisive and significant warfare possible, provided that the armies engaged remained relatively small and self-contained.

Notes

1   *Somer's Tracts*, xi. 462–71, 'Remarks upon the London Gazette relating to the Straits' Fleet and the Battle of Landen in Flanders'; R. B. Walker, 'The newspaper press in the reign of William III', *HJ*, xvii. (1974), pp. 706–7; E. S. de Beer, 'The English newspapers from 1695 to 1702', in, *William III and Louis XIV*, eds. Hatton & Bromley, pp. 118–19.

2   Hubert van Houtte, 'Les Conférences Franco-Espagnoles de Deynze, 1676 to 1678', *Revue d'Histoire Moderne*, ii. (1927), pp. 191–215.

3   G. N. Clark, 'The character of the Nine Years' War, 1688–1697', *Cambridge Historical Journal*, xi. (1953), pp. 168–71, 175–6; Richard Kane, *Campaigns of King William and the Duke of Marlborough . . . from 1689 to 1712* (London, 1747), p. 22; HMC, *Finch MSS.*, iv. 73.

4   Clark, *The Dutch Alliance and the War against French Trade*, pp. 120–40.

5   HMC, *Portland MSS.*, iii. 460; ARA, Raad van State, 489, ff. 214–15; BL, Stowe MSS. 481, f. 7; D'Auvergne, *1694*, p. 8.

6   *LG*, no. 3159; *Chronicles of an Old Campaigner, Monsieur de la Colonie, 1692–1717*, ed. W. C. Horsley (London, 1904), p. 26; HMC, *Bath MSS.*, iii. 2–3; HMC, *Denbigh MSS.*, pp. 91–2; *Archives d'Orange-Nassau*, i. 307.

7   BL, Stowe MSS. 481, f. 6.

8   Japikse, iii. 224, 19 Mar. 1691; ARA, Heinsius, 2172.

9   Japikse (Welbeck), ii. 81–5; *Parliamentary Diary of Luttrell*, p. 257. On the linguistic ability of the English gentry and aristocracy see, K. H. D. Haley, *An English Diplomat in the Low Countries: Sir William Temple and John De Witt, 1665–1672* (Oxford, 1986), pp. 11, 23–4.

10 Claude Alexander, Comte de Bonneval, *Memoirs of the Bashaw Count Bonneval* (London, 1750), pp. 15–16; BL, Egerton MSS. 3359, f. 3; BCRO, Trumbull Add. MSS. 103; *LG*, no. 3188; Luttrell, ii. 536; *Dangeau*, p. 199.

11 Müller, ii. 184.

12 BL, King's MSS. 229; LUL, MSS. 12, 'Livre des marches fait par les Armées de sa Majesté de la Grand Bretagne depuis l'an 1689 jusques a la fin de la Campagne 1695'; Heim, ii. pp. xlvix–lii; *Mémoires du Maréchal de Villars*, ed. C. J. Melchior de Mis (Paris, 1884), i. 134–9; *Memoirs of the late Marquis de Feuquières* (London, 1737), ii. 63–6; Bonneval, *Memoirs*, pp. 8–9.

13 ARA, Raad van State, 489, ff. 74–8, 168.
14 WO 24/10, f. 19.
15 G. Perjés, 'Army provisioning, logistics and strategy in the second half of the seventeenth century', *Acta Historica Academiae Scientarium Hungaricae*, xvi. (1970), pp. 4–14; Martin van Creveld, *Supplying War: Logistics from Wallenstein to Patton* (Cambridge, 1980), p. 24.
16 Perjés, 'Army provisioning', pp. 14–18.
17 D'Auvergne, *1693*, p. 46.
18 *CJ*, ix. 451–3; x. 295–6; *HMC, Finch MSS.*, iv. 82; Waddell, pp. 49–52.
19 Violet Barbour, *Capitalism in Amsterdam in the 17th century* (Michigan, 1963), pp. 30–1.
20 L. A. Vega, *Het Beth Haim van Ouderkerk aan de Amstel* (Assen, 1979), p. 44.
21 Albert M. Hyamson, *The Sephardim of England* (London, 1951), pp. 67–8; GAA, Notarial Protocollen, NP 2259, f. 189.
22 David Franco Mendes, *Memorias do Estabelecimento e Progresso des Judeos Portuguezes e Espanhoes nesta famosa citade de Amsterdam*, eds. L. Fuks & R. G. Fuks-Mansfeld (Amsterdam, 1975), pp. 87–8; ARA, Heinsius, 142, 5/15 Apr. 1689, Waldeck to Heinsius.
23 DCRO, Ilchester MSS., D. 124, Establishment, Ireland, 1690.
24 ARA, Heinsius, 142, 5/15 Apr. 1689, Waldeck to Heinsius; GAA, Archief der Portugees-Israelietsche gemeente te Amsterdam, PA 334/727, ff. 207–21, Machado and Pereira's accounts for supplying the auxiliary troops on the Maas, June–Oct. 1697.
25 GAA, PA 334/727, f. 204.
26 GAA, NP 2259, f. 189; GAA, NP 7532, f. 721.
27 ARA, Raad van State, 489, ff. 73–4, 168–72; *The Marlborough–Godolphin Correspondence*, ed. H. L. Snyder (Oxford, 1975), i. 435, 439; *CSPD 1690–1*, p. 7 et passim; BL, Add. MSS. 9,724, f. 45.
28 *Nieuw Nederlandsch Biografisch Woordenboek* (Leiden, 1924), vi. 982–3, 1106–7.
29 BL, Add. MSS. 9,725, f. 93; BL, Add. MSS. 9,735, f. 61; *CTP 1697–1702*, pp. 17, 218; BL, Add. MSS. 9,730, ff. 81–2.
30 BL, Add. MSS. 9,735, f. 48; Luttrell, ii. 508, 604–5; iii. 202; BCRO, Trumbull Add. MSS. 103.
31 *CSPD 1693*, p. 278; *HMC, Portland MSS.*, viii. 40; *CSPD 1697*, pp. 398–9; Tomlinson, *Guns and Government*, pp. 150–1.
32 BL, Add. MSS. 9,724, f. 129; BL, Stowe MSS. 444, ff. 16–22; *HMC, Various Collections*, ii. 176.
33 J. A. Lynn, 'The growth of the French Army during the Seventeenth Century', *Armed Forces and Society*, vi. (1979–80), pp. 568–85; Childs, *Armies and Warfare*, p. 41–2; Müller, ii. 255–6, Nov. 1688.
34 *Het Staatsche Leger, 1568–1795*, eds. F. G. J. Ten Raa & F. De Bas (The Hague, 1911–1959), vii. 6; Campana de Cavelli, *Les Derniers Stuarts a Saint-Germain-en-Laye* (Paris, 1871), ii. 447–8.
35 Japikse (Welbeck), i. 160–1; Erle–Drax MSS., 4/18, ff. 2–3; ARA, Heinsius, 2170; ARA, Raad van State, 1277.

36　*Het Staatsche Leger,* vii. 357–77.

37　Onno Klopp, *Der Fall der Hauses Stuart* (Vienna, 1875–88), vi. 173–4; BL, Add. MSS. 9,724, ff. 156–7; *CJ,* xi. 24–5; BL, Harl. MSS. 1,898, f. 40.

38　*CJ,* xi. 179; BL, Add. MSS. 9,724, f. 169; *CSPD 1695,* p. 334.

39　ARA, Raad van State, 1902/1; *CJ,* xi. 347–8; BL, Harl. MSS. 7,018, f. 171.

40　D. G. Chandler, 'Fluctuations in the strength of forces in English pay sent in Flanders during the Nine Years' War, 1688–1697', *War and Society,* i. (1983), pp. 1–19; WO 5/5, ff. 103–4; PRO, SP 8/17, f. 8.

41　*HMC, Bath MSS.,* iii. 17, 20; *CSPD 1695,* p. 233; *HMC, Le Fleming MSS.,* p. 333.

42　ARA, Raad van State, 489, f. 74; *Shrewsbury Correspondence,* pp. 32–3.

43　LUL, MSS. 12, ff. 206–31; NLI, MSS. 4166, ff. 24–6; *Mémoires du Maréchal de Berwick, écrits par lui-même* (Switzerland, 1778), i. 85–6.

44　Mark A. Thomson, 'Louis XIV and William III, 1689–97', *EHR,* lxxvi. (1961), pp. 45–6; Burnet, *History,* iv. 237–8; *HMC, Denbigh MSS.,* pp. 93–4.

45　*Locke Correspondence,* iv. 261, 15/25 May 1691, Rotterdam, Benjamin Furly to John Locke.

46　Daniel Defoe, *An Essay on Projects* (London, 1697), in, *The Earlier Life and the Chief Earlier Works of Daniel Defoe,* ed. Henry Morley (London, 1889), pp. 134–6.

XI

Reflections

The British standing army had lived through a chequered first forty-two years of life. It had initially come into existence in 1660 as a modest collection of royal guards, based on the French model, to give some guarantee of physical security both to the newly-restored monarchy and to its accompanying political and religious settlement. For the remainder of the seventeenth century, the army was to be dominated by political rather than by purely military factors. Until the time of the Exclusion Crisis, the restoration army had fulfilled its purpose of assisting in the maintenance of law and order and in defending the British Isles from attack by foreign powers but in 1681 its function began to alter. During the last four years of the reign of Charles II, the army drifted from its apolitical stance and commenced its transformation into a coercive, political police force intended to uphold an increasingly absolutist and centralised form of government, a tendency which reached its fullest expression under James II. The bogey of a militarised, catholic, absolute state which had deeply affected English political life since the later 1620s finally came close to fruition between 1685 and 1688. Fortunately for the development of English constitutional history, the role which James II demanded from his army was to bring about its impotence when faced with a Dutch invasion in November 1688. Its failure to face or fight William of Orange was directly consequent upon the purging of the officer corps which had been executed by the king and through that monarch's insistence upon political and religious loyalty. The dismal withdrawal from Salisbury to the environs of London in November and December 1688 witnessed the break-up of the old Stuart army and the history of the army under William III was one of partial recovery. Rapidly, the officer corps and the rank and file were stripped of political and religious malcontents and then the whole institution was placed upon a war footing, but the army was never subjected to a thorough overhaul and reform of its organisation, discipline, and methods and it carried its ancient malpractices and antique inefficiences forward into the new era. It was a victim of the king's indifference. To William, who perhaps did not fully appreciate the political depths to which the British military had sunk during James II's tenure of the throne, the army was an expendable tool for the furtherance of his short-term political schemes to maintain Dutch independence and to limit the extension of French power. Just as he was denied the means to establish a dynasty either in England or in the United Provinces and, as a corollary, lacked far-sighted vision in his foreign policy and tended to treat both domestic and international politics on a strictly limited and day-to-day basis, so one of his principal weapons for conducting that policy, the British army, was treated in the same, blinkered manner.

The political settlement which came into being during the 1690s to cement and take advantage of the Glorious Revolution was haphazard, characterised by immediate party and personal politics rather than by an ideological dream of the future. On the contrary, it was conservative and retrogressive, with politicians seeming anxious to secure their regained positions by turning the clock back. The army was a victim of the current political system. It bobbed and bounced in this political wash, as much a sufferer from the instability and uncertainty of the new order as its protector and defender. Its legal status within the constitution was only partially clarified, its very existence was still loathed and deeply feared, and the temporary power and influence which some of its officers and officials gained through the medium of the War of the Grand Alliance was greatly resented. Not surprisingly, it ended the reign flat on its back. By 1700, following the reactionary policy of vicious and exaggerated disbandment, it was smaller than at any time since the 1660s and much of the experience, expertise, and professionalism which had been nurtured during the most adverse circumstances over the previous forty years appeared to be in jeopardy. An institution which had positive uses as an aid to the civil power in obtaining law and order, which protected exposed and vulnerable colonies, which helped to secure the new political order after 1688, and which served as an important instrument in the conduct of foreign affairs was hacked down and emasculated. It was only through the misjudgements of Louis XIV that war returned to Europe within two years of the final series of disband-ments, a sufficiently short period to enable the half-pay officers and unemployed soldiers to flood back to the colours and to recreate the mature army of William III for the benefit of Queen Anne and the Duke of Marlborough. Under that leadership, the army was to prove vital in gaining a general European peace which brought tangible commercial and political gains to the United Kingdom. Ironically, the parlous state of the British military establishment was one of the factors which induced Louis XIV to renounce the Partition Treaty, endorse the will of Carlos II of Spain and undertake the pre-emptive occupation of the Dutch Barrier fortresses in the Spanish Netherlands. The demobilisation of the British army helped to cause the French king's miscalculations, although these errors of judgement brought the army back from the dead.

The ups and downs in the army's fortunes set the pattern for the next 240 years. Great Britain has never loved or respected its army. It has customarily been the prey of suspicion and the first target for financial economy, leading to constant uncertainty about its size, shape, or role from one decade to the next. Usually, it has been unprepared for war because politicians have never permitted it to remain effective between bouts of international hostility. Only with the advent of mass conscription for the two world wars of the twentieth century has a loose affinity between the British army and its public become apparent. Regular, professional armies should be invi-sible and silent when in the British Isles but ready to perform feats of glorious arms in the colonies and, less often, on mainland Europe. In King William's time, the British army was still in a transitional state and its relationship with its parent government and society was unclear. Prima facie, the army was funded by the taxpayer but con-siderable elements of the methods and systems of the old Germanic mercenary bands still persisted and the state refused to assume total responsibility for its own armed forces. It would not, or could not, feed its soldiers or provide them with barracks and decent lodgings, partly because no one could make up their minds whether the army was to be an integral part of the British social and political fabric or entirely removed into a world of its own. Even the clothes on the soldiers' backs were purchased from the state through its agents and middlemen, the commissioned officers. Pay was incredibly low but was then reduced to a ludicrous level through the blood money which the state permitted to its appointed officers. The peculation of Har-bord, Ranelagh, and Crawford, the endless series of fictitious musters, and the illegal stoppages from the subsistence money, all represented the fees charged to the state by the officers as their price for organising and running the state's army and for saving the government the task of administering the entire military machine and from having to meet its full costs. Perhaps, as in most of western Europe, underdeveloped economies run by governments which regarded minimal intervention as the norm could do no more than hire out their armies on trust to their officers. Inevitably, that trust was grossly abused and yet it had to be condoned as there existed no alternative system of control. Not until the end of the eighteenth century did British army officers come to see themselves as servants of the state rather than as individual entrepreneurs whose business was the extraction of a maximum profit from the state's soldiers.[1] The purchase system tended to enhance this view of an army commission as a commercial enterprise. Consequently, the army never quite understood what it was supposed to be or what it was supposed to do. Was it the right-hand of the monarch, to do his bidding, as had seemed to be the case between 1681 and 1688, or was it a national army answerable to the common law and parliament with the responsibility for the defence of the realm in time of war and emergency? By 1702, this question had just about been resolved in favour of the latter but it was not yet an absolutely clear answer. In 1688, England had enjoyed a lucky escape from the perils of militarism and military government, trends which were all too apparent in France, Scandinavia, and Germany. The British army was supposed to be a body of volunteers, yet its ranks were full of pressed conscripts and the victims of kidnapping. Although its political opponents insisted that it was a standing army, it was no such thing. When in England, most of the officers absented themselves from duty and the soldiers wandered off in search of part-time jobs in order to earn enough money to pay for the staff of life. Even the Mutiny Act was so vague that it was a moot point as to whether a distinct and constitutionally legal military law did actually exist in England in conjunction with the common law. In effect, the standing army of William III was unofficially a territorial army. It did not go as far as the Swedish, Prussian, or Hessian cantonal systems which accepted that the regular, native soldiery were territorials, but it was moving, de facto, along similar lines.[2] Yet, by 1702 there was a discernible feeling that the worst years of the apprenticeship were over. Ends were untied, threads remained crossed, much was in a tangle, but everything seemed to be gradually turning to point in a uniform direction towards a future where the army would play a much reduced role in the politics of the state and develop its own atmosphere complete with its own law, concerning itself more and more with the strictly military business of its employer. The War of the Grand Alliance and the Glorious Revolution marked a noticeable change in the history of the British army. Its slide towards politicisation was halted and its role as England and Great Britain's defence force commenced.

This change of course must not be laid solely at the feet of the Glorious Revolution. The very fact that the army was as small in 1699 as it had been in 1661 meant that the military had failed to develop into a permanent institution in England, Scotland, and Ireland. The armies of Cromwell and the Interregnum and those of James II had been politicised by excluding many of the traditional landed gentry and aristocracy from their officer corps. They were lower class, more plebeian formations, which threatened the hegemony of the English political élites. Both the Restoration in 1660 and the Glorious Revolution of 1688 marked the recapture of the army by the gentlemen and peers and the latter event was to prove a permanent captivity. Militarism and the militarisation of political and social life stood no chance of success in England because there were ample alternative bases for political power. Just when the Prussian, Swedish, French, and many Germanic aristocracies were being persuaded that the standing army was the new fundamental of political and monarchical authority, the English landed classes were discovering the joys of productive estate management, the 'Financial Revolution', and investment in an ever-increasing foreign and colonial trade. For much of Europe, militarism was but a substitute for lost economic and political power. In England, the fruits of commerce were enhancing the independent political power of landed society.

One of the major problems which has occurred in discussing the affairs of William III's army has been that of creating a sensible relative standard for its conduct and general efficiency. It has proved extremely difficult, if not impossible, to find out what contemporaries expected from a late seventeenth century army; permanent, mass armed forces were a new phenomenon and Englishmen possessed no clear yardstick with which to measure the performance of their soldiers. Much that appears to the modern historian as inefficient or indisciplined when compared with a twentieth century army, was perfectly acceptable in the 1690s. After all, military discipline is but an exaggerated version of the rules currently governing civilian society, and William's army should not be judged too harshly. Armies became a menace in England, and all over western Europe, during the course of the seventeenth century simply because the emergence and rapid growth of the standing army had been so sudden that no country had been able properly to assimilate its armed forces by building up support and adequate resources. Public attitudes also took decades, if not centuries, to adjust to the change. The engorged standing army of the seventeenth century was a cuckoo-in-the-nest, a creature which had outgrown its parent society, and really belonged to the post-industrial era rather than the rural Europe of the 1600s. This process lay at the root of the poor relations between the civilians and the military during William's reign. Although there was the omnipresent political dimension, William's army was loathed and resented not because it was particularly badly behaved or fought poorly in the field, but simply through the fact that the England of the 1690s was totally unprepared for the demands made by a large standing force on the public purse, on householders and innkeepers, on the delicate balance of the common law, and on manpower. Despite the unhappy apprenticeship to armies and war between 1642 and 1660, the story of civil-military relations between 1660 and 1702 was one of a conservative society trying to come to terms with the growing serpent in its midst.

Notes

1 Guy, *Oeconomy and Discipline,* pp. 162–8; Childs, *Armies and Warfare,* pp. 63–4, 78–9, 193–4.
2 Late in 1697, the Williamite government seriously considered building a network of barracks across England in order to accommodate the cadres remaining after the initial disbandment. However, a preliminary survey indicated that the cost of building and equipping one set of barracks and stables for one troop of horse or dragoons, complete with its three officers, would have amounted to £542 1s 8d (BL, Add. MSS. 38,703, f. 52). Faced with this scale of expenditure, the privy council threw up its hands in horror and abandoned the scheme leaving the army to continue, de facto, as a territorial force.

APPENDIX A

Rates of Pay

General Officers	per diem	per annum
General of the Foot	£6	£2,190
General of the Horse	£6	£2,190
Lieutenant-General	£4	£1,460
Major-General	£2	£730
Brigadier-General	£1 10s	£547 10s

Staff Officers		
Paymaster-General	£1	£365
Secretary-at-War	£1	£365
Commissary-General of the Musters	£1 5s 8¾d	£461 5s
Deputy Commissary-General of the Musters	£1 3s	£419 15s
Deputy Commissary of the Musters (8)	10s	£182 10s
Clerk	2s 6d	£45 12s 3d
Adjutant-General	£1	£365
Quartermaster-General	£1	£365
Assistant Quartermaster-General (2)	10s	£182 10s
Judge Advocate	£1	£365
Deputy Judge Advocate in Channel Isles	2s 6d	£45 12s 3d
Physician-General	10s	£182 10s
Chirurgeon-General	10s	£182 10s
Apothecary-General	10s	£182 10s

The Cavalry	Daily pay	Servant allowance	Total annual pay
The Life Guards			
Captain	£1	4 at 4s each	£657
Lieutenant	15s	2 at 4s each	£419 15s
Cornet	14s	2 at 4s each	£401 10s
Guidon	12s	2 at 4s each	£365
Exempt	12s	2 at 4s each	£365
Brigadier	10s	1 at 4s	£200
Sub-Brigadier	5s		£91 5s
Adjutant	7s		£127 15s
Chaplain	6s 8d		£121 13s 4d
Surgeon	6s	1 horse at 2s	£146
Trumpeter	5s		£91 5s
Kettledrummer	5s		£91 5s
Private Gentleman	4s		£73
Other Cavalry Regiments			
Colonel as Colonel	12s	2 at 2s 6d each	£310 5s
Lt. Col. as Lt. Col.	8s		£146
Major as Major	5s 6d		£100 7s 6d
Adjutant	5s		91 5s
Chaplain	6s 8d		£121 3s 4d
Kettledrummer	3s		£54 15s
Captain	14s	2 at 2s 6d each	£346 15s
Lieutenant	10s	1 at 2s 6d	£228 2s 6d
Cornet	9s	1 at 2s 6d	£209 17s 6d
Quartermaster	4s	1 horse at 2s	£109 10s
Corporal	3s		£54 15s
Trumpeter	2s 8d		£48 12s 6d
Trooper	2s 6d		£45 12s 6d
Dragoons			
Colonel as Colonel	15s	2 at 1s 6d each	£328 10s
Lt. Col. as Lt. Col.	9s		£164 5s
Major as Major	5s		£91 5s
Chaplain	6s 8d		£121 13s 4d
Captain	11s	2 at 1s 6d each	£255 10s
Lieutenant	6s	1 at 1s 6d	£136 17s 6d
Cornet	5s	1 at 1s 6d	£118 2s 6d
Quartermaster	4s		£73
Sergeant	1s 6d	1 horse at 1s	£45 12s 6d
Corporal	1s	1 horse at 1s	£36 10s

Drummer	1s	1 horse at 1s	£36	10s
Hautbois	1s	1 horse at 1s	£36	10s
Private	1s 6d		£29	14s 2½d

The Foot

The First Foot Guards and the Coldstream Guards

Colonel as Colonel	£1	2 at 10d each	£395	8s 4d
Lt. Col. as Lt. Col.	12s		£219	
Major as Major	8s		£146	
Chaplain	6s 8d		£121	3s 4d
Surgeon	4s	2 mates at 2s 6d each	£164	5s 0d
Adjutant (2)	4s		£73	
Quartermaster (2)	4s		£73	
Solicitor (agent)	4s		£73	
Drum-Major	1s 6d		£27	7s 6d
Deputy-Marshal (provost)	1s		£18	5s
Captain	14s	2 at 10d each	£285	18s 4d
Lieutenant	7s	1 at 10d	£142	19s 2d
Ensign	5s	1 at 10d	£106	9s 2d
Sergeant	1s 6d		£27	7s 6d
Corporal	1s		£18	5s
Drummer	1s		£18	5s
Private	10d		£15	4s 0½d

Other Foot Regiments

Colonel as Colonel	12s	2 at 8d each	£243	6s 8d
Lt. Col. as Lt. Col.	7s		£127	15s
Major as Major	5s		£91	5s
Chaplain	6s 8d		£121	13s 4d
Quartermaster & Adjutant	4s		£73	
Surgeon	4s	1 mate at 2s 6d	£118	12s 6d
Drum-Major	1s 6d		£27	7s 6d
Captain	8s	2 at 8d each	£170	6s 8d
Lieutenant	4s	1 at 8d	£85	3s 4d
Ensign	3s	1 at 8d	£66	18s 4d
Sergeant	1s 6d		£27	7s 6d
Corporal	1s		£18	5s
Drummer	1s		£18	5s
Private	8d		£12	1s 8d

Note. Only colonels received servant allowances in their capacity as field officers in addition to the servants permitted them as captains of their troops and companies. Lieutenant-colonels and majors received only their servant allowances as captains.

Source: DCRO, Ilchester MSS., D. 124, Army Establishment, 1699; Box 278, Army Establishment, 1694.

APPENDIX B

The Size of the British Corps in Flanders

1689	10,972
1690	5,360
1691	11,144
1692	21,000 + 19,000 foreign troops in British pay
1693	21,720 + 19,000 foreign troops in British pay
1694	29,100 + 27,209 foreign troops in British pay
1695	29,100 + 27,209 foreign troops in British pay
1696	29,100 + 27,209 foreign troops in British pay
1697	29,100 + 27,209 foreign troops in British pay

All figures are for privates and non-commissioned officers only. Commissioned officers are excluded.

Sources: Chandler, 'Fluctuations', pp. 1–19; WO 5/5, ff. 103–4; BL, Add. MSS. 9,730, f. 15; Japikse (Welbeck), ii. 73; BCRO, Trumbull Add. MSS. 103; PRO, SP 8/17, f. 8.

APPENDIX C

The annual cost of the army

The annual cost of the army's pay and contingencies was:

5 Nov. 1688 to 29 Sept. 1691	£3,481,585 6s 7½d
30 Sept. 1691 to 29 Sept. 1692	£1,895,942 15s 11d
28 Sept. 1692 to 28 Sept. 1693	£2,345,548 6s 7½d
29 Sept. 1693 to 28 Sept. 1694	£2,881,194 16s 3d
28 Sept. 1694 to 28 Sept. 1695	£2,558,924 6s 7½d*
29 Sept. 1695 to 28 Sept. 1696	£2,709,713 12s 10d
1697	£2,709,713 12s 10d
26 Mar. 1699 to 24 Dec. 1699	£278,803 19s 6d
29 Sept. 1698 to 28 Sept. 1699	£312,357
24 Dec. 1699 to 24 Dec. 1700	£384,778 6s 7d
25 Dec. 1700 to 25 Dec. 1701	£331,466 5s 8½d

*of this sum, £1,421,379 19s 5d was for the native, British troops, and the remainder was for the pay of the foreign troops.

An estimate of 1699, considered that between 1689 and 1699, £10 million had been raised for the pay of the army, £4 million for its clothing, and £3 million for its transportation. During the same period, the navy cost an estimated £33 million (Bod. Lib. Rawlinson MSS. A. 245, f. 30b).

Sources: HMC, House of Lords MSS., iii. 357–8; iv. 163; n.s. i. 67; n.s. ii. 163; Chandler, *Debates*, ii. 421; iii. 28; Davies, 'Reduction', p. 15; *CTrB 1695–1702*, p. dlii–dlv; DCRO, Ilchester MSS., D. 124, Army Establishment, 1699; BL, Harl. MSS. 7,018, ff. 169, 173–4.

INDEX